Progress in Physiological Psychology

Volume 5

Contributors to This Volume

Cassius B. Bordelon

Jennifer S. Buchwald

Perer L. Carlton

Carol Diakow

Robert Edelberg

Charles G. Gross

Gordon L. Humphrey

Melvyn Keiner

Catherine Lewis

Annabel G. Liebelt

Robert A. Liebelt

Barbara Markiewicz

Donald Pfaff

Gerard P. Smith

Progress in
PHYSIOLOGICAL PSYCHOLOGY

Edited by ELIOT STELLAR and JAMES M. SPRAGUE

*Institute of Neurological Sciences
and Department of Anatomy
The School of Medicine
University of Pennsylvania
Philadelphia, Pennsylvania*

Volume 5

1973

ACADEMIC PRESS   New York ● London
A Subsidiary of Harcourt Brace Jovanovich, Publishers

ACADEMIC PRESS, INC.
111 Fifth Avenue, New York, New York 10003

United Kingdom Edition published by
ACADEMIC PRESS, INC. (LONDON) LTD.
24/28 Oval Road, London NW1

LIBRARY OF CONGRESS CATALOG CARD NUMBER: 66-29640

PRINTED IN THE UNITED STATES OF AMERICA

Contents

An Analysis of Habituation in the Specific Sensory Systems

Jennifer S. Buchwald and Gordon L. Humphrey

Inferotemporal Cortex and Vision

Charles G. Gross

Studies of the Physiological Bases of Memory

Peter L. Carlton and Barbara Markiewicz

Mechanisms of Electrodermal Adaptations for Locomotion, Manipulation, or Defense

Robert Edelberg

The Adipose Tissue System and Food Intake

Robert A. Liebelt, Cassius B. Bordelon, and Annabel G. Liebelt

Contents

Neurophysiological Analysis of Mating Behavior Responses as Hormone-Sensitive Reflexes

Donald Pfaff, Catherine Lewis, Carol Diakow, and Melvyn Keiner

Adrenal Hormones and Emotional Behavior

Gerard P. Smith

Numbers in parentheses indicate the pages on which the authors' contributions begin.

Cassius B. Bordelon,* Departments of Cell and Molecular Biology and Medicine, Medical College of Georgia, Augusta, Georgia (211)

Jennifer S. Buchwald, Departments of Physiology and Psychiatry, Brain Research Institute and Mental Retardation Center, UCLA Medical Center, Los Angeles, California (1)

Peter L. Carlton, Department of Psychiatry, College of Medicine and Dentistry of New Jersey, Rutgers Medical School, Piscataway, New Jersey (125)

Carol Diakow, Rockefeller University, New York, New York (253)

Robert Edelberg, College of Medicine and Dentistry of New Jersey, Rutgers Medical School, New Brunswick, New Jersey (155)

Charles G. Gross, Department of Psychology, Princeton University, Princeton, New Jersey (77)

Gordon L. Humphrey, Departments of Physiology and Psychiatry, Brain Research Institute and Mental Retardation Center, UCLA Medical Center, Los Angeles, California (1)

Melvyn Keiner, Rockefeller University, New York, New York (253)

Catherine Lewis, Rockefeller University, New York, New York (253)

Annabel G. Liebelt, Departments of Cell and Molecular Biology and Medicine, Medical College of Georgia, Augusta, Georgia (211)

Robert A. Liebelt, Departments of Cell and Molecular Biology and Medicine, Medical College of Georgia, Augusta, Georgia (211)

Barbara Markiewicz, Department of Psychiatry, College of Medicine and Dentistry of New Jersey, Rutgers Medical School, Piscataway, New Jersey (125)

* Present address: Department of Anatomy, Baylor College of Medicine, Houston, Texas.

Donald Pfaff, Rockefeller University, New York, New York (253)

Gerard P. Smith, Department of Psychiatry, Cornell University Medical College, and Edward W. Bourne Behavioral Research Laboratory, New York Hospital, Westchester Division, White Plains, New York (299)

As a "continuing handbook of physiological psychology," this fifth volume of *Progress in Physiological Psychology* adds both diversity and depth to our coverage of scientific problems in the field. There are two new contributions to previous articles on the basis of learning and memory. The article by Buchwald and Humphrey on habituation in sensory systems is a significant contribution to our understanding of the plasticity of the central nervous system. In a very different vein, Carlton and Markiewicz address themselves to the disruption of the memory of a simple operant response by suppressing electrical activity of the brain with topical application of KCl. Previous articles also dealing with learning and memory are those of Adey in Volume 1, of Rowland and of Jasper and Doane in Volume 2, of Adey in Volume 3, and of Rowland and Anderson and of James C. Smith in Volume 4.

The article by Gross in the present volume on inferotemporal cortex and vision adds to previous articles concerned with central neural mechanisms involved in perceptual processes: Worden's article and Riesen's in Volume 1 and Weiskrantz and Cowey's contribution to Volume 3.

Edelberg's article on electrodermal changes in locomotion, manipulation, and defense covers new material in that it deals with the basis of peripheral psychophysiological measures classically used in the study of emotional responsiveness.

Adding to previous contributions to our understanding of appetite and obesity (Le Magnen's, Epstein's, and Teitelbaum's articles in Volume 4) is an article by Liebelt, Bordelon, and Liebelt on the role of adipose tissue in the regulation of food intake.

The contribution by Pfaff, Lewis, Diakow, and Keiner, which analyzes neurological mechanisms sensitive to changes in the internal environment, especially hormonal changes and mating behavior, belongs with the group of articles dealing with the physiological basis of motivated behavior: Andersson in Volume 1, Satinoff in Volume 3, and four articles in Volume 4 by Fitzsimons, Le Magnen, Epstein, and Teitelbaum.

Finally, an unusual contribution by Gerard P. Smith on adrenal hormones and emotional behavior should be read in the light of the articles by Snyder and by Ratcliffe in Volume 2; also pertinent are the articles by McCleary (Volume 1) and by Thomas, Hostetter, and Barker (Volume 2). Future volumes will continue in this vein, coming back occasionally to the same authors for updating of their previous contributions, going to new authors for new and different viewpoints on fields already covered, and always moving forward into new topics as they mature in the hands of our colleagues and become ready for definitive treatment. Whenever possible, we will try to collect articles on different aspects of the same field in single volumes.

ELIOT STELLAR
JAMES M. SPRAGUE

An Analysis of Habituation in the Specific Sensory Systems

Jennifer S. Buchwald and Gordon L. Humphrey
*Departments of Physiology and Psychiatry,
Brain Research Institute and Mental Retardation Center,
UCLA Medical Center, Los Angeles, California*

I. Introduction

The hyperactive child has been described as showing a syndrome which includes constant overactivity, distractibility, and short attention span (Ounsted, 1955). Although named after its most characteristic sign, this behavioral complex is believed to reflect dysfunction in the sensory processing systems rather than a deficit in motor function. For example, when hyperactive and normal children were placed in a room environment with minimal sensory stimulation, the exploratory motor activity of both groups was approximately the same (Hutt and Hutt, 1964). However, as environmental stimulation was increased by the introduction of a box of colored blocks, significant behavioral disparities developed between the groups. After an initial period of repeated visual and tactile contacts with the new stimuli, the normal children showed decreased sensory sampling and a parallel increase in attention span directed toward a particular activity, e.g., block building. In contrast, the hyperactive children continued to make unabated repetitive stimulus contacts, with little or no decrement, and showed no evolution of task-oriented attention. These data are interpreted to suggest that a problem of fundamental importance to the hyperactive child is an inability to habituate to sensory stimuli.

"As soon as each stimulus has been explored, its central effects are lost, and the child comes back to it as though it were a fresh stimulus" (Hutt and Hutt, 1964). Similarly, during repeated presentations of visual stimuli, hyperactive children showed an exaggerated initial response of alpha-wave desynchronization (arousal) and a decreased capacity to habituate to the stimulus (Milstein *et al.,* 1969), and, during repeated acoustic stimulation, the galvanic skin response of hyperactive children showed no habituation, as typically occurred among normal children (Tizard, 1968).

An even more complex behavioral syndrome, that of infantile autism, is likewise believed to reflect a deficit in sensory information processing rather than in motor function (Ornitz and Ritvo, 1968b). In the excitatory phase, the autistic child shows overreactivity to all types of sensory stimuli, an accentuated startle response, and aberrant hand-flapping and circling movements; in the inhibitory phase, the individual shows prolonged immobility and nonresponsiveness (Ornitz and Ritvo, 1968a). These alterating behavioral states are believed to reflect a fundamental failure of homeostatic regulation in the central nervous system so that there is either too much or too little sensory input, a suggestion which has some experimental support from the abnormally large amplitudes of auditory evoked potentials recorded from autistic children during REM sleep (Ornitz *et al.,* 1968), and from the inability of autistic children to show normal behavioral and electroencephalographic habituation (Hutt *et al.,* 1965).

These complex pathologies indicate that profound maladaptive behavior can occur without any specific involvement of motor pathways but, rather, may be due to deficient processing of sensory information, e.g., the inability to habituate to environmental stimuli. Although our present understanding of sensory function includes fine electrophysiological distinctions between, for example, the resting membrane potential of cells at the first central relay of the auditory pathway (Gerstein *et al.,* 1968) as compared with that of the more central, medial geniculate cells (Nelson and Erulkar, 1963), it is still difficult to assess the contribution of sensory systems to the adaptive behavior of the individual. By definition, behavioral adaptation requires response modulation so that any direct role played by the specific sensory systems in this process would require response plasticity within the sensory systems. However, there is at present little consensus among neurophysiologists as to whether response modulations develop within the relay nuclei of the sensory pathways or are exclusively the product of nonspecific convergence systems. Even in the simplest, most controllable experimental situation, i.e., repeated presentations of a single, constant stimulus, there is no general agreement as to whether response decrements do or do not occur within the sensory pathways. Thus, it is to the issue of sensory response plasticity, in particular, the decremental response or "habituation" induced by repetitious stimulus contacts, that the present paper is addressed.

Habituation, most simply defined as a response decrement to repeated stimulation (Harris, 1943), is generally considered to represent a simple form of learning, since habituated responses are mediated by the central nervous system and persist over a relatively long time course (Thorpe, 1963). The initial descriptions of habituation, which were made in the early part of this century, focused on the decremental behavior of the total organism (Jennings, 1906; Humphrey, 1933; Pavlov, 1941) or upon some somatic reflex component (Sherrington, 1898; Prosser and Hunter, 1936) during repeated presentations of a stimulus sufficiently strong to induce an overt response. This relatively simple approach to the study of learning rapidly became popular among behavioral and biological scientists, and several "model" responses began to enjoy a focus of attention by virtue of the fact that they represented an easily observed, relatively simple form of motor output, they could be predictably elicited, and, with repeated stimulation, they decremented markedly. Among the most studied of these models have been the *orienting reflex,* originally described by Pavlov (1941) as a diffuse complex of somatic and autonomic responses without specificity to quality or intensity of stimulus but with specificity of habituation to a repeated stimulus; the *startle reflex,* described by Landis and Hunt

(1939) as a response to a sudden intense auditory stimulus, e.g., gunshot, characterized by generalized contraction of the somatic musculature which tended to disappear after repeated acoustic stimulations; and the *flexion reflex,* decrement of which was first described in the spinal animal by Sherrington (1898).

Such overt motor responses provided the only means available in the early twentieth century to study a tangible manipulatable aspect of learning, i.e., relatively long-lasting response decrements. However, stimuli intense and repetitive enough to induce overt movements which gradually habituate are relatively rare outside of the laboratory, and even in an experimental setting novel stimuli may be unaccompanied by any observable motor response (Sokolov, 1963; Johnson and Lubin, 1967; Bernstein, 1968). Behavior, in turn, has become increasingly recognized as a phenomenon more subtle than overt activity. For example, the behavior of the adult has been distinguished from that of the child, and normal behavior distinguished from hyperactive, on the basis of acquired unresponsiveness to environmental stimuli which may or may not have had any initial motor component (Hutt and Hutt, 1964; Milstein *et al.,* 1969). Like the visible tip of an iceberg, overt activity reflects only a minor part of the information processing functions of the nervous system. Moreover, in an environment of continuous sensory stimulation, minimal physiological responsiveness to this background "noise" is essential for the efficient functioning and survival of the organism. Unresponsiveness is, indeed, the most prominent, sustained behavior pattern of mammalian life.

An understanding of this acquired, reversible unresponsiveness is, we feel, the important *behavioral* extrapolation of habituation studies. Such an orientation is in contrast to the study of behavioral habituation by the use of "model" motor response systems. Moreover, with the electrophysiological techniques which have evolved over the past several decades, it has become possible to look at responses within the nervous system in addition to the output of the final common path. Indeed, the promise of such enlarged observational capacities in relation to behavior was suggested a decade ago by physiologists trained in the Pavlovian School as well as by behaviorally oriented electrophysiogists (Galambos, 1961). Thus, in the study of acquired sensory unresponsiveness, electrophysiological measures within the nervous system may be able to reveal phenomena more closely allied to adaptive behavior than the overt motor end points of traditional behavioral habituation studies.

In this paper we shall attempt to survey the literature relating to plasticity within the major sensory systems during repeated stimulation procedures. We shall then summarize data from our own experiments which have utilized different recording techniques, stimulus parameters, and control procedures than found in prior studies. We shall subsequently make parametric comparisons between sensory response decrements and motor response habituation. Finally, we shall attempt to relate sensory habituation to the behavioral adaptation of daily existence.

II. What Is a Sensory System?

Defining a sensory system is difficult. Livingston (1960), in discussing this issue, has referred to the preferred definitions of others and suggested that, in the end, all definitions are arbitrary. "It is readily agreed that nature deals in functional differences but that definitions belong only to the investigator: we are, therefore, well advised to be aware of whatever intellectual conventions we assume" (p. 366). This problem is perhaps most important when it is responsible for divergent views with differences based primarily on definitions. For example, those neurons in layers I to IV of the dorsal horn of the spinal cord which readily habituate when stimulation is repeatedly given to the primary afferent fibers have been described as "interneurons" (Wickelgren, 1967b; Groves and Thompson, 1970). This is reasonable in that the cells lie between the primary afferent fiber terminals and the motor neurons of the anterior horn. However, Rexed (1964) has described these layers as constituting the *sensory* area of the spinal cord gray matter with second- and third-order sensory neurons receiving input from the cutaneous innervation of the trunk and extremities. Thus, one could conclude that habituation of second- and third-order "sensory" neurons was demonstrated in the previously cited studies.

While there is evidence that habituation can be mediated by extremely simple circuitry (Kandel and Spencer, 1968), we do not intend to imply that records of activity taken from specific points of the classical pathways are indicative of changes taking place solely, or mainly, at that particular location. The classical sensory systems were originally described on anatomical evidence. Since our present knowledge points to the existence of complex feedback circuits from higher levels of the pathway as well as from nonspecific systems, and since a certain amount of circuit complexity even at lower levels is involved in coding, extraction and integration of information important for perceptual functions, we are obviously discussing data derived from "interneurons" as well as from simple chains of "sensory" neurons involved in transmitting data to other points in the central nervous system. Whitfield (1967), in regard to such complex integrative effects has made this point:

> . . . it will no longer be worthwhile to treat the auditory system as if it were a one-way system proceeding to higher and higher degrees of elaboration. These centrifugal pathways take origin from all levels, from the cortex to the medulla, and interconnect intermediate nuclei in a complex way (p. 140).

Within the sensory systems, therefore, interneurons are involved in the elaboration of responses (*a*) to the extent that all stages of transmission beyond the first-order sensory neuron are defined as "interneuronal" and (*b*) to the extent that complex integrative or feedback circuitry, whether properly considered as part of a direct, or classical, sensory pathway or not, significantly modulates the relayed sensory information. Within these latitudes of anatomical and physiological definition, we have included data in the subsequent literature review recorded from the *classical sensory systems*. For reasons enumerated in context, we have also included studies of units in the optic tectum and data concerning the human vertex potential.

III. Literature Review: Sensory System Responses during Repeated Stimulation

This review is organized chronologically in order to trace the development of disagreements in the experimental literature and the subsequent attempts to resolve conflicting data.

A. THE AUDITORY SYSTEM

1. Animal Studies

Artemiev (1951) observed progressive decrements at the auditory cortex with repeated presentation of a sound stimulus, a phenomenon which he found to occur in the awake, but not in the anesthetized, preparation. The later discovery that sensory transmission in various systems is blocked at relatively peripheral levels by reticular formation activation (Hernández-Peón and Hagbarth, 1955; Hernández-Peón *et al.,* 1956c) led Hernández-Peón to examine the question of whether this reticular blockade of sensory input might account for sensory response decrements such as that seen by Artemiev.

Hernández-Peón and Scherrer (1955) first reported progressive decrements in click-evoked responses from the dorsal cochlear nucleus in unrestrained cats. The process took a number of hours to achieve with continuous click stimulation at interclick intervals of approximately two seconds. The decrement grew only as long as the *same* stimulus was continued, but was wiped out by any novel acoustic stimulus. The evoked potential regained its original height when the animal was given Nembutal, but was reduced again when tested after the drug had worn off. The response, even to novel auditory stimuli, became immediately smaller whenever the animal *attended* to stimuli of any other modality, as, for example, in the classic case of mouse-in-the-cage (Hernández-Peón *et al.*, 1956b). Habituation was impossible, also, after lesions of the mesencephalic tegmentum, a most significant finding for, together with the discovery that habituation was blocked under barbiturate anesthesia, it suggested that the response reduction was neither receptor adaptation nor fatigue but rather selective inhibition of sensory input as a direct result of reticular activation.

Galambos *et al.* (1956) reported decrements after many hours or even days of continuous day and night stimulation by clicks at a rate of one per 3 seconds in unrestrained cats. Habituation was measured by a drop in the amplitude of click evoked potentials recorded at widespread auditory and nonauditory brain sites including the cochlear nucleus. Dishabituation in cochlear nucleus by conditioning was shown to occur within 10–20 presentations of click paired with electric shock to the chest of the cats.

These data were extended in a subsequent study (Hernández-Peón *et al.*, 1957a) in which the very rapid habituation of the orienting response was compared with that of the evoked auditory potential at the cochlear nucleus, the full decrement of which took several thousands (several hours) of clicks. It was found that auditory habituation was faster with less intense stimulation, and that recovery of response amplitude could be brought about by rest, by presentation of novel or intense sounds, by conditioning procedures using meaningful unconditioned stimuli, as well as by anesthesia and gross reticular lesions. Habituation was reported to occur faster at higher levels of the auditory system, e.g., auditory cortex, and rehabituation progressed more rapidly than the original habituation. It was suggested that dishabituation involved simply the removal of the inhibition which produced response decrement. The decrement itself was characterized as "afferent neuronal habituation" (Hernández-Peón, 1960).

One of the puzzling aspects of these findings involved dishabituation. Hernández-Peón was able to show dishabituation at the cochlear nucleus when loud or sudden room noises occurred during the course of the habituation procedures; even sudden changes in the rhythmicity or intensity characteristics of the habituating click stimulus caused a recovery of the initial evoked response amplitude (Hernández-Peón, 1960). Nonauditory stimuli, however, had no such dishabituating effect. It took 1100 pairings of click and foot shock to return the cochlear nucleus response to its initial level; obviously the foot shock did not produce a strong dishabituation. This was a surprising result considering the wide variety of environmental stimuli which are known to produce dishabituation of behavioral responses quickly and easily.

It followed from Hernández-Peón's theory of attention that only auditory stimuli should be capable of dishabituating auditory responses. This theory proposed that activity would be uninhibited in that sensory system which was carrying information to which the animal was attending. Thus, if the evoked response were reduced by repeated presentation of a click and then a novel light flash was introduced, it would be expected that visual activity would be facilitated, but that auditory activity would remain depressed until new significance was attached to the habituated stimulus or until a novel acoustic stimulus was presented. The finding by Hernández-Peón *et al.* (1957a) that room noises caused recovery of a click-evoked response was interpreted to mean that new significance had been attached to auditory information.

In our own laboratory, however, we have achieved dishabituation of multiple-unit responses at the cochlear nucleus in intact cats by shock stimulation of the foot (see Section IV), and Buño *et al.* (1966) obtained dishabituation in the guinea pig cochlear nucleus by nonauditory extrastimuli. Two studies reported that conditioning procedures in which clicks were paired with shock (Galambos *et al.*, 1956) or puffs of air to the face (Marsh *et al.*, 1961) effectively reversed habituation after a very few pairings. To our knowledge, no other studies reporting significant habituation at the cochlear nucleus attempted dishabituation by any means, although Altman (1960) found rapid dishabituation of the eighth nerve N_1 potential following single skin shocks. It is thus unclear why Hernández-Peón was unable to dishabituate evoked responses at the cochlear nucleus with other than auditory extrastimuli.

Desmedt (1960), using procedures similar to Hernández-Peón and Galambos, reported habituation in the superior olivary complex after thousands of clicks at a rate of one per 3 seconds. Desmedt did not believe that the reticular formation was responsible, since electrical stimulation of this structure had no suppressive effect on the cochlear nucleus responsiveness to clicks. Activation of the extrareticular acoustic efferent system, which had been described by Desmedt and Mechelse (1958), was invoked to explain acoustic habituation. Stimulation of this efferent pathway lateral to the reticular formation led to a reduction in the size of evoked potentials at the ventral cochlear nucleus; since the auditory nerve potential and round window microphonic were unchanged by the electrical stimulation, the olivocochlear bundle (Rasmussen, 1946) was thought not to be involved.

By this time, habituation to repeated acoustic stimulation had been demonstrated at cochlear nucleus, superior olive, auditory cortex, and several nonauditory areas of the brain, although there was some disagreement about control mechanisms. Huttenlocher (1960), however, reported a lack of habituation of click-evoked potentials in the waking cat in both the cochlear nucleus and in the reticular formation after 1000 continuous clicks in a 1-hour period. It should be pointed out that 1000 clicks in 1 hour was considerably less stimulation than any of the previous experiments had used and might explain the cause of this first negative result. Bach-y-Rita *et al.* (1961) subsequently reported data which contradicted Desmedt's belief that inhibition of sensory input was due to activation of the descending efferent system. They found that lesions of the midbrain lateral to the reticular formation, which interrupted the descending efferents described by Desmedt, had no noticeable effect on the evoked potential amplitude decrements in the cochlear nucleus, which still developed after "several hours" of stimulation at a rate of one click per second. Moreover, electrical stimulation of the reticular formation caused recovery of a previously habituated response. Similar response decrements were recorded in the cochlear nucleus of decerebrate cats, although dishabituation was difficult to achieve in this preparation; those results agree well with our own unit data from decerebrate cats (see Section IV).

At about the same time, Altman (1960) found some decrement of the N_1 component of the eighth nerve potential recorded from the round window and of evoked potentials recorded from the medial geniculate body and auditory cortex after 5 hours of click stimulation at a rate of one per 3 seconds. The round window microphonic, however, did not change, which indicated that the decrements were not due to receptor adaptation or to damage to the cochlea. In agreement with Hernández-Peón's findings, response decrements appeared considerably sooner at the cortex than at the more peripheral locations, and were absent during barbiturate anesthesia but present in physiological sleep. On the other hand, Altman reported faster habituation with high-intensity stimulation, data which was opposite to the results reported by Hernández-Peón *et al.* (1957a). It was found that a single shock to the skin brought about dishabituation of the decremented response at all levels, including the auditory nerve. Altman attributed this to a nonspecific, widespread release of adrenaline by the sympathetic nervous system. In an important control experiment, similar decrements were observed by Altman at all sites after section of the ear muscles.

Altman's report of a habituated N_1 component suggests possible involvement of the olivocochlear bundle, although this neither supports nor negates the existence of other decremental processes at the second- or third-order neurons in the cochlear nucleus. Additional evidence in favor of the participation of the olivocochlear bundle was later provided by Buño *et al.* (1966) in the guinea pig. Like Altman, these investigators recorded the cochlear microphonic and auditory nerve potentials. They showed *both* responses were depressed after less than 1 hour of 70- to 90-dB click or tone burst stimulation at one per second. Midline sections through the brain stem at the level of the fourth ventricle, interrupting the crossed olivocochlear bundle, prevented the manifestation of the previously observed decrements. The decrements were not due to a fatigue process as brief stimulation by other, nonauditory, modalities caused a return of the evoked response to or above its original, prehabituation, level.

Another mechanism of auditory evoked response modulation was suggested by Hugelin *et al.* (1960) who demonstrated that cochlear nucleus potential were no longer reduced by reticular formation stimulation after section of the middle ear muscles. These authors believed that the habituation of cochlear nucleus responses observed by others was due to contractions of the middle ear muscles. Galambos *et al.* (1956), Altman (1960), and Bach-y-Rita *et al.* (1961), however, felt that ear muscle contractions were not totally responsible for the response decrement recorded in their experiments.

Thus, at this point, there was direct support for habituation in peripheral relays of the auditory pathway from four laboratories, one negative report, and at least three suggested mechanisms to account for the findings. The middle ear muscle explanation was reinforced by experiments of Guzmán-Flores and his collaborators (Guzmán-Flores *et al.,* 1960; Guzmán-Flores, 1961; Alcaraz *et al.,* 1962). Recording from the medial geniculate body and from the auditory cortex, this group found habituation of click-evoked potentials after 2–3 hours of clicks of one per 5 seconds only if the ear muscles were intact. No habituation was found when the cats were paralyzed, i.e., when neuro-muscular transmission was blocked and ear muscle contractions were absent. Even in intact cats, they found response decrements only when clicks were presented at an even rate and none if they were sounded at irregular intervals. These authors suggested that the response decrements did not reflect feedback inhibition of afferent transmission but, rather, reflected conditioned contractions of the middle ear muscles resulting from temporal conditioning. If the clicks were regular, the cat "expected" each click, and the ear muscles contracted prior to its occurrence.

In apparent contradiction of Guzmán-Flores's group, Moushegian *et al.* (1961) studied cats with severed ear muscles and found that the cortical evoked potential habituated even when a slow stimulus rate of one click per 10 seconds was utilized over a 10-day period. Alcaraz *et al.* (1962) attributed this discrepancy to the difference between the relatively fast habituation studied within 3–6 hours in their experiments, and the slow habituation observed over many days in the Moushegian *et al.* experiments. They admitted that a slow, centrally mediated habituatory process might be unaffected, for the most part, by middle ear muscle contractions.

Marsh *et al.* (1961), the first authors to state specific sound intensity values, recorded evoked potentials from the cochlear nucleus, superior olive, inferior colliculus, medial geniculate body, and auditory cortex, elicited by 80- to 90-dB clicks during click habituation, conditioning (with a puff of air to the face as the conditioning stimulus) and extinction. Clicks were presented to intact unrestrained cats at a rate of one click every 10 seconds, 24 hours per day, for 5–7 days at which time habituation was judged "stable." During this habituation procedure, auditory-evoked potentials were reduced in the cochlear nucleus as well as in the superior olive and auditory cortex. In some cases, however, the superior olive showed enhanced responses or no change, results also typical of the inferior colliculus and medial geniculate body. Conditioning procedures usually induced restoration of the response to its initial amplitude after very few pairings of click and air puff. For the cochlear nucleus, this study generally confirmed earlier reports of response habituation. The authors suggested that the reticular formation might either suppress or enhance information at higher levels of the auditory pathway so as to produce the varied effects they observed during habituation. They recognized important problems in the use of the evoked potential as a measure of neuronal responsiveness, particularly if analyses of change concentrated only on amplitude without regard for component patterns, and in the use of implanted unrestrained animals, whose behavior over any length of time is variable.

A thoroughly distressing result for believers in cochlear nucleus response habituation was subsequently published by Worden and Marsh (1963). After presenting 70-dB clicks at rates of one per 10 seconds or one per second for 6 or 7 hours, some cats showed a significant increase while others showed a significant decrease in cochlear nucleus response amplitude. Even when stimulation was continued for 5 days, consistent response decrements were not observed. The cochlear nucleus evoked potential was found to be generally larger in the alert subject than in the sleeping subject, an effect attributed to the alteration of ear position relative to the sound source in sleeping subjects rather than to arousal per se. There was no obvious correlation between location of recording site within the cochlear nucleus and direction or degree of evoked potential change. The authors concluded that habituation is a process restricted to higher loci.

To check the possibility that variations in head position in the sound field can account for considerable evoked potential variability, previously emphasized by Marsh *et al.* (1962), earphones were developed by Worden *et al.* (1964) for use with chronic unrestrained cats. These were employed by Marsh and Worden (1964) who again tested for evoked potentials in the cochlear nucleus and auditory cortex as well as in the flocculus of the cerebellum. Using a click intensity of 65 dB delivered at a rate of one click per 10 seconds for 6 hours, the auditory cortex and cerebellum showed significant response decrements in both "alert" and "nonalert" states, while the cochlear nucleus showed no significant change during either condition. Since middle ear muscle activity was known to produce alterations in the cochlear nucleus evoked response, the lack of observable cochlear nucleus response decrement suggested that the cortical response decrements developed independently of middle ear muscle activity.

Worden and Marsh and their collaborators thus relegated habituation at the cochlear nucleus to the status of nonexistence. There remained the two theories of peripheral relay habituation proposed by Hernández-Peón and Desmedt; but no theory was needed if no phenomenon existed. With the exception of earphones, there had been to this time no sweeping procedural variations since the original report (Hernández-Peón and Scherrer, 1955). There had evolved a general recognition of the importance of certain controls, such as arousal level, position of head, and condition of ear muscles, all of which were agreed to have some effect on the click-evoked response, yet no one of which was held solely responsible for previously observed response "habituation." Additionally, considerable care was taken by this time to state stimulation parameters.

The significance of the animal's head position in the test cage was pointed out by Webster and Dunlop (1965). In their experimental box the N_1 component of the auditory nerve response, measured from the round window, ranged from 250 μV to 400 μV as the cat raised its head toward the loudspeaker delivering the clicks. These data reemphasized the necessity for monitoring behavior in all experiments using unanesthetized, unrestrained cats.

This precaution of careful behavior observation was utilized by Dunlop *et al.* (1964b), although neither earphone stimulation nor ear muscle inactivation were employed. In a study of the effect of click intensity on amount of habituation, these authors gave clicks every 2 seconds for 95 minutes at 85, 95, or 105 dB to unrestrained cats. Evoked potentials recorded from the inferior colliculus showed a progessive decrement within 95 minutes, which was significant for all intensities except 105 dB. The percent decrement was less with more intense stimulation and most of the drop was seen in the first 20 minutes of stimulation, findings which agree well with parametric studies of overt behavioral habituation. Unfortunately, in a later publication, Dunlop *et al.* (1966) stated that a statistical test of trend applied to these same data resulted in a lack of significance of the intensity factor; nevertheless, a tendency toward more habituation with weaker intensity at the inferior colliculus was apparent. Dunlop, Webster, and Day suggested possible sources of artifacts in previous investigations and attempted to avoid these by procedures which restricted control-evoked responses to the first few responses elicited at the beginning of habituation, and by utilizing more sensitive devices for the measurement of click intensity. They believed, for example, that the 80–90 dB intensity reported by Marsh *et al.* (1961) might actually have been as high as 105 dB, which could explain the lack of response habituation in the inferior colliculus reported in this study in light of the report by Dunlop *et al.* (1964b) of lack of colliculus response habituation at 105 dB stimulation.

Dunlop *et al.* (1964a; see also Dunlop *et al.*, 1966) found less habituation at the cochlear nucleus than at the inferior colliculus and less at the latter than at the medial geniculate body when a 75-, 85-, 95-, or 105-dB click was delivered every 2 seconds for 95 minutes to unrestrained cats. Control amplitude was the mean of the first four responses in any one session. Most of the decrement at each site was achieved within 40 minutes, although in some cases additional decrements developed when the period of stimulation was extended from 95 minutes to 8 hours. Habituation did not significantly vary with stimulus intensity in the inferior colliculus or cochlear nucleus, although there was a tendency at these sites for more habituation to occur with weaker stimulus strength. At the medial geniculate body, more habituation was achieved at higher intensities; here, 105 dB was significantly *more* effective than the lower intensities.

In 20-minute sessions, a new low for duration of stimulation justified on the basis of their earlier discovery of rapid habituation in the first few minutes of click presentation, Webster *et al.* (1965) delivered 85-dB clicks at each of five different rates: one per 20 seconds, one per 10 seconds, one per 5 seconds, one per second, or 10 per second, and evoked responses were recorded from the cochlear nucleus. Behavior was rigidly monitored. The three slowest rates were ineffective, but habituation was seen at rates of both one per second and 10 per second. Together with the evidence of Dunlop *et al.* (1964a) and Dunlop *et al.* (1966) who had previously found decrements at the cochlear nucleus using a rate of one click every 2 seconds, it seemed clear that the degree of evoked response decrement at the cochlear nucleus was directly related to rate of click presentation. However, even at these high rates of stimulus delivery cochlear nucleus response decrements do not inevitably develop, as demonstrated by the results of Worden and Marsh (1963) who had failed to see response habituation at this site with a one per second click presentation rate.

Webster *et al.* obtained similar response decrements regardless of whether clicks were presented at regular or irregular intervals, a result confirmed later by Cook *et al.* (1968) at the cortex, and eliminated ear muscle contractions by Flaxedil paralysis without affecting cochlear nucleus response decrements; these findings refuted the claim of Guzmán-Flores (1961) that habituation necessitated both a regular presentation of clicks and intact ear muscles. Webster *et al.* also attempted to provide further evidence against a reticular feedback role in habituation. Cochlear nucleus responses which were habituated were then tested after an anesthetic dose of Nembutal. Evoked potentials showed the same amplitude post-Nembutal as they had in the habituated, preanesthetic state. It is not clear that the response level during anesthesia reflected any carry-over of habituation or whether it simply indicated a depressed activity level induced by the barbiturate, nor was it clear that habituation could have occurred had stimulus delivery been carried out from the beginning under Nembutal, an important question, since Hernández-Peón *et al.* (1957a) had reported an inability to achieve habituation of cochlear nucleus responses during barbiturate anesthesia. In a later report, however, Webster (1969) demonstrated that habituation at the medial geniculate body could develop under barbiturate anesthesia. As the barbiturate is known to depress the reticular formation, it was suggested that reticular-mediated inhibition of auditory habituation might thus be ruled out.

In a final parametric study Simons *et al.* (1966) found habituation of click-evoked potentials in the cochlear nucleus, inferior colliculus, and medial geniculate body after 1 hour of stimulation using 80-dB clicks at one per second, one per 5 seconds, and one per 10 seconds. Amount of habituation was generally greatest at higher auditory sites. Again, regularity of click presentation was not important, nor, at the cochlear nucleus, was stimulus rate significant in determining amount of decrement. As discussed above, Webster *et al.* (1965), however, reported that rates of one per 5 seconds and one per 10 seconds were ineffective in producing habituation at the cochlear nucleus. Simons *et al.* (1966) explained these contradictory results by suggesting that quite different effects might be produced by the 0.5 and 0.1-msec clicks of their study and the 20-msec clicks employed by Webster *et al.*, i.e., that very brief clicks can bring about habituation at slower rates of presentation than can clicks of longer duration, at least in the cochlear nucleus.

At both the inferior colliculus and medial geniculate body, the greatest amount of response decrement was induced by the fastest stimulation rates. The same laboratory had previously reported that at the level of the medial geniculate body habituation was directly related to stimulus *intensity* (Dunlop *et al.*, 1966). The findings that faster rates and more intense stimulation produced greater habituation in a given amount of time could indicate a mechanism of receptor adaptation or simple neural fatigue (Ward, 1966). Simons *et al.* (1966) suggested an intrinsic inhibitory mechanism to account for acoustic habituation. They postulated that a period of decreased excitability followed each stimulus, with the effect of reduced neural responsiveness to subsequent click presentations. The mechanism was thought to be inherent in the auditory pathway itself; Webster (1969) has elaborated on this hypothesis.

At the time of these publications, the evidence favoring habituation in lower sites of the auditory pathway was substantial. However, Wickelgren (1968a) subsequently offered evidence which again argued against this conclusion. Utilizing a rather complicated paradigm of slightly more than 6 seconds of five per second, 85-dB clicks during each minute, he noted evoked potential decrements in the medial geniculate body and auditory cortex but not in the cochlear nucleus, superior olive, or inferior colliculus after less than 1 hour of stimulation. The middle ear muscles were severed in one animal without substantially affecting the results. The author suggested that well-controlled experiments preclude the observation of habituationlike decrements at levels below the thalamus, and that most likely "the neural events which cause behavioral habituation are located at higher brain sites." The technique of delivering stimuli during only 6 seconds of each minute may, however, have precluded evoked potential modification at lower sites without impeding the decrements at higher levels. This explanation, of course, necessitates different processes or at least different rates of the same neural process at the two levels. This is not unreasonable. Habituation is clearly more readily observable at the thalamus and cortex than at subthalamic locations.

A report of some interest in regard to the question of cortical habituation is that of Teas and Kiang (1964), who failed to observe systematic changes in either early or late components of auditory evoked potentials in cats presented with clicks for a number of days. Late components did change with arousal level, however, and the authors suggested that prior studies which reported decrementing cortical responses may have simply been dealing with late component alterations in drowsy animals. Wickelgren (1968a) was careful to avoid data derived from subjects whose EEG records were indicative of sleep, although he did report decrements primarily of the late components of the evoked responses.

An important study in regard to the question of component decrements is that of Key (1965) who found large, significant, and *rapid* decrements in the *late,* or *secondary,* surface-positive component of the auditory cortex evoked potential in awake cats. Stimuli were either tone bursts of 30 msec duration or 5-second long tones delivered at 1- to 2-minute intervals. The behavioral arousal response induced by the initial stimuli, and the late component of the evoked response showed marked, parallel reductions within 30 stimulus presentations; this provided an important correlation between the secondary cortical component and the arousal response. The *primary* component of the cortical response remained unchanged during the decrements of the secondary component but did subsequently habituate after additional tone presentations.

Hall (1968) reported similar differential decrements of evoked response components. In a conditioning procedure, rats were trained to remain motionless with food as reinforcement. Trains of 60 clicks at one per second were then presented, with a 10-minute interval between each train; the clicks were not associated with reinforcement and were therefore not significant to the subjects. Only late components of the click-induced cortical potential showed clear amplitude reduction over days. Both early and late components in the medial geniculate body response showed similar changes, but no decrements were found in the potentials recorded from inferior colliculus or ventral cochlear nucleus. In a subsequent measurement of the click-evoked potentials during active bar-pressing, the late cortical potential was reduced, but no change was seen in ventral cochlear nucleus sites. Because several hundred potentials were averaged in this study to obtain a response amplitude for each day, the rapid decrements seen by others at the cochlear nucleus would, if they were present, have been missed by this technique. Hall's data showing no collicular or cochlear nucleus response decrements are similar to those of Wickelgren (1968a); as in Wickelgren's paradigm, Hall's stimuli were not continuously delivered but, rather, groups of stimuli were separated by 10-minute breaks.

As Teas and Kiang (1964) had previously suggested for cortical response decrements, Hall interpreted previous reports of cochlear nucleus evoked potential decrements as due to variations in arousal, a condition which was held constant by behavioral training methods in his experiment. Cochlear nucleus evoked response amplitude has been shown to vary with arousal levels (Winters *et al.,* 1967) as has the auditory nerve potential (Baust *et al.,* 1964). On the other hand, Huttenlocher (1960) and Wickelgren (1968b) were unable to see changes in the size of cochlear nucleus-evoked responses with varying levels of arousal; and Worden and Marsh (1963) attributed cochlear nucleus response variations with arousal to differences in ear position relative to the click source exhibited by aroused and drowsy subjects.

In agreement with Key (1965), cortical auditory-evoked response decrements of both early and late components were readily observed in moderately restrained, unparalyzed cats by Cook *et al.* (1968). In this study, asymptotic levels were generally reached after 10 earphone-delivered clicks. The asymptote of the early component, at least, was lower with faster click presentation rates. Arousal level was well controlled.

An extensive survey of the effects, throughout the brain, of repetitive 60-dB clicks at rates varying from 1 to 20 per second was made by Jaffe *et al.* (1969). Evoked responses were recorded in numerous auditory and nonauditory sites from rostral forebrain to pontine levels in unanesthetized spinal cats; clicks were delivered through the earbars which held the cat in a stereotaxic device. Response decrements ranged from partial reductions to complete disappearance of the evoked potential and developed in widespread parts of the brain during the first few clicks. There was no apparent difference between auditory and nonauditory sites in terms of rate of habituation, although the more rostral the electrode the more likely were the potentials to decrement. The observed decrements were thought to reflect neural processing related to the habituation of the orienting response. In argeement with others, the authors suggested that habituation which develops only after several hours or even days of constant stimulation is unrelated to overt behavioral habituation.

Progressive decrements in cortical potentials were observed by Meschersky and Rosenschtein (1969) using *encephale isole* cats; in the same preparation Weinberger *et al.* (1969) found little correlation between evoked responses recorded from the trapezoid body, superior olive, lateral lemniscus, or mesencephalic tegmentum and the habituation of eye movements. During repeated monaural, one per second, 85-dB trains of clicks or tone bursts, the eye movements disappeared after fewer than 30 trials, but no consistent modification of evoked potentials was seen at the peripheral relay levels of the auditory pathway.

Holstein *et al.* (1969a), Kitzes and Buchwald (1969), and Humphrey *et al.* (1970) reported progressive changes in *multiple-unit activity* at the cochlear nucleus, inferior colliculus, and medial geniculate body as a result of repeated stimulation with relatively long (at least 1.5-second) tones or white noise. These experiments were carried out on normal awake cats in both paralyzed and unparalyzed conditions, as well as on decerebrate, paralyzed cats. Both monaural and binaural sound stimulation were employed. Data from these studies will be discussed in detail in Section IV. In general, they indicated that *unit responses to repeated presentation of relatively long duration stimuli decrement at all levels of the specific auditory pathway.*

2. Human Studies

There have been a number of habituation studies focused upon the human, sound-elicited, vertex potential (Davis *et al.*, 1966; Ritter *et al.*, 1968; Butler, 1968; Butler *et al.*, 1969; Roth and Kopell, 1969; Fruhstorfer *et al.*, 1969, 1970). This response has been shown to habituate rapidly, often reaching asymptotic levels after as few as three click stimuli; fast stimulus rates (one per second) produced greater and more rapid decrements than slower ones (one per 3 seconds). The response was found to recover spontaneously but appeared difficult to dishabituate with other stimuli. This latter phenomenon has been related to the remarkable generalization of the vertex potential which can be similarly elicited not only by varied stimuli within one modality (Butler, 1968) but by stimulation of varied afferent systems as well (Fruhstorfer *et al.*, 1970). Because of this convergence, focused perhaps in the nonspecific sensory projection paths, habituation to one sensory stimulus would also result in smaller potentials subsequently elicited by some other stimulus modality (Fruhstorfer *et al.*, 1969).

Perceptual aftereffects in humans following auditory stimulation, particularly those of temporary threshold shifts, e.g., temporary deafness, may reflect phenomena importantly related to habituation. These data have been reviewed by Ward (1966) and Lawrence (1968). One interpretive difficulty at present is that there appears to be more than one mechanism responsible for such temporary shifts in sound threshold, and it is unclear whether these mechanisms are functioning at the cochlear receptor level or more centrally.

3. Summary

One would hope that from the foregoing investigations, concrete conclusions could be reached regarding the degree to which the classical auditory system can reflect or mediate response decrements, or habituation. In spite of the considerable effort expended in the analysis of habituation in this system, conclusions derived from it often seem to be based on impressions due to frequent, seemingly unresolvable contradictions. We have derived the following rough percentages of studies which have reported progressive decrements of at least one component of the evoked potential with iterative acoustic stimulation at the given sites: auditory cortex, 87%; medial geniculate body, 88%; inferior colliculus, 67%; superior olive, 67%; cochlear nucleus, 54%. In addition, in two examinations of the auditory nerve potentials, both have reported progressive decrements; and one of two examinations of changes in the cochlear microphonic has reported a reduction in the amplitude of this response, as well. These figures were arrived at by simply dichotomizing the data into those cases reporting the presence and those reporting the absence of progressive decrements without regard to controls, parametric considerations, or conclusions of the authors. Thus, while there are numerous studies that do not support the existence of progressive modulation of electrical activity along the classical auditory pathway, there are others that do. As a general statement, it appears clear that *the more rostral the locus, the more readily observable are modifications of evoked potentials;* and that *later, secondary components of the evoked response, usually recorded only at thalamic and cortical levels, are more likely to reflect changes than is the short latency, primary component.*

Perhaps the most prominent characteristic of the evoked potential, the classical recording utilized in these studies, is variability. The amplitude, for example, is often reported to wax and wane. The following variables have been implicated as determinants of evoked potential modifications: state of arousal, including anesthetic state; movements of the subject; condition of middle ear muscles; presence and location of brain lesions; interstimulus interval; intensity of stimulation; source of sound stimulus if earphones have not been utilized, i.e., the location of the animal in the experimental chamber relative to the loudspeaker, and the acoustic characteristics of the recording box; location of electrodes along the auditory pathway; recording position within a nucleus; and the component of the evoked potential measured. Except for occasional use of anesthesia, paralyzing agents, and middle ear muscle section, the experimental animals were generally awake and unrestrained, a condition which, while "physiological," is nevertheless most difficult to interpret. For example, ear muscle contractions to nonacoustic events, e.g., body movement or vocalization, are known to affect evoked response amplitudes in the auditory pathway (von Békésy, 1949; Carmel and Starr, 1963, 1964; Salomon and Starr, 1963; Simmons, 1964; Starr, 1964); lower levels are most susceptible to such peripheral influences, and it is response habituation at these lower levels which is most often questioned. The responsiveness of the auditory cortex is more affected by other "extraneous" influences. Heights of the cortical evoked responses are known to vary with arousal states (Gumnit and Grossman, 1961; Steriade and Demetrescu, 1962; Gerkin and Neff, 1963; Wickelgren, 1968b), fear (Hall and Mark, 1967), attention (Donchin and Cohen, 1967), movement (Starr, 1964), and even hunger (Saunders and Chabora, 1969).

In our own experiments (see Section IV) we combined the following procedures in an attempt to reduce the influence of these variables: (*a*) stimuli delivered by earphones; (*b*) monaural stimulation; (*c*) elimination of ear muscle effects (by paralysis); and (*d*) decerebration. In addition, these experiments differed from precedent studies in that we measured neural responsiveness by recording multiple-unit activity rather than the evoked potential, and utilized long duration tones (usually 1.5 seconds) rather than brief clicks. Procedures (*a*), (*c*), and (*d*) have been employed at least once in the habituation studies cited, but none has been used universally. Since all of these factors can, if not controlled, contribute singly and in combination to complicate the development and analysis of response habituation, it is not surprising that the evoked potential studies have yielded such inconsistent results.

However, many investigators since the study by Worden and Marsh (1963) have been careful to monitor behavior so as to avoid data during movements or vocalization or during trials in which the effective stimulus intensity varied due to altered head position. Many of these investigators reported consistent progressive decrements in evoked response amplitude to repetitive stimulation *even at the lower levels of the auditory pathway.*

B. THE VISUAL SYSTEM

1. The Retinocortical Pathway

During presentation of hundreds or thousands of light flash stimuli to unrestrained, unanesthetized cats over a 4-hour period, Hernández-Peón and his collaborators (Hernández-Peón *et al.,* 1956a, 1958; Palestini *et al.,* 1959) recorded optic tract, lateral geniculate body, and visual cortex evoked potentials; they reported clear decrements of the late-evoked potential components, especially in the lateral geniculate body and visual cortex, which were said to persist for 24 hours. Small decrements were occasionally seen at the optic tract when flashes were presented at rates of one per second. Evoked potentials were clearly reduced at all points along the visual pathway whenever the animal attended to acoustic or olfactory stimuli (Hernández-Peón *et al.,* 1957b). Responses recovered with rest and were dishabituated by changes in flash intensity or in background illumination and by pairings of flash and paw shock. Acoustic stimuli were also capable of dishabituating the visual evoked response; as discussed in our review of Hernández-Peón's auditory habituation experiments, his theory of attention implies that dishabituation by one stimulus mode (auditory in this case) of responses in another sensory system (visual in this case) can apparently be accomplished only if the animal does not *attend* to the dishabituating stimulus. It was believed that the reticular formation acted to suppress retinal activity during attention to stimuli of other modalities, and that during habituation suppression of sensory activity occurred at the lateral geniculate body, probably also mediated by the reticular formation.

Similarly, John and Killam (1959, 1960) found a reduction in amplitude of lateral geniculate body and visual cortex evoked responses to flickering light of 10 per second delivered daily, as 20 15-second periods of flicker, to unrestrained cats during a period of several days of "familiarization" prior to conditioning. Visual relays at thalamic and cortical levels showed response reduction but only after precedent decrements of rhinencephalic, reticular, and superior collicular responses. All decrements were readily reversed by conditioning procedures.

Mancia *et al.* (1959a) confirmed these findings of evoked potential diminution in the lateral geniculate body and visual cortex during flash presentations of one per second to the *cerveau isolé* cat, a preparation with little or no reticular influence on higher levels. All response components became depressed after many fewer stimuli than the Hernández-Peón group had found necessary to induce response decrements in the intact animal. In the *encephale isolé* preparation, on the other hand, with reticulocortical connections intact, almost one day of continuous flashes of one per second flashes were required before response decrements could be seen (Mancia *et al.*, 1959b). In both the *cerveau isolé* and the *encephale isolé* preparations the cortical responses were more quickly depressed than those of the lateral geniculate body. EEG synchronization paralleled evoked potential reduction, and EEG desynchronization accompanied enhancement of the evoked response. These results supported earlier observations but argued against an essential role for the reticular formation during response habituation in the visual system. In a contemporary study, it was also suggested that depression of the ascending reticular system was necessary for photic habituation (Cavaggioni *et al.*, 1959), while activation of the reticular formation played a significant role in *dishabituation*.

In an important control experiment, Naquet *et al.* (1960) demonstrated a direct relationship between degree of pupil dilation and evoked response amplitude in the optic tract and lateral geniculate body. Subsequently, Fernández-Guardiola *et al.* (1960, 1961) showed that response decrements in the optic tract and lateral geniculate nucleus no longer developed to flashes of four to six per second in intact or *encephale isolé* cats when pupillary dilation was held constant by atropine; a moderate amount of habituation was still apparent in the evoked potentials recorded from the visual cortex. Similarly Affanni *et al.* (1962; see also Mancia, 1961) recorded from the optic tract, lateral geniculate body, and visual cortex in *cerveau isolé* cats and found no change in response amplitude at any site when a number of peripheral factors were ruled out by control procedures. Pupillary dilation was held constant with atropine, by lesioning the oculomotor nucleus, or by cutting the ciliary nerve which innervates the pupil; the tendons of the extrinsic eye muscles were severed to prevent eye movements; the eyelids were held open; the nictitating membrane was resected; and a contact lens with an artificial pupil (slit) was fitted to the eye. Although Affanni *et al.* did not deny that some habituation of the visual pathway, independent of peripheral factors, was possible, previous positive results were attributed mainly to pupillary and other ocular variations.

Similar findings were reported by Palestini *et al.* (1964) who found that the evoked visual cortex responses, which completely disappeared in intact but restrained cats after 3–4 hours of flashes of one per second stimulation, did not show similar decrements when eyelid, eyeball, and pupil variations were precluded. The close correspondence between pupil size, ocular movements, and neural activity in the optic chiasma was discussed by Fernández-Guardiola *et al.* (1964a).

Bogacz *et al.* (1960) found clear habituation of the cortical visual evoked response of human subjects within 30 minutes using flash rates of two per second or one per 2 seconds with no pupillary control. This effect was observed whether or not the eyes were closed. There was greater change in response amplitude recorded from parietal and temporal regions, but all components of striatal visual responses showed some decrement with repetition of flash stimuli. Subsequent to the implication of peripheral influences in visual system habituation, García-Austt *et al.* (1963) tested normal human subjects, as well as two subjects with aniridia and one with ocular paralysis. One eye only was stimulated with light flashes and EEG was monitored to indicate general arousal levels. Progressive decrements of the visual cortex evoked response was observed with and without pupil dilation (by atropine, homatropine, or phenilephrine) or constriction (by pilocarpine), in all subjects with ocular abnormalities, under conditions of control by artificial pupil, and with and without the lids closed. Data from instances of head, eye, or lid movement (determined photographically at each flash) were rejected. These positive results were thought to be due in part to an averaging technique, utilizing successive series of 40 responses, which made small decrements more readily observable. These findings were discussed more extensively by García-Austt (1963).

Using computer analyses of their data, Perry and Copenhaver (1965) also reported habituation of cortical-evoked responses to flash stimulation in human subjects, and presented evidence favoring faster and greater percentage decrement to stimulation of the retina peripheral to the fovea than that to foveal stimulation. Pupil size was said to effect neither rate nor degree of habituation.

In an additional refutation of pupillary alterations as the primary cause of visual response decrements, Macadar *et al.* (1963) showed evoked response amplitude diminution at the visual cortex of both normal rats (with and without atropine-induced mydriasis) and iridectomized rats after 2–5 hours of flashes of one per 2 seconds; late components showed the most change. Dishabituation was achieved by brief (20- to 50-second) periods of darkness, by a change in the flash intensity or rate, or by stimulation of some other sensory modality.

Fernández-Guardiola *et al.* (1964b, 1968) showed that, while optic tract activity is directly related to pupil size, lateral geniculate and cortex responses vary independently of the pupil in both intact curarized, and *encephale isolé* cats. When a brief train of stimuli was presented every 15 seconds to paralyzed preparations with pupils atropinized, the cortical-evoked response *increased* in amplitude, while responses recorded from lateral geniculate simultaneously decreased. These changes occurred only during nonaroused states, indicated by synchronous EEG activity, and only with trains of stimulation; repeated single stimuli, at two per second, were without effect. The authors postulated a dual process in photic habituation whereby, in the absence of arousal, the pupillary motor centers gradually lost reticular inhibition with a resultant increase in pupillary constriction while, concurrently, cortical feedback circuits progressively modulated responsiveness within the lateral geniculate body.

Additional evidence of habituation of lateral geniculate activity is that of Arden (1963), who found some units in rabbit lateral geniculate which habituated very rapidly to a moving spot of light; these units required so few stimulus presentations before decrementing that they were difficult to detect.

Using unrestrained cats with nictitating membranes resected and with an elaborate contact light-shield device with an internal light source positioned next to the cornea, Steinberg (1965) observed no consistent decrement of any component of computer-analyzed cortical visual-evoked responses after 2–9 hours of flash stimulations of one per second or one per 4 seconds. In the striate cortex of freely moving cats, Horn (1965b) found no units whose responsiveness diminished with repeated diffuse light stimulation, although only a small proportion of the units studied were sensitive to this type of stimulus (see Hubel and Wiesel, 1962). Whether repetitive presentations of complex patterns would be more or less likely to cause response decrements is not known.

Hall (1968), on the other hand, found 50–60% day-to-day attenuation of the late evoked response components recorded from the visual cortex of rats; early components of the cortical response were unchanged. The behavior of the subjects was controlled by requiring them to hold a foot bar down for 15-second periods. Movement was restricted by cage dimensions so that the animals were forced to retain an orientation toward the small light source. Flashes were given at a rate of one per second for the final 13 seconds of the response. Many hundreds of potentials were averaged in this study to obtain the response amplitude for each day.

2. The Optic Tectum

Several studies of habituation of superior colliculus and pretectum single-unit responses to various visual stimuli have been reported in cat

(Sprague *et al.*, 1968; Harutiunian-Kozak *et al.*, 1968), rabbit (Horn and Hill, 1964, 1966a,b), rat (Humphrey, 1968), opossum (Goodwin and Hill, 1968; Hill and Goodwin, 1968), and monkey (Humphrey, 1968). The units often responded to moving spots or bars of light, and their response decrements were typically fast, often within three presentations of such moving stimuli. The unit response decrements were frequently seen in collicular layers containing fiber terminals of the retinal ganglion cells and third-order cells with which these terminals synapse. Sprague *et al.* (1968), however, found more units which habituated in the deeper collicular layers (*stratum griseum intermediale* and *stratum griseum profundum*).

Horn and Hill (1966b) reported stimulus-specific habituation in which some units, sensitive to tactile and/or acoustic stimuli as well as to visual stimuli, showed response decrements to one modality without similar decrements during repeated presentations of other stimulus modalities. Dishabituation of these decreased responses was difficult or impossible, but spontaneous recovery generally occurred after a period without stimulation.

3. Summary

Evaluation of neural habituation in the visual pathway has had a history not unlike that of the auditory system. It has progressed from a series of positive results through a continuing analysis of peripheral influences on these early findings. With adequate controls for pupillary stability and other variables, evoked response decrements in the optic tract during stimulus repetition have not been shown. On the other hand, in the lateral geniculate body and visual cortex, evoked potential reductions have been reported under well-controlled peripheral conditions; these changes are not inevitably seen, however, and the conditions which favor their manifestation remain elusive. There is general agreement that unit discharges in the optic tectum rapidly and consistently decrease during repeated visual stimulation.

Certain observations cannot easily be explained if peripheral mechanisms are assumed to be sole arbitors of visual response habituation: (a) activity in the lateral geniculate body and/or cortex showed a diminution with stimulus repetition, while no change was seen in the optic tract (Hernández-Peón *et al.*, 1956a, 1958); (b) response decrements were not temporally coincident, i.e., visual cortex decrements preceded the later decrements in lateral geniculate body (Cavaggioni *et al.*, 1959; Mancia *et al.*, 1959a,b; Fernández-Guardiola *et al.*, 1968); (c) the complete disappearance of the cortical-evoked response, frequently seen in habituation, was difficult to achieve simply by varying retinal illumination, even, for example, in extreme pupillary miosis (Affanni *et al.*, 1962); moreover, Naquet *et al.* (1960) found atropine-induced mydriasis produced increased visual-evoked responses in the optic chiasma and lateral geniculate body but had no effect on response size in the visual cortex.

Sprague *et al.* (1968) found closely corresponding decrements in superior colliculus unit discharge and the EMG of the superior rectus muscle; this suggests that some units in this tectal region may be involved, directly or indirectly, in motor function (see Wurtz and Goldberg, 1971). Harutiunian-Kozak *et al.* (1968), however, questioned whether the pretectal units which they found to habituate were involved in motor activities, e.g., the pupillary light reflex, or whether these units were solely sensory. Many units which have shown visual response decrements, both in the superior colliculus itself and in the pretectum, are located very close to optic tract input (Humphrey, 1968) and thus can reasonably be considered sensory. Sprague *et al.* (1968) suggested that, anatomically, the superficial layers of the superior colliculus are comparable to third-order units throughout the lateral geniculate body in that they both receive projections from second-order retinal cells. The lateral geniculate body relays to the cortex, while the superficial layers of the colliculus project to deeper parts of the optic tectum or to brainstem motor nuclei. Among these structures, habituation is most readily observed at the visual cortex and deep in the optic tectum, both of which receive multisynaptic inputs, while habituation is less probable but still present in the superficial layers of the superior colliculus and in the lateral geniculate body which receive second-order projections from the retina.

Thus, as appears to be true of the auditory pathway, the visual system is more likely to show habituatory response decrements the more centrally the neurons are located. Whether this indicates summation of decremental processes occurring at each synapse between the point of stimulation and the point of recording, whether it reflects a greater opportunity for integrative feedback mechanisms to operate on the more central cells, or whether it simply results from the different cellular characteristics at various central levels is not known.

C. The Somatosensory System

The extensive literature which has developed over the past 70 years on the subject of motor response habituation to repeated somatic stimulation probably contains several thousands of papers. Many of these data have been recently reviewed (Kandel and Spencer, 1968; Groves and Thompson, 1970). In contrast to this wealth of experimental investigation, information on plasticity within the somatosensory system *per se* during repeated somatic stimulation is almost nonexistent.

Concurrently with studies of auditory and visual system response plasticity, Hernández-Peón and Brust-Carmona (1961) examined the effects of repeated somatic stimulation on the somatosensory system. This work was confined to relatively few experiments carried out on high spinal animals with electrodes chronically implanted in the lateral funiculus of the spinal cord. Although response habituation and dishabituation were reported in the spinal-evoked response, the recording site was not specifically identified. Thus, it is not clear whether an ascending somatic pathway, a propriospinal relay, or possibly an internuncial pool was the significant source of response modulation. A subsequent study of the ventrobasal thalamic relay and somatosensory cortex of intact animals indicated that, during repeated electrical stimulation of the paw or cutaneous nerve, decrement of the secondary component of the cortical response occurred, although little or no change developed in the primary-evoked response at either level (Santibañez *et al.*, 1963). Little further investigation of somatosensory habituation occurred until recordings were made in paralyzed spinal animals of motoneuron response decrements during repeated cutaneous stimulation (Buchwald *et al.*, 1965b; Spencer *et al.*, 1966b; Wickelgren, 1967a). In order to determine the origin of the habituated motor response, discharges of the primary afferent fibers, dorsal horn cells, and ascending somatic spinal tracts were subsequently examined during repeated cutaneous stimulation. Recordings of the cord dorsum potential in the paralyzed spinal cat indicated that small but significant decrements occurred in the N_1, N_2, and P components (Spencer *et al.*, 1966a). The N_1 component has been ascribed to the postsynaptic potential of somatosensory neurons lying within the dorsal horn which give rise to ascending projections, while the N_2 wave represents the discharge of dorsal horn sensory neurons related to segmental reflex connections; the P wave is related to the depolarization of primary afferent fibers responsible for presynaptic inhibition. Additional evoked response recordings by Spencer *et al.* (1966a) were carried out from the dissected dorsolateral and ventral columns of the spinal cord. In both funiculi, ascending polysynaptic somatic relays showed small response decrements to repeated cutaneous stimulation, but the monosynaptic response of the dorsolateral column showed no change. When a strong dishabituating stimulus was presented, a partial restoration of the P wave, i.e., in the relays mediating presynaptic inhibition, occurred but no restoration occurred in the N_1 or

N_2 components, nor in the ascending tract potentials. In all cases spontaneous recovery occurred. Under the same stimulus conditions, the motor reflex responses showed much greater decrements and clear-cut restoration following a dishabituating stimulus. As the motoneurons themselves did not show marked decrements in excitability, the internuncial pool was considered to be the locus of greatest response plasticity.

Subsequently, several studies were carried out in which the responses of dorsal horn interneurons were recorded during repeated cutaneous stimulation in paralyzed spinal cats (Wall, 1967; Wickelgren, 1967b; Groves *et al.*, 1969). Because dorsal horn laminae I–V receive the primary afferent terminals of cutaneous fibers, the cells within these laminae can be considered second- and third-order somatosensory relays of either ascending or segmental projection pathways (Rexed, 1964). Among 72 units studied in dorsal horn layers IV and V, generally agreed to contain most of the cells responding to cutaneous input, response decrements to repeated cutaneous stimulation were frequently recorded; none of the habituating units, however, showed a monosynaptic response to the cutaneous stimulus (Wickelgren, 1967b). The habituating cells were characterized as responding to a wide range of somatic stimuli with a spontaneous discharge rate of more than 10 per second, a polysynaptic response latency, and a relatively repetitive discharge to a single shock stimulus. These data are in agreement with the response decrements of "novelty" units in lamina V (Wall, 1967), and have been reconfirmed in a subsequent study of units in lamina I–V during repeated cutaneous stimulation (Groves *et al.*, 1969).

Somewhat deeper in the internuncial pool, e.g., spinal layers VI–VIII, other interneurons have been noted to show transient response increments during repeated cutaneous stimulation (Frank and Fuortes, 1956; Kolmodin and Skoglund, 1960; Eccles *et al.*, 1961; Mendell and Wall, 1965) which may subsequently be followed by a decremental response (Groves *et al.*, 1969); both incremental and decremental responses may follow a time course which parallels similar response alterations in the concurrently induced flexion reflex (Groves and Thompson, 1970).

The most striking aspect of these data, in the perspective of habituation experiments in other systems, is the complete agreement among all investigators that somatosensory units in the dorsal horn show response decrements to repeated peripheral stimulation. Decrements were not found in the responses of monosynaptic cells, but the abundant number of units which did show decrements represented third-order or higher sensory relay neurons. In relation to the primary afferent input, such cells would be comparable to third-order neurons in, for example, the cochlear nucleus, inferior colliculus, or lateral geniculate body.

D. The Vestibular System

Although there is increasingly great interest in the vestibular system, as illustrated by the recent first review of vestibular function in the *Annual Review of Psychology* (Clark, 1970), studies of vestibular response plasticity have not focussed on the sensory pathway *per se*. A formidable mass of data has evolved which characterizes alterations in nystagmus during repetitive or prolonged vestibular stimulation, but we have not noted recordings from the central vestibular pathway during such stimulation procedures. As the present survey has been confined to studies of plasticity within the specific sensory systems, experiments utilizing motor reflexes as indices of sensorimotor plasticity have not been included. For comprehensive discussions of current work on habituation of nystagmus, several recent reviews are available (Jongkees, 1969; Young, 1969; Clark, 1970).

E. General Summary

A great flurry of excitement in the 1950s and early 1960s was directed toward the possibility that sensory inflow was modulated within the specific sensory systems. This notion had, in turn, been triggered by the description of feedback loops to the sensory pathways from cortical and subcortical levels, which suggested a mechanism for response modulation within the sensory nuclei. Efferent control systems had, by the early 1960's, been described anatomically for the auditory (Rasmussen, 1955) and vestibular (Gacek, 1960) systems, and physiologically for the visual (Granit, 1955; Hernández-Peón *et al.,* 1956c) and somatosensory (Hagbarth and Kerr, 1954; Hernández-Peón *et al.,* 1956c) systems. Almost concurrently with these studies came investigations of response habituation in these sensory systems. The resultant data, derived largely from awake cats with implanted electrodes, showed evoked response decrements not only in the specific sensory cortical projection area but also at the level of the first relay nucleus for the incoming sensory fibers. Response decrements in the sensory relay nuclei were interpreted as secondary to the more central, i.e., reticular formation or cortical, response modulations, which were believed to alter the lower level response by a build-up of inhibitory feedback.

This "afferent inhibition" theory of sensory habituation was quickly challenged by other investigators who attempted to repeat the original findings without complete success. A wide range of variability in response decrements to repeated sensory stimulation was reported, and this variability was soon attributed to alterations in peripheral control mechanisms, such as the ear muscles and pupil. These data gave rise to a "peripheral control" theory and triggered, in turn, further studies which were carried out under conditions of constant peripheral input, i.e., the ear muscles were cut or paralyzed, the iris was paralyzed, or an artificial pupil was used. Additional variables were defined, such as the effect of altered head position on the received decibel level, or the effects of body movements on neural activity in the sensory pathways.

Although there is now an awareness of these peripheral variables and attempts are made to control them, the format of sensory system habituation experiments has remained essentially unchanged. The evoked response is still the measure of activity most commonly used, although the neuronal counterparts of its various wave components are generally unidentified (Mackay *et al.*, 1969). It is clear that the earliest, or primary, component of the evoked potential reflects discharge of incoming fibers, resultant synaptic potentials and postsynaptic discharge of the neurons innervated most directly. As evidenced by the precedent data, such primary responses decrement less easily than the later, secondary components. It is difficult to determine the source of these later components at any specific site without careful experimental analysis. Such potentials could, in part, represent (*1*) the later arrival of discharges over nonspecific, multisynaptic pathways, e.g., relays through reticular formation, thalamic, or cortical levels, or (*2*) long-latency discharges mediated by interneuronal circuitry within the specific nucleus. In addition to these and other complicating factors, such as the arousal state of the subject and the parametric features of stimulation, the appearance of sensory response habituation seems to vary with the central level. Thus, after 15 years of experimentation, during which evoked potential recordings have been used chiefly in the intact awake cat to study sensory response habituation, existence of response alterations in specific auditory and visual pathways has general agreement only at the level of the cortex and thalamus.

On the other hand, recordings of unit discharge show general agreement that response modulations also occur at the more peripheral levels of the sensory pathways. Recordings from dorsal horn somatosensory neurons in the spinal cord have shown that responses of third-order neurons decrement significantly during repeated cutaneous stimulation, although the response of neurons making monosynaptic connections with the incoming primary afferent fibers do not show such changes. In the cochlear nucleus, inferior colliculus, lateral geniculate body, and superior colliculus, examples of other nuclei with numerous third-order neurons, significant decrements of unit discharge have been demonstrated during repeated acoustic or visual stimulation. Such data indicate that with appropriate experimental procedures, response modulations can be observed in the peripheral relay nuclei of the sensory pathways as well as at more central levels.

Thus, recent experimental literature supports the concept of sensory response habituation from the level of third-order sensory neurons through the more centrally situated cells of the thalamus and cortex where this characteristic becomes increasingly pronounced. It is obvious that further experimentation must be carried out to delineate the variables which permit or prevent the appearance of such decrements. In the next section, evidence from recent studies of the auditory system will be presented in which multiple-unit recordings, long-duration stimuli, and a variety of control procedures have been used; this experimental format has been utilized in an attempt to induce and evaluate responses less restricted than those elicited by stimulus onset. In the subsequent section (Section V), possible neuronal processes underlying sensory response decrements will be discussed.

IV. Response Plasticity Reflected by Multiple-Unit Recording and Long-Duration Stimuli

A. Introduction

Our interest in sensory response plasticity stems from electrophysiological observations initially made on awake animals during behavioral conditioning (Buchwald *et al.,* 1965a, 1966a). In these experiments, animals were exposed to several sessions of tone stimulation before the tone (CS) was paired with shock to the paw (US) to establish a conditioned flexion reflex. In contrast to the ventrobasal thalamic relay of the US, where no tone responses occurred before or after conditioning, tone responses in the medial geniculate body and inferior colliculus were markedly changed by the onset of tone-shock pairings (Fig. 1). These altered responses within the auditory pathway were paralleled by response alterations in the mesencephalic reticular formation. For both systems, conditioning sessions during complete Flaxedil paralysis were as effective as in the normal, awake animal.

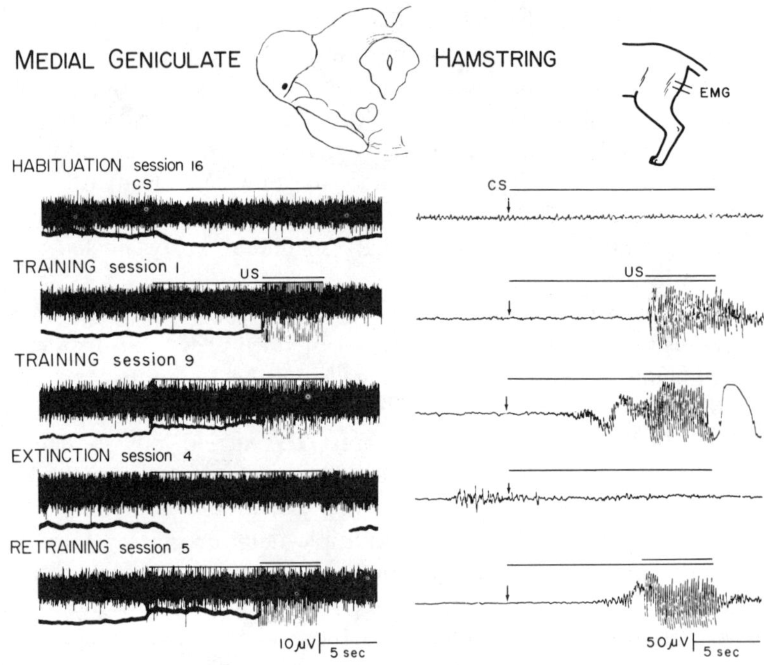

FIG. 1. Recordings from the principal nucleus of the medial geniculate body in a cat with implanted electrodes. Paired traces to the left indicate the multiple-unit activity (above) and its integration (below) for the training sequence and sessions indicated. Traces to the right indicate EMG activity during corresponding trials recorded from the hamstring muscles of the reinforced leg. Bars and arrows above the traces indicate onset and duration of CS (tone) and US (shock to the hindpaw). Electrode placement for unit recordings is illustrated in the midbrain insert (from Buchwald *et al.*, 1966a).

Thus, motor activity was not essential for the development or maintenance of the sensory response modulations.

B. RECORDING AND STIMULATION TECHNIQUES

Because the preceding effects were obtained during a complex conditioning paradigm, a simpler, more analyzable experiment seemed necessary if the apparent response plasticity of the auditory system were to be further investigated. Thus we began to study responses within the auditory pathway induced by a single repeated acoustic stimulus. In order to relate these data to the conditioning experiments, auditory stimuli with durations of 1–1.5 seconds, similar to those of the acoustic CS, were utilized. These stimuli were in contrast to the ultrashort clicks or tone pips traditionally used in studies of "acoustic habituation." Tone frequencies from 500 to 3000 Hz and white noise were utilized with intensities ranging from 65 to 80 dB re 0.0002 dyn/cm^2. Stimuli were presented by small speakers mounted in a head set which could be snugly adjusted to fit each cat and which minimized alterations in intensity due to variations in the animals' orientation to the sound source (Worden *et al.*, 1964).

Moreover, instead of the standard evoked potential recordings of acoustic habituation studies, multiple-unit activity was utilized as an index of electrophysiological activation and/or change. This measure, which had been used in the conditioning studies, clearly indicated alterations in response to training which had not been apparent in the concurrently recorded electroencephalogram and evoked potentials (Buchwald *et al.*, 1965a, 1966a,b). While multiple-unit activity cannot be equated with the precise behavior of a single discharging neuron, it is believed to represent primarily the action potential discharge of cells and fiber elements around the recording electrode (Arduini and Pinneo, 1962; Schlag and Balvin, 1963; Buchwald and Grover, 1970; Grover and Buchwald, 1970) and, where comparable studies have been carried out, close correspondences between multiple-unit and single-unit data have been reported (Podvall and Goodman, 1967; Holstein *et al.*, 1969a,b; Kitzes and Buchwald, 1969). Thus, multiple-unit recordings provide a summary of activation at the recording site based primarily upon net change in discharge frequency of local action potentials. (See Buchwald *et al.* (1973) for a review of this technique.)

In our experiments, the multiple-unit data was analyzed by first integrating the activity, either through a resistance–capacitance or a frequency integration system (Weber and Buchwald, 1965; Buchwald *et al.*, 1969), and then measuring the area of each response (Fig. 2). In many cases the integrated activity was computer averaged over five-trial series before such areal measurements were made. These measurements were then used for regression and variance analyses to determine whether progressive response modulations were significant. The response decrements reported below have been verified by such statistical analyses.

The discussion which follows summarizes data from several series of experiments in which 23 cats with chronically implanted electrodes, 22 cats with acutely implanted electrodes, and 32 decerebrated cats have been utilized. In all cases electrode placements were histologically verified. Data on binaural conditioning and habituation have been previously published (Buchwald *et al.*, 1965a, 1966a; Holstein *et al.*, 1969a; Kitzes and Buchwald, 1969), as have reports of monaural

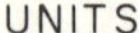

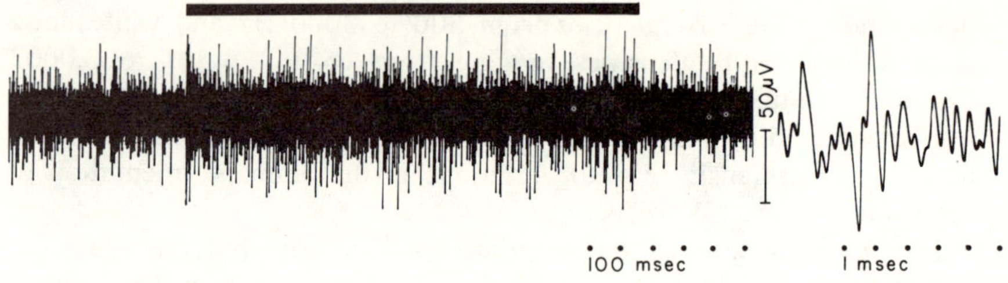

FREQUENCY INTEGRATION

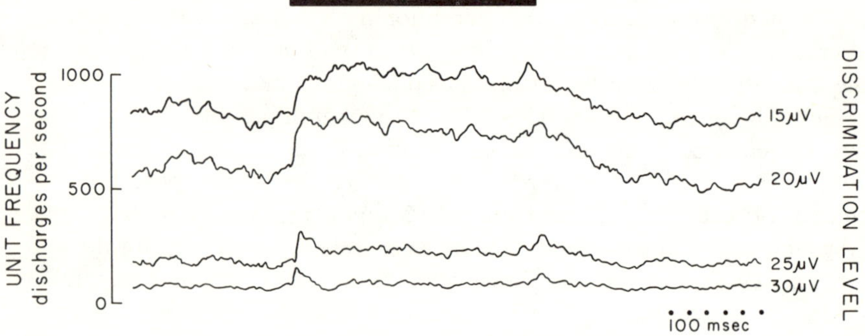

Fig. 2. Recordings from the medial geniculate body of an awake cat with implanted electrodes. Multiple-unit activity during a 1.5-second binaural tone is illustrated in the top trace; a segment of this activity is shown at a faster sweep speed in the insert to the right. Tone duration is indicated by black bar over the trace. Frequency integration of this activity at four different voltage levels is shown in the traces below. Unit frequency in discharges per second is indicated by the ordinate to the left, the discrimination level at which each integration was carried out is indicated to the right. Note differences in time bases as indicated by calibrations under the traces (from Buchwald *et al.*, 1969).

and decerebrate habituation (Buchwald, 1970; Buchwald and Humphrey, 1972; Humphrey *et al.*, 1970; Humphrey and Buchwald, 1972).

C. Binaural Stimulation of the Awake Cat

An initial series of animals was implanted with electrodes bilaterally placed throughout the extent of the subcortical auditory pathway, i.e., in the cochlear nucleus, inferior colliculus, medial geniculate body, pars principalis, and par magnocellularis. Characteristic multiple-unit tone response patterns were found for each relay nucleus which corresponded to the predominant patterns of single-unit discharge recorded by others (Holstein *et al.*, 1969b; Kitzes and Buchwald, 1969); as

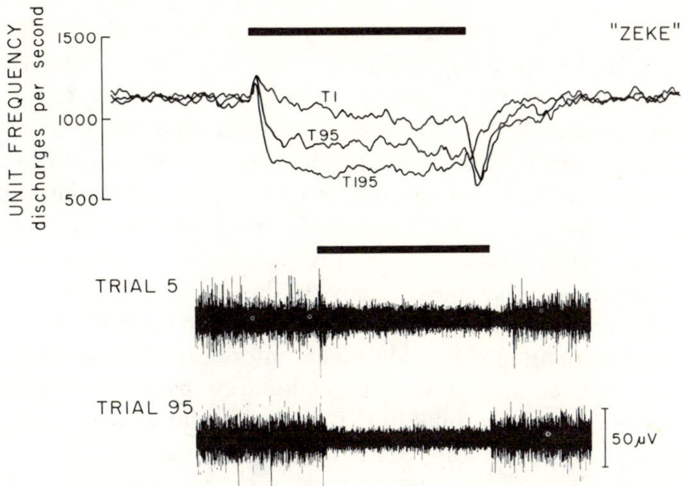

FIG. 3. Increasing inhibition of inferior colliculus responses during binaural tone presentations in a normal, waking cat. Traces of frequency integration (top) and corresponding multiple-unit fast activity (bottom) show changing form of the responses elicited by a 2500-Hz tone. Duration of the 1.5-second tone is indicated by bars over traces (from Holstein *et al.*, 1969a).

the acoustic pathway was ascended, more inhibition and less acceleration of unit discharge was produced by acoustic stimuli, and the range of effective tones became narrower.

The animals remained awake in the training hammock throughout acoustic habituation sessions in which 1.5-second tones were delivered *binaurally* at 5-second intervals through the earphones. In general, there was no overt stimulus-elicited movement of these animals. In the cochlear nucleus, the accelerated discharge to tone often increased, in other cases it decreased, and in other cases it showed little change with stimulus repetition; in contrast, in the inferior colliculus and medial geniculate body, the inhibition of unit discharge induced by acoustic stimulation became progressively more pronounced during repeated tones (Fig. 3).

D. Binaural Stimulation during Neuromuscular Paralysis

Although the field of the acoustic stimulus was controlled in these animals, the acoustic input was not, as the ear muscles were intact. The varied response modulations recorded from the cochlear nucleus indicated the necessity of controlling against fluctuating ear muscle contractions; thus, the habituation procedures were repeated during complete neuromuscular paralysis. Chronic tracheal fistulae were established in the preceding and other animals so that artificial respiration could easily be initiated following Flaxedil injection without precedent anesthesia for tracheal intubation and without panic or stress to the animal. This technique has been used extensively in our laboratory and animals subjected to repeated paralytic training become quite accustomed to it and developed no behavioral abnormalities (Buchwald *et al.*, 1964).

In the absence of ear muscle activity, the cochlear nucleus showed a greater accelerated discharge to tones and a decrement of this response during tone repetition (Fig. 4). The inferior colliculus and medial geniculate body continued to show inhibitory patterns which usually *increased* (became more inhibitory) during habituation, and resembled the responses shown in Fig. 3 for the unparalyzed cat.

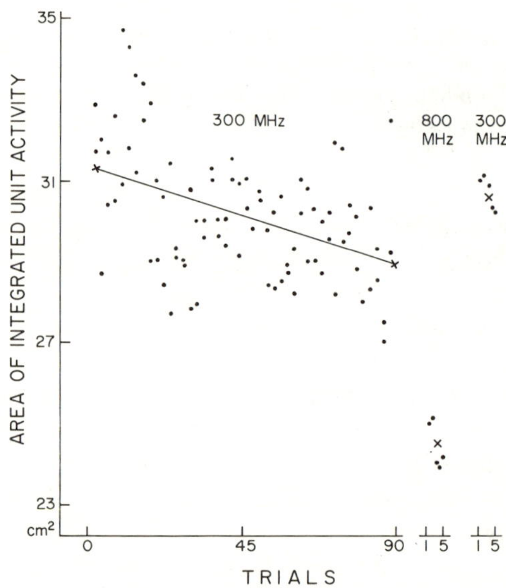

FIG. 4. Regression analysis of cochlear nucleus responses to repeated presentations of a 300-Hz tone in cat maintained under neuromuscular paralysis. The area of integrated multiple-unit activity measured for each tone response has been plotted against its corresponding habituation trial. The response decrement is significant at the 1% level, and the line corresponds to those values predicted from the regression equation with the X at each end equal to the predicted initial and final values ($F = 22.0$). After 90 habituation trials, a series of five 800-Hz dishabituating tones induced responses as shown on the graph with the average level indicated by an X. Subsequent presentations of the 300-Hz habituating tone elicited enhanced responses, the average of which is shown by an X (from Kitzes and Buchwald, 1969).

E. Monaural Stimulation

Although these response modulations during repeated acoustic stimulation were consistent from one cat to another, they reflected the complexity of binaural interaction at all levels of the acoustic pathway (Whitfield, 1967). In order to avoid this problem and to simplify the responsive system, a monaural stimulus, delivered through one earphone, was utilized in another habituation series with the contralateral earphone serving as a sound attenuation earplug. This group of cats was implanted with bilateral electrodes in dorsal or ventral cochlear nucleus, superior olivary complex, inferior colliculus, and medial geniculate body, pars principalis. When *monaural* tones were presented to the *paralyzed* cat, the cochlear nucleus showed accelerated unit discharge to ipsilateral stimulation and inhibition or no response to contralateral stimulation (Fig. 5). At the olivary level and at the level

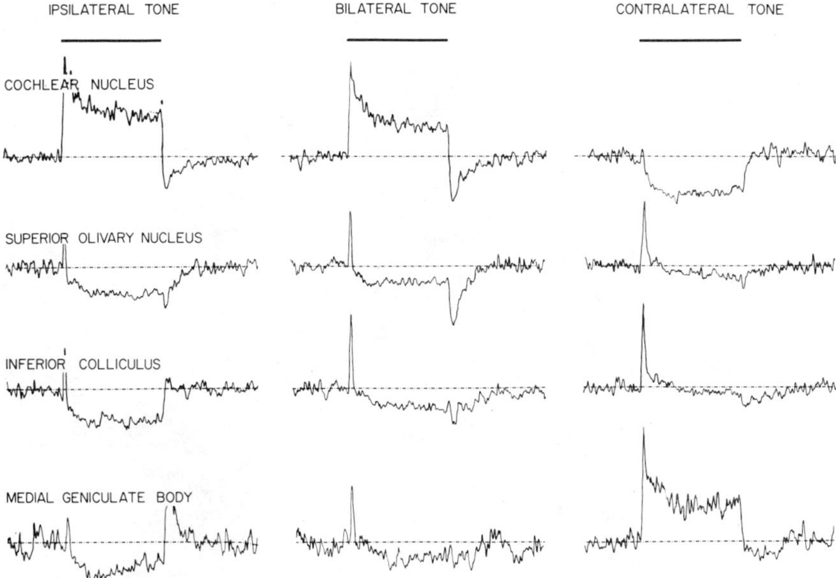

Fig. 5. Integrated multiple-unit activity from four levels of the auditory pathway in response to ipsilateral, bilateral, and contralateral presentations of a 2500-Hz, 80-dB tone to cat maintained under neuromuscular paralysis. These patterns are typical of those generally induced at each site, although some quantitative variation occurred as a function of tone frequency and intensity. The summed pattern of excitatory and inhibitory effects during bilateral stimulation was often imperfect, reflecting prepotency of input from one ear over that from the other. Bars over the traces represent duration of the 1.5-second tone; resistance–capacitance (RC) integration was utilized.

of the inferior colliculus and medial geniculate body, the responses to ipsilateral tone generally showed inhibited unit discharge, while those to contralateral tone showed acceleration (Fig. 5). These data are in general agreement with single-unit recordings during monaural stimulation (Whitfield, 1967). *These opposing effects tended to sum during binaural stimulation so as to produce the characteristic binaural response patterns previously observed* (Fig. 5).

Repeated presentations of the 1.5-second monaural tone at 5-second intervals resulted in progressive response *decrements* at all levels in the paralyzed cat. Thus, accelerated cochlear nucleus discharge to repeated ipsilateral tones decreased (Fig. 6), and inhibited discharge to contralateral tones also decreased during repeated stimulations (Fig. 7). (Both Figs. 6 and 7 illustrate data from decerebrate cats, but similar results have been obtained from the paralyzed intact cat.)

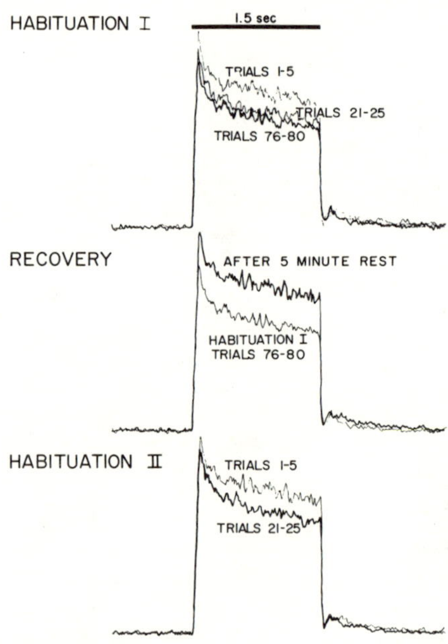

FIG. 6. Habituation, recovery, and rehabituation of cochlear nucleus accelerated discharge during presentations of a 1500-Hz, 80-dB tone to the ipsilateral ear of a paralyzed, decerebrated cat. Tone trials were repeated at 5-second intervals. The response decrements are statistically significant by linear regression analyses ($p < .05$). Bar over the traces represents duration of the 1.5-second tone; RC integration of multiple-unit activity was utilized.

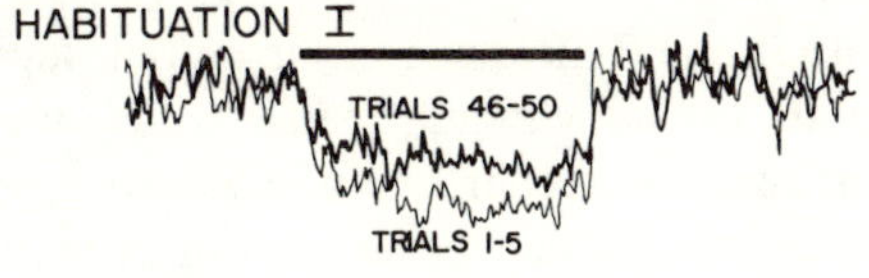

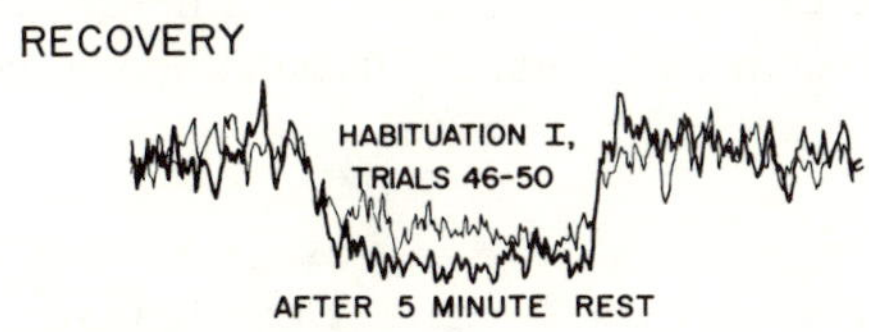

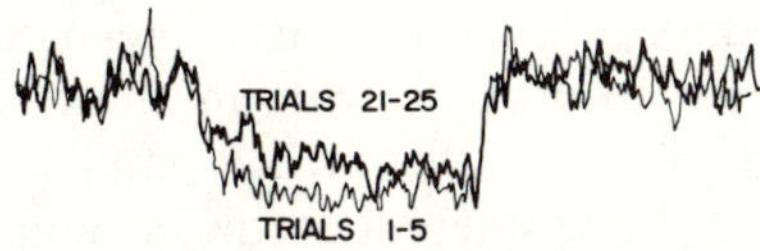

FIG. 7. Habituation, recovery, and rehabituation of cochlear nucleus inhibited discharge during presentations of a 1650-Hz, 80-dB tone to the contralateral ear of a paralyzed, decerebrated cat. Tones were repeated at 5 second intervals. The response decrements are statistically significant by linear regression analyses ($p < .05$). Bar over traces represents duration of the 1.5-second tone; RC integration of multiple-unit activity was utilized.

In the inferior colliculus and medial geniculate body, with repetition of an ipsilateral monaural stimulus, the typical inhibited response decreased (became *less* inhibited, as opposed to the increasing inhibition seen with binaural stimulation); the typical accelerated response to repeated contralateral stimulation also decreased.

Just as patterns of activity induced by binaural sounds reflect a combination of separate ipsilateral and contralateral effects, so too, *the repeated presentation of binaural tones resulted in progressive changes which are best interpreted as reflecting the sum of separate ipsilateral and contralateral progressive changes.* While we cannot discuss these effects in detail, it is clear that monaural stimulation results in data which are considerably easier to interpret than that produced by binaural stimulation.

We have only recently had the occasion to examine the patterns of multiple-unit activity and the progressive changes of that activity with iterative monaural sound stimulation in the unparalyzed intact cat. It is obvious that at the cochlear nucleus, and to some extent at the inferior colliculus, the ear muscles have a substantial effect on response variability. Initial evidence favors a complex action determined by several factors. The ear muscles initially habituate, probably in parallel with arousal habituation. This causes an initial increase in cochlear nucleus discharge to tones, which, if few trials are given, gives the appearance of sensitization rather than habituation of neural activity. This peripheral effect may influence the pattern of activity at the inferior colliculus to some extent, although we have never seen an ear muscle influence as high as the geniculate. Investigation is continuing on this problem.

F. Monaural Stimulation of the Decerebrate Cat

The preceding data indicated that response decrements occur at all levels of the auditory pathway during repeated monaural acoustic stimulation. In order to procede with an analysis of these decremental phenomena, it was necessary to further simplify the complexity of the pathway with its multiple efferent feedback loops. A step toward this simplification was accomplished by brain stem transection at the level of the inferior colliculus, a procedure which rendered the latter non-functional and eliminated all supracollicular influences on the brain stem (Buchwald and Humphrey, 1972; Humphrey and Buchwald, 1972). In such acutely prepared cats, maintained under Flaxedil paralysis, the multiple-unit response pattern of the cochlear nucleus to monaural tone was essentially the same as in the paralyzed intact cats, i.e., an acceleration to ipsilateral tone and inhibition to contra-lateral tone. During the same repeated stimulation procedures as those previously employed, similar response decrements were observed in the decerebrate cochlear nucleus. Significant and consistent decreases in acceleration to repeated ipsilateral tones occurred (Fig. 6) as well as decreases in inhibition to repeated contralateral tones (Fig. 7). *The decrements in these preparations are generally larger and faster than in the intact cat.* We have on several occasions seen reversals of the decrement ("spontaneous dishabituation") after 50–75 trials in the intact (and paralyzed) cat but have never observed this phenomenon in the decerebrate cat. It is clear that supracollicular areas tend to retard the progress of habituation of auditory system neurons, although the response patterns of the lower relay nuclei are essentially the same in the intact and decerebrate preparations.

G. Control Procedures

In six of these experiments, concurrent recordings from the ipsilateral round window accompanied the stimulation procedures. In some experi-ments the microphonic potential was stable throughout the experiment,

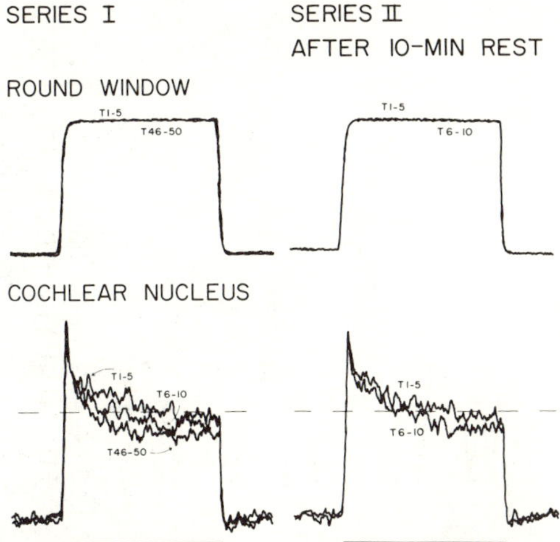

FIG. 8. Integrated round window microphonic (top) and cochlear nucleus multiple-unit activity (bottom) during presentations of a 1250-Hz, 70-dB tone to a paralyzed, decerebrate cat. Tones were repeated at 5-second intervals; a 10-minute rest period separated series I from series II. During both series I (left side) and series II (right side) the microphonic response remained constant while the neural activity progressively diminished ($p < .05$). Bars below traces represent duration of the 1.5-second tone; RC integration was utilized.

in others it fluctuated over time. However, cochlear nucleus response decrements commonly occurred while the microphonic potential remained constant, which indicated that the central decrements were independent of any change at the receptor level (Fig. 8).

Intravenous strychnine was routinely administered as a terminal phase in most of the preceding experiments. The doses used (0.2–0.8 mg/kg) were sufficient to block any strychnine sensitive postsynaptic inhibition such as that transmitted by the olivocochlear bundle to the cochlear hair cells (Desmet and Monaco, 1962). In the cochlear nucleus, acceleration to tone was enhanced and inhibition was reduced following strychnine; little or no change occurred in the acceleratory or inhibitory responses of the inferior colliculus and medial geniculate body. During repeated stimulation, response decrements continued to occur at all sites (Buchwald and Humphrey, 1972; Humphrey and Buchwald, 1972).

H. SPONTANEOUS RECOVERY

Response decrements which developed during repeated acoustic stimulation in the auditory relay nuclei disappeared following a rest period in both intact and decerebrate preparation. The response recovery

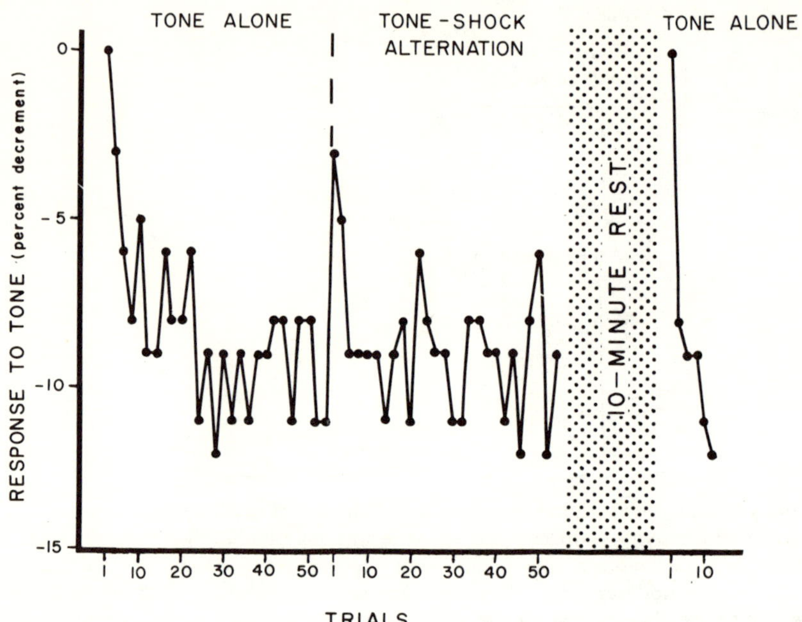

Fig. 9. Habituation, dishabituation, and recovery of cochlear nucleus multiple-unit activity in an intact cat paralyzed with Flaxedil. Following 50 1.5-second tones, a 0.5-second paw shock was interjected between each of the next 50 tones; all tones were presented at 5-second intervals. The initial shock induced a partial dishabituation but gradually lost effectiveness. Recovery was complete after a 10-minute rest, and rehabituation was readily produced.

followed an exponential course. In general, a 1- to 5-minute rest permitted at least 50% recovery following 50 tones at 5-second intervals, while an additional 15–25 minutes were often needed to complete the recovery process (Fig. 9). Almost never did the recovered response exceed its prestimulation level.

I. Dishabituation

In the *intact* cat, dishabituation was observed at all levels of the auditory pathway following response decrements induced by repeated acoustic stimulation. *In the decerebrate cat (cochlear nucleus only) little or no dishabituation has been demonstrated.* The dishabituating stimulus routinely used was a 0.5-second electrical shock train delivered to one forepaw. When shock stimulation was delivered during the intertrial intervals of one-per-5-second tone trials, decremented tone responses initially returned to or toward their initial value. As shown in Fig. 9, if the alternated tone-shock stimuli were continued, the dishabituating stimulus lost its effectiveness, i.e., it also habituated.

J. Summary

Although many puzzles remain to be solved, these data indicate that reversible sensory response decrements can occur throughout the auditory pathway during repeated acoustic stimulation. These changes are believed to develop independently of peripheral mechanisms which were controlled in a number of ways: the acoustic stimulus field was held constant by use of earphones attached to the animal's head; fluctuating ear muscle contractions were deleted by Flaxedil paralysis; alterations in hair cell activity produced by the olivocochlear bundle were blocked by strychnine injection, and the round window microphonic was recorded and observed not to change.

V. Mechanisms of Response Decrements in Specific Sensory Nuclei

The variety of theories which attempt to provide a general functional framework for motor response habituation have recently been summarized and compared (Kandel and Spencer, 1968; Groves and Thompson, 1970). We shall not attempt to reexamine in detail those concepts which are geared to system interactions and overt behavioral output. Rather, we shall direct this discussion to possible mechanisms of response decrements within mammalian sensory systems.

With respect to mechanisms underlying the response decrements of specific sensory neurons, Hernández-Peón (1960) postulated in his "afferent inhibition theory" that the response decrements observed in specific auditory, visual, and somatosensory relays were the result of recurrent inhibitory projections. These were thought to emanate from rostral levels of the reticular formation and to impinge upon synapses as far peripherally as the first synaptic relay; with stimulus repetition this peripheral inhibition would become increasingly effective. Desmedt (1960) supported a mechanism of inhibitory blockade, or gating, of input at the level of the cochlear nucleus but stressed the importance of feedback pathways which did not project through the reticular formation.

The concept that feedback projections from central levels such as mesencephalic reticular formation or cortex are necessary before response decrements can occur at the more peripheral sensory relays does not appear to have been supported experimentally, although recurrent loops have been clearly shown for all the sensory systems. For example, in the cochlear nucleus of decerebrate animals, response decrements have been found to develop during repeated acoustic stimulation (Bach-y-Rita *et al.*, 1961; Buchwald and Humphrey, 1972; Humphrey and Buchwald, 1972; see also this paper, Section IV) and, similarly, in the isolated spinal cord somatosensory relays within the dorsal horn show response decrements during repeated cutaneous stimulation (Spencer *et al.*, 1966a; Wall, 1967; Wickelgren, 1967b; Groves *et al.*, 1969).

Locally, blockade of the sensory responses could be accomplished (a) by an actual increase in neuronal inhibition, either pre- or postsynaptic, or (b) by a decrease of neuronal excitability, either a presynaptic transmitter depletion or a subsynaptic loss of receptor sensitivity. Hernández-Peón (1960) felt that inhibition actually built up at the sites of response decrement, and Desmedt (1960) may have had a similar process in mind when he said that the gating probably "depends on the activation of descending fibers exerting an inhibitory influence on the nerve cells in the cochlear nucleus." Simons *et al.* (1966) proposed that auditory habituation might be due to an inhibitory process intrinsic to nuclei along the auditory pathway, and Fruhstorfer *et al.* (1970) indicated that inhibition developing at synapses within the unspecific auditory pathway would adequately describe the habituation of the human vertex potential. Webster (1969) suggested a specific inhibitory mechanism, recurrent postsynaptic inhibition, as underlying the habituation of evoked potentials recorded from the medial geniculate body. Wickelgren (1967b) also postulated a build-up of postsynaptic inhibition as the source of the response decrements of dorsal horn somatosensory units.

This concept of summating inhibition as an explanation for sensory response decrements has no direct experimental support at the present time. In fact, the relevant data collected thus far indicate that in the absence of active inhibitory processes, response decrements still continue to develop. Somatosensory response decrements of the spinal cord dorsal horn cells have been shown to develop without concurrent increases in presynaptic inhibition (Groves *et al.*, 1970), and response decrements to repeated cutaneous stimulation continue to occur after picrotoxin blockade of presynaptic inhibition and strychnine blockade of postsynaptic inhibition (Spencer *et al.,* 1966b). In the cochlear nucleus, decrements also continued to appear after blockade of strychnine-sensitive postsynaptic inhibition (Buchwald and Humphrey, 1972; Humphrey and Buchwald, 1972). Moreover, while the neurons of central sensory levels have distinctly different electrical characteristics than more peripherally situated cells (Nelson and Erulkar, 1963; Gerstein *et al.,* 1968), and can be more strikingly inhibited by a sound stimulus (Holstein *et al.,* 1969b), there are still no data at these levels to support increasing neuronal inhibition as the mechanism responsible for progressive response decrements. Even the apparent strengthening of inhibited multiple-unit discharge in the inferior colliculus and medial geniculate body produced by repeated binaural sound stimulation (Fig. 3) seems to be a paradoxical result of progressive *weakening* of the accelerated, contralaterally induced discharge (Fig. 5) masking, or overwhelming, the simultaneous *weakening* of the concurrent, ipsilaterally induced inhibition of discharge (Fig. 5). Thus, even in the case of an initially inhibited response, there is no clear indication that inhibitory build-up or summation occurs during repeated stimulation.

As an alternative to increasing neuronal inhibition, *decreasing excitation* becomes the most obvious mechanism to account for the short-term phasic response decrements exhibited by sensory neurons. Both depletion of transmitter from the presynaptic terminals and loss of subsynaptic receptor sensitivity have been suggested as likely processes underlying the development of such decrements in mammalian systems (Spencer *et al.,* 1966b; Kandel and Spencer, 1968); strong supporting data which particularly emphasizes transmitter depletion as a significant mechanism of response habituation has accumulated from invertebrate studies on a variety of preparations (Kandel and Spencer, 1968; Bruner and Kennedy, 1970). Temporal distinctions between the response decrements of different systems, such as the maximum interstimulus interval over which decrements develop, might thus depend upon the time constants of each cell type for replenishment of transmitter or for recovery of subsynaptic sensitivity, in addition to other bioelectrical properties, e.g., membrane time constant, input impedance, and after-potential duration. While other mechanisms could be postulated to satisfy the short-term requirements of sensory neuron response decrements, the hypothesis of decreased excitation would seem the most attractive candidate for experimental scrutiny at the present time.

VI. Parametric Comparisons between Sensory and Motor Response Decrements

The preceding sections have indicated that reversible response decrements induced by repeated sensory stimulation can consistently be recorded from all central levels of the specific sensory systems if recording and stimulation procedures are employed which reveal more than stimulus "onset" responses. The failure of some experimenters to observe such modulations may largely be explained by their use of ultrashort stimuli, e.g., clicks, and electrical recordings which, at many sites, measure only the primary evoked potential. Our data, as well as that of others, indicate that reversible sensory response decrements are observed when the recording technique allows observation of polysynaptic events in the response and when stimuli have durations long enough to elicit sustained discharges.

Habituation has generally been equated with the *decrement of a specific motor response* induced by a specific suprathreshold stimulus. As a result of this emphasis, criteria have evolved to distinguish the motor reflex decrements mediated by a central learning process, i.e., "habituation," from those induced by trauma, maturational change, and peripheral receptor or effector fatigue, although peripheral fatigue can no longer be so clearly separated from central decremental processes as was once supposed (Bruner and Kennedy, 1970). Consequently, several parametric characteristics of motor response decrements have been enumerated and proposed to serve as an operational definition of habituation; moreover, the extent to which these characteristics are satisfied has been suggested as the determinant of whether other response decrements do or do not exemplify this simple type of learning (Thompson and Spencer, 1966). Presumably, sensory response decrements must also satisfy these characteristics before they can be said to exemplify a central learning process, i.e., habituation.

There are few data presently available for determining the extent to which sensory decrements fulfill the "requirements" for habituation. This is due, in part, to the unrecognized and uncontrolled variables in the earlier studies of sensory plasticity so that these results remain equivocal. Among the better controlled recent studies, moreover, a body of negative data has accumulated as a result of restrictive recording and stimulation procedures. Finally, in a number of studies primarily concerned with sensory function, motor, rather than sensory, responses have been used to suggest sensory system plasticity; this is particularly evident in the use of nystagmus habituation to suggest alterations in vestibular function. Such inferential involvement of the sensory systems does not provide data explicit enough for the present requirements.

In the following analysis, only positive data recorded from the specific sensory pathways with attention directed toward peripheral controls have been included. In an attempt to supplement these data, we have carried out parametric studies of response decrements to repeated auditory stimuli in the cochlear nucleus of five normal implanted cats and of six decerebrate cats. The technical procedures utilized were similar to those described in the preceding section. Our parametric data are presented in some detail where no other relevant data have been found in the literature.

A. Characteristics of Motor Response Habituation

1. Given That a Particular Stimulus Elicits a Response, Repeated Applications of the Stimulus Result in Decreased Response (Habituation)

Progressive decrements in response to repeated auditory stimulation have been recorded in the cochlear nucleus (Dunlop *et al.*, 1964a, 1966; Webster *et al.*, 1965; Simons *et al.*, 1966; Holstein *et al.*, 1969a; Kitzes and Buchwald, 1969; Buchwald and Humphrey, 1972; Humphrey and Buchwald, 1972; also see this paper), inferior colliculus (Dunlop *et al.*, 1964a,b, 1966; Simons *et al.*, 1966; Holstein *et al.*, 1969a; Jaffe *et al.*, 1969; Kitzes and Buchwald, 1969), medial geniculate body (Altman, 1960; Dunlop *et al.*, 1964a, 1966; Simons *et al.*, 1966; Hall, 1968; Holstein *et al.*, 1969a; Jaffe *et al.*, 1969; Kitzes and Buchwald, 1969; Webster, 1969), and auditory cortex (Altman, 1960; Moushegian *et al.*, 1961; Marsh and Worden, 1964; Key, 1965; Cook *et al.*, 1968; Ellinwood *et al.*, 1968; Hall, 1968; Wickelgren, 1968a; Meschersky and Rosenschtein, 1969).

Sensory response decrements to repeated visual stimuli have been recorded in the lateral geniculate body (Arden, 1963; Fernández-Guardiola *et al.*, 1964b, 1968) and visual cortex (Fernández-Guardiola *et al.*, 1960; Macadar *et al.*, 1963; García-Austt *et al.*, 1963; Perry and Copenhaver, 1965).

Sensory response decrements to repeated somatic sensory stimuli have been recorded in the N_1, N_2, and P deflections of the cord dorsum potential (Spencer *et al.*, 1966a), in the primary sensory dorsal horn lamina I, II, III, IV, and V (Wall, 1967; Wickelgren, 1967b; Groves *et al.*, 1969), in the ascending dorsolateral and ventral spinal tracts mediating cutaneous input (Spencer *et al.*, 1966a), and in the ventrobasal thalamus (Buchwald *et al.*, 1969).

In none of these experiments were stimulus repetition rates faster than those commonly used to study motor response decrements, i.e., one to three per second and, in many cases, stimulus presentations were much slower, e.g., one per 5 seconds. Thus, sensory response decrements can develop over interstimulus intervals similar to those of motor response habituation.

2. If the Stimulus Is Withheld, the Response Tends to Recover Over Time (Spontaneous Recovery)

Observations concerning spontaneous recovery following the development of response decrements were included in several of the studies cited above. Following cessation of repeated auditory stimulation, spontaneous recovery of the decremented acoustic response was observed in the cochlear nucleus (Holstein *et al.,* 1969a; Kitzes and Buchwald, 1969; Buchwald and Humphrey, 1972; Humphrey and Buchwald, 1972; also see this paper), inferior colliculus (Holstein *et al.,* 1969a; Kitzes and Buchwald, 1969), medial geniculate body (Altman, 1960; Holstein *et al.,* 1969a), and auditory cortex (Altman, 1960; Cook *et al.,* 1968). Following cessation of repeated somatic stimulation, recovery of the decremented responses was observed in the N_1, N_2 and P deflections of the cord dorsum potential (Spencer *et al.,* 1966a), in the dorsal horn laminae III, IV, and V (Wickelgren, 1967b; Groves *et al.,* 1969), in the ascending dorsolateral and ventral spinal tracts (Spencer *et al.,* 1966a), and in the ventrobasal thalamus (Buchwald *et al.,* 1969). Visual response decrements have been observed to recover in the lateral geniculate body (Fernández-Guardiola *et al.,* 1968) and visual cortex (Perry and Copenhaver, 1965). In many studies, no indication of spontaneous recovery is given following the demonstration of response decrements. In the absence of this index, or some other means of ascertaining the state of the experimental preparation, the development of response decrements over time could simply indicate central irreversible deterioration.

3. If Repeated Series of Habituation Training and Spontaneous Recovery Are Given, Habituation Becomes Successively More Rapid (Rehabituation)

Although rarely looked for in studies of sensory response decrements, some savings, or "memory," of repeated stimulation effects is suggested in the study of Holstein *et al.* (1969a). Both in inferior colliculus and medial geniculate body, recordings made over 4 consecutive days of acoustic habituation sessions showed increasingly rapid habituation to relatively constant asymptote.

4. Presentation of Another (Usually Strong) Stimulus Results in Recovery of the Habituated Response (Dishabituation)

Although this characteristic is often considered crucial in the distinction of "habituation" from "fatigue," few studies of sensory response decrements have utilized dishabituating stimuli as part of their experimental procedure.

In the auditory system, Kitzes and Buchwald (1969) found dishabituation of cochlear nucleus and inferior colliculus responses using tones of a different frequency as the dishabituating stimulus, and Altman (1960) reported rapid dishabituation of evoked response amplitude at the medial geniculate and auditory cortex. Both of these investigators used intact cats.

In the visual system, dishabituation has been reported by Macadar *et al.* (1963) of rat cortical evoked responses, by García-Austt *et al.* (1963) of the human visual evoked response (cortical), and by Fernández-Guardiola *et al.* (1968) of the lateral geniculate evoked response of intact curarized and *encephale isolé* cats. In the somatosensory system, a strong cutaneous stimulus was found to dishabituate the response decrements of the P-wave component of the cord dorsum response potential but did not influence the reduced N_1 component, nor were the decremented responses of the ascending dorsolateral and ventral spinal tracts reversed by this stimulus (Spencer *et al.,* 1966a).

In recent data recorded from intact, paralyzed cats with implanted electrodes, we found that decremented cochlear nucleus responses were reversed, or dishabituated, by an electric shock to one forepaw (Fig. 9). In contrast, in decerebrated cats, little or no dishabituation was induced by forepaw shock. The effects of the shock stimulus apparently project to the cochlear nucleus through a loop originating above the level of the decerebration which suggests an important role for supramedullary levels in response dishabituation (Buchwald and Humphrey, 1972).

If the cochlear nucleus response decrements dishabituate in the intact animal and do not in the decerebrate, does this mean that habituation has developed in the one case and not in the other? Obviously, the decremental process may be identical in both cases, but decerebration prevents the projections of a dishabituating stimulus from reaching the cochlear nucleus. Thus, dishabituation can supply elaborative data concerning the nature of the habituation process, i.e., that the decremented cells are still responding when a different input pathway is utilized. However, absence of dishabituation (where it has been attempted) may simply indicate an inability for the dishabituating stimulus to converge upon the habituated cells.

5. Upon Repeated Application of the Dishabituating Stimulus, the Amount of Dishabituation Produced Habituates

Rarely has repeated dishabituation been carried out in the studies reviewed. In our own experiments, repeated presentations of a dishabituating stimulus were found to result in diminished effectiveness, as indicated in Fig. 9. The cochlear nucleus response amplitude following the initial presentation of shock can be seen to quickly diminish during the subsequent period of tone-shock alternation.

6. The More Rapid the Frequency of Stimulation, the More Rapid and/or Pronounced Is Habituation

A somewhat confusing aspect in evaluating this characteristic is the semantic use of stimulation frequency in habituation studies. In most cases, this parameter is referenced to the interstimulus interval while the stimulus *per se* remains constant. In other studies, the interstimulus interval is held constant but the stimulus frequency is varied.

We are aware of no studies of habituation in the visual pathway where the rate of flash stimulation has been varied.

Somatic stimulation at one per min induced no decrement in cord dorsum potentials or in the dorsolateral and ventral column potentials, whereas significant decrements occurred with one-per-second stimulation (Spencer *et al.*, 1966a). Recordings of dorsal horn cell responses to cutaneous stimulation indicated frequency dependent decrements which occurred with a constant interstimulus interval and were maximal with 0.5-second shock trains of 50–100 pulses per second. However, increasing frequency still further to 400 pulses per second resulted in a somewhat lessened decremental effect (Wickelgren, 1967b).

In the auditory system, studies of the effect of stimulation frequency at the cochlear nucleus (Webster *et al.*, 1965) and auditory cortex in cats (Cook *et al.*, 1968) have shown faster or greater habituation with faster rates of stimulus presentation, i.e., with shorter intertrial intervals. Similar results were obtained by Fruhstorfer *et al.* (1970) for decrements of the human vertex potential.

In our studies of cochlear nucleus response decrements in intact and decerebrate cats (with monaural stimulation), we found a direct relationship between rate of stimulation (i.e., intertrial interval) and

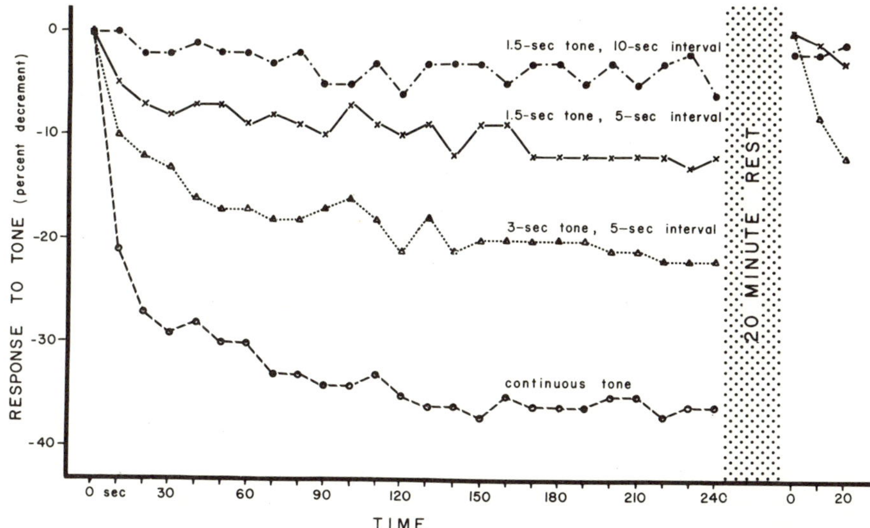

FIG. 10. Effects of increased stimulation duration per unit time on cochlear nucleus response decrements in a paralyzed, decerebrated cat. A 2500-Hz, 70-dB tone was presented to the ipsilateral ear at the durations and intervals indicated. Increased stimulus duration per unit time produced progressively more substantial decrements. After a 20-minute rest period, recovery was essentially complete for the three series of intermittent stimulus presentations. Recovery after continuous tone is not shown as this stimulation was continued for 1 hour; recovery did occur subsequently, however.

response decrement. The graduated rate of response decrement produced by several rates of stimulation are plotted for the cochlear nucleus in Fig. 10. Small, slowly developing response decrements occurred when a 1.5-second, 2500-Hz tone was presented with an interstimulus interval of 10 seconds. More pronounced and rapid decrements occurred when stimulation was more frequently presented and/or was of longer duration.

7. The Weaker the Stimulus, the More Rapid and/or More Pronounced Is Habituation

Stimulus intensity has recently been shown to be inversely related to response habituation only in a relative sense and to be directly related in an absolute sense (Davis and Wagner, 1968). In other words, greater absolute response decrements are revealed by neutral test stimuli after an intervening habituation sequence utilizing a strong rather than a weak intensity stimulus, even though the response decrements during strong stimulus presentations are relatively less than those during weak stimulus presentations. In general, only comparisons of the relative effect of stimulus intensity have been made in studies of sensory response decrements.

In the cochlear nucleus, weak acoustic stimulation was reported to lead to greater habituation (Dunlop *et al.,* 1964a) than intense stimulation, whereas, in a later investigation, Dunlop *et al.* (1966) found that stimuli of 75-, 85-, 95- and 105-dB intensity each produced a decrement of 5–15% and did not produce significantly different effects. At the inferior colliculus, amount of habituation has been reported to vary inversely with stimulus intensity (Dunlop *et al.,* 1964a,b), or to be independent of intensity (Dunlop *et al.,* 1966). The difference between these data at the level of the colliculus was attributed to differences in statistical testing procedures rather than to inconsistencies in the data. At the medial geniculate body, on the other hand, habituation has twice been reported to vary directly with intensity by these same authors (Dunlop *et al.,* 1964a; Dunlop *et al.,* 1966).

In our recordings from intact paralyzed cats, we found an inverse relationship between tone intensity (70 *vs.* 80 dB) and percent of response decrement in recordings of medial geniculate and inferior colliculus. However, concurrent recordings from the cochlear nucleus in the same cats showed no decrement at the lower stimulus intensity but, as if some "habituation threshold" had been reached, a very marked response decrement developed with the higher intensity stimulation; these responses subsequently showed spontaneous recovery and dishabituation.

Thus, the data are quite contradictory. Evoked-potential results have been inconsistent and they differ from the multiple-unit results. We can only say that further investigation is needed to resolve these differences.

An additional question is raised in our minds as a result of these investigations, namely, whether comparisons of *percent* decrement or *actual amount* of decrement is the more meaningful from the point of view of information handling. For example, if a large and a small response, induced by a strong and a weak stimulus, show the same percent drop in unit activity, does that mean that intensity of stimulation is not a significant variable; or is the larger actual amount of decrement of the large response the more significant modification? There may be cases in which a small response shows a greater percent change, while a large response shows a greater actual change. Which measure should be used to determine the relationship of response decrement to stimulus intensity?

While this relationship has been indicated as one of the most important characteristics of motor response habituation, we feel that it is the most potentially misleading because of the difficulties inherent in the expression of response decrement (i.e., percent change *vs.* actual decrease) and in the testing for decremental differences (i.e., either a relative inverse relationship or an absolute direct relationship between stimulus intensity and response decrement can be indicated depending upon the testing procedure utilized).

8. Habituation of a Response to a Given Stimulus Exhibits Generalization to Other Stimuli

Although frequently tested in human audiometric procedures, generalization of the effects of repeated stimulus presentations has not been widely looked for in studies of the specific sensory pathways. Among dorsal horn cells, a one-way generalization between two receptive fields was noted (Wickelgren, 1967b). Response decrements which resulted from repeated stimulation of one cutaneous site on the paw continued to occur when an area with overlapping receptive fields was subsequently stimulated. However, when the order of paw stimulation was reversed, a similar generalization did not take place. A somewhat different form of generalization was obtained from the cochlear nucleus following repeated tone presentations. In the one intact cat in which this procedure has thus far been carried out, response decrements induced by 200 presentations of a 2500-Hz, 70-dB tone were reflected by decrements in 2000-Hz and 2250-Hz test tones but not in 2750-Hz or 3000-Hz test tones.

9. The Effects of Habituation May Proceed beyond the Zero of Asymptotic Level

We have too little information on this point to provide any comments.

B. Summary

Few, if any, specific motor responses have been examined for their display of all of the preceding parameters during habituation procedures; rather, these characteristics represent a collage shown by many different responses under widely varying circumstances. As a matter of fact, when tested for, specific motor response decrements may not show these parametric characteristics. For example, Askew *et al.* (1969) found no evidence of faster rehabituation of the rat head shake response with repeated daily sessions. Davis and Wagner (1968) showed greater absolute habituation of the startle response with high, rather than low, stimulus intensity. It is thus quite remarkable that response decrements within the auditory system, as well as in the other sensory systems, share many if not all of the characteristics ascribed to motor response habituation. The term "habituation" would therefore seem equally applicable to both sensory and motor decremental phenomena.

On the other hand, all the parametric characteristics of many habituated motor responses need not be shown by a specific motor or sensory response, in order for each to exemplify a relatively long-lasting, centrally mediated change. For example, the cochlear nucleus response decrement in the intact and decerebrate cat was generally the same; in the former case, however, dishabituation by forepaw shock was possible, whereas, in the latter case, it was not. This does not mean that habituation occurred in the intact but not in the decerebrate preparation. Rather, it simply indicates that where there is no opportunity for convergence between the habituated neurons and the dishabituating stimulus, dishabituation will not occur.

While we recognize the necessity for standards against which phenomena can be measured as exemplifying or not exemplifying "learning," our present knowledge of central plasticity may be too rudimentary to justify or support a large number of rigid parametric requirements. Thus, we would think the term "habituation" could be reasonably applied to any electrophysiological response which shows a centrally mediated, progressive, but reversible, decrement to repeated stimulation.

If sensory system response decrements do really reflect underlying processes relating to a basic form of learning, i.e., if they can legitimately be said to habituate, questions regarding how these phenomena relate to behavior still remain. Indeed, one characteristic of sensory-evoked response decrements is that they may require repetitive stimulation prolonged beyond the number needed to habituate the arousal or orienting response and often show *continued* progressive decrements long after any behavioral response has disappeared. In the next two sections we shall attempt to relate specific sensory response decrements to arousal habituation and both processes to behavioral adaptation, the acquired unresponsiveness which predominates in successful behavior patterns.

VII. Relation of Response Decrements in Specific Sensory Nuclei to Arousal Habituation

In their classical study of the arousal reaction, Sharpless and Jasper (1956) showed that presentation of a loud acoustic stimulus initially induced behavioral arousal and EEG desynchronization in mesencephalic reticular formation and neocortex; however, repeated acoustic presentations resulted in habituation of the behavioral response and, concurrently, a loss of the EEG desynchronization at both reticular and cortical recording sites. It has been shown that this arousal reaction may include an orienting response toward the stimulus (Sokolov, 1963), or there may be an absence of any overt response. In either case, continued presentation of the arousal stimulus results in a complex of correlated changes: behavioral arousal ceases, with a loss of gross muscle activity (Sharpless and Jasper, 1956) and middle ear muscle relaxation (Carmel and Starr, 1963); desynchronization of reticular and cortical slow wave activity disappears; and the secondary component of the auditory cortex evoked response becomes markedly reduced (Key, 1965; Cook *et al.,* 1968).

Both a "phasic" and a "tonic" component of the arousal habituation process were distinguished by Sharpless and Jasper, similar to the "phasic" and "tonic" components noted during habituation of the orienting response (Sokolov, 1963). The "tonic" component of the EEG arousal response habituated rapidly, recovered slowly over a period of minutes to days, varied in duration from seconds to minutes, and often showed a long latency (Sharpless and Jasper, 1956). This component was believed to be mediated by the mesencephalic reticular formation. Subsequent studies have generally confirmed these characteristics of "tonic" habituation as common to habituation of reticular formation responses to sensory stimuli (Bell *et al.,* 1964; Scheibel and Scheibel, 1965; Horn and Hill, 1966b).

In contrast, the "phasic" component of the arousal response rarely outlasted the stimulus by more than 10–15 seconds, had a short latency, was resistant to habituation, and, once habituated, recovered within a few minutes; this component was believed to be mediated by the thalamic extension of the reticular formation (Sharpless and Jasper, 1956). However, specific sensory response decrements noted in our experiments and those of other investigators have essentially the same characteristics as those of "phasic" habituation, which suggests that the sensory relay nuclei themselves might be primarily responsible for this component. This interpretation is even more strongly suggested by the disappearance of the "phasic" component when bilateral lesions interrupted the lateral lemniscus or the inferior colliculus brachia (Sharpless and Jasper, 1956).

In an attempt to determine whether changes in the acoustic pathway contributed to habituation of arousal, Sharpless and Jasper studied the primary-evoked response recorded from auditory cortex during behavioral and EEG habituation to an acoustic stimulus. No concurrent decrement was observed in the primary evoked potential, and it was concluded that the auditory system *per se* played no role in the progressive response decrements. However, these authors did not test for reduction of the primary evoked potential during habituation of the higher threshold "phasic" arousal component. Since habituation of the "phasic" component appeared only after habituation of the "tonic" component of arousal and, as indicated above, shows characteristics of response habituation within the specific sensory relay nuclei, sensory response decrements might be expected during this later "phasic" habituation period. This was indeed indicated to be the case by a subsequent study. In agreement with previous work, habituation of behavioral arousal and reduction in the secondary component of the evoked potential recorded from auditory cortex occurred concurrently, even when an acoustic stimulus of 5-second duration was repeatedly presented (Key, 1965). In this experiment, however, stimulus presentations were continued after arousal habituation reached asymptote. A subsequent reduction in the primary component of the acoustic evoked potential was recorded, and this decrement was interpreted as indicating response reduction within the auditory system *per se*. The absence of this sensory decrement until after arousal habituation was essentially complete, its high threshold, and its relatively transient nature again suggest specific sensory response decrements as a substrate of the "phasic" habituation of Sharpless and Jasper.

Our own data indicate that marked response decrements develop within the auditory nuclei if the arousal mechanisms are deleted by mid-collicular decerebration. In this preparation, the response decrements seem to occur more clearly and consistently than in the intact, aroused animal. "Spontaneous dishabituation" often seen in the auditory nuclei of the intact animal has not been seen in the decerebrate cat. Moreover, whenever an arousing stimulus is presented, e.g., shock to the paw, dishabituation of the auditory responses occurs in the intact but not in the decerebrate animal. Further support for this viewpoint is provided by habituation data derived from intact cats in which thalamic nuclei were directly stimulated (Wester, 1971). Without involvement of the arousal systems, behavioral and electroencephalographic responses induced by discrete stimulation of the specific sensory nuclei were found to habituate rapidly. However, dishabituation readily occurred with the presentation of an arousing stimulus, e.g., ringing bells or light flashes.

These data correspond to the rapid and distinct response decrements within the auditory relay nuclei to repeated tone stimuli which also develop most clearly in the absence of arousal.

If, indeed, the most prominent aspect of response decrements within the auditory pathway appears *subsequent* to habituation of the arousal response, as is suggested by the preceding discussion, what function is subserved? If the arousal reaction induced by a novel stimulus habituates as the stimulus continues to be presented, the stimulus has obviously lost physiological significance to the organism. If the stimulus lacks significance, the neural responses it induces are simply "noise" introduced into the system. A mechanism to reduce such "noise," as is provided by the response decrements of the auditory relay nuclei, would, in turn, leave higher levels freer for more complex functions. Such a phasic decremental function would seem extremely well suited to the response characteristics of the sensory system itself. Spontaneous recovery is relatively rapid and complete, as is the dishabituation produced by an arousal stimulus. Thus, the sensory relays show no long-lasting "memory" for a repeated, nonsignificant stimulus but can damp the "noise" it interjects into the nervous system until new significance is attached to it, as for example, by a dishabituating stimulus.

VIII. Relation of Sensory Response Decrements to Behavioral Adaptation

The ontogeny of behavioral adaptation would seem to begin with the initial exposures of the newborn to light, sound, and somatic stimulation. After repetitive sensory exposures, the stimuli gradually become nonarousing, and the responses they induce become habituated. This concept is illustrated by a study of young children who were found to habituate to specific sensory stimuli after repeated stimulus exposures and, thereafter, to develop a generalized sensory habituation to the total stimulus environment (Hutt and Hutt, 1964). Such acquired unresponsiveness would, we believe, reflect an initial habituation of arousal responses induced by novel stimuli and, thereafter, response decrements would develop within the specific sensory nuclei to some asymptotic level. However, in order for the even more sophisticated quiescence of adult behavior to evolve, it would seem necessary for these specific short-term habituation sequences, mediated by mesencephalic reticular structures and specific sensory nuclei, to become increasingly generalized and retained as long-term habituation under headings such as "non-significant environmental stimuli." Such a phylogenetically ubiquitous phenomenon might be expected to involve significantly the older parts of the vertebrate brain, e.g., the limbic lobe.

Rich representation of sensory responsiveness has been found throughout the rhinencephalon, particularly in hippocampus and amygdala (Green and Machne, 1955; Machne and Segundo, 1956; Creutzfeldt *et al.*, 1963; Sawa and Delgado, 1963; Vinogradova, 1966; O'Keefe and Bouma, 1969). This physiological activation by sensory stimuli may result from anatomical connections which project either directly from sensory nuclei to limbic structures (Gloor, 1960; Sutin, 1963) or to the mesencephalic reticular formation (Bell *et al.*, 1964; Scheibel and Scheibel, 1965), which in turn projects heavily into the rhinencephalon (Scheibel and Scheibel, 1958; Nauta, 1960). A number of additional studies have demonstrated that limbic structures may influence transmission through the classical sensory relay nuclei, and anatomical and electrophysiological projections from limbic nuclei to sensory relay nuclei have been described (Long, 1959; Cazard and Buser, 1963; Powell and Hoelle, 1967; Redding, 1967; Parmeggiani and Rapisarda, 1969; Powell *et al.*, 1970). Thus, reciprocal interactions between the sensory nuclei and the limbic system seem possible at many different levels with or without the interposed mediation of the reticular formation.

Structures within the limbic lobe have been viewed as sensory analysors (MacLean, 1949, 1969; McLardy, 1959; Hilton, 1966; Gergen, 1967; Meissner, 1967; Pribram, 1967; O'Keefe and Bouma, 1969) with information storage capacities (Milner and Teuber, 1968; MacLean, 1969; Olds and Hirano, 1969; Turner, 1969), functions which are not carried out in the specific sensory pathways but which are necessary if behavioral habituation to environmental stimuli is to occur. Thus, as a result of many short-term or "phasic" sensory habituation experiences, involving first the loss of a generalized arousal response and, secondarily, specific sensory response decrements, information would be relayed to the limbic nuclei where generalization and storage of habituated sensory response blocks would occur.

This would suggest that one aspect of behavioral adaptation might develop through repetitions of a three-step sequence: habituation of the nonspecific arousal reaction, primarily involving the mesencephalic reticular activating system; habituation of the specific sensory response, primarily involving the sensory relay nuclei; and storage of generalized blocks of these habituated experiences, primarily involving the nuclei of the limbic system. Subsequently, arousal to similar stimuli would be reduced by the effects of these stored, habituated response blocks; exposure to a previously habituated stimulus would release stored habituation effects which would, in turn, damp arousal and thus permit the phasic response decrements within the sensory nuclei. In a simple experimental situation, it has been noted that the tone response recorded from the inferior colliculus becomes habituated increasingly rapidly as the habituation procedure is extended over days (Holstein *et al.*, 1969a). We would postulate that this effect did not reflect a "memory" function of the inferior colliculus, but rather that the limbic storage of habituation to the specific tone stimulus had become increasingly stable or "overtrained"; after 50 tone presentations of each of 4 days, little or no arousal would be induced by the habituated tone, so that the inferior colliculus response would decrement rapidly, reflecting a phasic habituation of sensory neurons in the absence of other "dishabituating" or arousal influences.

The concept of "stored habituated response blocks" is similar to the model hypothesis of Sokolov (1963) who suggests that stimulus patterns form a "model" in the cortex during the habituation process. Thereafter, stimuli similar to the model would be prevented from inducing arousal by an inhibition of their collateral input to the arousal system, although specific sensory responses would occur; unfamiliar stimuli would not match any model, access to the arousal system would therefore not be inhibited, and arousal and orienting would result. We differ from this general notion insofar as we stress the probability of the limbic system as the locus of "habituated model" storage and emphasize the contribution of the sensory systems to the formation and reinforcement of the habituated model. Response specificity, elicited by any stimulus complex, is due to the patterning capacities of the specific sensory pathways; the arousal response, in contrast, is very generalized and involves a system with little response specificity. Therefore, storage of a habituated response specific enough to block the arousal effects of certain "familiar" stimulus patterns and not other "novel" stimuli requires the detail that only the specific sensory systems provide. Stimulation continued after the disappearance of arousal or other overt behavioral responses, i.e., habituation beyond the asymptotic level (Thompson and Spencer, 1966) might serve to facilitate the ingraining of specificity.

In summary, sensory pathway response decrements subsequent to loss of arousal would not only reduce *noise* of insignificant stimuli coming into the system but they would also serve to imprint the *specific patterns* of the insignificant stimulus complexes upon the stored habituation, or "model," in the limbic lobe.

These speculations lead to the further suggestion that from birth onward we exist in a constantly developing, constantly changing state of partial habituation to blocks of commonly encountered sensory stimuli, e.g., familiar faces, background noises, body postures. When a dishabituating stimulus occurs, the ongoing habituation is abolished by a generalized arousal and specific environmental stimuli are transiently perceived at a nonhabituated level. Moreover, when familiar stimuli cease to be encountered for an extended period of time, so that the habituation is no longer reinforced, subsequent exposure to the same stimuli may result in a nonhabituated initial response, i.e., a partial spontaneous recovery. Environments of minimal explorable stimuli and maximal stimulus repetition have been shown to favor sensory response habituation and, concurrently, to induce an increased attention span for a particular task (Piaget, 1952; Hutt and Hutt, 1964). This suggests that sensory response habituation not only plays an important role in the development of normal adaptive behavior but, thereby, also becomes an important foundation for the evolution of attention and more complex learning phenomena.

IX. Summary

A common conclusion of reviewers of habituation in sensory systems is that response plasticity at the more peripheral levels has not as yet been conclusively shown (Horn, 1965a; Thompson and Spencer, 1966) or that, if habituation does occur within the sensory systems, it has no obvious relationship to the much faster habituation of overt behavior or arousal (Groves and Thompson, 1970; Milner, 1970). Thus, there has been a popular conviction that integration of information relevant to the survival of the organism or to the meaningfulness of environmental stimuli is confined to the complex neural circuitry and memory-storing capabilities of higher, e.g., cortical, levels. On the other hand, it has been established that simple neural networks show response decrements with repeated use (Kandel and Spencer, 1968), and doubt has been expressed that such a ubiquitous phenomenon as habituation requires the higher centers of the brain (Sharpless, 1964). The importance of the specific sensory systems to adaptive behavior has been dramatically indicated by the aberrant activities of cats in which the medial, lateral, trigeminal, and spinal lemnisci were interrupted at the rostral brain stem level (Sprague *et al.*, 1961, 1963). Although visual and olfactory sensory systems, as well as extraleminiscal auditory and somatic relays, remained essentially intact and the adjacent reticular formation was undamaged, such animals were hyperactive, inattentive, and emotionally volatile for the 2½ years of postoperative observations. These aberrancies were attributed in part to an inability to utilize sensory information in making adaptive responses to the environment, and not to simple sensory deficits alone. Such data strongly suggest that the peripheral levels of the sensory systems contribute significantly to the elaboration of normal adaptive behavior.

Cognizant of these divergent implications, we have attempted, within the scope of this paper, to examine and evaluate the role of the specific sensory systems in relation to response plasticity and, ultimately, to behavioral adaptation. We have suggested that the normal behavior of adult life is not dominated by arousal and motor responses to the commonplace, i.e., environmental stimuli, but rather an acquired unresponsiveness develops, a form of adaptive behavior which is essential for the successful survival of the individual. In order to understand the genesis of this acquired unresponsive behavior, it seems insufficient to study the habituation of "model" motor responses, since most novel environmental stimuli do not induce repeated motor actions which gradually disappear, but simply an enhanced arousal level which subsequently diminishes. Present electrophysiological techniques permit examination of processes within the central nervous system, subthreshold for motor activity but relevant to the adaptive behavior pattern of the individual.

The question of whether acquired unresponsiveness develops within the specific sensory systems during repeated stimulus presentations has been examined rather intensively over the past decade but has received equivocal answers. Initially, this was because of numerous unrecognized variables, e.g., alterations in pupillary or ear muscle contractions, which led to a mass of contradictory and often uninterpretable data. Definition of these sources of response fluctuation and attempts to control them have subsequently been incorporated into studies of sensory system response plasticity.

Only relatively recently, in the era of recognized and controlled variables, have single- and multiple-unit recordings been utilized to measure sensory neuron responses during repeated stimulation. In contrast to the conflicting results of the more common evoked potential studies, the unit data, although not voluminous, are in general agreement. Studies of unit responses in somatosensory, auditory, and visual systems during repeated stimulation procedures have indicated that decremental phenomena may occur at the level of third-order afferent neurons, as well as at levels more central in the sensory pathways. Evoked response data have been more controversial, and many interpretive problems remain unresolved. While some of these studies have not found consistent progressive evoked potential modification, others have clearly indicated that evoked response decrements can be obtained as peripherally as the dorsal horn in the somatosensory pathway, the lateral geniculate body in the visual pathway, and the cochlear nucleus in the auditory system, all levels which contain numerous third-order neurons. In neither unit nor evoked potential studies have response decrements been shown for second-order sensory neurons, i.e., those making monosynaptic contacts with the primary afferent fibers. Generally, the sensory neuronal response decrements seem to develop more readily the more centrally located the relay level.

Decremental processes of the sensory neurons *per se* are relatively phasic or short-term, in that recovery is essentially complete within a brief time period. The mechanisms underlying these decrements are not presently known. Although a build-up of inhibition has been frequently postulated, there has been no direct experimental support for this concept. Response decrements have been shown to continue in the absence of pre- or postsynaptic inhibition, so that decreased excitation, either through transmitter depletion or decreased subsynaptic sensitivity, is more consistent with present experimental data. In spinalized and decerebrated preparations, response decrements of sensory neurons within the more peripheral relay nuclei have been shown to develop without the necessity of feedback loops or other modulation from the deleted higher levels, e.g., cortex, thalamus, or reticular formation.

A number of parametric characteristics have evolved which are presently used to determine whether or not the decrement of an overt behavioral response represents a centrally mediated simple form of learning, i.e., "habituation." These characteristics, e.g., spontaneous recovery, dishabituation, generalization, etc., also typify response decrements within the specific sensory systems. Since sensory and motor decremental phenomena show similar parametric characteristics, the term "habituation" would seem valid for both. However, the use of a rigid parametric definition to determine whether a phenomenon qualifies as habituation seems basically invalid, insofar as distinct neuroanatomical loci mediating the habituation process might not necessarily display all the parametric characteristics recorded from the final common path. We would, therefore, suggest that any progressive response decrement which is reversible and centrally mediated should, at this time, qualify as a phenomenon of habituation.

On the grounds that arousal or overt behavioral habituation occurs relatively rapidly, the significance of response habituation mediated by the sensory systems *per se* has been questioned, since these latter decrements may only subsequently appear clearly and may continue long after the arousal or overt response has reached asymptote. Long latency components of the sensory-evoked responses, recorded from thalamic and cortical levels of the sensory pathways, may show response decrements which generally correlate in time with those of arousal and overt behavioral habituation, and may remain reduced for long periods of time after habituation. These temporal characteristics are distinctly different from those of the sensory systems and suggest that the long latency components may reflect neural activity, influenced largely by extrasensory, nonspecific reticular and cortical systems, which is a part of the arousal response. On the basis of current data, we suggest that within the specific sensory systems, generalized arousal produces excitatory, or dishabituating, stimulation. As the arousal response habituates, the sensory systems receive less dishabituating excitation, so that *subsequent* to arousal habituation, a phasic response decrement of the sensory neurons develops. This development has two suggested functions. First, as a stimulus loses significance and becomes "noise," indicated by the loss of the arousal response, the sensory response decrements serve to reduce such noise. Second, sensory response decrements would provide specificity and reinforcement for the gradual storage of repeated habituation experiences which take place continually from birth onward. In this way, the process is extended to behavioral adaptation. Such stored information would serve, in turn, to block arousal to a subsequently encountered familiar stimulus configuration and thereby permit faster rehabituation of sensory responses. Dishabituation, attention, and conditioning could be expected to reverse or override both the inhibition of arousal and the reduced sensory responses. The close anatomical and physiological interrelationships between the specific sensory systems and structures known to have information storage functions within the limbic lobe suggest this primitive part of the vertebrate brain as the likely candidate for storing this essential but simple form of "learning."

Thus, we propose that response decrements which are mediated by the specific sensory pathways would serve to *reduce noise* generated by nonsignificant background stimuli, and to *provide specificity* to stored complex models of habituation experiences. In these ways the sensory systems would seem to contribute importantly not only to the immediate adaptive behavior required by novel stimuli but also to the acquired unresponsiveness which develops throughout life to commonly encountered environmental stimuli.

Acknowledgments

The authors would like to thank Mrs. Glow Holland for her assistance in the preparation of this manuscript.

This work has been supported by U. S. Public Health Service Grants NB 05437 and MH 06415. Bibliographic assistance was obtained from UCLA Brain Information Service supported by NIH Grant 70-2063. Computing assistance was obtained from the Health Sciences Computing Facility, UCLA, sponsored by NIH Special Research Resources Grant RR-3.

References

Affanni, J., Mancia, M., and Marchiafava, P. L. (1962). Role of the pupil in changes in evoked responses along the visual pathways. *Archives Italiennes de Biologie* **100**, 287–296.

Alcaraz, M., Pacheco, P., and Guzman-Flores, C. (1962). Changes in acoustic habituation following severance of the intrinsic ear muscles in chronic preparations. *Acta Physiologica Latino Americana* **12**, 1–7.

Altman, I. A. (1960). Electrophysiological examination of different parts of the auditory system in the cat during sustained rhythmical stimulation. *Sechenov Physiological Journal of the USSR* **46**, 617–629.

Arden, G. B. (1963). Complex receptive fields and responses to moving objects in cells of the rabbit's lateral geniculate body. *Journal of Physiology (London)* **166**, 468–488.

Arduini, A., and Pinneo, L. R. (1962). A method for the quantification of tonic activity in the nervous system. *Archives Italiennes de Biologie* **100**, 415–424.

Artemiev, V. V. (1951). Electric responses of the cerebral cortex to acoustic stimuli in anesthetized and unanesthetized animals. *Fiziologicheskii Zhurnal SSSR imeni I. M. Sechenova* **37**, 688–702.

Askew, H. R., Leibrecht, B. C., and Ratner, S. C. (1969). Effects of stimulus duration and repeated sessions on habituation of the head-shake response in the rat. *Journal of Comparative and Physiological Psychology* **67**, 497–503.

Bach-y-Rita, G., Brust-Carmona, H., Peñaloza-Rojas, J., and Hernández-Peón, R. (1961). Absence of para-auditory descending influences on the cochlear nucleus during distraction and habituation. *Acta Neurologica Latinoamericana* **7**, 73–81.

Baust, W., Berlucchi, G., and Moruzzi, G. (1964). Changes in the auditory input in wakefulness and during the synchronized and desynchronized stages of sleep. *Archives Italiennes de Biologie* **102**, 657–674.

Bell, C., Sierra, G., Buendia, N., and Segundo, J. P. (1964). Sensory properties of neurons in the mesencephalic reticular formation. *Journal of Neurophysiology* **27**, 961–987.

Bernstein, A. S. (1968). The orienting response and direction of stimulus change. *Psychonomic Science* **12**, 127–128.

Bogacz, J., Vanzulli, A., Handler, P., and García-Austt, E. (1960). Evoked responses in man. II: Habituation of photic responses. *Acta Neurologica Latinoamericana* **6**, 353–362.

Bruner, J., and Kennedy, D. (1970). Habituation: Occurrence at a neuromuscular junction. *Science* **169**, 92–94.

Buchwald, J. S. (1970). Sensory convergence in the classical auditory pathway. *Proceedings of the International Congress of Anatomists, 9th, Leningrad* p. 20.

Buchwald, J. S., and Grover, F. S. (1970). Amplitudes of background fast activity characteristic of specific brain sites. *Journal of Neurophysiology* **33**, 148–159.

Buchwald, J. S., and Humphrey, G. L. (1972). Response plasticity in the cochlear nucleus of decerebrate cats during acoustic habituation procedures. *Journal of Neurophysiology* **35**, 864–878.

Buchwald, J. S., Standish, M., Eldred, E., and Halas, E. S. (1964). Contribution of muscle spindle circuits to learning as suggested by training under Flaxedil. *Electroencephalography and Clinical Neurophysiology* **16**, 585–594.

Buchwald, J. S., Halas, E. S., and Schramm, S. (1965a). A comparison of multiple-unit and EEG activity recorded from the same brain site in chronic cats during behavioral conditioning. *Nature (London)* **205**, 1012–1014.

Buchwald, J. S., Halas, E. S., and Schramm, S. (1965b). Progressive changes in efferent unit responses to repeated cutaneous stimulation in spinal cats. *Journal of Neurophysiology* **28**, 200–215.

Buchwald, J. S., Halas, E. S., and Schramm, S. (1966a). Changes in cortical and sub-cortical unit activity during behavioral conditioning. *Physiology & Behavior* **1**, 11–22.

Buchwald, J. S., Halas, E. S., and Schramm, S. (1966b). Relationships of neuronal spike populations and EEG activity in chronic cats. *Electroencephalography and Clinical Neurophysiology* **21**, 227–238.

Buchwald, J. S., Weber, D. S., Holstein, S. B., and Schwafel, J. A. (1969). Quantified unit background activity in the waking cat during paralysis, anesthesia and cochlear destruction. *Brain Research* **15**, 465–482.

Buchwald, J. S., Holstein, S. B., and Weber, D. S. (1973). Multiple unit recording: technique, interpretation and experimental applications. *In* "Bioelectric Recording Techniques: Cellular Processes" (R. Thompson and M. Patterson, eds.), Vol. I. Academic Press, New York.

Buño, W., Jr., Velluti, R., Handler, P., and García-Austt, E. (1966). Neural control of the cochlear input in the wakeful free guinea-pig. *Physiology & Behavior* **1**, 23–35.

Butler, R. A. (1968). Effect of changes in stimulus frequency and intensity on habituation of the human vertex potential. *Journal of the Acoustical Society of America* **44**, 945–950.

Butler, R. A., Spreng, M., and Keidel, W. D. (1969). Stimulus repetition rate factors which influence the auditory evoked potential in man. *Psychophysiology* **5**, 665–672.

Carmel, P. W., and Starr, A. (1963). Acoustic and non-acoustic factors modifying middle ear muscle activity in waking cats. *Journal of Neurophysiology* **26**, 598–616.

Carmel, P. W., and Starr, A. (1964). Non-acoustic factors influencing activity of middle ear muscles in waking cats. *Nature (London)* **202**, 195–196.

Cavaggioni, A., Giannelli, G., and Santibañez, G. (1959). Effects of repetitive photic stimulation on responses evoked in the lateral geniculate body and the visual cortex. *Archives Italiennes de Biologie* **97**, 266–275.

Cazard, P., and Buser, P. (1963). Modification des réponses sensorielles corticales par stimulation de l'hippocampe dorsal chez le lapin. *Electroencephalography and Clinical Neurophysiology* **15**, 413–425.

Clark, B. (1970). The vestibular system. *Annual Review of Psychology* **21**, 273–306.

Cook, J. D., Ellinwood, E. H., Jr., and Wilson, W. P. (1968). Auditory habituation at primary cortex as a function of stimulus rate. *Experimental Neurology* **21**, 167–175.

Creutzfeldt, O., Bell, F., and Adey, W. (1963). The activity of neurons in the amygdala of the cat following afferent stimulation. *Progress in Brain Research* **3**, 31–49.

Davis, H., Mast, T., Yoshie, N., and Zerlin, S. (1966). The slow response of the human cortex to auditory stimuli: Recovery process. *Electroencephalography and Clinical Neurophysiology* **21**, 105–113.

Davis, M., and Wagner, A. R. (1968). Startle responsiveness after habituation to different intensities of tone. *Psychonomic Science* **12**, 337–338.

Desmedt, J. E. (1960). Neurophysiological mechanisms controlling acoustic input. *In* "Neurological Mechanisms of the Auditory and Vestibular Systems" (G. L. Rasmussen and W. F. Windle, eds.), pp. 152–164. Thomas, Springfield, Illinois.

Desmedt, J. E., and Mechelse, K. (1958). Suppression of acoustic input by thalamic stimulation. *Proceedings of the Society for Experimental Biology and Medicine* **99**, 772–775.

Desmedt, J. E., and Monaco, P. (1962). The pharmacology of a centrifugal inhibitory pathway in the cats' acoustic system. *Proceedings of the International Pharmacological Meeting, 1st, Stockholm, 1961* **8**, 183–188.

Donchin, E., and Cohen, L. (1967). Averaged evoked potentials and intramodality selective attention. *Electroencephalography and Clinical Neurophysiology* **22**, 537–546.

Dunlop, C. W., McLachlan, E. M., Webster, W. R., and Day, R. H. (1964a). Auditory habituation in cats as a function of stimulus intensity. *Nature (London)* **203**, 874.

Dunlop, C. W., Webster, W. R., and Day, R. H. (1964b). Amplitude changes of evoked potentials at the inferior colliculus during acoustic habituation. *Journal of Auditory Research* **4**, 159–169.

Dunlop, C. W., Webster, W. R., and Rodger, R. S. (1966). Amplitude changes of evoked potentials in the auditory system of unanesthetized cats during acoustic habituation. *Journal of Auditory Research* **6**, 47–66.

Eccles, J. C., Hubbard, J. E., and Oscarssan, O. (1961). Intracellular recordings from cells of the ventral spinocerebellar tract. *Journal of Physiology (London)* **158**, 486–516.

Ellinwood, E. H., Cook, J. D., and Wilson, W. P. (1968). Habituation of evoked response to unilateral clicks. *Brain Research* **7**, 306–309.

Fernández-Guardiola, A., Roldán, E., Fanjul, L., and Castells, C. (1960).

Papel del receptor en el proceso de la habituación en la via visual. *Boletin del Instituto de Estudios Medicos y Biologicos* [*Universidad Nacional Autonoma de Mexico*] 18, 1–28.

Fernández-Guardiola, A., Roldán, E., Fanjul, L., and Castells, C. (1961). Role of the pupillary mechanism in the process of habituation of the visual pathways. *Electroencephalography and Clinical Neurophysiology* 13, 564–576.

Fernández-Guardiola, A., Harmony, T., and Roldán, E. (1964a). Modulation of visual input by pupillary mechanisms. *Electroencephalography and Clinical Neurophysiology* 16, 259–268.

Fernández-Guardiola, A., Toro, A., Aquino-Cias, J., and Guma, E. (1964b). Evolution of chiasmatic, thalamic and cortical electrical responses during photic habituation. *Boletin del Instituto de Estudios Medicos y Biologicos* [*Universidad Nacional Autonoma de Mexico*] 22, 39–69.

Fernández-Guardiola, A., Toro, A., Aquino-Cias, J., and Guma, E. (1968). Peripheral and central modulation of visual input during "habituation." *Progress in Brain Research* 22, 388–399.

Frank, K., and Fuortes, M. G. F. (1956). Unitary activity in spinal interneurons of cats. *Journal of Physiology* (*London*) 131, 424–435.

Fruhstorfer, H., Jarvilehto, T., and Soveri, P. (1969). Short-term habituation and dishabituation of the sensory evoked response in man. *Acta Physiologica Scandinavica* 76, 14A–15A.

Fruhstorfer, H., Soveri, P., and Jarvilehto, T. (1970). Short-term habituation of the auditory evoked response in man. *Electroencephalography and Clinical Neurophysiology* 28, 153–161.

Gacek, R. R. (1960). Efferent component of the vestibular nerve. *In* "Neural Mechanisms of the Auditory and Vestibular Systems" (G. L. Rasmussen and W. F. Windle, eds.), pp. 276–284. Thomas, Springfield, Illinois.

Galambos, R. (1961). Processing of auditory information. *In* "Brain and Behavior" (M. A. B. Brazier, ed.), Vol. 1, pp. 171–203. Amer. Inst. Biol. Sci., Washington, D. C.

Galambos, R., Sheatz, G., and Vernier, V. G. (1956). Electrophysiological correlates of conditioned responses in cat. *Science* 123, 376–377.

García-Austt, E. (1963). Influence of the states of awareness upon sensory evoked potentials. *Electroencephalography and Clinical Neurophysiology* Supplement 24, 76–89.

García-Austt, E., Vanzulli, A., Bogacz, J., and Rodríguez-Barrios, R. (1963). Influence of the ocular muscles upon photic habituation. *Electroencephalography and Clinical Neurophysiology* 15, 281–286.

Gergen, J. A. (1967). Functional properties of the hippocampus in the subhuman primate. *Progress in Brain Research* 27, 442–461.

Gerkin, G. M., and Neff, W. D. (1963). Experimental procedures affecting evoked responses recorded from auditory cortex. *Electroencephalography and Clinical Neurophysiology* 15, 947–957.

Gerstein, G. L., Butler, R. A., and Erulkar, S. D. (1968). Excitation and inhibition in cochlear nucleus. I. Tone burst stimulation. *Journal of Neurophysiology* 31, 526–536.

Gloor, P. (1960). Amygdala. *In* "Handbook of Physiology, Sect. 1: Neurophysiology" (J. Field, H. W. Magoun, and V. E. Hall, eds.), Vol. 2, pp. 1395–1420. Amer. Physiol. Soc., Washington, D. C.

Goodwin, H. E., and Hill, R. M. (1968). Receptive fields of a marsupial visual system. I. The superior colliculus. *American Journal of Optometry* **45**, 358–363.

Granit, R. (1955). Centrifugal and antidromic effects on ganglion cells of retina. *Journal of Neurophysiology* **18**, 388–411.

Green, J. D., and Machne, X. (1955). Unit activity of rabbit hippocampus. *American Journal of Physiology* **181**, 219–221.

Grover, F. S., and Buchwald, J. S. (1970). Correlation of cell size with amplitude of background fast activity in specific brain nuclei. *Journal of Neurophysiology* **33**, 160–171.

Groves, P. M., and Thompson, R. F. (1970). Habituation: A dual process theory. *Psychological Review* **77**, 419–450.

Groves, P. M., DeMarco, R., and Thompson, R. F. (1969). Habituation and sensitization of spinal interneuron activity in acute spinal cat. *Brain Research* **14**, 521–525.

Groves, P. M., Glanzman, D. L., Patterson, M. M., and Thompson, R. F. (1970). Excitability of cutaneous afferent terminals during habituation and sensitization in acute spinal cat. *Brain Research* **18**, 388–392.

Gumnit, R. J., and Grossman, R. G. (1961). Potentials evoked by sound in the auditory cortex of the cat. *American Journal of Physiology* **200**, 1219–1225.

Guzmán-Flores, C. (1961). Discussion. *In* "Brain and Behavior" (M. A. B. Brazier, ed.), Vol. 1, pp. 232–240. Amer. Inst. Biol. Sci., Washington, D. C.

Guzmán-Flores, C., Alcaraz, M., and Harmony, T. (1960). Role of the intrinsic ear muscles in the process of acoustic habituation. *Boletin del Instituto de Estudios Medicos y Biologicos* [*Universidad Nacional Autonoma de Mexico*] **18**, 135–149.

Hagbarth, K. E., and Kerr, D. J. B. (1954). Central influences on spinal afferent conduction. *Journal of Neurophysiology* **17**, 295–307.

Hall, R. D. (1968). Habituation of evoked potentials in the rat under conditions of behavior control. *Electroencephalography and Clinical Neurophysiology* **24**, 155–165.

Hall, R. D., and Mark, R. G. (1967). Fear and the modification of acoustically evoked potentials during conditioning. *Journal of Neurophysiology* **30**, 893–910.

Harris, J. D. (1943). Habituatory response decrement in the intact organism. *Psychological Bulletin* **40**, 385–422.

Harutiunian-Kozak, B., Kozak, W., and Dec, K. (1968). Single unit activity in the pretectal region of the cat. *Acta Biologiae Experimentalis* (*Warsaw*) **28**, 333–343.

Hernández-Peón, R. (1960). Neurophysiological correlates of habituation and other manifestations of plastic inhibition. *Electroencephalography and Clinical Neurophysiology Suppl.* **13**, 101–114.

Hernández-Peón, R., and Brust-Carmona, H. (1961). Functional role of subcortical structures in habituation and conditioning. *In* "Brain Mechanisms and Learning" (J. F. Delafresnaye, ed.), pp. 393–412. Thomas, Springfield, Illinois.

Hernández-Peón, R., and Hagbarth, K. (1955). Interaction between afferent and cortically induced reticular responses. *Journal of Neurophysiology* **18**, 44–55.

Hernández-Peón, R., and Scherrer, H. (1955). Habituation to acoustic stimuli in cochlear nucleus. *Federation Proceedings, Federation of American Societies for Experimental Biology* **14**, 71.

Hernández-Peón, R., Guzmán-Flores, C., Alcaraz, M., and Fernández-Guardiola, A. (1956a). Photic potentials in the visual pathway during "attention" and photic "habituation." *Federation Proceedings, Federation of American Societies for Experimental Biology* **15**, 91–92.

Hernández-Peón, R., Scherrer, H., and Jouvet, M. (1956b). Modification of electrical activity in cochlear nucleus during attention in unanesthetized cats. *Science* **123**, 331.

Hernández-Peón, R., Scherrer, H., and Velasco, M. (1956c). Central influences on afferent conduction in the somatic and visual pathways. *Acta Neurologica Latinoamericana* **2**, 8–22.

Hernández-Peón, R., Jouvet, M., and Scherrer, H. (1957a). Auditory potentials at cochlear nucleus during acoustic habituation. *Acta Neurologica Latinoamericana* **3**, 144–156.

Hernández-Peón, R., Guzmán-Flores, C., Alcaraz, M., and Fernández-Guardiola, A. (1957b). Sensory transmission in visual pathway during "attention" in unanesthetized cats. *Acta Neurologica Latinoamericana* **3**, 1–8.

Hernández-Peón, R., Guzmán-Flores, C., Alcaraz, M., and Fernández-Guardiola, A. (1958). Habituation in the visual pathway. *Acta Neurologica Latinoamericana* **4**, 121–129.

Hill, R. M., and Goodwin, H. (1968). Visual receptive fields from cells of a marsupial (*Didelphis Virginiana*) superior colliculus. *Experientia* **24**, 559–560.

Hilton, S. M. (1966). Hypothalamic regulation of the cardiovascular system. *British Medical Bulletin* **22**, 243–248.

Holstein, S. B., Buchwald, J. S., and Schwafel, J. A. (1969a). Progressive changes in auditory response patterns to repeated tone during normal wakefulness and paralysis. *Brain Research* **16**, 133–148.

Holstein, S. B., Buchwald, J. S., and Schwafel, J. A. (1969b). Tone response patterns of the auditory nuclei during normal wakefulness, paralysis, and anesthesia. *Brain Research* **15**, 483–499.

Horn, G. (1965a). Physiological and psychological aspects of selective perception. *In* "Advances in the Study of Behavior" (D. S. Lehrman, R. A. Hinde, and E. Shaw, eds.), Vol. 1, pp. 155–215. Academic Press, New York.

Horn, G. (1965b). The effect of somesthetic and photic stimuli on the activity of units in the striate cortex of unanesthetized, unrestrained cats. *Journal of Physiology (London)* **179**, 263–277.

Horn, G., and Hill, R. M. (1964). Habituation of the response to sensory stimuli of neurones in the brain stem of rabbits. *Nature (London)* **202**, 296–298.

Horn, G., and Hill, R. M. (1966a). Effect of removing the neocortex on the response to repeated sensory stimulation of the neurones in the midbrain. *Nature (London)* **211**, 754–755.

Horn, G., and Hill, R. M. (1966b). Responsiveness to sensory stimulation of units in the superior colliculus and subjacent tectotegmental regions of the rabbit. *Experimental Neurology* **14**, 199–223.

Hubel, D. H., and Wiesel, T. N. (1962). Receptive fields, binocular interaction and functional architecture in the cats' visual cortex. *Journal of Physiology (London)* **160**, 106–154.

Hugelin, A., Dumont, S., and Paillas, N. (1960). Tympanic muscles and control of auditory input during arousal. *Science* **131**, 1371–1372.

Humphrey, G. (1933). "The Nature of Learning." Harcourt, New York.

Humphrey, G. L., and Buchwald, J. S. (1972). Response decrements in the cochlear nucleus of decerebrate cats during repeated acoustic stimulation. *Science* **175**, 1488–1491.

Humphrey, G. L., Kitzes, M. I., and Buchwald, J. S. (1970). Progressive changes of acoustic reflex in decerebrate cats. *Federation Proceedings, Federation of American Societies for Experimental Biology* **29**, 324.

Humphrey, N. K. (1968). Responses to visual stimuli of units in the superior colliculus of rats and monkeys. *Experimental Neurology* **20**, 312–340.

Hutt, S. J., and Hutt, C. (1964). Hyperactivity in a group of epileptic (and some non-epileptic) brain-damaged children. *Epilepsia* **5**, 334–351.

Hutt, S. J., Hutt, C., Lee, D., and Ounsted, C. (1965). A behavioral and electroencephalographic study of autistic children. *Journal of Psychiatric Research* **3**, 181–197.

Huttenlocher, P. R. (1960). Effects of state of arousal on click responses in the mesencephalic reticular formation. *Electroencephalography and Clinical Neurophysiology* **12**, 819–827.

Jaffe, S. L., Bourlier, P. F., and Hagamen, W. D. (1969). Adaptation of evoked auditory potentials: A midline through frontal map in the unanesthetized cat. *Brain Research* **15**, 121–136.

Jennings, H. (1906). "Behavior of the Lower Organisms." Columbia University Press, New York.

John, E. R., and Killam, K. F. (1959). Electrophysiological correlates of avoidance conditioning in the cat. *Journal of Pharmacology and Experimental Therapy* **125**, 252–274.

John, E. R., and Killam, K. F. (1960). Electrophysiological correlates of differential approach-avoidance conditioning in cats. *Journal of Nervous and Mental Disease* **131**, 183–201.

Johnson, L. C., and Lubin, A. (1967). The orienting reflex during walking and sleeping. *Electroencephalography and Clinical Neurophysiology* **22**, 11–21.

Jongkees, L. B. W. (1969). Physiologie und Pathophysiologie des Vestibularorganes. (Normal and pathological function of the vestibular organ.) *Archiv für Klinische und Experimentelle Ohren-, Nasen- und Kehlkopfheilkunde* **194**, 1–110.

Kandel, E. R., and Spencer, W. A. (1968). Cellular neurophysiological approaches in the study of learning. *Physiological Review* **48**, 63–134.

Key, B. J. (1965). Correlation of behavior with changes in amplitude of cortical potentials evoked during habituation by auditory stimuli. *Nature (London)* **207**, 441–442.

Kitzes, M., and Buchwald, J. (1969). Progressive alterations in cochlear nucleus, inferior colliculus, and medial geniculate responses during acoustic habituation. *Experimental Neurology* **25**, 85–105.

Kolmodin, G. M., and Skoglund, C. R. (1960). Analysis of spinal interneurons activated by tactile and nociceptive stimulation. *Acta Physiologica Scandinavica* **50**, 337–355.

Landis, C., and Hunt, W. A. (1939). "The Startle Pattern." Rhinehart, New York.

Lawrence, M. (1968). Audition. *Annual Review of Psychology* **19**, 1–26.

Livingston, R. B. (1960). A discussion of research potentialities. *In* "Neural Mechanisms of the Auditory and Vestibular Systems" (G. L. Rasmussen and W. F. Windle, eds.), pp. 362–369. Thomas, Springfield, Illinois.

Long, R. G. (1959). Modification of sensory mechanisms by subcortical structures. *Journal of Neurophysiology* **22**, 412–427.

Macadar, O., Ginés, A., Bove, I. C., and García-Austt, E. (1963). Effect of habituation, interference and association of stimuli upon the visual evoked response in the rat. *Acta Neurologica Latinoamericana* **9**, 315–327.

Machne, X., and Segundo, J. P. (1956). Unitary responses to afferent volleys in amygdaloid complex. *Journal of Neurophysiology* **19**, 232–240.

MacKay, D. M., Evans, E. F., Hammond, P., Jeffreys, D. A., and Regan, D. (1969). Evoked brain potentials as indicators of sensory information processing. *Neurosciences Research Program, Bulletin* **7**, 181–276.

McLardy, T. (1959). Hippocampal formation of brain as detector-coder of temporal patterns of information. *Perspectives in Biology and Medicine* **2**, 443–452.

MacLean, P. D. (1949). Psychosomatic disease and the "viseral brain." Recent developments bearing on the Papez theory of emotion. *Psychosomatic Medicine* **11**, 338–353.

MacLean, P. D. (1969). The internal-external bonds of the memory process. *Journal of Nervous and Mental Disease* **149**, 40–47.

Mancia, M. (1961). Discussion. *In* "Brain and Behavior" (M. A. B. Brazier, ed.), Vol. 1, pp. 348–353. Amer. Inst. Biol. Sci., Washington, D. C.

Mancia, M. Meulders, M., and Santibañez, G. (1959a). Changes of photically evoked potentials in the visual pathway of the *cerveau isole* cat. *Archives Italiennes de Biologie* **97**, 378–398.

Mancia, M., Meulders, M., and Santibañez, G. (1959b). Changes of photically evoked potentials in the visual pathway of the midpontine pretrigeminal cat. *Archives de Italiennes de Biologie* **97**, 399–413.

Marsh, J. T., and Worden, F. G. (1964). Auditory potentials during acoustic habituation: Cochlear nucleus, cerebellum and auditory cortex. *Electroencephalography and Clinical Neurophysiology* **17**, 685–692.

Marsh, J. T., McCarthy, D. A., Sheatz, G., and Galambos, R. (1961). Amplitude changes in evoked auditory potentials during habituation and conditioning. *Electroencephalography and Clinical Neurophysiology* **13**, 224–234.

Marsh, J. T., Worden, F. G., and Hicks, L. (1962). Some effects of room acoustics on evoked auditory potentials. *Science* **137**, 280–282.

Meissner, W. W. (1967). Hippocampus and learning. *International Journal of Neuropsychiatry* **3**, 298–310.

Mendell, L. M., and Wall, P. D. (1965). Responses of single dorsal cord cells to peripheral cutaneous unmyelinated fibres. *Nature (London)* **206**, 97–99.

Meschersky, R. M., and Rosenschtein, G. S. H. (1969). Instability of the central nervous system. *Brain Research* **13**, 367–375.

Milner, B., and Teuber, H. L. (1968). Alteration of perception and memory in man: Reflections on methods. *In* "Analysis of Behavioral Change" (L. Weiskrantz, ed.), pp. 268–375. Harper, New York.

Milner, P. M. (1970). "Physiological Psychology." Holt, New York.

Milstein, V., Stevens, J., and Sachdev, K. (1969). Habituation of the alpha attenuation response in children and adults with psychiatric disorders. *Electroencephalography and Clinical Neurophysiology* **26**, 12–18.

Moushegian, G., Rupert, A., Marsh, J., and Galambos, R. (1961). Evoked cortical potentials in absence of middle ear muscles. *Science* **133**, 582–583.

Naquet, R., Regis, H., Fisher-Williams, M., and Fernández-Guardiola, A. (1960). Variations in the responses evoked by light along the specific pathways. *Brain* 83, 52–56.

Nauta, W. J. H. (1960). Some neural pathways related to the limbic system. *In* "Electrical Studies on the Unanesthetized Brain" (E. R. Ramey and D. S. O'Doherty, eds.), pp. 1–16. Harper (Hoeber), New York.

Nelson, P. G., and Erulkar, S. D. (1963). Synaptic mechanisms of excitation in the central auditory pathway. *Journal of Neurophysiology* 31, 44–61.

O'Keefe, J., and Bouma, H. (1969). Complex sensory properties of certain amygdala units in the freely moving cat. *Experimental Neurology* 23, 384–398.

Olds, J., and Hirano, T. (1969). Conditioned responses of hippocampal and other neurons. *Electroencephalography and Clinical Neurophysiology* 26, 159–166.

Ornitz, E. M., and Ritvo, E. R. (1968a). Neurophysiologic mechanisms underlying perceptual inconstancy in autistic and schizophrenic children. *Archives of General Psychiatry* 19, 22–27.

Ornitz, E. M., and Ritvo, E. R. (1968b). Perceptual inconstancy in early infantile autism. *Archives of General Psychiatry* 18, 76–98.

Ornitz, E. M., Ritvo, E. R., Panman, L. M., Lee, Y. H., Carr, E. M., and Walter, R. P. (1968). The auditory evoked response in normal and autistic children during sleep. *Electroencephalography and Clinical Neurophysiology* 25, 221–230.

Ounsted, C. (1955). The hyperkinetic syndrome in epileptic children. *Lancet* ii, 303–311.

Palestini, M., Davidovich, A., and Hernández-Peón, R. (1959). Functional significance of centrifugal influences upon the retina. *Acta Neurologica Latinoamericana* 5, 113–131.

Palestini, M., Gallardo, R., and Armengol, V. (1964). Peripheral factors in the study of the habituation of the cortical responses to photic stimulation. *Archives Italiennes de Biologie* 102, 608–615.

Parmeggiani, P. L., and Rapisarda, C. (1969). Hippocampal output and sensory mechanisms. *Brain Research* 14, 387–400.

Pavlov, I. P. (1941). A brief outline of higher nervous activity. *In* "Conditioned Reflexes and Psychiatry" (W. Horsley Gantt, ed. and transl.), Vol. 2, pp. 44–59. Int. Publ., New York.

Perry, N. W., and Copenhaver, R. M. (1965). Differential cortical habituation with stimulation of central and peripheral retina. *Perceptual and Motor Skills* 20, 1209–1213.

Piaget, J. (1952). "The Origins of Intelligence in Children" (M. Cook, transl.). Int. Univ. Press, New York.

Podvall, E. M., and Goodman, S. J. (1967). Averaged neural electrical activity and arousal. *Science* 155, 223–225.

Powell, E. W., and Hoelle, D. G. (1967). Septotectal projections in the cat. *Experimental Neurology* 18, 177–183.

Powell, E. W., Furlong, L. D., and Hatton, J. B. (1970). Influence of the septum and inferior colliculus on medial geniculate body units. *Electroencephalography and Clinical Neurophysiology* 29, 74–82.

Pribram, K. H. (1967). The limbic systems, afferent control of neural inhibition and behavior. *Progress in Brain Research* 27, 318–336.

Prosser, C. L., and Hunter, W. S. (1936). The extinction of startle responses and spinal reflexes in the white rat. *American Journal of Physiology* 117, 609–618.

Rasmussen, G. L. (1946). The olivary peduncle and other fiber projections of the superior olivary complex. *Journal of Comparative Neurology* 84, 141–219.

Rasmussen, G. L. (1955). Descending or "feed-back" connections of auditory system of the cat. *American Journal of Physiology* 183, 653.

Redding, F. K. (1967). Modification of sensory cortical evoked potentials by hippocampal stimulation. *Electroencephalography and Clinical Neurophysiology* 22, 74–83.

Rexed, B. (1964). Some aspects of the cytoarchitectonics and synaptology of the spinal cord. *Progress in Brain Research* 11, 58–90.

Ritter, W., Vaughan, H. G., and Costa, L. D. (1968). Orienting and habituation to auditory stimuli: A study of short term changes in average evoked responses. *Electroencephalography and Clinical Neurophysiology* 25, 550–556.

Roth, W. T., and Kopell, B. S. (1969). The auditory evoked response to repeated stimuli during a vigilance task. *Psychophysiology* 6, 301–309.

Salomon, G., and Starr, A. (1963). Electromyography of middle ear muscles in man during motor activities. *Acta Neurologica Scandinavica* 39, 161–168.

Santibañez, G., Trouche, E., and Albe-Fessard, D. (1963). Étude de l'évalution au cours du temps de l'amplitude des activités corticales et thalamiques évoquées par des stimuli somatique répétés. *Journal de Physiologie (Paris)* 55, 335–336.

Saunders, J. C., and Chabora, J. T. (1969). Effects of appetitive drive on evoked potentials in cochlear nucleus and auditory cortex in cats. *Journal of Comparative and Physiological Psychology* 69, 355–361.

Sawa, M., and Delgado, J. (1963). Amgdala unitary activity in the unrestrained cat. *Electroencephalography and Clinical Neurophysiology* 15, 637–650.

Scheibel, M. E., and Scheibel, A. B. (1958). Structural substrate of integrative patterns in the brainstem reticular core. *In* "The Reticular Formation of the Brain" (H. H. Jasper, L. D. Proctor, R. S. Knighton, W. C. Noshay, and R. T. Costello, eds.), pp. 31–55. Little, Brown, Boston, Massachusetts.

Scheibel, M. E., and Scheibel, A. B. (1965). The response of reticular units to repetitive stimuli. *Archives Italiennes de Biologie* 103, 279–299.

Schlag, J., and Balvin, R. (1963). Background activity in the cerebral cortex and reticular formation in relation to the electroencephalogram. *Experimental Neurology* 8, 203–219.

Sharpless, S. K. (1964). Reorganization of function in the nervous system—use and disuse. *Annual Review of Physiology* 26, 357–388.

Sharpless, S., and Jasper, H. (1956). Habituation of the arousal reaction. *Brain* 79, 655–680.

Sherrington, C. S. (1898). Experiments in the examination of the peripheral distribution of the fibers of the posterior roots of some spinal nerves. *Philosophical Transactions of the Royal Society of London, Series B* 190, 45–186.

Simmons, F. B. (1964). Perceptual theories of middle ear muscle function. *Annals of Otology, Rhinology, & Laryngology* 73, 724–739.

Simons, L. A., Dunlop, C. W., Webster, W. R., and Aitkin, L. M. (1966). Acoustic habituation in cats as a function of stimulus rate and the role of temporal conditioning of the middle ear muscles. *Electroencephalography and Clinical Neurophysiology* **20**, 485–493.

Sokolov, E. N. (1963). Higher nervous functions: The orienting reflex. *Annual Review of Physiology* **25**, 545–580.

Spencer, W. A., Thompson, R. F., and Neilson, D. R., Jr. (1966a). Alterations in responsiveness of ascending and reflex pathways activated by iterated cutaneous afferent volleys. *Journal of Neurophysiology* **29**, 240–252.

Spencer, W. A., Thompson, R. F., and Neilson, D. R., Jr. (1966b). Decrement of ventral root electrotonus and intracellularly recorded PSPs produced by iterated cutaneous afferent volleys. *Journal of Neurophysiology* **29**, 253–274.

Sprague, J. M., Chambers, W. W., and Stellar, E. (1961). Attentive, affective and adaptive behavior in the cat. *Science* **133**, 165–173.

Sprague, J. M., Levitt, M., Robson, K., Liu, C. N., Stellar, E., and Chambers, W. W. (1963). A neuroanatomical and behavioral analysis of syndromes resulting from midbrain lemniscal and reticular lesions in the cat. *Archives Italiennes de Biologie* **101**, 225–295.

Sprague, J. M., Marchiafava, P. L., and Rizzolatti, G. (1968). Unit responses to visual stimuli in the superior colliculus of the unanesthetized midpontine cat. *Archives Italiennes de Biologie* **106**, 169–193.

Starr, A. (1964). Influence of motor activity on click-evoked responses in the auditory pathway of waking cats. *Experimental Neurology* **10**, 191–204.

Steinberg, R. H. (1965). Alterations of averaged photic evoked potentials in cat visual cortex during repetitive stimulation. *Electroencephalography and Clinical Neurophysiology* **18**, 378–391.

Steriade, M., and Demetrescu, M. (1962). Reticular facilitation of responses to acoustic stimuli. *Electroencephalography and Clinical Neurophysiology* **14**, 21–36.

Sutin, J. (1963). An electrophysiological study of the hypothalamic ventromedial nucleus in the cat. *Electroencephalography and Clinical Neurophysiology* **15**, 786–795.

Teas, D. C., and Kiang, N. Y.-S. (1964). Evoked responses from the auditory cortex. *Experimental Neurology* **10**, 91–119.

Thompson, R. F., and Spencer, W. A. (1966). Habituation: A model phenomenon for the study of neuronal substrates of behavior. *Physiological Review* **73**, 16–43.

Thorpe, W. H. (1963). "Learning and Instinct in Animals." Methuen, London.

Tizard, B. (1968). Habituation of EEG and skin potential changes in normal and severely subnormal children. *American Journal of Mental Deficiency* **73**, 34–40.

Turner, E. (1969). Hippocampus and memory. *Lancet* **ii**, 1123–1126.

Vinogradova, O. S. (1966). Dynamic classification of the reactions of hippocampal neurons to sensory stimuli. *Federation Proceedings, Federation of American Societies for Experimental Biology* **25**, Trans. Suppl., T397–T403.

von Békésy, G. (1949). The structure of the middle ear and the hearing of one's own voice by bone conduction. *Journal of the Acoustical Society of America* **21**, 217–232.

Wall, P. D. (1967). The laminar organization of dorsal horn and effects of descending influences. *Journal of Physiology (London)* **188**, 403–423.

Ward, W. D. (1966). Audition. *Annual Review of Psychology* **17**, 273–308.

Weber, D., and Buchwald, J. S. (1965). A technique for recording and integrating multiple unit activity simultaneously with the EEG in chronic cats. *Electroencephalography and Clinical Neurophysiology* 19, 190–192.

Webster, W. R. (1969). Auditory habituation and barbiturate induced neural activity. *Science* 164, 970–971.

Webster, W. R., and Dunlop, C. W. (1965). Unanesthetized cats, auditory evoked potentials and test cage acoustics: A methodological study. *Journal of Auditory Research* 5, 11–25.

Webster, W. R., Dunlop, C. W., Simons, L. A., and Aitkin, L. M. (1965). Auditory habituation: A test of a centrifugal and a peripheral theory. *Science* 148, 654–656.

Weinberger, N. M., Goodman, D. A., and Kitzes, L. M. (1969). Is behavioral habituation a function of peripheral auditory system blockade? *Communications in Behavioral Biology* 3, 111–116.

Wester, K. (1971). Habituation to electrical stimulation of the thalamus in unanesthetized cats. *Electroencephalography and Clinical Neurophysiology* 30, 52–61.

Whitfield, I. C. (1967). "The Central Auditory Pathway." Arnold, London.

Wickelgren, B. G. (1967a). Habituation of spinal motorneurons. *Journal of Neurophysiology* 30, 1404–1423.

Wickelgren, B. G. (1967b). Habituation of spinal interneurons. *Journal of Neurophysiology* 30, 1424–1438.

Wickelgren, W. O. (1968a). Effect of acoustic habituation on click-evoked responses in cats. *Journal of Neurophysiology* 31, 777–782.

Wickelgren, W. O. (1968b). Effect of state of arousal on click-evoked responses in cats. *Journal of Neurophysiology* 31, 757–768.

Winters, W. D., Kenjiro, M., Spooner, C. E., and Kado, R. T. (1967). Correlation of reticular and cochlear multiple unit activity with auditory evoked responses during wakefulness and sleep. I. *Electroencephalography and Clinical Neurophysiology* 23, 539–545.

Worden, F. G., and Marsh, J. T. (1963). Amplitude changes of auditory potentials evoked at cochlear nucleus during acoustic habituation. *Electroencephalography and Clinical Neurophysiology* 15, 866–881.

Worden, F. G., Marsh, J. T., Abraham, F. D., and Whittlesey, J. R. B. (1964). Variability of evoked auditory potentials and acoustic input control. *Electroencephalography and Clinical Neurophysiology* 17, 524–530.

Wurtz, R. H., and Goldberg, M. E. (1971). Superior colliculus cell responses related to eye movements in awake monkeys. *Science* 171, 82–84.

Young, L. R. (1969). Biocybernetics of the vestibular system. *In* "Biocybernetics of the Central Nervous System" (L. D. Proctor, ed.), pp. 79–117. Little, Brown, Boston, Massachusetts.

Inferotemporal Cortex and Vision

Charles G. Gross
*Department of Psychology,
Princeton University,
Princeton, New Jersey*

I. Introduction

Our ignorance of the physiology of mental activity is almost total. Whereas we are beginning to understand the early stages of sensory processing and the final stages of the control of movement, the intervening mechanisms remain mysterious. Our knowledge of the physiological mechanisms of perception, cognition, and memory is largely confined to information about defects after brain damage: we know little of the neuronal processes that underlie normal mentation.

The study of inferotemporal cortex may provide a bridge from sensory physiology to the physiology of cognition. Inferotemporal cortex is "association" cortex on the inferior surface of the temporal lobe of primates. Its removal impairs visual, and only visual, learning while leaving basic visual sensory functions unchanged. Thus, inferotemporal cortex must have some perceptual, associative, or mnemonic functions. Recent advances in sensory physiology and cortical anatomy offer hope of understanding these functions in terms of the underlying neural events.

The first section of this article provides a brief summary of previous research on the behavioral effects of ablation of inferotemporal cortex. The second section describes the anatomical connections of inferotemporal cortex with other visual structures and discusses the possible roles of these connections. The third section is devoted to our experiments on the behavioral effects of lesions of inferotemporal cortex and of the adjacent "foveal" prestriate cortex. In the fourth section, we describe our electrophysiological studies on inferotemporal cortex, with emphasis on the visual properties of inferotemporal neurons and their anatomical bases.

II. Behavioral Effects of Inferotemporal Lesions

A. Localization of the Deficit

In the late 1930s, Klüver and Bucy (1937, 1938, 1939) reported a constellation of bizarre effects after removal of the temporal lobes in monkeys. Their monkeys failed to recognize objects visually and were deficient in learning and remembering visual discrimination habits. In addition, they compulsively touched and mouthed objects, were un- naturally tame and docile, and showed abnormal sexual behavior.

The "Klüver-Bucy syndrome," as these effects of temporal lobectomy were called, was subsequently fractionated by Karl Lashley's associates, particularly Chow and Pribram. They showed that components of the syndrome could be produced independently by smaller temporal lobe lesions. The impairment on visual discrimination tasks followed lesions of the neocortex of the temporal lobe, whereas the remaining aspects of the syndrome resulted from destruction of rhinencephalic structures of the temporal lobe, particularly the amygdala (Pribram and Bagshaw, 1953; Blum *et al.,* 1950; Chow, 1951, 1952). Subsequent studies dem- onstrated that the cortex crucial for normal visual discrimination learn- ing was "inferotemporal cortex"[1] (comprising most of the middle and

---

[1] In this paper, "inferotemporal cortex" and "Area TE" of von Bonin and Bailey (1947) are used synonymously. Inferotemporal cortex is equivalent to Brodmann's (1905) Areas 21 and 22, except that the latter also include the temporal pole (Area TG of von Bonin and Bailey).

inferior gyri of the temporal lobe, see Fig. 1). By contrast, lesions of other regions of the temporal lobe cortex (viz., superior temporal gyrus, temporal pole, fusiform gyrus, and hippocampal gyrus) had no effect on visual discrimination learning (Mishkin, 1954, 1966; Mishkin and Pribram, 1954; Pribram, 1954).

Bilateral inferotemporal lesions are required to obtain the full deficit. Unilateral inferotemporal lesions have had little (Ettlinger and Gautrin, 1971) or no effect (e.g., Mishkin and Pribram, 1954). An exception is in "split-brain" animals. That is, animals with unilateral inferotemporal lesions and section of the optic chiasm and corpus callosum show impaired discrimination when tested with the eye ipsilateral to the lesion, but normal performance when tested with the other eye (Butler, 1969). Henceforth in this article, "inferotemporal lesion" will mean a bilateral cortical lesion unless otherwise specified.

Visual discrimination learning is also impaired by electrical disruption of inferotemporal cortex. Two methods have been used: induction of epiliptiform discharges by implantation of alumina cream (Stamm and Pribram, 1961; Stamm and Knight, 1963) and direct electrical stimula-

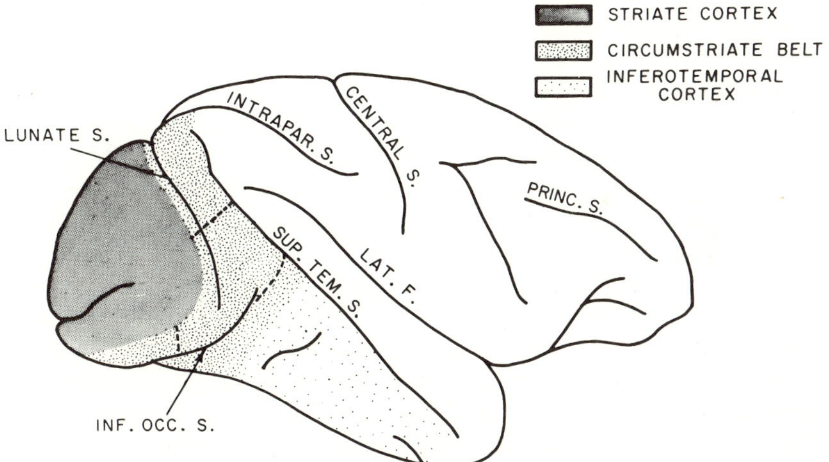

Fig. 1. Diagram of lateral view of cerebral hemisphere of *Macaca mulatta*. The circumstriate belt (or prestriate cortex) is shown after Kuypers *et al.* (1965). Von Bonin and Bailey (1947) divide this region into an Area OB, adjacent to striate cortex (Area OC) and a more rostral Area OA. The dashed lines indicate the approximate borders of the direct projections of foveal striate cortex onto the circumstriate belt; much of this projection lies in the lunate, inferior occipital, and superior temporal sulci (Zeki, 1969b; Cragg and Ainsworth, 1969). INTRAPAR.S., Intraparietal sulcus; PRINC.S., principal sulcus; LAT.F., lateral fissure; SUP.TEM.S., superior temporal sulcus; INF.OCC.S., inferior occipital sulcus. See also Figs. 2, 3, and 12, and footnotes 1 and 2.

tion (Chow, 1961a,c; Goldrich and Stamm, 1971; Reitz and Gerbrandt, 1971; Kovner and Stamm, 1972). Unilateral stimulation is only effective if it produces afterdischarge in both temporal lobes.

B. Characteristics of the Deficit

1. Sensory and Motor Status

The discrimination deficit that follows inferotemporal lesions is an exclusively visual deficit. Learning and retention of olfactory, auditory, tactile, and gustatory discrimination tasks are unaffected (Brown, 1963; Brown *et al.*, 1963; Pasik *et al.*, 1958; Pribram and Barry, 1956; Weiskrantz and Mishkin, 1958; Wilson, 1957). The deficit appears to exist in the absence of any sensory changes. Minimum separable visual acuity, the visual fields, critical flicker frequency, threshold for detection of a brief flash, and backward masking functions all remain normal after inferotemporal lesions (Cowey and Weiskrantz, 1963, 1967; Weiskrantz and Cowey, 1963; Symmes, 1965; Bender, 1973a,b,c; but cf. Pasik *et al.*, 1960). (In order to obtain these measurements of sensory capacity, extensive training was necessary, and the animals with inferotemporal lesions usually required far more training than the control animals. However, the final asymptotic performance was always indistinguishable from that of normal animals.) Thus, it is highly unlikely that a simple sensory impairment is the principal *cause* of the visual discrimination impairment after inferotemporal lesions. This suggests that the inferotemporal syndrome fits Freud's (1891) classic definition of agnosia: a modality-specific disturbance of a "higher-order" recognition function in the absence of any elementary sensory disturbances sufficient to account for the recognition deficit.

Monkeys with inferotemporal lesions show abnormal patterns of eye movements during acquisition of two-choice visual discrimination tasks. They tend to look longer at the discriminanda and shift their gaze between the discriminanda less than normal monkeys (Oscar-Berman *et al.*, 1971, 1973). When staring at one discriminandum, they show a greater rate of change of fixation within its borders (Oscar-Berman *et al.*, 1973). Furthermore, they show slower learning when the response required is fixation of one of two patterns (Bagshaw *et al.*, 1970). By contrast, the pattern of eye movements during spontaneous viewing of novel and familiar stimuli are normal after inferotemporal lesions (Bagshaw *et al.*, 1972). Thus, it is unlikely that an oculomotor disorder is the cause of the discrimination deficit. Rather, the abnormal pattern of eye movements during training, and the impairment in learning to fixate a particular stimulus are probably effects of the inability of the animals to recognize the discriminanda and respond appropriately to them.

2. Types of Visual Tasks Impaired

After inferotemporal lesions, monkeys are severely impaired in learning visual discrimination problems: they require many more trials than control animals to reach a learning criterion (e.g., Pribram, 1954). If trained on a visual discrimination prior to surgery, they show a severe loss in postoperative retention (e.g., Pribram, 1954). Inferotemporal lesions impair both the learning of individual problems and the rate at which monkeys improve their performance on successive problems, i.e., acquire visual discrimination sets (e.g., Chow, 1954a; Mishkin, 1966). The learning deficit is a permanent one: after years of postoperative training experience, animals with inferotemporal lesions will still acquire new discriminations more slowly than control animals with the same experience.

The inferotemporal deficit has been found with a great variety of discriminanda, including both ones differing in a single parameter such as hue, brightness, or size, and ones differing in several parameters such as two-dimensional patterns and three-dimensional objects (e.g., Mishkin, 1954; Mishkin and Hall, 1955; Wilson and Mishkin, 1959). The deficit has been found with a great variety of training methods such as simultaneous and successive presentation of the discriminanda, two-choice and multi-choice discriminations, and discrete trial and free operant paradigms (e.g., Pribram and Mishkin, 1955; Pribram, 1960; Butter *et al.,* 1965).

This deficit is not a total inability to learn any visual discrimination. Rather, the occurrence and severity of the impaired learning depends on the "difficulty" of the discrimination. Task "difficulty" is measured by the number of trials a normal monkey, with a comparable training history, requires to learn the discrimination. It usually depends on the degree of physical difference between the stimuli, on the training procedure used, and on the animal's previous experience. On a simple visual discrimination (one that normal monkeys learn in one to ten trials), animals with inferotemporal lesions often show little or no impairment. However, on a more difficult discrimination (one that normal monkeys require several hundred trials to learn), animals with inferotemporal lesions usually are severely impaired, often failing to learn in several thousand trials (e.g., Pribram, 1954; but cf. Ettlinger, 1962). Task difficulty may not be the sole determinant of the degree of inferotemporal impairment. Unfortunately, however, there have been no systematic studies varying stimulus parameters while keeping task difficulty constant.

What about retention of discriminations acquired after surgery? Do animals with inferotemporal lesions remember visual discriminations normally once they have learned them? Yes, but only if a stringent learning criterion is used. If animals with inferotemporal lesions and control animals are trained to a criterion of nine correct out of ten responses, the animals with inferotemporal lesions take longer than the controls to successively reach more stringent criteria of 18 correct out of 20, and 45 correct out of 90. But once they have reached a criterion of 90 correct out of 100, they will perform similarly to controls. This phenomenon is often reflected in a more negatively accelerating learning curve in animals with inferotemporal lesions. Thus, animals with inferotemporal lesions may appear to have a memory deficit for discriminations acquired postoperatively when tested for retention after learning to a weak criterion (e.g., nine out of ten) but will show normal retention when trained to a strong criterion (e.g., 90 out of 100) (Gross and Footnick, 1966; cf. Ettlinger, 1962).

3. Conditions that Prevent the Deficit

There are three conditions under which inferotemporal lesions do not impair the learning of even difficult visual discrimination tasks. The first is preoperative overtraining. If animals are overtrained on a particular discrimination prior to inferotemporal lesion, they will show normal postoperative retention of that discrimination, but impaired retention of nonovertrained ones (Chow and Survis, 1958; Orbach and Fantz, 1958; Meyer, 1958).

The second condition is lesion when young. Animals that receive posterior association cortex lesions (including inferotemporal and prestriate cortex) when 130 or 370 days old showed much better performance on visual discrimination tasks than animals receiving lesions when 900 days old (Raisler and Harlow, 1965). By contrast, in normal animals visual discrimination learning is superior at the older age (Harlow *et al.*, 1960).

The third condition is the use of shock punishment for incorrect responses. In all previous inferotemporal studies, food or water was used as reward for the correct response. However, when incorrect responses were punished with shock as well as correct responses rewarded with food, monkeys with inferotemporal lesions learned difficult visual discrimination tasks as well as normal monkeys, but continued to be impaired when trained under the conventional procedure of only food reward as shown in Fig. 9 (Manning, 1971a).

Presumably, under these three conditions other mechanisms are able to compensate for the absence of inferotemporal cortex. Whether the compensation is similar in all three cases, and whether it involves the surrounding tissue (Glees and Cole, 1950) or subcortical structures is unknown.

4. Functional Ablation

"Turning on and off" the inferotemporal deficit by electrical stimulation of inferotemporal cortex has provided interesting experimental possibilities. Reitz and Gerbrandt (1971) compared the effects of pre- and posttrial stimulation of inferotemporal cortex. Pretrial stimulation (in which the afterdischarges continue until or beyond the animal's response) severely impaired visual learning. However, posttrial stimulation had no effect. Kovner and Stamm (1972) investigated the effects of stimulation during segments of each trial of a delayed "match from sample" task. Stimulation during the delay period and at match onset impaired performance, but stimulation during the sample period or after the response had little or no effect. Taken together, these results seem to implicate inferotemporal cortex in some perceptual or short-term storage mechanism rather than in "long-term memory consolidation."

5. Analogies and Homologies

Lesions of other regions of "association cortex" besides inferotemporal cortex produce modality-specific deficits in discrimination learning by monkeys. Posterior parietal lesions impair somesthetic discrimination learning (e.g., Wilson, 1957), superior temporal lesions impair auditory discrimination learning (e.g., Weiskrantz and Mishkin, 1958), and temporal pole lesions impair olfactory discrimination (e.g., Brown *et al.,* 1963). However, it is not yet clear that these deficits are independent of sensory deficits as appears to be the case for the inferotemporal syndrome (Gross, 1972; Semmes, 1973). Thus, more information is required before it is certain that the apparent similarity of the functions of inferotemporal cortex to those of other regions of posterior association cortex is more than a superficial analogy.

Virtually all the research on the functions of inferotemporal cortex in animals has been done with macaques and (less commonly) baboons. Indeed, it is not clear whether homologous cortex exists outside of the primate order, and even within the primate order its exact location is often uncertain.

In man, the effects of temporal lobe damage depend on the hemisphere injured, reflecting the unique lateralization of the human brain. Damage to the temporal lobe of the dominant hemisphere produces language disturbances. By contrast, the temporal lobe of the nondominant hemisphere appears to have visual functions similar to those of inferotemporal cortex in the monkey. Support for this view comes from both the study of surgical excision (Milner, 1968) and of electrical stimulation of temporal cortex in man (Penfield and Perot, 1963) as well as from the study of temporal lobe pathology.

C. INTERPRETATIONS OF THE DEFICIT

Over the last 20 years, various investigators have offered various "explanations" and "interpretations" of the effects of inferotemporal lesions. Usually, this involved inferring a loss or deficit in some psychological function after inferotemporal lesions and then attributing that function to the normal activity of inferotemporal cortex. Among the functions attributed to inferotemporal cortex have been traditional ones such as "visual perception," "visual attention," "visual memory," and more contemporary ones such as "centrifugal control of visual redundancy" and "visual information processing" (see discussions by Wilson, 1968; Weiskrantz, 1967, 1970; Pribram, 1967, 1971). These interpretations have often been supported by the results of tests that afford more analytical possibilities than the standard two-choice visual discrimination tests. These include tests of stimulus equivalence (e.g., Butter, 1968, 1969; Butter and Gekoski, 1966; Iversen and Weiskrantz, 1967), stimulus generalization (Butter et al., 1965), matching from sample (Wilson et al., 1972; Weiskrantz, 1967), oddity discrimination (Iversen and Humphrey, 1971), discrimination reversal (Manning, 1972), size constancy (Humphrey and Weiskrantz, 1969), size transposition (Butter and Doehrman, 1968), visual memory (e.g., Wilson et al., 1968a,b; Iversen and Weiskrantz, 1964, 1970; Butler, 1969), visual attention (e.g., Butter and Hirtzel, 1970; Chow and Orbach, 1957), and variations in such parameters as intertrial interval (Riopelle and Churukian, 1958), number of discriminanda (e.g., Pribram, 1960), stimulus redundancy (Wilson and Kaufman, 1969), and type of response (e.g., Pribram and Mishkin, 1955).

However, it is not clear whether these experiments have revealed anything specific about the functions of inferotemporal cortex. Often, the performance of the animals with inferotemporal lesions was identical to that of the normal controls at an earlier stage of learning (cf. Weis-krantz, 1970). Thus, the effects on stimulus equivalence, stimulus generalization, discrimination reversal, and so on may simply have reflected the slower and poorer learning of visual discrimination by animals with inferotemporal lesions.

In the fourth section of this paper, experiments comparing the effects of inferotemporal and foveal prestriate lesions are described. Both lesions impair visual discrimination learning, but in different ways. Their comparison promises to specify and clarify the functions of each area in visually guided behavior.

In summary, inferotemporal lesions impair the learning of a variety of visual discrimination tasks, while leaving visual sensory function intact. Inferotemporal cortex appears to be involved in cognitive processes that underlie visual recognition and visual learning.

III. Afferent Connections of Inferotemporal Cortex

The behavioral effects of inferotemporal lesions indicate that inferotemporal cortex has visual functions. What are its connections with other visual structures? Are these connections necessary for normal visual learning?

A. Corticocortical Connections

Striate cortex projects to the ipsilateral circumstriate belt.[2] There are projections from the circumstriate belt to the ipsilateral inferotemporal cortex (see Fig. 2). Finally, each circumstriate belt projects both to the contralateral circumstriate belt and to the contralateral inferotemporal cortex, and the two inferotemporal cortices are connected to each other (Myers, 1965; Kuypers *et al.*, 1965, and earlier studies cited therein). However, these summary statements belie the extreme complexity of the topography of the projections, the number of synapses involved,

---

[2] The nomenclature for this area of occipitotemporal cortex varies with different authorities and methods. In this paper, "circumstriate belt" of Kuypers *et al.* (1965) and "prestriate cortex" are used synonymously. Von Bonin and Bailey (1947) divide this area into an Area OB, adjacent to striate cortex (i.e., Area OC) and a more anterior Area OA. Brodmann (1905) divided it somewhat differently into Areas 18 and 19. Areas OA and OB combined and Brodmann's Areas 18 and 19 combined are both approximately, but not exactly, the same as the circumstriate belt. Zeki's (1971b) subdivision of prestriate cortex is shown in Fig. 2. Following Kuypers *et al.* (1965), the anterior border of the circumstriate belt is taken as the posterior border of inferotemporal cortex (see Figs. 1 and 2).

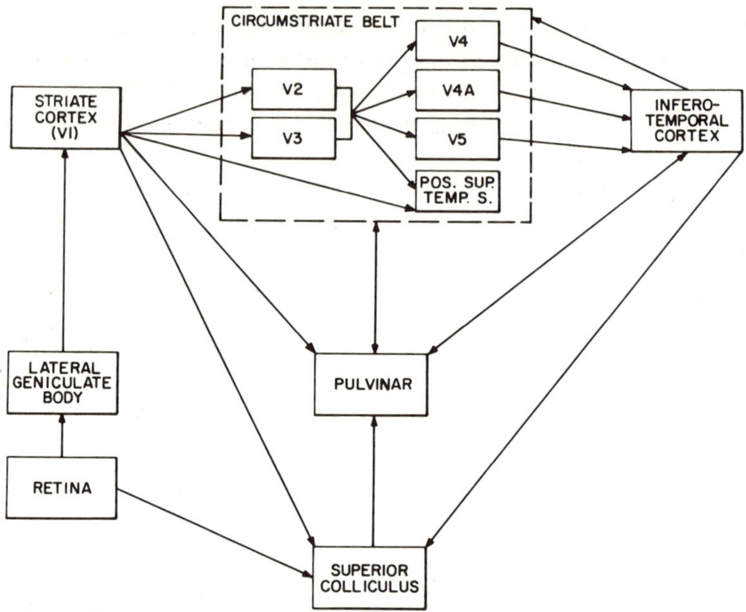

FIG. 2. Major ipsilateral afferent connections of the inferotemporal cortex in *Macaca mulatta*. Each arrowhead is not intended to indicate a single synapse. For example, axons from the superior colliculus may not terminate in the pulvinar on the same neurons that project from the pulvinar to inferotemporal cortex. V2, V3, V4, V4A, and the posterior bank of the superior sulcus (POS. SUP.TEMP.S.) are subdivisions of the circumstriate belt based on the antero-grade degeneration studies of Zeki (1971b) and others. A direct connection from the circumstriate belt to the superior colliculus has been omitted. See also Fig. 3.

and the number of subdivisions within the circumstriate belt that more recent studies have demonstrated. These more detailed results are sum-marized in the remainder of this section, which relies on the work of Zeki (1969b, 1970, 1971a,b), except where indicated otherwise, and largely uses his terminology. Essentially similar, but less complete find-ings have been reported by Cragg and Ainsworth (1969), Myers (1965), and Cowey (1971).

Striate cortex projects to at least three discrete areas of the circum-striate belt, viz., "V2," "V3," and the posterior bank of the superior temporal sulcus (Fig. 3). (Zeki identifies V2 with Area 18 and V3 with Area 19, but his Areas 18 and 19 are different from those of Brodmann and others.) At least V2 and V3 and perhaps the projection in the superior temporal sulcus are retinotopically organized (cf. Allman *et al.*, 1972). The foveal representations in V2 and V3 coincide in ventrolateral prestriate cortex (Fig. 1). V2 and V3 both project to four cortical areas. The first and second Zeki calls "V4" and "V4A." They both lie, dorsally, in the anterior bank of the lunate sulcus and,

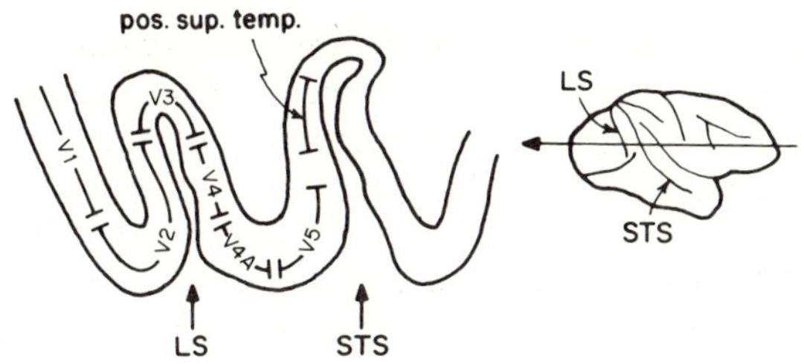

Fig. 3. Horizontal section showing approximate location of cortical visual areas according to the anterograde degeneration studies of Zeki (1971b). (The designation "V5" is not used by Zeki in the diagram from which this figure is adapted.) The level of the section is shown by the arrow on the small lateral view of the cerebral hemisphere. LS., Lunate sulcus; STS., superior temporal sulcus. See also Figs. 1 and 2 and footnotes 2 and 3.

ventrally, in or posterior to the posterior bank of the inferior occipital sulcus. V4A is located anterior to V4. The third site (which is here called "V5") lies, dorsally, in the anterior part of the prelunate gyrus and, ventrally, in the anterior bank of the inferior occipital sulcus and the posterior part of the inferior occipital gyrus.[3] The fourth site is the posterior bank of the superior temporal sulcus, which, as noted above, also receives a direct projection from striate cortex. The location of these projection fields is shown in Fig. 3, and their connections in Fig. 2.

There is a breakdown in retinotopic organization beyond Areas V2 and V3. Points within Areas V4 and V4A receive projections both from the representation of the vertical meridian and from the representation of the horizontal meridian in V2 and V3 as well as from intervening regions, and the upper and lower quadrant representations in V3 are interconnected.

Small lesions in the region of Areas V4, V4A, and V5 that receive projections from the foveal representation in V2 and V3 produce widespread anterograde degeneration in inferotemporal cortex (Cowey, 1971). Inferotemporal cortex, in turn, projects back to prestriate cortex and is reciprocally connected with lateral frontal cortex (Kuypers et al., 1965). There is no evidence for any retinotopic organization within Area TE.

There are extensive and complex interhemispheric projections of prestriate cortex. At least for Areas V2 and V3, a large portion of these connect the areas of midline representation. However, more anterior

---

[3] Area V5 corresponds to at least the posterior portion of what Petr et al. (1949) and Mishkin (1972) call Area TEO. Cytoarchitectonically, Area TEO is transitional between OA (prestriate) and TE (inferotemporal) cortex.

areas, such as V4 and V4A, which are not organized in a discrete retinotopic fashion, have heavy interhemispheric connections which presumably bring widespread representation of the ipsilateral visual field to each hemisphere. Interhemispheric connections of the circumstriate belt are carried by the splenium of the corpus callosum (Pandya *et al.*, 1971; Zeki, 1970). The posterior regions of inferotemporal cortex are connected through the corpus callosum, whereas the more anterior parts are connected across the anterior commissure, although there may be some overlap of these projection fields (Pandya *et al.*, 1971; Zeki, 1970; Myers, 1965; Fox *et al.*, 1948).

In summary, there are at least five representations of the retina in prestriate cortex. Some parallel each other, such as V2 and V3, whereas others, such as V4, are built from earlier representations. As one moves rostrally and more synapses away from striate cortex, the retinotopic organization of the representations breaks down, and there is an increased interhemispheric contribution from the ipsilateral visual field. By the time one reaches inferotemporal cortex, there is no longer any retinotopic organization, and there has been considerable contribution from the ipsilateral visual field.

B. Anatomic Basis of the Inferotemporal Deficit

Although the anatomical projections described in the previous section have only recently been demonstrated, the existence of a striate-circumstriate-inferotemporal pathway had been proposed some time ago (e.g., Mettler, 1935; Bailey *et al.*, 1943). Consequently, it was suggested quite early that the role of inferotemporal cortex in visual learning might be dependent on visual information transmitted along this route (e.g., Chow, 1951). The first positive evidence for this view came from a study in which Mishkin (1958, 1966) indirectly, but totally, interrupted this pathway. He did so in three surgical stages. First, he removed striate cortex on one side, then inferotemporal cortex on the other, and finally, he cut the corpus callosum. Thus, the third operation left the remaining inferotemporal cortex without any corticocortical connection with the remaining striate cortex. Retention of a visual pattern discrimination was tested after each surgical operation and was found to be severely impaired only after the third one. Thus, a corticocortical route from striate to inferotemporal cortex seems necessary for normal visual learning. [Ettlinger (1959) and Reitz (1969) obtained similar results when a unilateral optic tract section rather than a unilateral striate lesion was made.]

The major difficulty for the hypothesis that prestriate cortex is a crucial afferent route to inferotemporal cortex has been the repeated finding that large prestriate lesions, which should have interrupted this pathway, had little or no effect on visual discrimination learning (Lashley, 1948; Chow, 1951, 1952; Evarts, 1952; Meyer *et al.*, 1951; Riopelle *et al.*, 1951; Pribram *et al.*, 1969; Zeki, 1969a). However, in all these studies the lesions were incomplete.[4] Invariably, they spared some of the extensive buried cortex in the ventrolateral convexity, presumably because this cortex is difficult to reach and the lesions were already large. Although unknown at the time, this spared tissue invariably included large portions of the foveal representation on prestriate cortex.

Recently, Iwai and Mishkin (1968, 1969) have demonstrated, and we have confirmed (Cowey and Gross, 1970), that lesions of ventrolateral prestriate cortex extending to the posterior border of Area TE produce a massive pattern discrimination deficit, even greater than that after inferotemporal lesions. These lesions included most of the foveal portions of V2 and V3 as well as the more anterior regions to which this tissue projects, i.e., Areas V4, V4A, and V5. Furthermore, they included the buried tissue that had been spared in the previous investigations, in which prestriate lesions had little effect on visual learning. Cowey and I (Cowey and Gross, 1970) termed this lesion one of "foveal prestriate cortex"[5] (see Fig. 4). Foveal prestriate cortex appears to be a critical source of visual input for the functions of inferotemporal cortex in visual learning.

C. SUBCORTICAL CONNECTIONS

The pulvinar projects to inferotemporal cortex and to the circumstriate belt (Chow, 1950). Neurons in the inferior pulvinar have receptive fields that are retinotopically organized (Allman *et al.*, 1972). The pulvinar receives projections from both striate cortex (Myers, 1962) and the superior colliculus (Myers, 1962; Mishkin, 1972). Thus, inferotemporal cortex could receive visual information, by way of the pulvinar, from both the geniculostriate system and from the superior colliculus as shown in Fig. 2. However, neither superior colliculus lesions nor

[4] There are three early studies that reported considerable visual discrimination deficits after prestriate lesions, but they did not provide sufficient data to evaluate the lesion site (Ades, 1946; Ades and Raab, 1949; Riopelle and Ades, 1953).

[5] This lesion has also been called one of "posterior inferotemporal cortex" (e.g., Mishkin, 1972; Wilson, 1968; Wilson *et al.*, 1972). Cowey and I felt that this was a misleading designation because the lesion spares most of Area TE (which we prefer to keep as a synonym for inferotemporal cortex), and because most of the tissue removed was not in the temporal lobe.

pulvinar lesions impair performance of the visual discrimination tasks that are disrupted by inferotemporal lesions (Chow, 1954b, 1961a; Mishkin, 1972; Anderson and Symmes, 1969; Rosvold *et al.*, 1958). Thus, the subcortical input to inferotemporal cortex does not appear necessary for its role in visual discrimination learning.

What, then, might be the functions of the pulvinar projection to inferotemporal cortex? The primate superior colliculus seems to be involved in visual localizing and orienting functions (e.g., Schiller and Koerner, 1971; Trevarthen, 1968; Humphrey, 1970; Wurtz and Goldberg, 1972; Goldberg and Wurtz, 1972). Since inferotemporal cortex is an anatomical junction of the tectofugal visual system and the geniculostriate one, it is possible that one of its physiological functions is to integrate the localizing-orienting functions of the former with the stimulus analysis functions of the latter system. Unfortunately, there are no systematic studies of the effects of pulvinar or inferotemporal lesions on the ability to localize or orient toward visual stimuli. (Indeed, a major weakness of this entire area is the almost exclusive use of two-choice discrimination problems as the measures of visually guided behavior.) Perhaps the pulvinar will yield some of its mysteries to a more appropriate behavioral measure.

In summary, the corticocortical input to inferotemporal cortex from striate cortex by way of a series of stages in prestriate cortex is crucial for visual learning. In contrast, the functions of the subcortical input to inferotemporal cortex from the pulvinar remain obscure.

IV. Contrasting Effects of Inferotemporal and Foveal Prestriate Cortex Lesions

A. Pattern vs. Concurrent Discrimination

The study of inferotemporal cortex entered a new phase with the discovery by Iwai and Mishkin (1968, 1969; Mishkin, 1972) of a second extrastriate cortical area necessary for normal visual discrimination learning. This area lies in the ventrolateral portion of the circumstriate belt and the posterior portion of the temporal lobe. We have called it "foveal prestriate cortex" because it includes most of the foveal projection onto Areas 18 and 19 as well as projection fields of fibers arising from the foveal representation in Areas 18 and 19 (see Fig. 4).

Iwai and Mishkin found that inferotemporal and foveal prestriate lesions produced different kinds of visual discrimination deficits. The foveal prestriate lesions impaired postoperative retention of a pattern discrimination more than the inferotemporal lesions, but the infero-

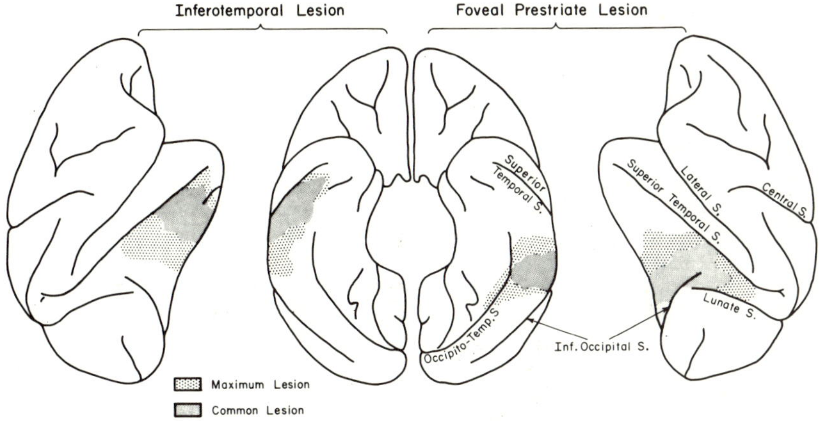

Fig. 4. Lateral and ventral view of cerebral hemispheres showing extent of inferotemporal (left) and foveal prestriate lesion (right) in monkeys used in several experiments described in this section, viz., Cowey and Gross (1970), Gross *et al.* (1971), and Manning *et al.* (1971). The foveal prestriate lesions were more extensive than appears because they included tissue in the inferior occipital, lunate, superior temporal, and occipitotemporal sulci. Reconstructions and cross sections of the individual lesions and thalamic degeneration are given in Cowey and Gross (1970).

temporal lesions produced slower acquisition of a "concurrent" discrimination task[6] than the foveal prestriate lesions.

After replicating Iwai and Mishkin's results (see Figs. 5a and 5b), Alan Cowey, Fredrick Manning, David Bender, and I set out to characterize the roles of these two areas in visual learning by comparing the effects of their removal on a variety of visual tasks. The two tasks used by Iwai and Mishkin to differentiate foveal prestriate and inferotemporal lesions had differed in three ways: (*a*) in the discriminanda used (objects *vs.* patterns); (*b*) in one being a test of postoperative acquisition and the other being a test of postoperative retention; and (*c*) in one involving multiple discrimination tasks and the other a single discrimination problem. To determine which of these variables was crucial, we tested monkeys with each lesion on postoperative acquisition of both individual object and individual pattern discrimination tasks (Cowey

---

[6] This task involved the parallel learning of eight two-choice discrimination tasks. The discriminanda were three-dimensional junk objects, and each discrimination would have been very easy if presented alone. In every daily session of 40 trials, each of the eight pairs of discriminanda were presented in a random sequence for a total of five trials per pair. The animals were trained until they made only one error in a session and thus had learned the eight intermingled discriminations.

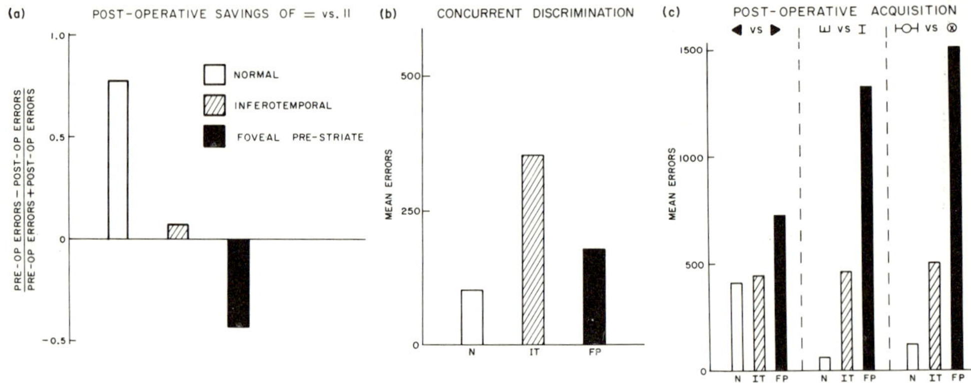

FIG. 5. Effects of inferotemporal and foveal prestriate lesions on performance of visual discrimination tasks. (a) Postoperative retention of a horizontal *vs.* vertical line discrimination task as measured by savings scores. (b) Postoperative acquisition of a concurrent discrimination involving eight pairs of three-dimensional objects. (c) Postoperative acquisition of three pattern discrimination tasks. The problems were given successively in the order shown. Postoperative retention and acquisition of the pattern discrimination tasks were more impaired by the foveal prestriate lesions (a) and (c), whereas acquisition of the concurrent discrimination (b) was more impaired by the inferotemporal lesions (from Cowey and Gross, 1970).

and Gross, 1970). The foveal prestriate lesions impaired performance of both types of task more than the inferotemporal lesions did (see Figs. 5c and 6a). Thus, the feature that made the concurrent tasks more difficult after inferotemporal lesions was that they involved several discriminations in parallel.

We then asked whether the greater inferotemporal impairment on the concurrent task occurred because the component discriminations had to be acquired concurrently, performed concurrently, or both. Monkeys with foveal prestriate lesions, monkeys with inferotemporal lesions, and normal controls were trained successively on five object discriminations and then tested for retention with all five discriminations presented intermingled in a single session, i.e., concurrently (Cowey and Gross, 1970). The object discriminations were chosen so as to be very easy, and thus, as expected, all groups learned them equally quickly. Furthermore, the groups showed equal and near perfect retention when the five discriminations were presented concurrently. Then, these five established discriminations were presented together with five new discriminations in a ten-problem concurrent paradigm. Now, the animals with inferotemporal lesions took about twice as many trials to reach criterion as the animals with foveal prestriate lesions. By contrast, the performance of the animals with foveal prestriate lesions did not differ significantly from the unoperated animals. (All the animals made most of their errors on the new problems, but those with inferotemporal lesions made many more than the other groups.) Thus, the difficulty of the concurrent paradigm after inferotemporal lesions lies in the parallel acquisition and not the parallel retention of the discriminations.

B. An Hypothesis: Attention/Perception vs. Memory/Association

"Noncontinuity" and "attention" learning theorists from Lashley (1929) and Krechevsky (1938) to Sutherland and Mackintosh (1971) have suggested that discrimination learning involves two stages, an attentional one and an associational one. We hypothesized that foveal prestriate cortex might be primarily involved in the attentional stage and inferotemporal cortex primarily in the associational one (Cowey and Gross, 1970). [Iwai and Mishkin (1968, 1969) have made a similar suggestion.] In previous studies of inferotemporal cortex, both an "attentional" deficit and an "associational" or "mnemonic" one had been offered as descriptions of the inferotemporal impairment. In many of these studies, the lesions had extended posteriorly to include part of what we have called foveal prestriate cortex. We thought this controversy might be resolved by showing that smaller lesions in occipito-temporal association cortex could produce an attentional/perceptual deficit and a mnemonic/associative deficit independently.

The experiments to be described below were influenced by this general hypothesis that foveal prestriate lesions might produce a more attentional or perceptual type of deficit and inferotemporal lesions a more mnemonic or associational deficit.

1. Retention as a Function of Interpolated Material

One type of mnemonic deficit that could underlie the inferotemporal impairment on the concurrent task is greater pro- or retroactive interference among the component problems. To test this, we measured retention of individual discriminations as a function of the type of discrimination interpolated between learning and retention of the original discrimination (Gross *et al.,* 1971). In a single session monkeys were (*a*) trained on either the discrimination of two-colored plaques or of

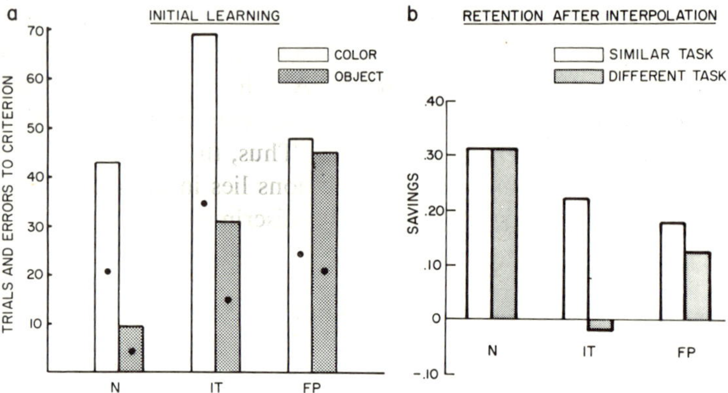

FIG. 6. Effects of inferotemporal and foveal prestriate lesions on (a) acquisition of color and object discriminations and (b) retention of color and object discriminations as a function of type of interpolated experience. In each of twenty daily sessions the animals (1) learned a color or object discrimination, (2) then learned a second color or object discrimination, and finally (3) were tested for retention of the first problem. SIMILAR TASK, color discrimination if the initial problem was a color discrimination and object discrimination if the initial problem was an object discrimination. DISSIMILAR TASK, a color discrimination if the initial problem was an object discrimination, and an object discrimination if the initial problem was a color discrimination. The animals with inferotemporal lesions were impaired relative to the normal monkeys on learning both the object and color discriminations, whereas the animals with foveal prestriate lesions were impaired only on the object discriminations (although the other two groups found the object discriminations less difficult than the color discriminations). On the retention tests, only the animals with inferotemporal lesions were impaired and then only when a dissimilar task was interpolated (after Gross *et al.*, 1971). Abbreviations as in Fig. 5.

two gray three-dimensional objects, (*b*) trained on a new color or object discrimination, and then (*c*) tested for retention of the original discrimination. Under all conditions, the retention performance of the foveal prestriate group was the same as that of the normal controls (Fig. 6b). By contrast, the animals with inferotemporal lesions showed impaired retention when the interpolated problem was dissimilar from the initial problem. That is, they were impaired on retention of a color discrimination only when an object problem was interpolated and on an object discrimination only when a color problem was interpolated. This suggests that inferotemporal lesions do produce greater interproblem interference, but only of a specific kind. There is greater interference between the strategies used ("color" or "object"), but not between the stimuli within one dimension ("red" or "pink").

2. Uniqueness of Color Cues

A totally unexpected result of this experiment was an interaction of lesion and discriminanda. The animals with the inferotemporal lesions were impaired (relative to normal monkeys) on initial learning of both the color and object problems, whereas the foveal prestriate group was only impaired on the object discriminations (see Fig. 6a). Yet for both the normal and inferotemporal groups, the color discriminations were much more difficult, requiring over twice as many trials to learn. The degree of impairment on visual learning tasks after inferotemporal lesions has usually been a function of the difficulty of the task for normal monkeys whatever the discriminanda or training procedure. However, this relation between task difficulty and relative impairment did not hold across different classes of stimuli for the foveal prestriate group. The color discriminations were more difficult than the object ones for the normal and inferotemporal groups, and yet the foveal prestriate group was impaired on the object problems relative to the normal group, but not on the color ones. Thus, the foveal prestriate deficit appears to depend on the nature of the discriminanda and not simply on the difficulty of the discrimination. This supports the hypothesis that the foveal prestriate discrimination deficit, unlike the inferotemporal one, is a perceptual or attentional one.

3. Relevant and Irrelevant Cues

Further support for a perceptual or attentional dysfunction after foveal prestriate lesions comes from two experiments in which we studied the effect of adding or subtracting stimuli from the discriminanda. In the first experiment, normal monkeys and monkeys with inferotemporal or foveal prestriate lesions were trained to discriminate two patterns and then were tested for retention when irrelevant color cues were added to the background (Gross *et al.*, 1971). The normal and inferotemporal groups showed similar and virtually perfect retention of the original pattern problem after the background cues were added, whereas the addition of the irrelevant cues produced a severe deficit for the foveal prestriate animals. Repeat of the experiment with a new pattern and with background intensity as the irrelevant cue yielded similar results (Fig. 7).

Thus, the animals with foveal prestriate lesions appeared to be more distractable, or to put it more specifically, they may have paid more attention to the irrelevant background cues than the inferotemporal

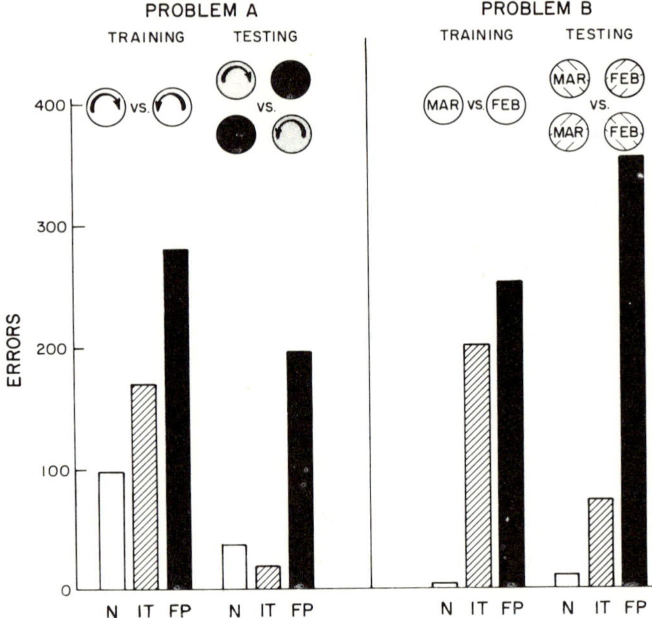

FIG. 7. Effects on performance on a visual discrimination task of adding irrelevant stimuli. In problem A, the monkeys were trained to discriminate an arrow and its mirror image and then tested for retention when one arrow had a red background and the other a green one. The color of the background varied randomly from trial to trial and was not correlated with the orientation of the arrow. Problem B was identical except that the training stimuli were the trigrams FEB and MAR, and the irrelevant stimuli used in testing were the intensities of the backgrounds. On both problems, the addition of the irrelevant background stimuli disrupted the performance of the monkeys with foveal prestriate lesions more than it did the performance of the other groups (after Gross *et al.*, 1971). Abbreviations as in Fig. 5.

lesion or normal groups. Support for this interpretation comes from the second experiment, which involved a similar set of operated and normal monkeys (Manning, 1971b). The animals were first trained on a color discrimination, then a different pattern was added to each color cue so that the patterns were "relevant" and "redundant" with the color cues. In both these stages of the experiment, the performance of the groups was similar. In the third stage, the colors were removed, leaving the pattern cues and here, the performance of the foveal prestriate group was superior to that of the inferotemporal group. That is, the animals with foveal prestriate lesions and the normal animals appeared to have noticed and learned more about the added cues than the animals with inferotemporal lesions. Taking these experiments together, the foveal prestriate lesions appear to produce an alteration of selective attention, perhaps one that results in a "diffusing" or spread of attention. This alteration hindered the animals with foveal prestriate lesions in the first (irrelevant cue) experiment, but helped them in the second (relevant cue) experiment.

4. Partial Reinforcement

The experiments described in the previous section suggested a specific change in selective attention after foveal prestriate lesions, viz., a diffusing or spreading of attention. We examined this possibility further by using a procedure known to spread attention in normal animals, namely partial reinforcement. Rats and birds trained on a discrimination involving multiple cues subsequently transfer to a greater number of the component cues if they had been trained under partial reinforcement rather than under continuous reinforcement (McFarland, 1966; Sutherland, 1966). That is, under partial reinforcement these animals notice more features of the stimulus situation. They also acquire discriminations more slowly under partial reinforcement, apparently because although they are learning about more cues, they are learning less about each. If monkeys with foveal prestriate lesions are already attending to more aspects of the discriminanda than normal monkeys, then partial reinforcement should have less effect on their learning than on that of normal monkeys. We trained monkeys with foveal prestriate or inferotemporal lesions and unoperated monkeys on four discrimination tasks with either 100% or 25% reinforcement for the correct response (Manning et al., 1971). As compared with continuous reinforcement, acquisition under partial reinforcement was slower for the normal group, and much slower for the inferotemporal group, but the schedule of reinforcement had no effect whatsoever on the foveal prestriate group (Fig. 8).

One interpretation of these results is that foveal prestriate lesions produce monkeys "functionally" under partial reinforcement, and that is why they show slower learning, more diffuse attention, and, assuming a ceiling effect, no additional learning impairment under partial reinforcement. But if monkeys with foveal prestriate lesions are functionally under partial reinforcement, they should show slower extinction, and they do not (Butter et al., 1965). Thus, it appears that foveal prestriate lesions produce "diffused attention" for some other reason, and diffusing it further by partial reinforcement has no additional effect.

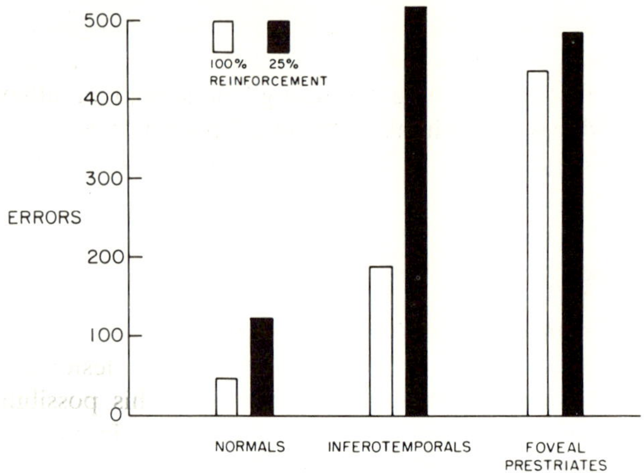

Fig. 8. Effects of reinforcement schedule on learning of visual discrimination tasks. Each animal was trained on two pattern discrimination problems with 100% reinforcement for correct responses and two-pattern discrimination problems with 25% reinforcement for correct responses. Partial reinforcement slowed learning by the normal monkeys and those with inferotemporal lesions, but had no effect on the monkeys with foveal prestriate lesions (from Manning *et al.*, 1971).

5. Punishment

The greater sensitivity of the inferotemporal group to reinforcement condition demonstrated in the partial reinforcement experiment was shown much more dramatically in another experiment by Manning (1971a). Animals with foveal prestriate, inferotemporal, or no lesion were trained on a series of visual discriminations in which they were shocked for making incorrect responses in addition to receiving the conventional food reward for making correct ones. The results were surprising. When shocked for errors, the animals with inferotemporal lesions learned as quickly as the normal controls. However, the use of shock had no effect on the performance of the animals with foveal prestriate lesions: they continued to be as impaired relative to normal controls as they had been when trained with food reinforcement alone (Fig. 9).

These results support the hypothesis that inferotemporal lesions interfere with an associative or mnemonic function rather than a purely perceptual one. Perhaps, in some way associative bonding is weaker after inferotemporal lesions and is brought to a normal level by the addition of punishment.

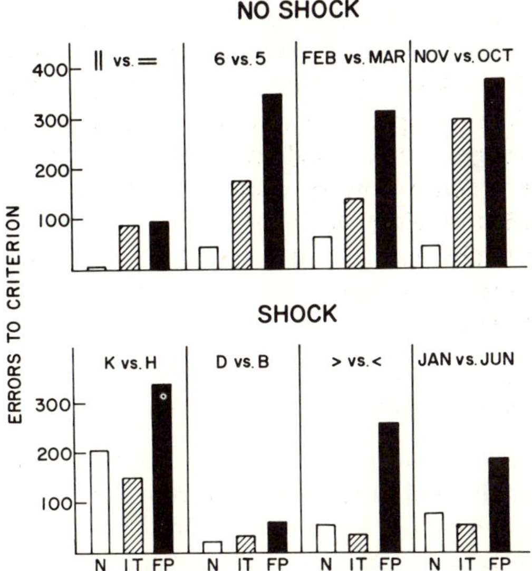

FIG. 9. Effects of shock punishment on learning of visual discrimination tasks. The monkeys were trained on four-pattern discrimination problems with food reward for every correct response ("NO SHOCK") and on four pattern discrimination problems with food reward for correct responses and electric shock for incorrect responses ("SHOCK"). Note that the use of shock punishment eliminated the visual discrimination deficit of the animals with inferotemporal lesions (after Manning, 1971a). Abbreviations as in Fig. 5.

6. Sensory Capacity

The effects of foveal prestriate lesions that suggest a perceptual or attentional deficit might also have been due to some kind of sensory loss. Inferotemporal lesions do not produce changes in a variety of measures of sensory capacity, but perhaps foveal prestriate lesions, like striate lesions, would.

To test for sensory alterations after foveal prestriate lesions as well as to extend the psychophysical analysis of inferotemporal lesions, Bender compared monkeys with inferotemporal and foveal prestriate lesions on three sensory tasks. In the first, the absolute threshold for detection of a brief flash of light was determined (Bender, 1973a). In the second, detection of a brief flash on an adapting background was measured with a signal detection paradigm (Bender, 1973b). This afforded the independent measure of sensory capacity (d') and response bias (β). In the third study, backward masking of a pattern by a blanking flash was measured as a function of the interval between the target and masking stimuli (Bender, 1973c). In all three studies, the asymptotic performance of normal monkeys, monkeys with foveal prestriate lesions, and monkeys with inferotemporal lesions was indistinguishable. These preliminary results suggest that foveal prestriate lesions, like inferotemporal lesions, do not produce sensory changes of a magnitude sufficient to underlie the deficit in visual learning produced by these lesions. However, more psychophysical data, particularly of such functions as visual acuity, are required to rule out the possibility of sensory losses after foveal prestriate lesions.

C. Some Generalizations about the Two Areas

The impairment in visual discrimination learning produced by foveal prestriate lesions differed in several ways from that produced by inferotemporal lesions. Relative to inferotemporal lesions, foveal prestriate lesions produced slower learning of pattern and object, but not color discriminations, more disruption from the introduction of an irrelevant stimulus, and less sensitivity to both partial reinforcement and shock punishment. In contrast, the inferotemporal lesions produced a relatively greater impairment when a concurrent paradigm was used and when the discriminanda were colors, greater disruption after interpolation of a dissimilar problem, and greater sensitivity to both partial reinforcement and shock punishment.

These two constellations of deficits cannot readily be identified with the two stages of discrimination learning of attention theorists, nor, for that matter, do they easily fit any other psychological constructs. Yet, it is possible to make some tentative generalizations about the two deficits. The foveal prestriate lesions impaired performance on tasks in which foveal vision was important, such as pattern and object discriminations, but not on tasks in which foveal vision was not crucial, such as color discrimination, or tasks where the difficulty lay in a concurrent paradigm rather than in the discriminanda themselves. Furthermore, the animals with foveal prestriate lesions were more affected by the addition of extrafoveal (or background) stimuli. Thus, foveal prestriate lesions produced an inability to use foveal information and a greater dependence on extrafoveal information. However, this notion that foveal prestriate lesions produce a "functional foveal scotoma" may be too simplistic. Rather, the disorder may be a more attentional one: the inability to maintain (foveal) attention to specific details of the discriminanda. Or, is "visual attention" identical to foveal fixation?

The hypothesis that foveal prestriate lesions produce a functional foveal scotoma does have the virtue of being readily testable. Why should a functional foveal scotoma produced by foveal prestriate lesions severely impair visual discrimination when an actual foveal scotoma produced by removal of lateral striate cortex does not? After foveal striate lesions, both monkeys and humans fixate eccentrically and apparently substitute the extrafoveal portions of the retina and geniculostriate system for the foveal portions (Cowey, 1967; Cowey and Weiskrantz, 1963; Teuber *et al.,* 1960). Thus, information is processed by extrafoveal striate cortex and then, presumably, by extrafoveal prestriate cortex. However, if a monkey has no foveal prestriate cortex, it may continue to fixate foveally. Thus, information arriving at foveal striate cortex could not be processed in the corresponding prestriate cortex, resulting in a discrimination deficit. This explanation of the foveal prestriate deficit predicts that (*a*) monkeys with foveal prestriate lesions continue to fixate foveally, and (*b*) forcing an animal with a foveal prestriate lesion to fixate extrafoveally (perhaps by inflicting foveal retinal or foveal striate lesions) should reduce or eliminate its visual discrimination deficit (Cowey and Gross, 1970).

The characterization of the inferotemporal deficit is more difficult. In contrast to the foveal prestriate deficit, the inferotemporal one does not seem to be perceptual or attentional. Rather, since inferotemporal lesions produce greater sensitivity to both interproblem interference and reinforcement condition, inferotemporal cortex probably plays a role in the storage of visual experience. Whether inferotemporal cortex is primarily involved in short-term or in long-term storage is unclear. Similarly, whether either or both storage mechanisms are confined to inferotemporal cortex or involve circuits including the hippocampus, amygdala, or other structures remains to be determined (Gross, 1973).

What are the functional relations of foveal prestriate and inferotemporal cortex? The anatomy suggests that prestriate cortex operates on the outputs of striate cortex and, in turn, inferotemporal cortex operates on the outputs of prestriate cortex. However, the processing may not be strictly serial. The connections from inferotemporal cortex back to prestriate cortex suggest recycling of information from inferotemporal to prestriate cortex for further analysis.

In conclusion, the comparison of the effects of foveal prestriate and inferotemporal lesions suggests that foveal prestriate cortex contains mechanisms involved in attentional or foveal aspects of visual learning, whereas inferotemporal cortex is concerned with mnemonic or associative functions. Inferotemporal cortex may be viewed as processing the output of prestriate cortex, the foveal portion of this being particularly important for pattern discrimination learning.

V. Electrophysiology of Inferotemporal Cortex

Inferotemporal cortex, like most other regions of "association cortex" in the monkey, was a neurophysiological *terra incognita* when we began our studies. Our first aim was to demonstrate that visual information arrives at inferotemporal cortex, first with macroelectrode and then with microelectrode recording. Since then, we have been investigating the visual properties of single neurons in inferotemporal cortex in both paralyzed and behaving monkeys, and the anatomic bases of these properties.

A. Visual-Evoked Responses

Visual-evoked responses were recorded from macroelectrodes (monopolar and bipolar) placed on inferotemporal cortex in both anesthetized and awake monkeys (Vaughan and Gross, 1969; Gerstein *et al.,* 1968). These responses were small and usually had to be averaged to be detected. They consisted of a negative deflection at about 45 msec followed by a complex positive wave with one to three peaks in the period 68–136 msec after the stimulus (Fig. 10). Activity time locked to the stimulus continued for up to 400 msec. This response was differentially altered by unilateral optic tract section and unilateral removal of striate cortex, suggesting that both corticocortical and subcortical input to inferotemporal cortex may have contributed to the response recorded from inferotemporal cortex.

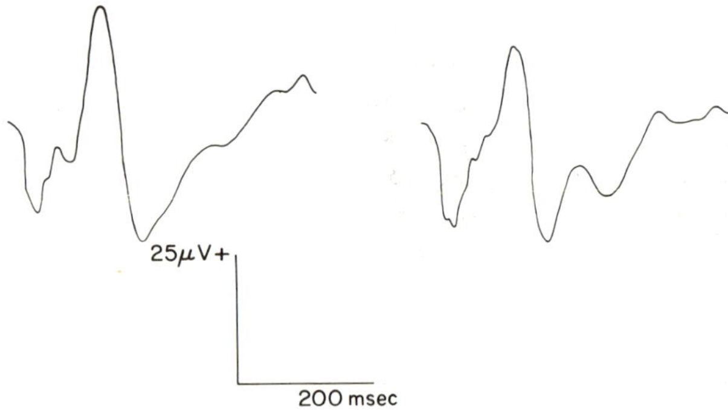

Fig. 10. Visual-evoked responses recorded monopolarly from an electrode on inferotemporal cortex. Responses from the left and right hemispheres are shown on the left and right, respectively. Each trace is based on eight averages of 100 responses. The stimulus was a brief illumination of the entire visual field (after Vaughan and Gross, 1969).

We looked for evoked response correlates of learning by recording the responses evoked by discriminanda during the acquisition and reversal of pattern discrimination tasks (Gerstein *et al.*, 1968). The waveforms of the responses recorded from inferotemporal cortex were not related to the nature of the task, the stage of learning, the significance of the stimulus, or the subject's subsequent response.

Although these evoked response studies were consistent with the notion that inferotemporal cortex receives visual information, they indicated little more. Gross evoked responses are characteristically very difficult to interpret: it is not clear how or where they are generated, or what type of information processing or other function, if any, they reflect.

Several workers, including ourselves, have reported transient changes in the inferotemporal electrocorticogram during the course of visual learning (Chow, 1961a,b; Stamm and Mahoney, 1962; Gerstein *et al.*, 1968). The transient, inconsistent, and relatively rare nature of these changes suggest that they reflect some arousal process rather than a mechanism fundamental to visual perception or learning.

B. Visual Properties of Inferotemporal Neurons[7]

1. Modal Specificity

About three quarters of the neurons sampled were responsive to visual stimuli. None responded to auditory, somesthetic, or olfactory stimuli.

The latency of the inferotemporal unit response to light was surprisingly long: no neurons responded before 70 msec, and the mean of the earliest response was about 120 msec. In many units, time-locked activity continued for 400 msec or longer after the stimulus offset (see Fig. 11).

[7] From Gross *et al.* (1967, 1969, 1972, 1973; Bender *et al.*, 1972; Rocha-Miranda *et al.*, 1973). The results described in this section were obtained in experiments in which rhesus monkeys were immobilized with gallamine triethiodide and anesthetized with nitrous oxide and oxygen. Similar properties were observed in a much smaller sample of cells when local anesthesia was used and in chronically implanted animals. In the latter, the head was fixed and eye movement eliminated by section of the third, fourth, and sixth cranial nerves. However, under barbiturate anesthesia, most inferotemporal neurons were unresponsive to light or responded in a weak and nonspecific fashion.

    Charles G. Gross

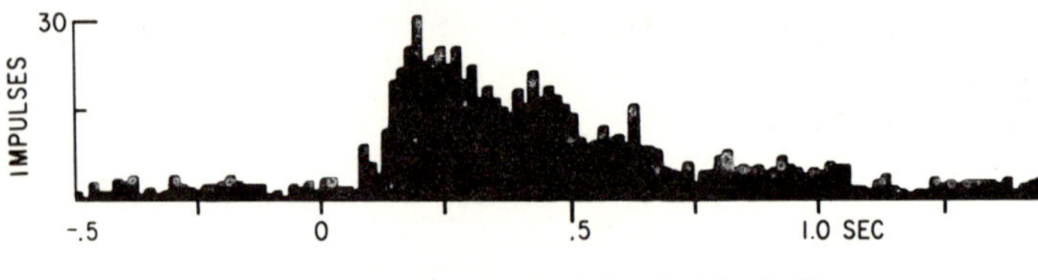

FIG. 11. Poststimulus time histogram for a unit in inferotemporal cortex. The stimulus was a vertical $1° \times 70°$ black slit on a white background oriented along the vertical meridian and presented 20 times for a duration of 1 second, with an interstimulus interval of 10 seconds. The horizontal line indicates the stimulus duration. The vertical scale indicates total impulses per bin. The bin width was 15.6 msec. The long latency of the response was typical of inferotemporal neurons.

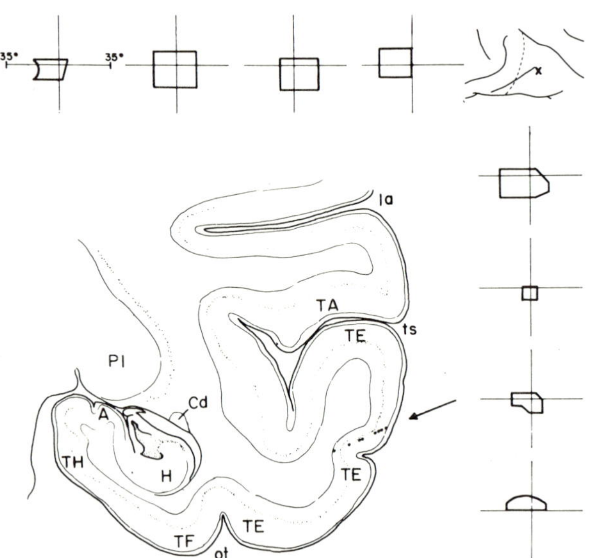

FIG. 12. Coronal section in plane of electrode pass (arrow) in the inferotemporal cortex showing approximate location of eight representative cells recorded on the pass and the size and location of their receptive fields. The receptive fields recorded at increasing depth are shown clockwise starting from the top left. In these and all following receptive field maps, the axes represent the horizontal and vertical meridia of the visual field, and the half-field contralateral to the recording electrode is on the left. The scale is in degrees of visual angle. In the inset brain drawing, x marks the site of entry of the electrode pass (see Fig. 1). la, Lateral fissure; ot, occipitotemporal sulcus; ts, superior temporal sulcus; Cd, caudate nucleus; H, hippocampus; Pl, pulvinar; TA, TE, TF, TH, and A refer to cytoarchitectonic areas of von Bonin and Bailey. Note that all fields include the fovea and that some extend well into both visual half-fields (from Gross *et al.*, 1971).

2. Receptive Fields

We were able to plot receptive fields for most of the responsive neurons. Every receptive field included the fovea (center of gaze). Over half extended well into both visual half-fields, about one third were in the half-field contralateral to the electrode, and the rest were in the ipsilateral half-field. This is in striking contrast to receptive fields in the lateral geniculate body, striate cortex, and Areas 18 and 19, where the receptive fields are confined (within a few degrees) to the contralateral half-field (e.g., Hubel and Wiesel, 1961, 1962, 1965, 1967, 1968, 1970).

Another difference with receptive fields in the geniculostriate system was the large size of the inferotemporal receptive fields. They were usually more than $10° \times 10°$ with a median area of 418 square degrees and an interquartile range of 150–1410 square degrees. A few extended beyond $35°$ in all directions from the fovea (see Figs. 12 and 13).

3. Trigger Features

For all neurons, the strength of response varied as a function of several parameters of the stimulus. Among these were movement, contrast, size and shape, orientation and direction of movement, and wavelength. Most neurons responded more vigorously to a moving stimulus than a stationary one. About three quarters of the responsive neurons could be driven by dark stimuli on a white background, about three quarters by light stimuli on a dark background, and about half of them were responsive to both contrast conditions. For the great majority of the neurons, a white, dark, or colored slit about $1°$ in width was a more adequate stimulus than other rectangular or circular stimuli. About half of the units were sensitive to the direction of movement. Most of these were "bidirectional," i.e., they fired equally well to both directions of movement in the optimal orientation of the stimulus and had null directions $90°$ to the optimal one (e.g., Fig. 13); other units were "unidirectional," i.e., they fired best to one direction of movement and had null directions $180°$ from the optimal one.

We found a number of neurons which fired more strongly to a colored stimulus than to white stimuli presented over a great range of intensities. "Red sensitive" neurons were far more common than either "blue" or "green" ones.

Perhaps the most salient characteristic of the inferotemporal neurons was the heterogeneity of their properties and the difficulty of finding their "adequate stimulus" or "optimum trigger feature." Although we

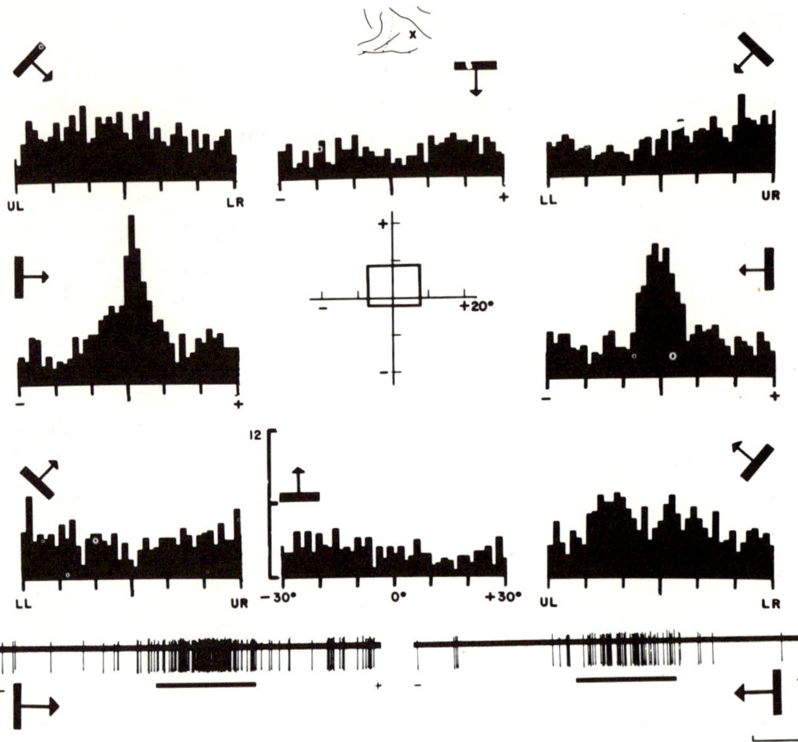

FIG. 13. Receptive field and responses of an inferotemporal neuron which showed "bidirectional sensitivity." The histograms indicate unit activity as a function of retinal locus of a 1° × 70° white slit moving at 5° per second in the direction indicated above each histogram. Each histogram was generated by seven sweeps of the stimulus. For the eight histograms, the vertical scale indicates total number of neuron discharges summed over the seven sweeps. The bin width was 293 msec. The horizontal scale indicates degrees of visual angle. The middle of each horizontal scale (0°) represents the center of gaze. The receptive field of this unit is shown in the center of the array of histograms. Plus (+) in all parts of the figure indicates upper or right of the visual field; minus (−) indicates lower or left; UL, upper left; LR, lower right; LL, lower left; UR, upper right. The lower part of the figure shows responses of the unit to a single sweep of the stimulus in the direction indicated. The lines below each trace correspond to the horizontal extent of the receptive field. The marker indicates 8° or 1.6 seconds. The histograms and trace in which the arrow is shown on the left were generated from left to right, whereas the converse was true where the arrow is shown on the right. The site of the pass on which this unit was recorded is shown on the brain drawing, the dotted line indicating the typical border between Area OA and Area TE. See also Fig. 1 and legend to Fig. 12 (after Gross et al., 1971).

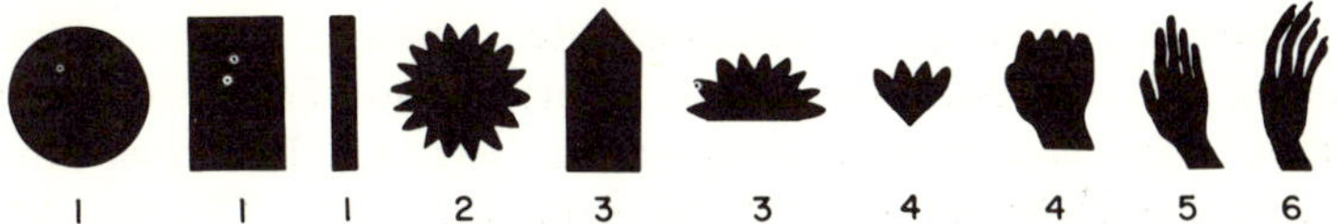

FIG. 14. Examples of shapes used to stimulate an inferotemporal unit apparently having very complex trigger features. The stimuli are arranged from left to right in order of increasing ability to drive the neuron from none (1) or little (2 and 3) to maximum (6) (from Gross *et al.*, 1971).

could show variations in response strength with variations in the parameters described above, we often could not be sure that we had found the best possible stimulus conditions. This difficulty is underlined by our finding of a few dozen neurons with highly complex and specific trigger features which we often discovered accidentally. Among these were neurons whose best stimulus appeared to be the shadow of a monkey hand (Fig. 14), a bullet-shaped form, the shadow of a hemostat forceps, and a bottle brush. Some neurons preferred a particular three-dimensional stimulus over any two-dimensional representation of it.

The existence of such cells with highly specific trigger features raises the possibility that we may never have found the appropriate trigger feature for other of our cells. Thus, a (more typical) neuron that responded best to a $1° \times 5°$ red slit oriented at $45°$ within its receptive field may not have been "coding" this size, shape, color, and orientation. Rather, its trigger feature might have been a far more specific, complex, and perhaps meaningful stimulus that we never used and that happened to share some of the stimulus parameters of the stimulus we did use. Thus, in searching for the adequate stimulus and systematically varying the length, width, color, etc. of a slit we may have been like Kipling's proverbial blind men examining an elephant. Another possibility suggested by the highly specific trigger features that we found for some cells is that adequacy of a stimulus for inferotemporal neurons may be a function of the meaning of a stimulus as well as of the physical parameters of the stimulus actually falling on the retina.

C. Comparison of Foveal Prestriate and Inferotemporal Neurons

The neurons whose properties were described in the previous section were all recorded from the middle and posterior portions of Area TE. We also studied units located more posteriorly in the temporal lobe, namely the strip of circumstriate cortex extending from the ascending inferior occipital sulcus anteriorly to the posterior border of inferotemporal cortex (Gross *et al.,* 1972). [This strip overlaps with Areas V4, V4A, and V5 of Zeki and Area TEO of Mishkin (1972). Cytoarchitectonically, it is OA cortex or cortex transitional between OA and TE.] We termed neurons in this area "OA units" to distinguish them from the "TE units" we recorded in inferotemporal (TE) cortex.

In general, the OA neurons had similar properties to the TE neurons: their receptive fields always included the fovea; bilateral, ipsilateral, and contralateral receptive fields were found. Like the TE units, the OA units were sensitive to at least some of the following parameters of the visual stimulus: contrast, wavelength, size, shape, orientation, and direction of movement. However, the OA units differed from

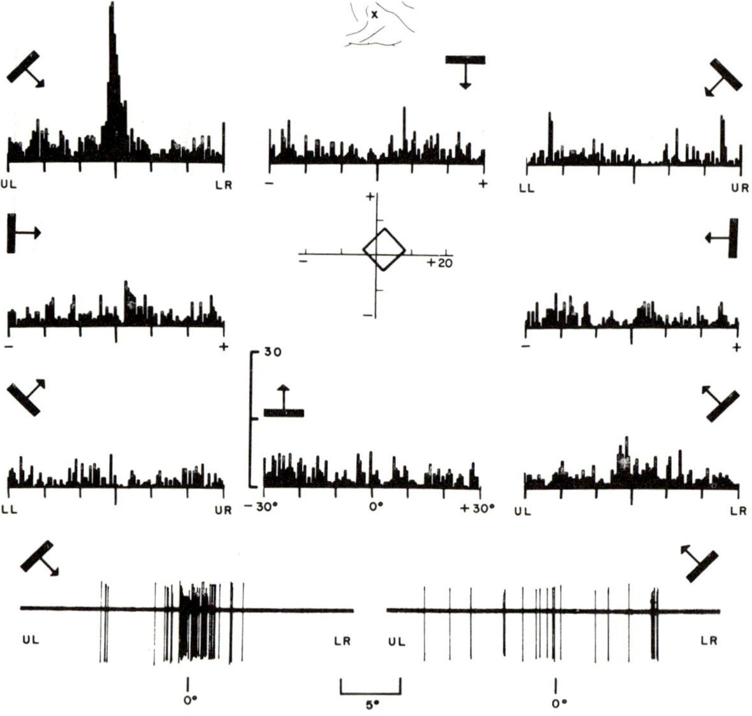

FIG. 15. Receptive field and responses of a Group OA neuron which showed "unidirectional sensitivity." Each histogram was generated by ten sweeps of a 1° × 70° red slit moving in the indicated direction at 5° per second. The bin width in the histograms was 117 msec. See also legends to Figs. 12 and 13 (from Gross *et al.,* 1971).

the TE units in the incidence of certain properties. OA units had much smaller receptive fields, and a higher proportion showed differential sensitivity to direction of movement of the stimulus (see Fig. 15). If directionally sensitive, OA units were more likely to be unidirectional. Among the OA units, bilateral receptive fields were slightly less common. Finally, units with highly specific and complex trigger features were found less often in the OA group than in the TE one.

The anatomical projection of this cortex to inferotemporal cortex (Cowey, 1971) suggests that the properties of inferotemporal neurons may derive, in part, from converging inputs from OA units.

D. ANATOMIC BASES OF PROPERTIES OF INFEROTEMPORAL NEURONS

The hypothesis that the visual responsiveness of inferotemporal neurons is due to the projections they receive from prestriate cortex offers explanations for several of the unusual properties of these neurons. The invariable inclusion of the fovea in the receptive fields would be due to the projections from the regions of V4, V4A, and V5 onto which the foveal representation in V2 and V3 projects. The large size of the receptive fields would follow from the breakdown in retinotopic specificity as one proceeds from V1 through V2 and V3 to V4, V4A, and V5, and then to inferotemporal cortex. The ipsilateral receptive fields and the ipsilateral portion of the bilateral receptive fields would derive from interhemispheric connections of V4, V4A, and V5 through the corpus callosum and possibly the interhemispheric connections of Area TE through both the corpus callosum and the anterior commissure.

We studied the afferent basis of the visual properties of inferotemporal neurons in three experiments in which we made lesions in various routes to inferotemporal cortex (Bender *et al.,* 1972; Gross *et al.,* 1973; Rocha-Miranda *et al.,* 1973).

In the first experiment, we totally removed the striate cortex of one hemisphere. If the visual properties of inferotemporal cortex were dependent on striate cortex, then after unilateral ablation of striate cortex, inferotemporal units should be responsive only to visual stimulation in the half-field contralateral to the remaining striate cortex. This hypothesis was confirmed: in the animals with unilateral striate lesions, all the receptive fields were unilateral and confined to the visual half-field contralateral to the intact striate cortex, whereas in normal animals over half the receptive fields had extended well into both visual half-fields. The properties of the neurons were otherwise the same as in normal monkeys.

In the second experiment, the corpus callosum and anterior commissure were completely sectioned to determine if these pathways contributed to the responsiveness in the ipsilateral half-fields that characterized a majority of inferotemporal neurons. As predicted, after section of the interhemispheric commissures, all fields were unilateral and confined to the half-field contralateral to the recording electrode (Fig. 16). Again the neurons appeared normal in other respects.

Although these experiments demonstrate that inferotemporal cortex receives visual information from striate cortex, they do not establish the specific route (except that it must include the corpus callosum or

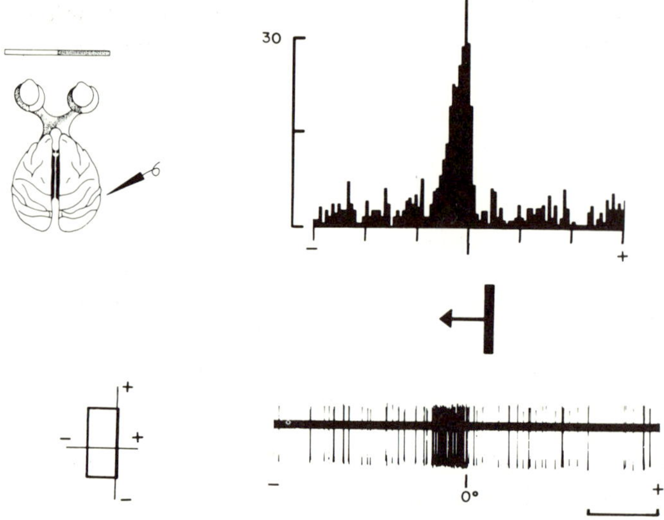

Fig. 16. Typical receptive field (lower left) and responses of a neuron in inferotemporal cortex in an animal with previous section of the corpus callosum and anterior commissure. The histogram was generated by ten sweeps of a 1° × 70° white slit moving in the indicated direction at 5° per second. The bin width in the histogram was 117 msec, and each subdivision on the horizontal scale is 10°. The scale of the receptive field plot is the same as the horizontal scale of the histogram. Both the histogram and the trace were generated from right to left. The scale for the trace is 10°, or 2 seconds. See also legends to Figs. 12 and 13. As in this case, all inferotemporal neurons in animals with interhemispheric section had receptive fields confined to the half-field contralateral to the electrode (after Bender *et al.*, 1972).

anterior commissure). Inferotemporal cortex could receive input from striate cortex along three known anatomical routes: cortical, subcortical, and combined subcortical-cortical. The cortical route involves synapses in the circumstriate belt. The subcortical route involves projections from the pulvinar to inferotemporal cortex. The pulvinar can receive information from striate cortex either directly or by way of the superior colliculus. There are several possible subcortical routes. All involve synapses in both prestriate cortex and the pulvinar. The three types of possible routes are shown in Fig. 2.

In the third experiment exploring the afferent pathways to inferotemporal cortex, we studied the effects of bilateral pulvinar lesions to decide between the first possibility (a strictly corticocortical route) and the second and third possibilities (a route involving the pulvinar). After pulvinar lesions, both the incidence of responsive neurons in inferotemporal cortex and their trigger features were similar to those in intact monkeys. Thus, the pulvinar cannot be crucial for the visual responsiveness of inferotemporal neurons to light, nor for their stimulus specificities. These properties must depend on the corticocortical connections between striate and inferotemporal cortex.

There was, however, a dramatic and unexpected effect of the pulvinar lesions. In the monkeys that had received pulvinar lesions, virtually none of the inferotemporal neurons had discrete receptive fields; rather, they responded to visual stimulation any place on the $64° \times 64°$ area of the tangent screen used to present visual stimuli (see Fig. 17). This occurred only when the portion of the pulvinar destroyed included the ventral and caudal portions of the pulvinar which according to retrograde degeneration studies project to inferotemporal cortex.

These results suggest that information about local sign, or about the location of visual stimuli, may be sent by the pulvinar to inferotemporal cortex. This sort of information may have been lost through the degeneration of retinotopic organization in visual areas V3 to V5. The pulvinar is retinotopically organized (Allman *et al.,* 1972), and this organization may serve to delimit receptive field boundaries in inferotemporal cortex. The retinotopic organization of the pulvinar (or whatever mechanism in the pulvinar is necessary for the discrete receptive fields in inferotemporal cortex) could derive from either striate cortex or the superior colliculus, as both project to the pulvinar. The superior colliculus appears to be involved in visual localization and orientation functions (p. 90), and thus, the pulvinar lesions may have interfered with the transmission of such information to inferotemporal cortex, resulting in the absence of localized responses to light.

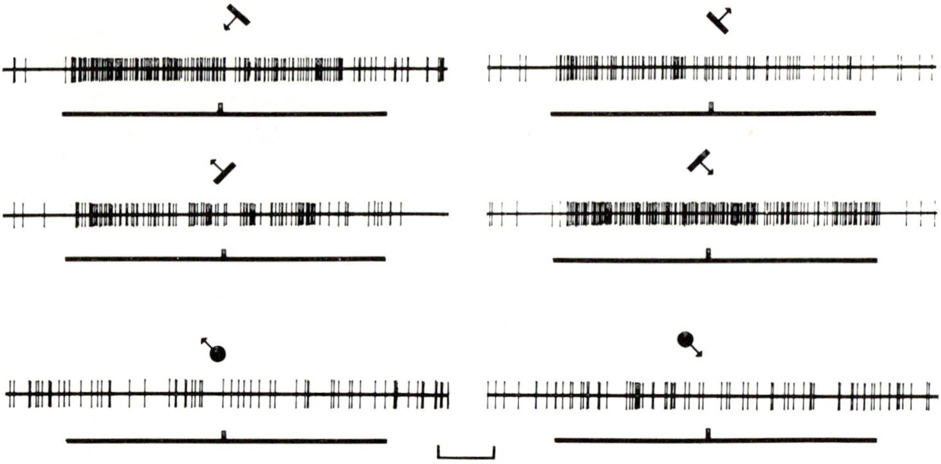

FIG. 17. Typical responses of a neuron in inferotemporal cortex in an animal that had previously received bilateral pulvinar lesions. These lesions included the regions of the inferior pulvinar that project to the region of the inferotemporal cortex in which this neuron was recorded. The upper four traces show the responses to a 1° × 64° white slit moving at 7° per second in the directions indicated. The lower two traces show responses to a white circle of 7.5° diameter also moving at 7° per second. The horizontal line below each trace indicates when the stimulus was traversing the 64° tangent screen and visible to the animal. The marker indicates 10° or 1.4 seconds. Note that the unit responds to the slits of light everywhere on the tangent screen independent of the direction of movement, but does not respond to the circle (from Rocha-Miranda *et al.,* 1973).

E. Functions of Inferotemporal Cortex

1. Pattern Recognition

What does inferotemporal cortex do with the information it receives from the circumstriate belt? One possibility is that inferotemporal cortex is a further stage in the hierarchy of pattern recognition mechanisms proposed by Hubel and Wiesel. They have shown that the geniculostriate system consists of a series of converging and diverging connections such that at each successive tier of processing mechanism, single neurons respond to increasingly specific visual stimuli falling on an increasingly wider area of the retina (Hubel and Wiesel, 1962, 1968). This hierarchy continues into Areas 18 (V2) and 19 (V3) where cells with still more specific trigger features and larger receptive fields are found (Hubel and Wiesel, 1965, 1970). Since the visual feature detectors they have found could provide only the first stages of pattern analysis and pattern recognition, there must be other regions of the brain where this processing is carried further. The rest of prestriate cortex (V4, V4A, V5, and the posterior superior temporal sulcus) and inferotemporal cortex are the obvious candidate sites for further pattern recognition mechanisms as they receive projections from Areas V1, V2, or V3 and as their removal impairs the learning of visual discriminations.

What is the nature of the further transformation of the stimulus input carried out in the visual areas beyond V1, V2, and V3? One possibility is that it continues along similar principles, yielding individual neurons with more specific trigger features and larger receptive fields. Another possibility is that some fundamentally different mechanism of pattern recognition ensues, such as one involving Fourier-like analysis (cf. Pollen *et al.*, 1971) or one involving ensembles of cells.

Some of the properties of many inferotemporal cells do appear to continue the trends seen in the geniculostriate system. Virtually all inferotemporal neurons had receptive fields that were much larger than those in Areas 18 and 19. Furthermore, many inferotemporal neurons had more specific trigger features than have been reported for more posterior visual areas. Other inferotemporal cells appeared to be less sensitive to such stimulus parameters as length, width, and orientation than cells in striate and prestriate cortex. This apparent lack of specificity may have been because these cells had complex and specific trigger features that we never found. The existence of other cells in our sample with very complex trigger features supports this possibility. The observation that three-dimensional objects were far more adequate stimuli than two-dimensional patterns for some neurons also suggests that a wider range of stimuli might have revealed a greater stimulus specificity. On the other hand, these apparently less specific cells may be involved in some fundamentally different type of pattern recognition mechanism.

2. Beyond Stimulus Analysis

It is possible that inferotemporal cortex is involved in more than further analysis of the retinal stimulus. One such function may be to integrate the geniculostriate and tectofugal visual systems. The primate superior colliculus seems to be concerned with orientation and localization functions, particularly involving eye movements (e.g., Schiller and Koerner, 1971; Humphrey, 1970; Wurtz and Goldberg, 1972;

Goldberg and Wurtz, 1972). Thus, it is possible that information about the relation of visual stimuli to the position and movement of the monkey's head and eyes may be projected corticopetally to inferotemporal cortex by way of the pulvinar. That is, inferotemporal cortex may integrate the pattern analysis functions of the geniculostriate system with the orientation functions of the tectofugal system. "Adequacy" of stimulus for inferotemporal neurons may depend on more than the retinal stimulus; it may also depend on the orientation of the animal or its eyes toward the stimulus. Perhaps the absence of discrete receptive fields after the pulvinar lesions is related to this possibility.

Another possible function of inferotemporal cortex is suggested, indeed demanded, by results of analysis of the behavioral effects of inferotemporal lesions. The visual discrimination deficit that follows inferotemporal lesions depends on several nonsensory factors such as the animal's prior experience, the training procedure used, and the type of reinforcement (pp. 80–85). Rather than producing a sensory, perceptual, or attentional deficit, inferotemporal lesions seem to interfere with some mnemonic or associative function (pp. 93–101). Thus, adequacy of a stimulus for inferotemporal units may depend on its meaning for the animal, that is, on the animal's previous experience. This is also suggested by the extreme specificity of the trigger features of some of the inferotemporal units we studied. At least some neurons in inferotemporal cortex may, in Konorski's (1967) terms, be "gnostic units."

In summary, it is possible that stimulus adequacy for inferotemporal neurons may depend on more than the retinal stimulus. It may also depend on the orientation of the animal toward the stimulus and on the meaning of the stimulus for the animal. These speculations remain to be tested in behaving, discriminating monkeys.

VI. A Final Comment

The study of the effect of brain lesions on learning in animals sometimes seems to exist in a limbo outside physiology, anatomy, and psychology. Too often, little is known of the anatomical connections of the ablated region or the type of information it receives, processes, or sends. Consequently, we are often confined to describing the effect of a brain lesion in such quasi-Aristotelian terms as "memory" and "attention," in pseudo-physiological terms such as "inhibition" and "activation," or perhaps in cybernetic ones such as "redundancy" and "feedback." Such formulations do not often increase our understanding of the neuronal mechanisms of behavior. The difficulty of drawing inferences from the behavioral effect of a brain lesion still plagues the study of inferotemporal cortex, as sections of this essay demonstrate. Yet, we are beginning to emerge from a phenomenology of inferotemporal lesions and can see the possibility of a physiological anatomy of inferotemporal cortex. The afferent inputs to inferotemporal cortex and their roles in visual discrimination learning are becoming clear. The first steps in understanding the processing of information in inferotemporal cortex itself are being made.

Acknowledgments

The behavioral experiments described in Part IV were done in collaboration with Alan Cowey, Fredrick J. Manning, and David B. Bender. The electrophysiological studies described in Part V were carried out in collaboration with Carlos Eduardo Rocha-Miranda, David B. Bender, Susan Volman, and Laura Frishman, and some of the earlier ones with Peter Schiller, George L. Gerstein, and Herbert Vaughan, Jr.

I would like to thank the following for their detailed comments of earlier drafts of this article or for otherwise assisting with its preparation: Robert W. Baker, David B. Bender, Alan Cowey, Laura Frishman, Richard Kovner, Diane A. MacKinnon, Fredrick J. Manning, Mortimer Mishkin, and Michael V. Sullivan. Preparation of the paper and research of the laboratory cited therein were supported by grants from the National Institute of Mental Health and the National Science Foundation.

References

Ades, H. W. (1946). Effects of extirpation of prestriate cortex on learned visual discrimination in monkeys. *Journal of Neuropathology and Experimental Neurology* **5**, 60–65.

Ades, H. W., and Raab, D. H. (1949). Effect of preoccipital and temporal decortication on learned visual discriminations in monkeys. *Journal of Neurophysiology* **12**, 101–108.

Allman, J. M., Kaas, J. H., Lane, R. H., and Miezin, F. M. (1972). A representation of the visual field in the inferior nucleus of the pulvinar in the owl monkey (*Aotus trivirgatus*). *Brain Research* **40**, 291–302.

Anderson, K. V., and Symmes, D. (1969). The superior colliculus and higher visual functions in the monkey. *Brain Research* **13**, 37–52.

Bagshaw, M. H., Mackworth, N. H., and Pribram, K. H. (1970). The effect of inferotemporal cortex ablations on eye movements of monkeys during discrimination training. *International Journal of Neuroscience* **1**, 153–158.

Bagshaw, M. H., Mackworth, N. H., and Pribram, K. H. (1972). The effect of resections of the inferotemporal cortex or the amygdala on visual orienting and habituation. *Neuropsychologia* **10**, 153–162.

Bailey, P., von Bonin, G., Garol, H. W., and McCulloch, W. S. (1943). Functional organization of the temporal lobe of monkey (*Macaca mulatta*) and chimpanzee (*Pan satyrus*). *Journal of Neurophysiology* **6**, 121–128.

Bender, D. B. (1973a). Visual sensitivity following inferotemporal and foveal prestriate lesions in the rhesus monkey. *Journal of Comparative and Physiological Psychology* (in press).

Bender, D. B. (1973b). Signal detection in the rhesus monkey. Unpublished manuscript.

Bender, D. B. (1973c). Visual masking in man and monkey. Unpublished manuscript.

Bender, D. B., Rocha-Miranda, C. E., Gross, C. G., Volman, S., and Mishkin, M. (1972). Effects of striate lesions and commissure section on the visual response of neurons in the inferotemporal cortex. *Physiologist* **15**, 84.

Blum, J., Chow, K. L., and Pribram, K. H. (1950). A behavioral analysis of the organization of the parieto-temporo-preoccipital cortex. *Journal of Comparative Neurology* **93**, 53–100.

Brodmann, K. (1905). Beiträge zur histologischen Lokalisation der Grosshirnrinde. Dritte Mitteilung: Die Rindefelder der niederen Affen. *Journal für Psychologie und Neurologie* **4**, 177–226.

Brown, T. S. (1963). Olfactory and visual discrimination in the monkey after selective lesions of the temporal lobe. *Journal of Comparative and Physiological Psychology* **56**, 764–768.

Brown, T. S., Rosvold, H. E., and Mishkin, M. (1963). Olfactory discrimination after temporal lobe lesions in monkeys. *Journal of Comparative and Physiological Psychology* **56**, 190–195.

Butler, C. R. (1969). Is there a memory impairment in monkeys after inferior temporal lesions? *Brain Research* **13**, 383–393.

Butter, C. M. (1968). The effect of discrimination training on pattern equivalence in monkeys with inferotemporal and lateral striate lesions. *Neuropsychologia* **6**, 27–40.

Butter, C. M. (1969). Impairments in selective attention to visual stimuli in monkeys with inferotemporal and lateral striate lesions. *Brain Research* **12**, 374–383.

Butter, C. M., and Doehrman, S. R. (1968). Size discrimination and transposition in monkeys with striate and temporal lesions. *Cortex* **4**, 35–46.

Butter, C. M., and Gekoski, W. L. (1966). Alterations in pattern equivalence following inferotemporal and lateral striate lesions in rhesus monkeys. *Journal of Comparative and Physiological Psychology* **61**, 309–312.

Butter, C. M., and Hirtzel, M. (1970). Impairment in sampling visual stimuli in monkeys with inferotemporal lesions. *Physiology & Behavior* **5**, 369–370.

Butter, C. M., Mishkin, M., and Rosvold, H. E. (1965). Stimulus generalization following inferotemporal and lateral striate lesions in monkeys. *In* "Stimulus Generalization" (D. Mostofsky, ed.), pp. 119–133. Stanford Univ. Press, Stanford, California.

Chow, K. L. (1950). A retrograde cell degeneration study of the cortical projection field of the pulvinar in the monkey. *Journal of Comparative Neurology* **93**, 313–340.

Chow, K. L. (1951). Effects of partial extirpations of the posterior association cortex on visually mediated behavior. *Comparative Psychology Monograph* **20**, 187–217.

Chow, K. L. (1952). Further studies on selective ablation of associative cortex in relation to visually mediated behavior. *Journal of Comparative and Physiological Psychology* **45**, 109–118.

Chow, K. L. (1954a). Effects of temporal neocortical ablation on visual discrimination learning sets in monkeys. *Journal of Comparative and Physiological Psychology* **47**, 194–198.

Chow, K. L. (1954b). Lack of behavioral effects following destruction of some thalamic association nuclei in monkey. *AMA Archives of Neurology and Psychiatry* **71**, 762–771.

Chow, K. L. (1961a). Anatomical and electrographical analysis of temporal neocortex in relation to visual discrimination learning in monkeys. *In* "Brain Mechanisms in Learning" (J. F. Delafresnaye, ed.), pp. 507–525. Blackwell, Oxford.

Chow, K. L. (1961b). Changes of brain electropotentials during visual discrimination learning in monkey. *Journal of Neurophysiology* **24**, 377–390.

Chow, K. L. (1961c). Effect of local electrographic after-discharges on visual learning and retention in the monkey. *Journal of Neurophysiology* **24**, 391–400.

Chow, K. L., and Orbach, J. (1957). Performance of visual discriminations presented tachistoscopically in monkeys with temporal neocortical ablations. *Journal of Comparative and Physiological Psychology* **6**, 636–640.

Chow, K. L., and Survis, J. (1958). Retention of overlearned visual habit after temporal cortical ablation in monkey. *AMA Archives of Neurology and Psychiatry* **79**, 640–646.

Cowey, A. (1967). Perimetric study of field defects in monkeys after cortical and retinal ablations. *Quarterly Journal of Experimental Psychology* **19**, 232–245.

Cowey, A. (1971). Personal communication.

Cowey, A., and Gross, C. G. (1970). Effects of foveal prestriate and inferotemporal lesions on visual discriminations by rhesus monkeys. *Experimental Brain Research* **11**, 128–144.

Cowey, A., and Weiskrantz, L. (1963). A perimetric study of visual field defects in monkeys. *Quarterly Journal of Experimental Psychology* **15**, 91–115.

Cowey, A., and Weiskrantz, L. (1967). A comparison of the effects of inferotemporal and striate cortex lesions on the visual behavior of rhesus monkeys. *Quarterly Journal of Experimental Psychology* **19**, 246–253.

Cragg, B. G., and Ainsworth, A. (1969). The topography of the afferent projections in the circumstriate visual cortex of the monkey studied by the Nauta method. *Vision Research* **9**, 733–747.

Ettlinger, G. (1959). Visual discrimination following successive temporal ablations in monkeys. *Brain* **82**, 232–250.

Ettlinger, G. (1962). Relationship between test difficulty and the visual impairment in monkeys with ablations of temporal cortex. *Nature (London)* **196**, 911–912.

Ettlinger, G., and Gautrin, D. (1971). Visual discrimination performance in the monkey: the effect of unilateral removals of temporal cortex. *Cortex* **7**, 317–331.

Evarts, E. V. (1952). Effects of ablation of prestriate cortex on auditory-visual association in monkey. *Journal of Neurophysiology* **15**, 191–200.

Fox, C. A., Fisher, R. R., and Desalva, S. J. (1948). The distribution of the anterior commissure in the monkey (*Macaca mulatta*). *Journal of Comparative Neurology* **89**, 245–278.

Freud, S. (1891). "Zür Auffassung der Arphasien; eine kritische Studie." Deuticke, Leipzig. ["On Aphasia: A Critical Study" (transl. by E. Stengel). International Univ. Press, New York, 1953.]

Gerstein, G. L., Gross, C. G., and Weinstein, M. (1968). Inferotemporal evoked potentials during visual discrimination performance by monkeys. *Journal of Comparative and Physiological Psychology* **65**, 526–528.

Glees, P., and Cole, J. (1950). Recovery of skilled motor functions after small repeated lesions of motor cortex in macaque. *Journal of Neurophysiology* **13**, 137–148.

Goldberg, M. E., and Wurtz, R. H. (1972). Activity of superior colliculus in behaving monkey. II. Effect of attention on neuronal responses. *Journal of Neurophysiology* **35**, 560–574.

Goldrich, S. G., and Stamm, J. S. (1971). Electrical stimulation of inferotemporal and occipital cortex in monkeys: effects on visual discrimination and spatial reversal performance. *Journal of Comparative and Physiological Psychology* **74**, 448–458.

Gross, C. G. (1973). Visual functions of inferotemporal cortex. *In* "Handbook of Sensory Physiology" (R. Jung, ed.), Vol. 7/3B. Springer-Verlag, Berlin and New York.

Gross, C. G., and Footnick, R. (1966). Unpublished data.

Gross, C. G., Schiller, P. H., Wells, C., and Gerstein, G. L. (1967). Single unit activity in temporal association cortex of the monkey. *Journal of Neurophysiology* **30**, 833–843.

Gross, C. G., Bender, D. B., and Rocha-Miranda, C. E. (1969). Visual receptive fields of neurons in inferotemporal cortex of the monkey. *Science* **166**, 1303–1306.

Gross, C. G., Cowey, A., and Manning, F. J. (1971). Further analysis of visual discrimination deficits following foveal prestriate and inferotemporal lesions in rhesus monkeys. *Journal of Comparative and Physiological Psychology* **76**, 1–7.

Gross, C. G., Rocha-Miranda, C. E., and Bender, D. B. (1972). Visual properties of neurons in inferotemporal cortex of the macaque. *Journal of Neurophysiology* **35**, 96–111.

Gross, C. G., Bender, D. B., and Rocha-Miranda, C. E. (1973). Inferotemporal cortex: A single unit analysis. *In* "The Neurosciences: A Third Study Program." M.I.T. Press, Cambridge, Massachusetts.

Harlow, H. F., Harlow, M. K., Rueping, R. R., and Mason, W. A. (1960). Performance on discrimination learning, delayed response and discrimination learning set. *Journal of Comparative and Physiological Psychology* **53**, 113–121.

Hubel, D. H., and Wiesel, T. N. (1961). Integrative action in the cat's lateral geniculate body. *Journal of Physiology* (*London*) **155**, 385–398.

Hubel, D. H., and Wiesel, T. N. (1962). Receptive fields, binocular interaction and functional architecture in the cat's visual cortex. *Journal of Physiology* (*London*) **160**, 106–154.

Hubel, D. H., and Wiesel, T. N. (1965). Receptive fields and functional architecture in two nonstriate visual areas (18 and 19) of the cat. *Journal of Neurophysiology* **28**, 229–289.

Hubel, D. H., and Wiesel, T. N. (1967). Cortical and callosal connections concerned with the vertical meridian of visual fields in the cat. *Journal of Neurophysiology* **30**, 1561–1573.

Hubel, D. H., and Wiesel, T. N. (1968). Receptive fields and functional architecture of monkey striate cortex. *Journal of Physiology* (*London*) **195**, 215–243.

Hubel, D. H., and Wiesel, T. N. (1970). Stereoscopic vision in macaque monkey. *Nature (London)* **225**, 41–42.

Humphrey, N. K. (1970). What the frog's eye tells the monkey's brain. *Brain, Behavior and Evolution* **3**, 324–337.

Humphrey, N. K., and Weiskrantz, L. (1969). Size constancy in monkeys with inferotemporal lesions. *Quarterly Journal of Experimental Psychology* **21**, 225–238.

Iversen, S. D., and Humphrey, N. K. (1971). Ventral temporal lobe lesions and visual oddity performance. *Brain Research* **30**, 253–263.

Iversen, S. D., and Weiskrantz, L. (1964). Temporal lobe lesions and memory in the monkey. *Nature (London)* **201**, 740–742.

Iversen, S. D., and Weiskrantz, L. (1967). Perception of redundant cues by monkeys with inferotemporal lesions. *Nature (London)* **214**, 241–243.

Iversen, S. D., and Weiskrantz, L. (1970). An investigation of a possible memory defect produced by inferotemporal lesions in the baboon. *Neuropsychologia* **8**, 21–36.

Iwai, E., and Mishkin, M. (1968). Two visual foci in the temporal lobe of monkeys. *In* "Neuropsychological Basis of Learning and Behavior" (N. Yoshii and N. A. Buckwald, eds.). Osaka Univ. Press, Osaka.

Iwai, E., and Mishkin, M. (1969). Further evidence on the locus of the visual area in the temporal lobe of the monkey. *Experimental Neurology* **25**, 585–594.

Klüver, H., and Bucy, P. C. (1937). "Psychic blindness" and other symptoms following bilateral temporal lobectomy in rhesus monkeys. *American Journal of Physiology* **119**, 352–353.

Klüver, H., and Bucy, P. C. (1938). An analysis of certain effects of bilateral temporal lobectomy in the rhesus monkey, with special reference to "psychic blindness." *Journal of Psychology* **5**, 33–54.

Klüver, H., and Bucy, P. C. (1939). Preliminary analysis of functions of the temporal lobe in monkeys. *Archives of Neurology and Psychiatry* **42**, 979–1000.

Konorski, J. (1967). "Integrative Activity of the Brain," Univ. of Chicago Press, Chicago, Illinois.

Kovner, R., and Stamm, J. S. (1972). Effects of electrical stimulation of inferotemporal cortex on short-term visual memory. *Journal of Comparative and Physiological Psychology* **81**, 163–172.

Krechevsky, I. (1938). A study of the continuity of the problem-solving process. *Psychological Review* **45**, 107–133.

Kuypers, H. G. J. M., Szwarcbart, M. K., Mishkin, M., and Rosvold, H. E. (1965). Occipito-temporal cortico-cortical connections in the rhesus monkey. *Experimental Neurology* **11**, 245–262.

Lashley, K. S. (1929). "Brain Mechanisms and Intelligence: A Quantitative Study of Injuries to the Brain." Univ. of Chicago Press, Chicago, Illinois. [Reprinted by Dover, New York, 1965.]

Lashley, K. S. (1948). The mechanism of vision. XVIII. Effects of destroying the visual "associative areas" of the monkey. *Genetic Psychology Monograph* **37**, 107–166.

McFarland, D. J. (1966). The role of attention in the disinhibition of displacement activities. *Quarterly Journal of Experimental Psychology* **18**, 19–30.

Manning, F. J. (1971a). Punishment for errors and visual-discrimination learning by monkeys with inferotemporal cortex lesions. *Journal of Comparative and Physiological Psychology* **75**, 146–152.

Manning, F. J. (1971b). The selective attention "deficit" of monkeys with ablations of foveal prestriate cortex. *Psychonomic Science* **25**, 291–292.

Manning, F. J. (1972). Serial reversal learning by monkeys with inferotemporal or foveal prestriate lesions. *Brain Research* **8**, 177–181.

Manning, F. J., Gross, C. G., and Cowey, A. (1971). Partial reinforcement: effects on visual learning after foveal prestriate and inferotemporal lesions. *Physiology & Behavior* **6**, 61–64.

Mettler, F. A. (1935). Corticofugal fiber connections of the cortex of *Macaca mulatta*. The occipital region. *Journal of Comparative Neurology* **61**, 221–256.

Meyer, D. R. (1958). Some psychological determinants of sparing and loss following damage to the brain. *In* "Biological and Biochemical Basis of Behavior" (H. F. Harlow and C. N. Woolsey, eds.), pp. 173–192. Univ. of Wisconsin Press, Madison.

Meyer, D. R., Harlow, H. F., and Ades, H. W. (1951). Retention of delayed responses and proficiency in oddity problems by monkeys with preoccipital ablations. *American Journal of Psychology* **64**, 391–396.

Milner, B. (1968). Visual recognition and recall after right temporal-lobe excision in man. *Neuropsychologia* **6**, 191–209.

Mishkin, M. (1954). Visual discrimination performance following partial ablations of the temporal lobe: II. Ventral surface vs. hippocampus. *Journal of Comparative and Physiological Psychology* **47**, 187–193.

Mishkin, M. (1958). Visual discrimination impairment after cutting cortical connections between the inferotemporal and striate areas in monkeys. *American Psychologist* **13**, 414. (Abstr.)

Mishkin, M. (1966). Visual mechanisms beyond the striate cortex. *In* "Frontiers of Physiological Psychology" (R. Russell, ed.), pp. 93–119. Academic Press, New York.

Mishkin, M. (1972). Cortical visual areas and their interaction. *In* "The Brain and Human Behavior" (A. G. Karczmar and J. C. Eccles, eds.), pp. 187–208. Springer-Verlag, Berlin and New York.

Mishkin, M., and Hall, M. (1955). Discrimination along a size continuum following ablation of the inferior temporal convexity in monkeys. *Journal of Comparative and Physiological Psychology* **48**, 97–101.

Mishkin, M., and Pribram, K. H. (1954). Visual discrimination performance following partial ablations of the temporal lobe. I. Ventral vs. lateral. *Journal of Comparative and Physiological Psychology* **47**, 14–20.

Myers, R. E. (1962). Striate cortex connections in the monkey. *Federation Proceedings, Federation of American Societies for Experimental Biology* **21**, 352.

Myers, R. E. (1965). Phylogenetic studies of commissural connexions. *Ciba Foundation Study Group* [*Papers*] **20**, 138–143.

Orbach, J., and Fantz, R. L. (1958). Differential effects of temporal neocortical resections on overtrained and nonovertrained visual habits in monkeys. *Journal of Comparative and Physiological Psychology* **51**, 126–129.

Oscar-Berman, M., Heywood, S. P., and Gross, C. G. (1971). Eye orientation during visual discrimination learning by monkeys. *Neuropsychologia* **9**, 351–358.

Oscar-Berman, M., Heywood, S. P., and Gross, C. G. (1973). Effects of inferotemporal lesions on eye orientation during visual learning by monkeys. Submitted for publication.

Pandya, D. N., Karol, E. A., and Heilbronn, D. (1971). The topographical distribution of interhemispheric projections in the corpus callosum of the rhesus monkey. *Brain Research* **32**, 31–43.

Pasik, P., Pasik, T., Battersby, W. S., and Bender, M. B. (1958). Visual and tactual discrimination by macaques with serial temporal and parietal lesions. *Journal of Comparative and Physiological Psychology* **51**, 427–436.

Pasik, T., Pasik, P., Battersby, W. S., and Bender, M. B. (1960). Factors influencing visual behavior of monkeys with bilateral temporal lobe lesions. *Journal of Comparative Neurology* **115**, 89–102.

Penfield, W., and Perot, P. (1963). The brain's record of auditory and visual experience: a final summary and discussion. *Brain* **86**, 595–696.

Petr, R., Holden, L. B., and Jirout, J. (1949). The efferent intercortical connections of the superficial cortex of the temporal lobe (*Macaca mulatta*). *Journal of Neuropathology and Experimental Neurology* **8**, 100–103.

Pollen, D. A., Lee, J. R., and Taylor, J. H. (1971). How does the striate cortex begin the reconstruction of the visual world? *Science* **173**, 74–77.

Pribram, H., and Barry, J. (1956). Further behavioral analysis of the parieto-temporo-preoccipital cortex. *Journal of Neurophysiology* **19**, 99–106.

Pribram, K. H. (1954). Toward a science of neuropsychology: (Method and data). *In* "Current Trends in Psychology and the Behavioral Sciences" (R. A. Patton, ed.), pp. 115–152. Univ. of Pittsburgh Press, Pittsburgh, Pennsylvania.

Pribram, K. H. (1960). The intrinsic systems of the forebrain. *In* "Handbook of Physiology, Sect. 1: Neurophysiology, Vol. II" (J. Field, H. W. Magoun, and V. E. Hall, eds.), pp. 1323–1344. Amer. Physiol. Soc. Washington, D. C.

Pribram, K. H. (1967). Neurophysiology and learning: I. Memory and the organization of attention. *In* "Brain Function and Learning" (D. B. Lindsley and A. A. Lumsdaine, eds.), pp. 79–112. Univ. of California Press, Berkeley.

Pribram, K. H. (1971). "Languages of the Brain; Experimental Paradoxes and Principles in Neuropsychology." Prentice-Hall, Englewood Cliffs, New Jersey.

Pribram, K. H., and Bagshaw, M. H. (1953). Further analysis of the temporal lobe syndrome utilizing fronto-temporal ablations. *Journal of Comparative Neurology* **99**, 347–375.

Pribram, K. H., and Mishkin, M. (1955). Simultaneous and successive discrimination by monkeys with inferotemporal lesions. *Journal of Comparative and Physiological Psychology* **48**, 198–202.

Pribram, K. H., Spinelli, D. N., and Reitz, S. L. (1969). The effects of radical disconnexion of occipital and temporal cortex on visual behavior of monkeys. *Brain* **92**, 301–312.

Raisler, R. L., and Harlow, H. F. (1965). Learned behavior following lesions of posterior association cortex in infant, immature, and preadolescent monkeys. *Journal of Comparative and Physiological Psychology* **60**, 167–174.

Reitz, S. L. (1969). Effects of serial disconnection of striate and temporal cortex on visual discrimination performance in monkeys. *Journal of Comparative and Physiological Psychology* **68**, 139–146.

Reitz, S. L., and Gerbrandt, L. K. (1971). Pre- and post-trial temporal lobe seizures in monkeys and memory consolidation. *Journal of Comparative and Physiological Psychology* **74**, 179–184.

Riopelle, A. J., and Ades, H. W. (1953). Visual discrimination performance in rhesus monkeys following extirpation of prestriate and temporal cortex. *Journal of Genetic Psychology* **83**, 63–77.

Riopelle, A. J., and Churukian, G. A. (1958). The effect of varying the inter-trial interval in discrimination learning by normal and brain-operated monkeys. *Journal of Comparative and Physiological Psychology* **51**, 119–125.

Riopelle, A. J., Harlow, H. F., Settlage, P. H., and Ades, H. (1951). Performance of normal and operated monkeys on visual learning tests. *Journal of Comparative and Physiological Psychology* **44**, 283–289.

Rocha-Miranda, C. E., Gross, C. G., Bender, D. B., Volman, S., Frishman, L., and Mishkin, M. (1973). Afferent bases of the visual properties of neurons in inferotemporal cortex. Unpublished.

Rosvold, H. E., Mishkin, M., and Szwarcbart, M. K. (1958). Effects of sub-cortical lesions in monkeys on visual-discrimination and single-alternation performance. *Journal of Comparative and Physiological Psychology* **51**, 437–444.

Schiller, P. H., and Koerner, F. (1971). Discharge characteristics of single units in the superior colliculus of the alert rhesus monkey. *Journal of Neurophysiology* **34**, 920–936.

Semmes, J. (1973). Somesthetic effects of damage to the central nervous system. *In* "Handbook of Sensory Physiology" (R. Jung, ed.). Springer-Verlag, Berlin and New York.

Stamm, J. S., and Knight, M. (1963). Learning of visual tasks by monkeys with epileptogenic implants in temporal cortex. *Journal of Comparative and Physiological Psychology* **56**, 254–260.

Stamm, J. S., and Mahoney, W. A. (1962). Electrical slow waves from tem-poral lobe during learning of complex tasks. *Exerpta Medica Foundation International Congress Series* **48**.

Stamm, J. S., and Pribram, K. H. (1961). Effects of epileptogenic lesions in inferotemporal cortex on learning and retention in monkeys. *Journal of Comparative and Physiological Psychology* **54**, 614–618.

Sutherland, N. S. (1966). Partial reinforcement and breadth of learning. *Quarterly Journal of Experimental Psychology* **18**, 289–301.

Sutherland, N. S., and Mackintosh, N. J. (1971). "Mechanisms of Animal Dis-crimination Learning." Academic Press, New York.

Symmes, D. (1965). Flicker discrimination by brain-damaged monkeys. *Journal of Comparative and Physiological Psychology* **60**, 470–473.

Teuber, H.-L., Battersby, W. S., and Bender, M. B. (1960). "Visual Field Defects After Penetrating Missile Wounds of the Brain." Harvard Univ. Press, Cambridge, Massachusetts.

Trevarthen, C. B. (1968). Two mechanisms of vision in primates. *Psychologische Forschung* **31**, 299–337.

Vaughan, H. G., Jr., and Gross, C. G. (1969). Cortical responses to light in unanesthetized monkeys and their alteration by visual system lesions. *Experimental Brain Research* **8**, 19–36.

von Bonin, G., and Bailey, P. (1947). "The Neocortex of *Macaca mulatta*." Univ. of Illinois Press, Urbana.

Weiskrantz, L. (1967). Central nervous system and the organization of behavior. *In* "The Organization of Recall" (D. P. Kimble, ed.), pp. 234–294. N. Y. Acad. Sci., New York.

Weiskrantz, L. (1970). Visual memory and the temporal lobe of the monkey. *In* "The Neural Control of Behavior" (R. E. Whalen, R. F. Thompson, M. Verzeano, and N. M. Weinberger, eds.), pp. 239–256. Academic Press, New York.

Weiskrantz, L., and Cowey, A. (1963). Striate cortex lesions and visual acuity of the rhesus monkey. *Journal of Comparative and Physiological Psychology* **56**, 225–231.

Weiskrantz, L., and Mishkin, M. (1958). Effects of temporal and frontal cortical lesions on auditory discrimination in monkeys. *Brain* **81**, 406–414.

Wilson, M. (1957). Effects of circumscribed cortical lesions upon somesthetic and visual discrimination in the monkey. *Journal of Comparative and Physiological Psychology* **50**, 630–635.

Wilson, M. (1968). Inferotemporal cortex and the processing of visual information in monkeys. *Neuropsychologia* **6**, 135–140.

Wilson, M., and Kaufman, H. M. (1969). Effect of inferotemporal lesions upon processing of visual information in monkeys. *Journal of Comparative and Physiological Psychology* **69**, 44–48.

Wilson, M., Rothblat, L., and Kirstein, E. (1968a). Frequency and recency of reward and inferotemporal lesions. *Psychonomic Science* **11**, 237–238.

Wilson, M., Wilson, W. A., Jr., and Sunenshine, H. S. (1968b). Perception, learning and retention of visual stimuli by monkeys with inferotemporal lesions. *Journal of Comparative and Physiological Psychology* **65**, 404–412.

Wilson, M., Kaufman, H. M., Zieler, R. E., and Lieb, J. P. (1972). Visual identification and memory in monkeys with circumscribed inferotemporal lesions. *Journal of Comparative and Physiological Psychology* **78**, 173–183.

Wilson, W. A., Jr., and Mishkin, M. (1959). Comparison of the effects of inferotemporal and lateral occipital lesions on visually guided behavior in monkeys. *Journal of Comparative and Physiological Psychology* **52**, 10–17.

Wurtz, R. H., and Goldberg, M. E. (1972). Activity of superior colliculus in behaving monkey. IV. Effects of lesions on eye movements. *Journal of Neurophysiology* **35**, 587–596.

Zeki, S. M. (1969a). The secondary visual areas of the monkey. *Brain Research* **13**, 197–226.

Zeki, S. M. (1969b). Representation of central visual fields in prestriate cortex of monkey. *Brain Research* **14**, 271–291.

Zeki, S. M. (1970). Interhemispheric connections of prestriate cortex in monkey. *Brain Research* **19**, 63–75.

Zeki, S. M. (1971a). Convergent input from the striate cortex (area 17) to the cortex of the superior temporal sulcus in the rhesus monkey. *Brain Research* **28**, 338–340.

Zeki, S. M. (1971b). Cortical projections from two prestriate areas in the monkey. *Brain Research* **34**, 19–35.

Studies of the Physiological Bases of Memory[1]

Peter L. Carlton and Barbara Markiewicz
Department of Psychiatry,
College of Medicine and Dentistry of New Jersey,
Rutgers Medical School, Piscataway, New Jersey

I. Introduction

Our interest in the physiological bases of memory began with two reports that dealt with possible biochemical factors in this process. In one of these (Flexner *et al.,* 1967), it was reported that intracerebral injections of an antibiotic, puromycin, could produce substantial retention deficits. This result suggests that, because puromycin injected in this way produces massive inhibition of protein synthesis, the integrity of this synthetic mechanism may be required for normal memory. On the other hand, the second report (Barondes and Cohen, 1966) suggested that these deficits might be due to the electrical silence of the brain produced by puromycin rather than to the inhibition of protein synthesis.

[1] Supported by NIMH Grant MH-08585 to Peter L. Carlton.

125

This latter possibility led to an obvious experiment: Might it be possible to produce retention deficits by inducing electrical silence in some way other than by the injection of puromycin? Because potassium chloride (KCl) is known to induce electrical silence, we undertook an experiment designed to determine whether KCl injections could induce retention deficits. In addition, we devised a simple technique for monitoring the electrical consequences of these injections and thus provided ourselves with a degree of experimental control that has been curiously absent from most studies involving direct chemical injections into the brain.

II. Procedures and Initial Findings

In the majority of our experiments, an extremely simple kind of learning has been used to index retention. Thirsty adult, male rats are initially placed in the chamber shown at the top of Fig. 1 and given the opportunity to take 110 licks at the drinking tube. On a subsequent day the animals are returned to the chamber; they have not been deprived of water, and the drinking tube is not available. In this second session each animal is given four presentations of a tone, the termination of which is coincident with a brief, inescapable, painful electric shock applied to the grid floor of the chamber. On the next day each animal is surgically anesthetized, placed in a stereotaxic instrument, and given bilateral injections of either isotonic saline or 25% KCl delivered via a microsyringe into the hippocampal area of the brain (see the bottom of Fig. 1). The microsyringe is connected to a 30-gauge needle that is lowered into the brain through a 23-gauge needle mounted on the carrier of the stereotaxic instrument. The larger 23-gauge needle is insulated except for about 1 mm at the tip. Thus, it is possible to obtain monopolar records of electrical activity of the brain (EEG) both before and after injection.

In a typical experiment, the EEG of an anesthetized animal that has previously been placed in the stereotaxic instrument is monitored for about 10 minutes. The 30-gauge needle is then inserted, and 4–11 μl of saline or KCl are slowly injected; the effects of such injections are concurrently monitored with the EEG recorder. More complete details of these procedures have been provided by Avis and Carlton (1968) and by Hughes (1969).

Following injection, the animals' scalps are sutured, the animals are then returned to their home cages and remain there for 2 days. On the third day water is removed and, on the fourth, each animal is returned to the test chamber and allowed to emit 100 licks at the

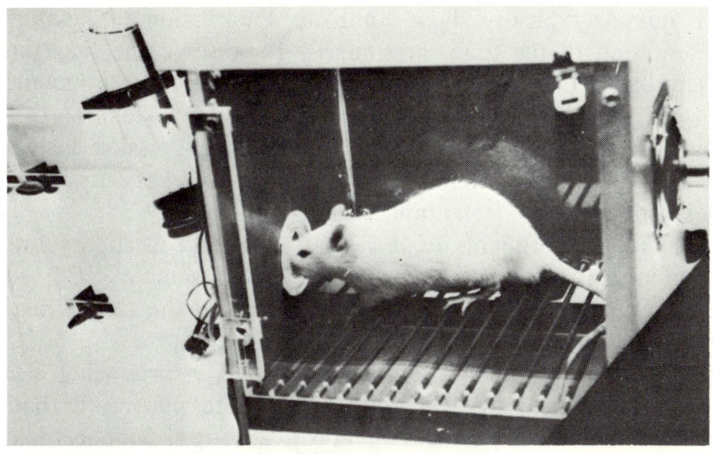

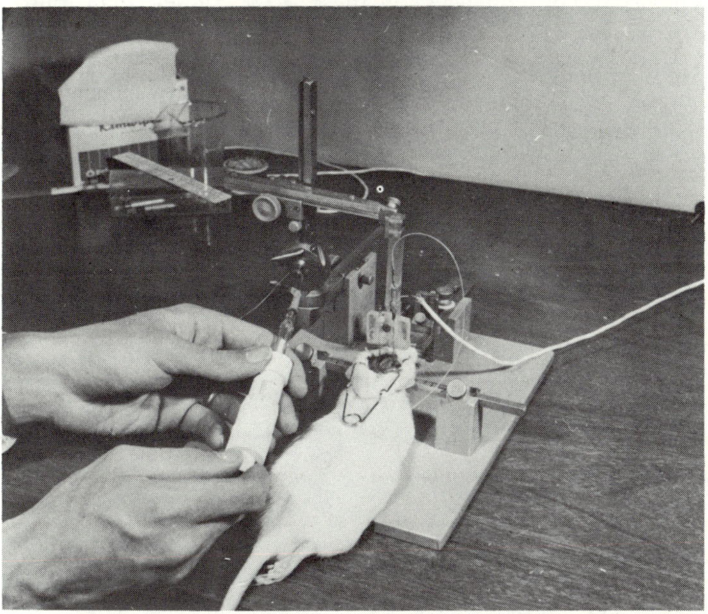

Fig. 1. Top: Rat in the chamber in which licking behavior is monitored and tone-shock pairings are administered. Bottom: Anesthetized rat in stereotaxic instrument. Solution is being injected into the right ventral hippocampus.

drinking tube, as in the first session. Upon completion of the one-hundredth lick, the tone that has previously been paired with shock is turned on. This tone remains on until the animal has made an additional ten licks at the tube, or until 300 seconds has elapsed.

Normal animals typically show complete suppression of licking upon the presentation of the tone, presumably because of the fear that has previously been conditioned to that tone as a result of its having been paired with inescapable shock. We have used the extent of this suppression as a measure of retention; complete suppression is taken as representing complete retention, whereas a lack of suppression is taken as representing a retention deficit.

In the initial experiments of this kind, Avis and Carlton found that KCl produced the expected electrical silence; sample EEG records showing the lack of effect of saline injection and the electrical silence produced by KCl are shown in Fig. 2.

In our initial experiment, we were interested in producing electrical silence by injections into that brain area where puromycin had produced retention deficits; hence we chose a ventral hippocampal site. The behavioral consequences of these KCl, rather than puromycin, injections were twofold.

First, animals given KCl showed essentially no suppression of licking, whereas those given saline showed normal suppression. Thus, there was an indication of a large-order retention deficit due to the injection of KCl, and the consequent electrical silence, given 24 hours after

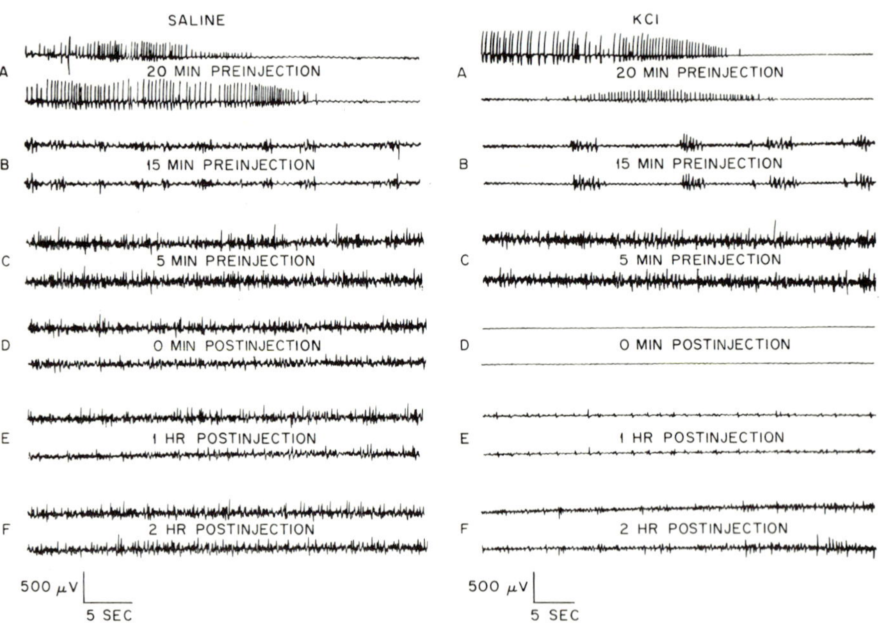

FIG. 2. Bilateral EEG records taken from rats being given either saline (left) or KCl injections (right) into the hippocampus.

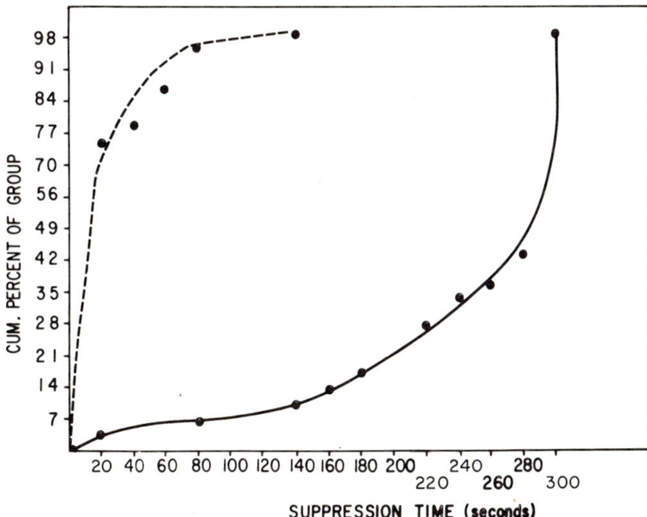

FIG. 3. Cumulative percentages of animals given saline (—) or KCl (- - -) plotted in relation to suppression time during test. Animals were injected bilaterally into the hippocampus with isotonic saline or 25% KCl solution 1 day after tone-shock pairing and 3 days before testing.

conditioning. Second, we found that there was a systematic relationship between the duration of this electrical silence and the magnitude of the retention deficit.

These initial observations have been amply confirmed in subsequent experimentation. The suppression data from a large number of animals are summarized in Fig. 3. In this figure the cumulative percentage of the animals showing various suppression times (on the abscissa) have been plotted. As the figure indicates, there is essentially no overlap of the scores of the two populations of animals; for example, only 5% of the animals given KCl have suppression times greater than 80 seconds, whereas only about 5% of those given saline have suppression times *less than* this value.

The relation between extent of EEG silence and suppression time is shown in Fig. 4. (Duration of EEG silence was measured by tabulating the number of minutes during which EEG was virtually absent bilaterally; unilateral silence was not sufficient.) Each of the plotted points is for a single rat; there is a reasonably orderly relationship between the duration of electrical silence and extent of suppression. In particular, very low levels of suppression (i.e., retention deficits) are reliably obtained only when about 11 minutes of silence have been induced. In all subsequent experiments this criterion of electrical silence

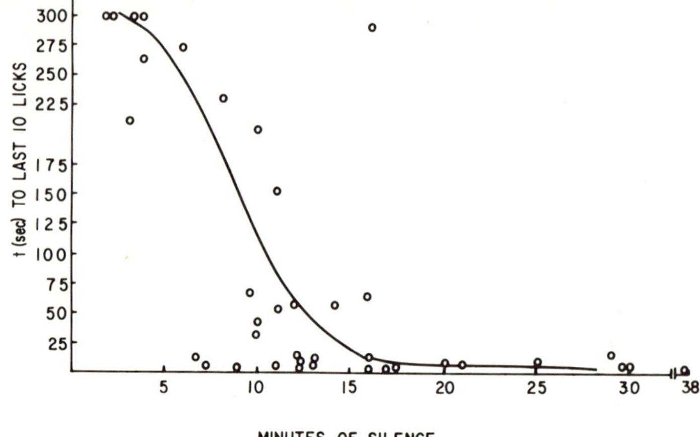

Fig. 4. Suppression time during test for individual KCl-treated animals plotted as a function of minutes of electrical silence.

was imposed by administering small supplemental doses of KCl whenever the concurrently monitored EEG began to show recovery before a total of 11 minutes of silence had been obtained.

III. Some Problems of Interpretation

There are seven questions concerning the interpretation of the effects that we have just described; each of these is discussed below.

A. Effects of Hypertonicity

The first question is whether the suppression deficits could be produced by the introduction of any hypertonic solution. An answer to this question is that we have found that injections of 25% sodium chloride (NaCl), in volumes comparable to those of KCl, do not produce protracted electrical silence and also do not produce retention deficits like those produced by KCl (see below). Recently, Kapp and Schneider (1971) independently confirmed this lack of effect of NaCl as well as the retention deficits due to KCl. Thus, as the relationship in Fig. 4 suggests, the suppression deficits are dependent upon electrical silence.

B. Role of Tissue Damage

The second question concerning the interpretation of the effects of KCl relates to the fact that KCl may cause lesions and that such damage could produce suppression deficits. Thus, there is a very real possibility that, if KCl produces lesions, then the suppression deficits could be due to those lesions rather than the electrical silence, although Kapp and Schneider have reported that animals given NaCl crystals are histologically indistinguishable from those given KCl. In our own analysis of the possible role of damage, the brains of 40 animals were sectioned and stained. The volume of damage, regardless of locus, was then approximated by projecting the most anterior section with damage and estimating the total area of damaged tissue, and repeating this process for the most posterior section as well as for that section falling in the middle anterior-posterior plane. The total damage in these three areas when then multiplied by the anterior-posterior extent of damage provides a crude estimate of volume of damage (VOD). Although this procedure is unsatisfactory for determining absolute amounts of damage, it does provide a rough index that can only be used to estimate *relative* tissue loss.

When the VODs for different animals that had been given KCl were correlated with their suppression scores, the resultant rank order r was $-.20$, a value that is not reliably different from zero. Thus, variations in tissue damage appear to account for only 4% of the variation in suppression scores.

Although damage tended to appear in hippocampus, tissue loss was quite widespread relative to that seen following passage of dc current, presumably because of the diffusion of KCl; it was this diffuseness that prompted our use of VOD for the entire brain. However, a parallel analysis restricted to ventral hippocampus produced a similarly low correlation of damage and suppression ($r = .13$).

In agreement with Kapp and Schneider, we also found that hypertonic NaCl or KCl produced comparable damage but very different suppression scores; the median VOD for animals given 25% KCl was 17.0 and for those given 25% NaCl it was 17.5, whereas the corresponding median suppression scores were 16.9 seconds and 283.5 seconds.

These lines of evidence agree with the relationship shown in Fig. 4 in indicating that the extent of the deficit is due to electrical silence rather than permanent damage due to injection. Finally, some of the temporal dependencies that we will be discussing later show no correlation with degree of damage.

C. Prolongation of Anesthesia

We have observed that animals anesthetized and given KCl are generally slower to recover from anesthesia than are those given saline; animals given KCl reflexively respond to foot pinch in about 1½ hours and show recovery of righting in about 3 hours, whereas the corresponding values for the saline animals are 40 minutes and 2¼ hours. We have also noted an even greater difference in recovery of normal locomotion. The KCl animals appear to be uncoordinated and somewhat ataxic for several hours more than are those given saline. This difference, one that we have not attempted to quantify, may be related to an interaction of anesthesia with a motor incapacitation like that uniformly observed following application of KCl to cortex (Bureš and Burešová, 1960).

The possibility that this augmented anesthesia can itself account for the retention loss due to KCl is an extremely remote one. Anesthesia induced at intervals greater than several minutes after training does not produce retention deficits (McGaugh, 1966). It is therefore difficult to see how a modest increase in the effects of anesthesia due to KCl given one or several days after training could produce such a dramatic difference in retention. More to the point, Kapp and Schneider administered KCl to unanesthetized rats through cannulas that had previously been implanted in the ventral hippocampus. These injections not only produced retention deficits but other features of the effects of our technique as well.

D. Duration of EEG Disruption

Although none of the animals show gross signs of debilitation within several hours of surgery, the duration of disruption of normal EEG activity could be more extended. As a check on this possibility we implanted the recording-injection cannulas, injected KCl in the usual way and recorded the EEG at daily intervals thereafter. At the time of injection, KCl produced the typically prolonged period of electrical silence but, when recorded 1 day later from the unanesthetized animals, the EEG was entirely normal. This waning of effect of KCl was also found by Kapp and Schneider. Thus, insofar as the extremely gross measure of brain activity that is provided by the EEG may be taken as an index, the electrical effects of KCl have dissipated long before its effects on retention have done so.

E. Does KCl Increase Thirst?

The fifth remaining question of the seven that we will discuss in this section is concerned with the possibility that KCl injections increase thirst and thereby decrease suppression. This possibility embodies the assumption that a thirstier animal would be less likely to suppress and thereby forego water.

That this possibility is a very unlikely one is indicated by data obtained in an experiment by Auerbach (1971). In this experiment, animals were given the usual KCl or physiological saline injections but had not been given prior tone-shock pairings. When these animals were subsequently tested, no differences in drinking patterns were noted as a consequence of kind of injection. Furthermore, these animals were presented with the tone after they had made 100 licks as in the usual test session; because they had not had prior tone-shock pairings, however, this was the first time these animals had been exposed to the tone. Thus, this presentation of the tone was, for these rats, a novel stimulus; its effect was to produce a pause in the ongoing drinking. Once again, the kind of previous injection did not differentiate the animals with respect to the duration of this pause. One would expect the thirstier animal to be less disrupted by the novel stimulus, but this differential effect was not obtained.

F. GENERALITY OF INHIBITORY DEFICITS

The sixth question with which we will be concerned is the possibility that KCl injections produce an animal that is incapable of inhibiting its ongoing behavior once that behavior has been initiated. That this is not the case is suggested by the data that we have just described. As we indicated before, animals that had been given saline showed brief but reliable pauses in ongoing drinking upon the presentation of the tone for the first time; in these animals a novel stimulus produced a transient inhibition of ongoing behavior. Precisely the same effect was obtained in animals that had been given KCl. Thus, it is reasonable to conclude that both groups were equally distractable, and that KCl does not produce a general inability to inhibit ongoing behavior.

G. INHIBITION OF PROTEIN SYNTHESIS

The final question of the seven with which we are concerned is whether the effects of KCl on retention are related to inhibition of protein synthesis. Our initial interest in KCl was based on the fact that it, like puromycin, can produce electrical silence. If KCl, unlike puromycin, does not produce inhibition of protein synthesis, then it could at least be concluded that such inhibition was not a necessary condition for the induction of retention deficits. Unfortunately, we have no direct evidence bearing on this question; there are, however, several indirect indications that these effects cannot be attributed to inhibition of protein synthesis.

The first indication comes from reports (Bennett and Edelman, 1969; Ruscak, 1961) showing that, although KCl does produce inhibition of protein synthesis in rat cortex, both the extent and the duration of this attenuation is far less than that which is evidently required to produce retention deficits following injections of puromycin (see Flexner *et al.*, 1967). A more direct evaluation of the possible role of inhibition of protein synthesis has been reported by Lim *et al.* (1970). In these experiments it was found that KCl produced a moderate and relatively brief inhibition of synthesis in fish brain, but that this degree of inhibition could not account for the observed retention deficits. In general, then, there is at least circumstantial evidence to suggest that the effects of KCl cannot be attributed to inhibition of protein synthesis, and thus that inhibition is not a necessary condition for retention deficits. [This conclusion is in general agreement with that of Flexner *et al.* (1966), who found no retention deficits due to profound inhibition with acetoxycycloheximide.] On the other hand, electrical silence appears to be an element common to the retention deficits due to both KCl and puromycin.

IV. Temporal Gradient of Effect

One of the critical aspects of studies of the physiological bases of retention is the demonstration of a temporal dependency in the relationship between training and the introduction of a subsequent treatment. In general, it has been found that the greater the interval between training and the introduction of a disruptive event like electroconvulsive shock, the less the retention deficit that appears in a subsequent test (McGaugh, 1966). Data of this kind have been taken as an indicant of some kind of "consolidation" process. The intervals involved in these dependencies have been on the order of minutes. On the other hand, the comparable dependency obtained with puromycin is measured in days. This latter finding prompted Hughes (1969) to investigate the effect of variations in the time intervening between training and injection of KCl.

Different groups of animals were given tone-shock pairings, as previously described, and were then given intrahippocampal KCl injections 1, 3, 7, or 21 days later; all groups of animals were tested

4 days after injection. Hughes found large-order suppression deficits at all intervals; that is, there was no temporal dependency in the effect of KCl injected after training.

Hughes' data are important in at least two ways. First, they indicate that, with our technique, deficits can be obtained with injections that lie well beyond the usual "consolidation" interval. Second, these data highlight a major difference between the effects of KCl and puromycin, as studied by Flexner *et al.* (see the following section). Both of these points require further elaboration.

With respect to the first point of importance, Kapp and Schneider (1971) have reported that KCl injections (via implanted cannulas) *can* produce deficits interpretable as disrupted "consolidation" if such injections are given within a few seconds after training. In the Kapp and Schneider experiment, rats were given injections 10 seconds or 24 hours after suppression training like that which we have used. When retention was measured 4 days later, large-order deficits were obtained. However, the results from a second pair of groups given injections at these two posttraining intervals were different. These two groups were tested 21 days after injections, but only the animals given the posttraining injection at 24 hours showed recovery of suppression. Thus, recovery after 21 days was contingent on the longer interval between training and injection.

These results are significant for two reasons. First, they provide an independent replication of both the phenomenon first reported by Avis and Carlton and of the recovery from retention deficits that Hughes had previously reported (see below). Second, these data indicate that the action of KCl is dual: When given shortly after training, it can produce a deficit that is evidently permanent (i.e., from which there is no recovery), and it can also produce a transient deficit when given at longer intervals. Both of these facets of the action of KCl will be discussed in greater detail in a subsequent section.

The second aspect of Hughes' results that we singled out for comment was the fact that KCl, unlike puromycin, can produce a deficit even though given at essentially any posttraining interval. We will discuss the possible significance of this result in the next section.

V. Generalized Electrical Silence due to Hippocampal KCl

KCl produces deficits when injected into the hippocampus as much as 21 days after training. Although our primary interest is not in protein synthesis and retention, the fact is that puromycin does produce silence and retention deficits. These latter deficits occur only when puromycin, unlike KCl, is injected into the hippocampus less than 6 days after training. Furthermore, puromycin, injected into widely distributed brain areas in addition to the hippocampal area, produces deficits when given as much as 11–60 days after training. Thus, KCl injected into the hippocampus is (*a*) *unlike* puromycin in terms of effective train–inject interval when puromycin is injected into the hippocampus, but is (*b*) *like* puromycin when it is given at multiple brain sites.

The parallelism in the long-term effects of multiple puromycin and KCl injections prompted Avis (1969) to study the effects of hippocampal injections of KCl on EEG activity at sites other than hippocampus. That is, the lack of temporal gradient obtained with KCl might be due to the fact that widespread rather than localized electrical silence was obtained. Thus, the injections of KCl, although given at a particular locus, might functionally spread widely in the brain and thereby produce effects comparable to those produced by multiple injections of puromycin.

Avis found marked depression of EEG in all areas of the brain that he sampled (amygdala, caudate, dorsal hippocampus, thalamus, and frontal cortex). These results indicate that the effects of KCl are very unrestricted, and that the long intervals between training and injection at which KCl produces deficits may be related to this diffuseness of action. Furthermore, these data pose a question as to whether the suppression deficits are peculiarly due to injections into the hippocampus per se or whether such deficits can be obtained by injecting into essentially any area of the brain. Although Avis obtained some preliminary data indicating that this was not the case, a systematic answer to this question is yet to be provided.

Nonetheless, the data at hand indicate that KCl injected into the ventral hippocampus can produce widespread silence in other areas of the brain but, paradoxically, that silence directly induced in those areas may not produce a suppression deficit. There is, therefore, the suggestion of an anatomical specificity involved in these effects. Furthermore, these data indicate that, although electrical silence may be a sufficient condition for inducing deficits, it is certainly not necessary. That is, it is possible to obtain silence without a suppression deficit if silence is induced in loci other than the ventral hippocampus.

VI. Generality of the Deficits

Thus far we have described profound deficits in conditioned suppression that can be produced by the intracerebral injection of KCl. All of the experiments that we have summarized were designed to examine various aspects of this phenomenon, and all involved measurement of the lack of suppression of ongoing drinking. This limitation in behavioral technique poses two general questions. The first of these is whether the behavioral deficits are specific to conditioned suppression or can be generalized to other kinds of behavior. The second question has to do with whether the deficits can only be reflected in ongoing skeletal responding or whether they can also be found in other physiological measures that may reflect the fear that is presumably conditioned to the tone by pairing it with shock.

With respect to the first question, we have attempted to obtain deficits in the performance of a variety of other learned behaviors. These have involved complex discrimination problems and operant behavior maintained by a variety of schedules of reinforcement including discrimination problems and differential reinforcement of both high and low rates. Although unusual behavior was occasionally seen in an animal that had been given KCl, none of these techniques proved to reliably discriminate animals given KCl from those given saline.

These failures can be reasonably attributed neither to the several days of training involved nor to overtraining. As far as duration of training is concerned, we have already noted that deficits due to KCl can be obtained as much as 21 days after the conditioning of suppression; thus, the relatively longer periods involved in the other learning techniques does not seem to be the basis of their insensitivity. With respect to overtraining, we explicitly varied the number of tone-shock pairings involved in the conditioned suppression procedure and also varied the relative distribution of these pairings. KCl was injected in the usual way and produced large-order deficits of the usual magnitude regardless of both distribution and number of tone-shock pairings (up to 40).

Further confirmation of the specific sensitivity of conditioned suppression to the effects of KCl was found in a study in which there was an explicit attempt to match responses that were rewarded, on the one hand, with those that were suppressed by electric shock, on the other. In particular, the animals were either rewarded for emitting a particular response or punished when that response was spontaneously emitted; other animals were neither rewarded nor punished. (The response involved was the poking of the rat's snout through a 2-in. diameter hole placed in the center of one of the shorter walls of the experimental chamber. The number of such responses in a 4-minute period was recorded.)

On the day following training the animals were anesthetized and given the usual injections of either isotonic saline or KCl. After an intervening 3 days, they were tested for the effects of the prior reward or punishment. This experiment thus involves the same temporal parameters that were used in the basic conditioned suppression experiments. The results are shown in Fig. 5.

As the figure indicates, the animals that had been rewarded and given saline injections emitted more responses than those that had not been rewarded and had also been given saline (the left hand values in the top panel of the figure). All that this result indicates is that prior reward will inflate the tendency of an animal to emit a rewarded response. The figure also indicates that KCl injections had no effect on this inflation of the tendency to respond (the values at the right of the upper portion of the figure). In contrast, the data in the bottom panel of the figure indicate that the animals that were shocked and given saline showed a large-order suppression of the tendency to respond, and that this suppression was reliably attenuated by KCl injections. Thus, an increase in the tendency to respond due to reward is unaffected by KCl and the resultant electrical silence, whereas the same injections markedly attenuate the suppression of the tendency to emit this same response.

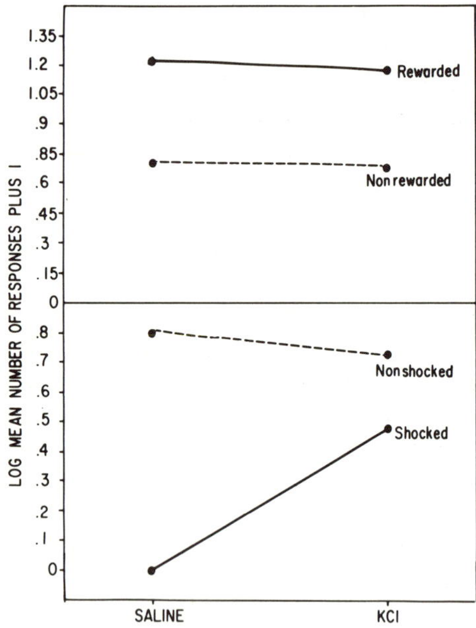

Fig. 5. Effects of KCl or saline injections on number of previously rewarded or punished responses.

In yet another experiment, Auerbach (1971) obtained data showing that animals not given tone-shock pairings and given injections of saline learned to approach the drinking tube more rapidly, i.e., the times to make contact with the tube were consistently less in the test session than in the initial session of the usual series. This index of learning was not reliably altered by KCl, as would be expected from the results of the experiment just described.

In a third experiment we altered the basic apparatus so that the drinking tube was made available only after the animal had depressed a lever inserted into the chamber. (Lever presses retracted a panel that blocked access to the tube mounted outside the chamber.) The animals were trained to emit 10 lever presses to receive their daily access to the drinking tube. Once their performance had stabilized, they were then given the usual tone-shock pairings (while undeprived and with the lever withdrawn) followed by KCl or saline injections.

All animals were then tested following the standard 3-day postoperative interval. Each animal was placed in the chamber (24 hours water deprived) and allowed to emit 10 responses, which provided access to the tube; once the rat had made 100 licks, the tone was turned on and the time required for 10 additional licks was recorded. The median time required for the 10 lever presses was 144.5 seconds in animals that had been given KCl and 259.8 seconds in those given saline; this difference, while not reliable, may reflect an attenuation of fear due to KCl and is certainly opposite to the effect one would expect if KCl produced a general retention deficit. In contrast to the data for lever pressing, the values for time to emit 10 licks in the tone showed marked differences; the median for the animals given KCl was 4.6 seconds and 191.2 seconds for those given saline, with no overlap between these sets of suppression times.

The second question that we raised above was whether the suppression deficits due to KCl would also be reflected in other physiological changes that are attendant upon the pairing of a stimulus with shock. One aspect of this question was investigated by Avis (1969), who measured the heart rate changes that occur during a tone that has previously been paired with shock. Avis used essentially the same procedure that we have used in the conditioned suppression experiments except that cardiac changes, rather than suppression of drinking, was used as the measure of the effect of KCl injections.

The results of this experiment are shown in Fig. 6. Avis found that animals that had been given tone-shock pairings 1 day prior to intrahippocampal injections of saline showed cardiac deceleration when the tone was presented in a test session given on the fourth day after

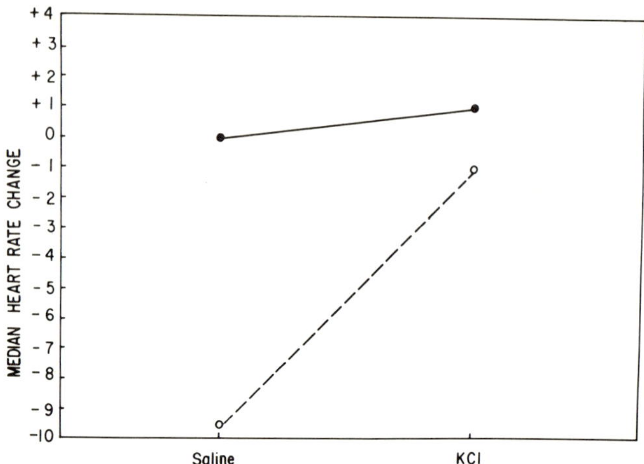

Fig. 6. The effects of shock (- - -) *vs.* no shock (—) and KCl *vs.* saline on subsequent changes in heart rate. Tone-shock pairings were given the day before hippocampal injections of either saline or KCl and 4 days before the change in heart rate was observed during the presence of tone.

injections (the shock-saline group in the figure). In contrast, the animals that had not been given tone-shock pairings and comparable saline injections (the no shock-saline group) showed essentially no change in heart rate. More to the point, the unshocked animals that were also given KCl failed to show a deceleration as did those that *had* been shocked and given KCl.

These results are in complete agreement with our previous findings concerning the interaction of KCl treatment with conditioned suppression, but they also amplify these findings in that they indicate that the deficits are not peculiar to measurements based on the suppression of ongoing behavior. Rather, they suggest that KCl injections can eliminate at least one physiological consequence of prior conditioning and that, therefore, the lack of suppression of drinking is a reflection of a lack of conditioned fear.

Recent experiments by Auerbach and Carlton (1971) point in the same direction. Briefly, they established that an increase in corticosterone extracted from blood or adrenal cortex was obtained when animals were exposed to the tone that had previously been paired with shock. (The animals were decapitated immediately after tone presentation.) This increase was essentially eliminated if intracerebral injections of KCl intervened between conditioning and subsequent test. This result once more suggests that the effects of KCl are not specific to deficits in the suppression of ongoing behavior but may be due to the more general deficit in conditioned fear that is reflected in the lack of such suppression.

VII. Permanence of the Suppression Deficit

One obvious question about the effects of KCl on suppression is whether the deficits it produces are permanent ones. Hughes (1969) addressed himself to this question by first giving animals the standard suppression training, injecting KCl or saline 1 day later, and varying the time that intervened between these injections and subsequent tests. Hughes found that, within 21 days, essentially complete recovery occurred. In supplementary experiments, we have confirmed Hughes' basic finding; the data from our experiments are given in Fig. 7.

One way of conceptualizing this effect of KCl is in terms of a tape recorder in which the tape ("memory") has been made but in which the volume control for playback ("retrieval") has been turned off (by KCl). Furthermore, we can conceive of recovery as being due to the gradual return of the volume control to its normal setting. Thus, recovery represents a return to normal of a retrieval process that controls behavior.

If the effects of KCl are viewed in this way, then one can ask a testable question about the effects of *retraining*. Regardless of precisely how much, if any, additional information is added to the tape in retraining, the availability of that information should vary with the

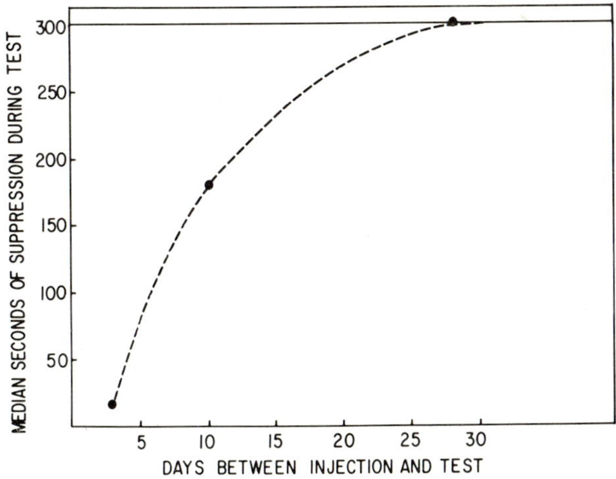

FIG. 7. Median suppression time (seconds) during the tone at different intervals after KCl (- - -) or saline (—) injections into the hippocampus. Injections were administered 24 hours after original tone-shock pairing.

interval between turning off the volume control and later retesting. That is, just as the extent of suppression varies as a function of the interval between injection and test, so should the suppression in *re*testing after interpolated retraining. Finally, one might expect that, if additional information is recorded as a result of retraining, then recovery from KCl should be somewhat more rapid in retest than it is in test; this expectation follows from an extension of the tape recorder idea to the supposition that, with increased information due to retraining, a relatively lower setting of the volume control would be adequate for retrieval and, therefore, suppression.

We examined this possibility by plotting retest data from a variety of experiments as a function of the injection–retest interval and found that there was indeed a temporal dependency in the extent of suppression subsequent to retraining. These data are shown in Fig. 8.

The data in this figure were taken from a number of different experiments in which the intervals between injection and initial testing, as well as between initial testing and subsequent retraining, varied. However, in all cases except one, retraining and subsequent retesting were separated by 4 days. As the figure indicates, there is a correlation between the time that elapsed after the administration of KCl and the subsequent suppression obtained with retesting that followed interpolated retraining. Furthermore, as might also be expected from the tape recorder analogy, the rate of rise in this function is somewhat more rapid than that in Fig. 7.

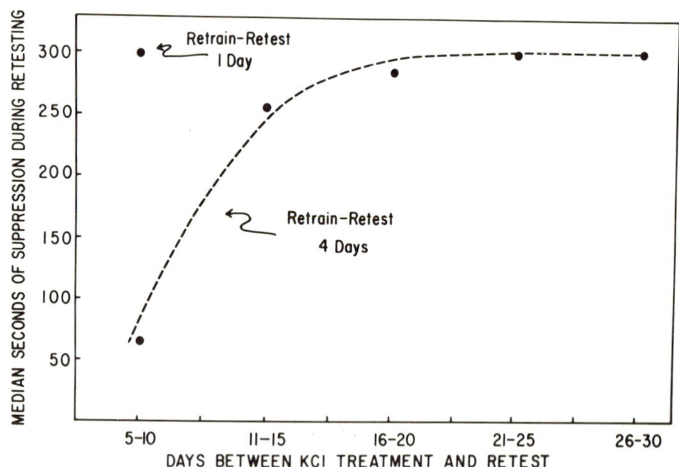

FIG. 8. Median suppression time during the tone when rats were retested at various intervals after KCl injection. As noted in the figure, the retraining and retesting were separated by 4 days except as noted.

There is, however, one value in Fig. 8 that is clearly anomalous; this point is at the upper left. In this case, high levels of suppression were obtained at a short interval between KCl and retraining, although the other values in the figure suggest that low levels of suppression should have been obtained. This value differs from all others in that retesting was on the day following retraining, whereas in all other cases retesting occurred 4 days later. This finding suggested to us that there might be a short-term process that would maintain suppression and that was relatively immune to the effects of KCl. The rationale for this speculation is elaborated below.

VIII. Short- and Long-Term Processes

In the preceding section, we described data that provided a basis for supposing that there might be a short-term process that could lead to suppression but was independent of the effect of KCl. That is, animals retrained and retested on the next day showed suppression at a time when such suppression would not be expected on the basis of data obtained from other animals; these latter animals had been retested on the fourth rather than the next day after retraining. Thus, there might be some process that would mediate suppression for only a day or so and wane thereafter.

This possibility is schematized in Fig. 9, which combines a hypothetical short-term process, the dashed curve, with a schematic representation of recovery from the effects of KCl, the solid curve.

The two processes are assumed to summate in determining suppression. Thus, with KCl on day 0, suppression would be low in the test on day 3. If the animals were than *re*trained on day 4, the short-term

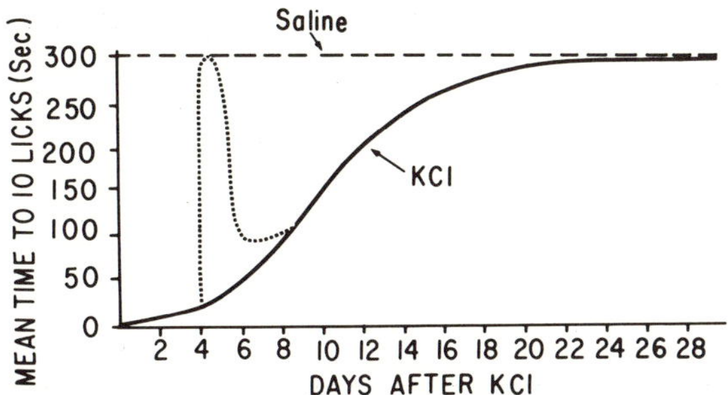

FIG. 9. Schematic diagram representing the fact that recovery from the effects of KCl occurs (—) and the hypothetical short-term process (- - -) that is proposed to account for a rat's ability to suppress 1 day after retraining in spite of the fact that KCl is active.

process would be initiated; if these animals were retested shortly there-after (e.g., day 5), suppression would be obtained. On the other hand, if retesting were given at longer intervals, levels of suppression would be a function of the recovery process. Thus, with long retrain–retest intervals, the retest function shown in Fig. 8 should be essentially the same as the recovery function in Fig. 7. As, in fact, it is.

This conceptualization generates three kinds of experiments, each of which are described below.

In the first of these, animals were initially trained, injected and tested in the usual way. The animals were then given additional tone-shock pairings a few hours after the initial test. They were then retested at various times after this retraining. In this experiment, the animals that had been given either saline or KCl were repeatedly tested at 1, 6, 24, 48, and again at 96 hours.

The results of this experiment are shown in Fig. 10. The values at the left indicate that the usual effect of KCl in the initial test was obtained (i.e., a large-order deficit in suppression). The figure also indicates that retraining led to substantial suppression both 1 and 6 hours later in the animals given KCl but that this effect waned so that, by 48 and 96 hours, the animals had returned to the low level of suppression that had characterized their behavior *prior* to retraining. The early suppression presumably reflects the action of a short-term process; because this process wanes and because recovery has not occurred, a lack of suppression subsequently appears.

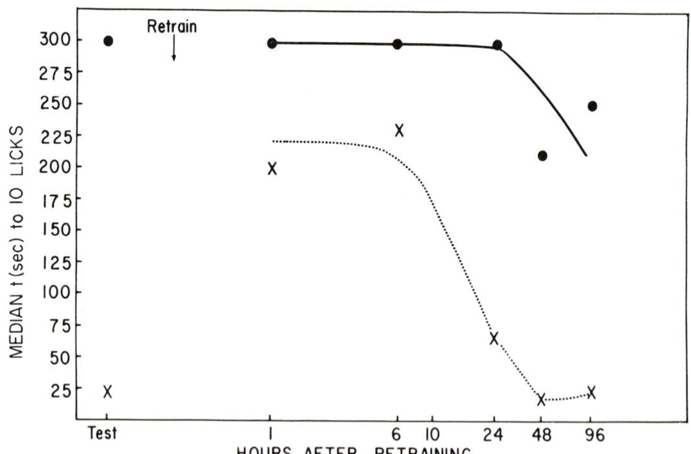

FIG. 10. The effect of KCl (- - -) or saline (——) given 1 day after tone-shock pairings on suppression time during initial test and subsequent retests at various intervals after interpolated retraining.

It is important to bear in mind that the later low level of suppression was obtained *despite* the fact that retraining had intervened. These data are, however, complicated by the fact that retesting was repeated in the same animals and are, therefore, contaminated by extinction of the tendency to suppress; this decline in suppression due to extinction is reflected in the data from the saline animals (see Fig. 10).

An obvious way to avoid this contamination would be to test different groups of animals at different times after retraining. The procedure in the experiment designed to examine the rcle of extinction in the saline animals was exactly the same as that in the previous experiment, except that different, rather than the same, groups of animals were tested 6 *or* 48 hours after retraining.

The results of the experiment are given in Fig. 11. It is once again clear that the animals given KCl are capable of suppression when they are retested shortly after retraining (i.e., 6 hours later). In contrast, the second group of animals fails to show suppression when the hypothetical short-term process has declined but recovery has not occurred (i.e., when they are retested 48 hours after retraining).

A particularly important aspect of this same experiment is the result of the histological comparison of the animals in the two groups. Although suppression times clearly discriminated the animals retested after 6 hours from those retested after 48 hours, damage did not (the median VODs were 14.8 and 16.0, respectively).

Yet a third way of examining the possibility of a short-term process

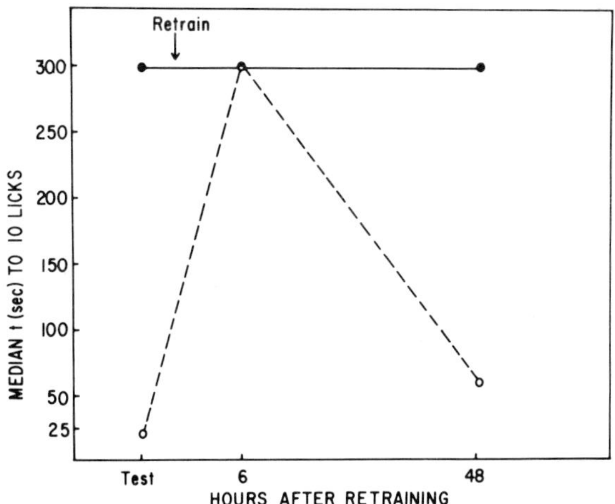

Fig. 11. The effects of KCl (- - -) and saline (——) given 1 day after tone-shock pairings on suppression time during initial test and subsequent retest either 6 hours or 48 hours after interpolated retraining.

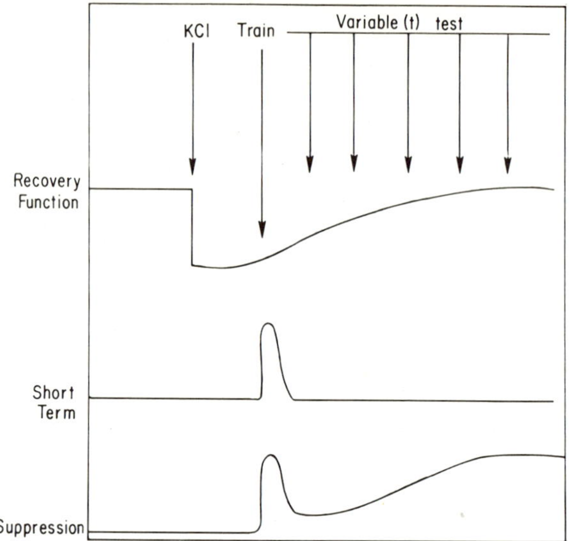

FIG. 12. Schematic representation of the effects of KCl in conjunction with a short-term process which functions briefly after training. The bottom curve depicts the levels of suppression to be expected when rats are given KCl, exposed to tone-shock pairings 3 days later and tested at various times after training.

is schematized in Fig. 12. In this figure, we have assumed that the action of KCl in producing deficits in suppression is not dependent on the time at which it is injected relative to the time of training. That is, we are assuming that KCl can act both proactively and retroactively to produce attenuated retrieval; this is one assumption that we examine in the experiment to be described below.

A second assumption, which we also evaluate, is that there is indeed a short-term process that can override the effects of KCl on suppression. Accordingly, Fig. 12 shows the injection of KCl, subsequent training and testing at various times thereafter, as well as the operation of a recovery process in conjunction with a short-term process that begins with training. The interaction of these latter two processes leads to the expectation that there should be large-order suppression shortly after the training that follows KCl, but that this suppression should wane only to gradually reappear as recovery takes place.

The results of an experiment designed to evaluate these possibilities is shown in Fig. 13. In this experiment, animals were injected with KCl and the usual electrical silence recorded. The animals were trained 3 days later and different groups were then tested 1, 3, 28, or 42 days thereafter. As the figure clearly indicates, suppression occurred 1 day

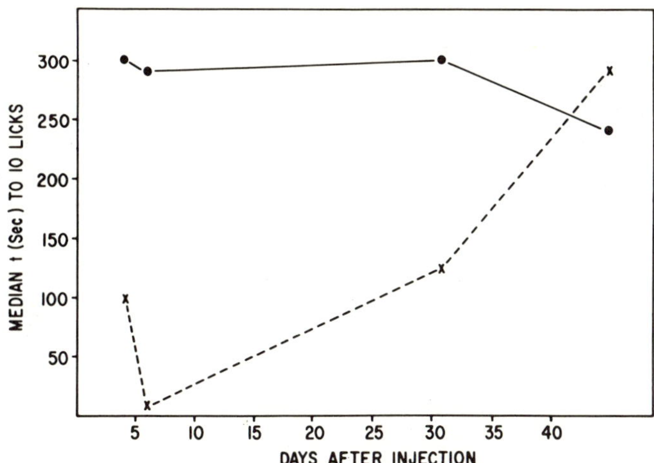

FIG. 13. Mean suppression times of rats given KCl or saline, exposed to tone-shock pairings 3 days later and tested at one of four intervals after KCl (- - -) or saline (—) treatment.

after training, presumably as a manifestation of a short-term process that is immune to KCl; suppression was again obtained at 42 days, presumably as a manifestation of recovery. Between these two times, lower levels of suppression were obtained because of the absence of a short-term process and because of incomplete recovery.

There are two features of these data that are especially important. First, the median suppression time obtained 3 days after injection (i.e., 1 day after training) approximates that which would be expected from the data in Figs. 10 and 11; the difference between this value and that obtained 6 days after injection (i.e., 3 days after training) is nonetheless a reliable one ($p < 0.02$ by two-tailed Mann-Whitney U-test). Second, recovery in this experiment is slow (e.g., compare the 32-day value in Fig. 13 with the value obtained at the longest interval in Fig. 7). This differential rate of recovery may reflect a proactive action of KCl that attenuates total input during training. If this were the case, then, in the context of the tape recorder model, one would expect that a greater return of the volume control toward normal (i.e., longer recovery time) would be required for full retrieval of the recorded signal.

IX. Some Final Considerations

The manipulations that we have discussed here are patently gross ones, although not substantially more so than those involved in other widely used techniques, whether these involve lesions, stimulation, or injection into brain. Nevertheless, it was the fact of this grossness that prompted our various control procedures, themselves something of a rarity in studies involving direct injection into the brain. These controls indicate that the effects of KCl cannot reasonably be attributed solely to inhibition of protein synthesis or hypertonicity, that they do show a temporal dependency on duration of silence, and they are surprisingly specific at a behavioral level.

This specificity raises a general question about studies purporting to bear on the problem of memory. In addition to a general lack of any histological or EEG considerations, where these are pertinent, such studies typically involve only one behavioral measure. Thus, it is not clear whether deficits represent an attenuation of memory, in some generally meaningful sense of that word, or whether they bear on only certain kinds of retention. If our studies are any indication, the use of single behavioral techniques is a dangerous procedure for, despite the diffuseness of the effects of KCl, the behavioral specificity and the correlated changes in cardiac and steroid activity indicate that we are justified in saying only that we are dealing with retention of fear rather than a more general process called memory.

Such specificity is not new, although the instances of it seem to have attracted less attention than they have deserved. For example, Chevalier (1965) reported that an attenuation of shock-suppressed motor activity could be obtained with another gross technique, electro-convulsive shock (ECS). He also reported that the decline in activity due to exploration, "habituation-suppressed" activity, was not attenuated by ECS administered in a manner identical to that used in the shock experiment. These latter data were reported in a footnote in Chevalier's paper; one is left to wonder why ECS should attenuate one kind of memory but not another, just as our data pose the same kind of question about KCl. It is that question to which we turn now.

A. The Concept of Potentiated Lesions[2]

The effects of KCl, except when it is given almost immediately after training, are clearly not on an encoding mechanism but are on some sort of retrieval process. We know this because recovery occurs. We have likened this process to the turning off of the volume control of a tape recorder.

Generally speaking, KCl acts as if it were producing a lesion in the

---

[2] The idea that the effects of KCl might be mediated by an interaction of electrical silence with localized lesion was suggested to us by Russell Leaf.

hippocampus. Although it is not doing so exclusively because of the extent of histologically determined damage, KCl may be producing a local "reversible lesion," of the kind obtained with cortical KCl, without producing massive tissue damage. The major fact that mitigates against this possibility is that the duration of such cortically induced effects are not measured in weeks, as are those that we have described.

Although extent of histologically determined tissue loss cannot account for the effects we have described in any direct way, the fact remains that KCl *does* produce damage. It may be that local insult, itself ineffective, may render the brain area in which that damage occurs hypersensitive to KCl, regardless of the extent of damage, and thereby lead to a prolongation of the effects of induced electrical silence.

A related kind of hypersensitivity was reported by Teitelbaum and Cytawa (1965), who studied the effects of cortical applications of KCl given to rats that had previously sustained lesions of the lateral hypothalamus and had recovered from the aphagia and adipsia that these lesions produce. They found that cortical KCl reinstated the typical lateral hypothalamic syndrome, and that full recovery did not occur until 10–27 days had elapsed. They also reported a comparable reinstatement of the hyperreactivity induced by prior septal lesions.

Teitelbaum and Cytawa suggest that, with recovery, the activity of the residual tissue that remains following lesioning could normally be facilitated by those structures that are later inactivated by cortical KCl. Such inactivation would therefore reinstate the prior syndrome for a period corresponding to the duration of abnormality due to KCl.

A version of this concept could be applied to our data as an alternative to the idea that a lesion induced hypersensitivity to KCl that is localized in that area where damage occurs. This alternative embodies the assumption that extrahippocampal tissue is somehow "engaged" by the lesion, and that this tissue would normally provide facilitation sufficient to override the lesion effect were it not for the concurrent depression due to KCl.

Both the alternative suggested by the Teitelbaum and Cytawa data and the hypothesis concerning localized hypersensitivity suggest that KCl effectively potentiates the effect of a small lesion that would otherwise go undetected. This concept accounts for the specificity of the behavioral deficits in a straightforward way: The specificity inheres, not in the KCl-induced silence, but in the locus of the lesions induced by the injection. But just as the concept of potentiated lesions accounts for specificity, it poses a major question.

Why should there have been a lack of effect of KCl on other behavioral indices? The resolution of this problem may simply lie in the fact that our earlier studies of other behaviors involved techniques relatively insensitive to hippocampal damage. We were, at that time, looking at the effects of KCl in terms of a general memory deficit, not hippocampal damage, and therefore expected to find effects on other retention as massive as that on conditioned suppression. That we failed to find such reliable effects may reflect the fact that these other techniques were simply insufficiently subtle to detect differences. Consistent with this possibility is the general finding that hippocampal damage is most reliably detected by techniques involving shock-induced suppression (see Grossman, 1967). Alternatively, the concept of potentiated lesions may be utterly wrong. In any case, the question can now be simply answered because, after the fact, it can be simply stated: Any behavioral index that is consistently sensitive to hippocampal lesions should be sensitive to hippocampal KCl; any index that is reliably sensitive to large lesions in *other* brain loci should be sensitive to KCl injected into such loci.

B. The Problem of Short-Term Retention

We have already suggested that some kind of hypersensitivity to KCl is induced by the small lesions concomitant with injection, and that these potentiated lesions account for the behavioral specificity we have observed. Short-term retrieval persists despite such disruptions; this maintenance of retrieval may be based on that tissue that is spared. That is, short-term retrieval may require less functionally normal tissue than does long-term retrieval.

This possibility was suggested to us by a consideration of the clinical literature concerning memory defects in man. The anterograde effects of traumatic head injury often contain a transitional period in which the patient may be able to retrieve new information for several hours but not thereafter (see, e.g., Barbizet, 1970). If the course of recovery from injury represents the return of progressively more normally functioning tissue (cf., recovery from KCl), then this transitional state implies that short-term retrieval can be normal with relatively less intact tissue. Although we have not examined the literature critically on this point, it also appears that a condition of short-term without long-term retrieval may be a fraction of the memory disorders associated with aging. Again, this differential may be due to a differential effect of tissue loss.

The point about memory defects in aging raises another possibility. Just as it is possible to usefully analyze the regulation of feeding from an ontogenetic point of view (Teitelbaum, 1971), the problem of retrieval and its possible dependency on functional tissue can be examined in this way. Feigley and Spear (1970) have reported on the beginnings of such a program; they found that retrieval in very young rats showed a much greater decline with time than did that of adult rats. This finding supports our conjecture, if it is assumed that less functionally intact tissue was available for retrieval in the immature animals. (This result is the complement of what may be seen at the opposite end of the spectrum with aging; it therefore suggests that the study of old as well as young rats could be a profitable one.)

There is yet another way to examine the short-term process and that is in terms of the "incubation of fear" and the so-called "Kamin-effect" (Brush, 1964). These transient phenomena have been little applied to the problem of memory (see, however, Pinel and Cooper, 1966). Emphasis on this mode of analysis raises a question about the role of factors not usually considered in the context of memory (e.g., steroids) as they may modulate retrieval (see Brush and Levine, 1966). In this context, it would be important to amplify the results of Auerbach and Carlton (1971), who found an absence of steroid mobilization at long intervals after training and KCl; the possibility remains that mobilization is possible for a short period following training, despite the action of KCl.

C. Relevance to Pathological Memory in Man

Thus far we have almost exclusively emphasized retrieval processes. But, as the work of Kapp and Schneider has made clear, KCl can produce retention deficits without recovery if it is administered early enough following training. KCl can thus be added to the catalog of treatments indicating that the brain must be normal if some sort of "consolidation" process is to take place.

The addition of this temporal dependency means that the three basic clinical phenomena involved in the pathology of human memory can be brought into the laboratory via the action of one agent, KCl. Thus, KCl can produce (*1*) retrograde amnesia, (*2*) protracted but reversible retrieval failures even when given at long intervals after the "to-be-remembered" event, and (*3*) a short-term process that maintains retrieval to be followed by recovery at longer intervals.

There is yet a fourth aspect of such clinical phenomena that may also be produced by KCl. If KCl is given very shortly after training, there is a retention deficit *without* recovery, unlike the deficits with recovery that occur with longer intervals between training and injection. We do not know, unfortunately, whether KCl given shortly after training would leave a short-term retrieval process intact, because Kapp and Schneider measured retention only after 4 or 21 days. If however, such a short-term process could be demonstrated at brief training–injection intervals, the resultant sequence would be retrieval followed by loss without recovery, a situation analogous to the clinical picture attendant upon temporal lobe lesions (see Milner, 1966).

That analogs of these clinical phenomena can be produced in the laboratory is, nonetheless, a hopeful sign. Because of the wider latitude of study possible with laboratory techniques, we may be in a better position to profitably analyze both pathological, as well as normal, retention processes. For example, our data dictated a conjecture about potentiated lesions that could account for the rather bewildering array of different but very specific retention deficits sometimes seen in different patients following traumatic head injury. If such injury can be assumed to induce a condition comparable to that produced by KCl, plus some minor focal injury, then a prolonged but specific deficit, with recovery, would be expected to ensue.

Acknowledgments

We are deeply indebted to Dr. Richard Katz and Mr. Sanford Waxman for their assistance.

References

Auerbach, P. P. (1971). Electrical silence in the CNS: Interference with conditioned suppression. M.S. Thesis, Rutgers Univ., New Brunswick, New Jersey.

Auerbach, P., and Carlton, P. L. (1971). Retention deficits correlated with a deficit in the corticoid response to stress. *Science* **173**, 1148–1149.

Avis, H. H. (1969). The effects of temporary disruption of the electrical activity of the brain on retention. Ph.D. Thesis, Rutgers Univ., New Brunswick, New Jersey.

Avis, H. H., and Carlton, P. L. (1968). Retrograde amnesia caused by hippocampal spreading depression. *Science* **161**, 73–75.

Barbizet, J. (1970). "Human Memory and Its Pathology." Freeman, San Francisco, California.

Barondes, S. H., and Cohen, H. D. (1966). Puromycin effect on successive phases of memory storage. *Science* **151**, 594–595.

Bennett, G. S., and Edelman, G. M. (1969). Amino acid incorporation into rat brain proteins during spreading cortical depression. *Science* **163**, 393–395.

Brush, F. R. (1964). Avoidance learning as a function of time after fear conditioning and unsignalled shock. *Psychonomic Science* **1**, 405–406.

Brush, F. R., and Levine, S. (1966). Adreno-cortical activity and avoidance learning as a function of time after fear conditioning. *Physiology & Behavior* **1**, 309–311.

Bureš, J., and Burešová, O. (1960). The use of Leao's spreading cortical depression in research on conditioned reflexes. *Electroencephalography and Clinical Neurophysiology Supplement* 13, 359–376.

Chevalier, J. A. (1965). Permanence of amnesia after a single posttrial electroconvulsive seizure. *Journal of Comparative and Physiological Psychology* 59, 125–127.

Feigley, D. A., and Spear, N. E. (1970). Effect of age and punishment condition on long-term retention by the rat of active and passive avoidance learning. *Journal of Comparative and Physiological Psychology* 73, 515–526.

Flexner, L. B., Flexner, J. B., and Roberts, R. B. (1966). Stages of memory in mice treated with acetoxycycloheximide before or immediately after learning. *Proceedings of the National Academy of Sciences, U. S.* 56, 730–735.

Flexner, L. B., Flexner, J. B., and Roberts, R. B. (1967). Memory in mice analyzed with antibiotics. *Science* 155, 1377–1383.

Grossman, S. P. (1967). "A Textbook of Physiological Psychology." Wiley, New York.

Hughes, R. A. (1969). Retrograde amnesia in rats produced by hippocampal injections of potassium chloride: Gradient of effect and recovery. *Journal of Comparative and Physiological Psychology* 68, 637–644.

Kapp, B. S., and Schneider, A. M. (1971). Selective recovery from retrograde amnesia produced by hippocampal spreading depression. *Science* 173, 1149–1151.

Lim, R., Brink, J. J., and Agranoff, B. W. (1970). Further studies on the effects of blocking agents on protein synthesis in goldfish brains. *Journal of Neurochemistry* 17, 1637–1649.

McGaugh, J. L. (1966). Time dependent processes in memory storage. *Science* 153, 1351–1358.

Milner, B. (1966). Amnesia following operation on the temporal lobes. *In* "Amnesia" (C. W. M. Whitty and O. L. Zangwill, eds.), pp. 109–133. Appleton, New York.

Pinel, J. P. J., and Cooper, R. M. (1966). Incubation and its implications for the interpretation of the ECS gradient effect. *Psychonomic Science* 6, 123–124.

Ruscak, M. (1961). Incorporation of ^{35}S-methionine into proteins of cerebral cortex in rats during spreading EEG depression. *Physiologia Bohemoslovenica* 9, 235–248.

Teitelbaum, P. (1971). The encephalization of hunger. *In* "Progress in Physiological Psychology" (E. Stellar and J. M. Sprague, eds.), Vol. 4, pp. 319–350. Academic Press, New York.

Teitelbaum, P., and Cytawa, J. (1965). Spreading depression and recovery from lateral hypothalamic damage. *Science* 147, 61–63.

Mechanisms of Electrodermal Adaptations for Locomotion, Manipulation, or Defense

Robert Edelberg

*College of Medicine and Dentistry of New Jersey,
Rutgers Medical School, New Brunswick, New Jersey*

I. Introduction

Although it has been suggested that the galvanic skin reflex, or *electrodermal activity* in general (EDA), may serve to sensitize tactile receptors by direct efferent modulation (Edelberg, 1961b; Wilcott, 1966), the prevailing view is that it reflects activity of the sweat gland (McCleary, 1950; Martin and Venables, 1966). Sudorific activity, by altering hydration, affects surface friction (Adams and Hunter, 1969), the resistance of the skin to abrasion (Wilcott, 1966), the pliability of the integument during movement of the underlying muscles, and, of course, evaporative heat loss. These have consequences on the effectiveness of a wide variety of motor and perceptual-motor activity, and as such may be considered in the light of their adaptive significance.

Darrow (1936) regarded EDA as reflecting a sudorific process which serves to facilitate grasping and tactile manipulation. Lacey (1959) concluded that EDA may serve the transactional process between an individual and his environment by facilitating intake of information. Despite these adaptive interpretations, the vast majority of behavioral studies that utilize this measure proceed on the assumption that it reflects "emotion" in some nonspecific way, and more often that it indicates anxiety or tension. Perhaps because the efforts of many behavioral scientists have been applied to the study of misbehavior rather than behavior, that is, to the nature of emotional problems and mental disease, their attention has for the most part been directed toward fear, anxiety, tension, or defensiveness. Thus electrodermal activity has to a considerable extent become identified with tension or anxiety, despite the fact that in the rare laboratory situation in which the subject enjoys himself, EDA may be at its peak. A perusal of the electrodermal literature shows that stimuli have overwhelmingly consisted of sudden loud noises, electrical shocks, mental arithmetic (aversive conditioning to this stimulus is apparently extinguished very slowly), cold pressor exposure, emotionally loaded words, etc. The use of such stimuli to the exclusion of the large array of potentially appetitive stimuli available to the experimenter surely implies some bias in his interpretation of changes in this measure. True, there have been occasional demonstrations (e.g., Shock and Coombs, 1937) showing that EDA occurs in response to pleasant as well as unpleasant stimuli, but these have been given scant attention. One notable exception is seen in the writings of Berlyne (1966) who defends the role of EDA in exploratory behavior.

Even if we discount the possibility that EDA directly modifies tactile sensitivity, the various effects brought about by sweat gland activity alone may clearly have advantages for mechanical protection, for locomotion, or for manipulation. An effectively functioning organism should appropriately call forth these functions according to situational requirements. Recent work (Edelberg, 1970, 1971b, 1972b) has, in fact, demonstrated qualitative differences in EDA according to the nature of the overt behavior.

This article is concerned with an examination of the specificity of these adaptations and especially with the nature of the peripheral mechanism by which they are differentially reflected in the electrodermal pattern. It will concern itself primarily with sudomotor activity, although some evidence exists to suggest that vascular processes may contribute directly or indirectly to the electrical properties which are commonly monitored (Schicht and Edelberg, unpublished data). A model of the electrodermal system will be developed on the basis of evidence from comparative physiology and behavior, central neural mechanisms, and peripheral physiology. This model will emphasize the central modulation of skin hydration to achieve an optimal state for the particular type of behavior called for or anticipated. The control of skin hydration will be shown to depend not only upon modulation of sweat secretion, but upon the variable rate of sweat reabsorption through an epidermal membrane. It will be argued that in the human, the water permeability of this membrane is under independent tonic neural control, and that variation in the tonic state of this membrane influences the waveform of both the potential and resistance response. The waveform, in particular the recovery limb of the conductance or resistance response, will accordingly be shown to carry information about the qualitative nature of the adaptation. The advantages of increased sweat reabsorption for manipulative activity and of its inhibition for defensive behavior will be highlighted.

It is perhaps in order, in view of the prevailing confusion in terminology, to outline the system to be used in this article. In recent years, a group of active investigators in this area have attempted to arrive at a measure of standardization; their recommendations are adopted here. The traditional terms, *psychogalvanic reflex* (PGR) and *galvanic skin reflex* or *response* (GSR), were considered too ambiguous, or even misleading, and the term *electrodermal response* (EDR), is replacing the older ones. This is a generic term which may refer to either conductance, resistance, or potential responses. An additional term that is even more general since it includes tonic activity as well as phasic changes, *electrodermal activity* (EDA), will be used as well. It was further agreed, in the interest of clarity, to use terms that indicate whether the measurement is of a response amplitude or of a tonic level, and whether it is one of conductance, resistance, or potential. The terms that accomplish this are: *skin conductance level* (SCL), *skin conductance response* (SCR), *skin resistance level* (SRL), *skin resistance response* (SRR), *skin potential level* (SPL), and *skin poten-*

tial response (SPR). Here "level" refers to an average value of the baseline between responses, while "response" refers to the amplitude of the change from base level just before onset of the response to the maximum conductance (or minimum resistance) reached at the peak of the change, usually 2 to 3 seconds after the onset.

Unlike the case for conductance or resistance, the potential response which is another concomitant of sudomotor activity may be negative, positive, or biphasic, and the term SPR is therefore frequently preceded by a notation of its polarity. For a biphasic response, the negative SPR, which almost always occurs first, is the amplitude of the potential change from onset to the peak of the negative-going deflection, while the positive SPR is usually measured as the potential difference between onset of the entire response and the most positive deflection of the complex. Like the conductance response, both the positive and negative SPR amplitudes are usually, though not always, highly correlated (within subjects) with the magnitude of the associated evolution of sweat (Wilcott, 1962b).

Finally, a new term, *neurodermal,* has been suggested (Edelberg, 1972a) for use in discussing this response system in a biological-behavioral sense, i.e., when its electrical manifestations are not relevant. The electrical effects are in this sense seen merely as epiphenomena of biological activity whose actual function is to alter the state of the skin for survival purposes.

The resistance measurements described in this article were for the most part made with a constant current bridge that applied 8 μA through a 1 cm^2 site, the circuit being completed via a large inactive arm electrode. Conductance measurements were made with a constant voltage bridge that imposed 0.75 V across two active sites in series. Skin potentials were measured between an active site and an inactive reference on the ear or forearm using silver-silver chloride electrodes and DC amplification. For a more comprehensive treatment of the electrical properties of the skin, their measurement and their physiological origins, the reader is referred to papers by Martin and Venables (1966), Montagu and Coles (1966), Venables and Martin (1967), Wilcott (1967a), Fowles and Venables (1970a), and Edelberg (1967, 1971a, 1972a).

II. Neurodermal Activity and Adaptive Behavior

A. Adaptive Requirements

Neurodermal activity is assumed to occur because it is of use to the organism in responding to the actual or *perceived* demands of the environment. Some of these demands are homeostatic, others of a more dynamic nature. In most instances there is an anticipatory aspect to this response which reflects the particular individual's assessment of imminent rather than present demands. Presumably these account for most of the more conspicuous changes which we observe in EDA. Among homeostatic requirements may be included thermoregulation and the role of the skin as an accessory kidney in control of water and electrolyte balance.

While thermoregulation at first glance appears to be a process which is continuous and which does not contribute appreciably to the sudden changes in EDA that are recognizable as *electrodermal responses* (EDR), there are some cases where homeostatic mechanisms must shift suddenly to deal with an emergency. For example, in a threatening situation an individual may exhibit widespread cutaneous vasoconstriction, perhaps as a preparatory adaptation to reduce bleeding in case of injury. He will very soon be under a considerable heat load due to the arrest of his usual mechanism for discharging heat at the skin surface. In such a case, the thermoregulatory mechanism would appropriately shift over to evaporative cooling with the help of enhanced sudorific activity, producing a condition commonly recognized as a "cold sweat."

The above is not the only conceivable cause for a rapidly occurring sudomotor adaptation which is thermoregulatory in nature. If an organism is activated by a stimulus which is the normal antecedent of considerable motor activity, that is, one which will involve any of the primary functions [fighting, escape, feeding (especially predatory) or sexual behavior], a useful adaptation for a biologically anticipated heat load is again an enhancement of evaporative heat loss by sudorific activity. It is thus reasonable to expect that the activity of limbic structures, whose processes are also concerned with these same functions, would be associated with enhanced discharge to the sudomotor apparatus, at least in those mammals which utilize this means of thermoregulation.

By the same token it is to be expected that inhibition of such behaviors, as occurs in the conservative process of sleeping, would, except for the homeostatic requirements of an idling system, be accompanied by inhibition of sudomotor activity in the interest of water conservation. For the land animal who may be prevented from replenishing his water supply for extended periods, it is obvious that radiation via the cutaneous circulation is the most advantageous means of heat loss. The marked cutaneous vasodilation occurring during sleep is understandable in these terms.

It is perhaps unfortunate that the most common mammal other

than man used in electrodermal studies, namely the cat, sweats only on its foot pads. Since the foot pads are in contact with the ground most of the time, it is obvious that this surface is not particularly effective for evaporative heat loss. Some evaporative heat loss could occur during ambulation. However, Adams *et al.* (1970) point out that the foot pads of the cat "represent so small a percentage of the total body surface area . . . and contain such relatively inactive sweat glands . . ., that even with full exposure to freely moving dry air, evaporation from these surfaces alone would not contribute effectively in heat balance." The cat's foot pad seems a poor model for the general study of EDA, a significant part of which may serve a thermoregulatory function in man.

Numerous observations show that either a cat or a human, in response to a threatening situation, manifests considerable sweating on the extremities. Such sweating in man could possibly be construed as anticipatory thermoregulatory sweating, since his hands have been shown to participate to some extent in thermoregulation (Wilcott, 1963). This explanation would not hold for the feet of either species; a more reasonable explanation would have to do with preparation of these surfaces for the special requirements of emergency locomotion.

There are still other conditions in the laboratory in which neither threat nor heat load exists; yet both cat and man evince considerable EDA on the extremities. In fact the conscious cat displays more EDA than man under similar mild laboratory conditions (Deckert and Edelberg, unpublished data), including those involving appetitive behavior. The neurodermal activity occurring on the hands under these conditions may be viewed as facilitating grasping or tactual behavior (Darrow, 1936). This interpretation may in a limited way hold for the cat's foot pad as well.

It seems improbable that the sweating which occurs on the foot of man functions to facilitate grasping. However, a study by this author has shown that the most active electrodermal area on the foot is at the junction of the sole with the medial aspect of the foot about midway between the malleolus and the toe (Edelberg, 1967). This is the area of the foot which is still used by humans in scaling palm trees to harvest coconuts. The other most active areas on the foot are the heel and the ball, that is, those surfaces which make the strongest frictional contact with the ground. A key function of sweating on the extremities is clearly to provide sure contact with the environment for locomotion. Locomotion is such a ubiquitous behavior, that we can expect this particular type of adaptation to show up in rather diverse activities.

A comparison of relative positive *skin potential response* (SPR) from various sites shows an interesting relation of such activity to the function of the site. The relative negative and positive SPR amplitudes in relation to that of the palmar surface of the finger are shown for the dorsal surface and for various parts of the foot in Table I. Negative SPR amplitudes on the palmar and dorsal surfaces of the finger are approximately equal. Those on the fleshy part of the palm (thenar and hypothenar eminences) and on the foot are considerably larger.

The distribution of positive SPRs shows a considerably different picture. All locations on the foot and the dorsum of the finger show positive amplitudes which are only 5–40% of those from the palmar surface of the finger and usually less than 10% of those from the thenar and hypothenar surfaces. Thus positive activity is represented predominantly on the grasping contact surface of the hand. This is consistent with the notion that positive SPR activity is associated with tactual motor activity. It also suggests that locomotion has different requirements than manipulation. The foot of the human behaves more like the pad of the cat than does the palm. Whether these relations are explainable in terms of the relative thickness of the corneum is a matter requiring some consideration. Relevant to these considerations is the conclusion reached by Kuno (1956) that the control of palmar and plantar sweating is independent of that on other parts of the body.

In the case of primates, the emergence of grasping and manipulative

TABLE I

COMPARISON OF AMPLITUDES OF NEGATIVE AND POSITIVE COMPONENTS
OF THE SKIN POTENTIAL RESPONSE FROM
VARIOUS SITES ON HUMAN SUBJECTS[a]

Site	N	Negative	Positive
Finger			
Palmar	All	1.00	1.00
Dorsal	12	.96	.35
Hand			
Thenar and hypothenar	7	2.5	3.8
Foot			
Plantar			
Heel	20	2.2	.18
Ball	20	2.6	.02
Toe	8	3.3	.4
Abductor hallucis muscle	11	1.6	.33

[a] Reference electrode was at a skin-drilled site. Values are expressed in terms of the median ratio of the amplitude of the response component to the corresponding component in the simultaneous recording from a palmar finger site for N subjects.

activity calls attention to the tactile properties of the skin. The cat in its manipulation of objects uses its paws essentially as flexible clubs, except for the use of its claws. It cannot be considered to grasp objects in the manner characteristic of the primate; any tactual manipulation of an object is either a crude test of hardness and response to pressure or an effort to move it for better olfactory or visual examination. By contrast the primate, and especially man, engages in delicate manipulation with considerable tactual exploration. This leads one to consider the possible role played by sudomotor activity in the adaptation for such behavior. Two factors may be subject to change, ease of grasping or manipulating, and tactual acuity or resolution.

Most of us have had occasion to moisten our index finger with our tongue before separating sheets of paper or turning pages, apparently to increase friction between skin and paper. It is also not unusual to observe someone wiping his hands on his pants before trying to unscrew the lid of a jar, or before grasping a baseball bat. I have also observed individuals who moisten their hand before grasping a bat. These conscious efforts to alter the wetness of the palmar surface are suggestive of a need to attain an optimum level of hydration. It is noteworthy in this regard that Adams and Hunter (1969) have demonstrated that the relation between level of hydration and the friction between the skin and a deglazed plastic surface is an inverted U-shaped function. Maximum friction is reached at rather low levels of hydration, compared to the total possible range.

The above examples pertain primarily to sureness of contact. There is little need for optimum tactual function in such tasks. In other situations the need to make fine distinctions between various surfaces places a somewhat different requirement on the skin. The peculiar "gloved" sensation that we experience after our palms have become coated with chalk dust testify to the importance of adequate cutaneous hydration in enabling optimum tactual performance. This everyday observation has recently received laboratory support in experiments involving artificial local alteration of surface moisture (Edelberg, Huber, and Beaver, unpublished data). It was found that performance in a tactile acuity task (one in which the surface was moved against the stationary finger, as well as one which involved active tactual scanning) improved with increasing levels of hydration. It was expected, too, that excess moisture would be detrimental to tactual resolution, but this phenomenon was exhibited by insufficient individuals in the test population to be statistically significant.

Perhaps as important for manipulative function as tactile acuity is the constancy of the skin's characteristics as a mechanical transducer.

A familiar object such as a piece of finished wood feels considerably different when felt with moistened as compared with dry fingers. When stroked with fingers which have been made unusually dry, it also feels different from usual, but not the same as when stroked with the wet finger. For optimum tactual recognition it serves the observer to have his skin at some relatively standard level of hydration.

B. COMPARATIVE NEURODERMAL BEHAVIOR

The above discussion implies that the adaptive function of sweating is often the same for the cat and the human, but may be considerably different in regard to exploratory behavior. Since differences may be observed in the electrical manifestations of neurodermal activity in these two species, as well as in the morphology, physiology, and histochemistry of their respective sweat ducts (Munger and Brusilow, 1961), it is tempting to consider whether such differences are consistent with the contrast in their manipulative behavior. Both cat and man show considerable EDA in response to a large variety of stimuli. Conductance (or resistance) changes in the cat have been studied by several investigators (Schwartz, 1934, 1937; Fujimori, 1955; Edelberg, 1967) and in general appear similar to those of man.

The potential responses of the two species are different in that the conscious cat has, to my knowledge, never been observed to produce positive waves, either alone or as part of a biphasic response. There are references in the literature to positive potential responses in the *anaesthetized* cat (Langworthy and Richter, 1930; Lloyd, 1961; Shaver *et al.*, 1962; Wilcott, 1965), but these reports may, for one reason or another, be questioned. They do not make a convincing case for concluding that the cat produces positive skin potential responses (SPRs) of the same type as man. Those reported by Lloyd and by Shaver and his coworkers were produced after long-term stimulation. They had a time course of the order of minutes. They appear to be of the sort that may be explained by increased hydration of the corneum (Edelberg, 1968). Wilcott (1965) reported positive SPRs from the anaesthetized cat, but these occurred only during the first 5–10 minutes of stimulation. His failure to elicit positive waves after this appears consistent with the supposition that the first responses were producing positive components by wetting the dry corneum. This "hydration" effect will be discussed later. After hydrating the corneum by successive sweat responses in the first several minutes, he presumably was unable to produce further hydration change and thereby lost the capacity to elicit positive responses.

One apparently convincing report of positive SPRs is that by Langworthy and Richter (1930). The allegation in their paper that positive responses could be elicited by cortical, but not by subcortical stimulation is of such fundamental importance to the interpretation of this type of response, that its acceptance should await replication. Wang has contended that positive SPRs have never been elicited by brain stimulation of the cat. Paradoxically, one of his studies on the anaesthetized cat (Wang and Lu, 1930, Fig. 5) does show what appear to be *bona fide* positive responses obtained with dc recording by stimulation of the cortex and with the dorsal and ventral roots sectioned.

A study by Deckert and Edelberg (unpublished data) showed that in 25 separate daily runs on seven conscious cats, with stimuli including petting, feeding, noises, the recorded barking of a dog, and the sight of a live rodent, there was no instance of a *bona fide* positive response. Many responses having an apparent positive component, were of a "pseudo" type resulting from the occurrence of a series of small, negative responses superimposed on the recovery limb of a larger negative response. It is possible that those reported by Langworthy and Richter (1930) were also of this type.

While the cat does not under ordinary circumstances manifest positive SPR activity, it is likely that it is capable of producing a weak positive wave, not attributable to the hydration effect. Wilcott (1965) shows illustrations of such responses obtained by recording from the mucous layer after removal of the corneum. They were of considerably lower amplitude than those obtained from a similar preparation in the human. Wilcott reports that responses from the conscious cat were always uniphasic negative. It may be relevant that the effect of superimposed external potentials on the SPR was different for the cat and the human.

The neurodermal apparatus of the cat appears to have evolved to the point at which the positive component, so conspicuous in man, can be observed under suitable (and unusual) conditions. However, the mechanism responsible for the production of positive SPRs has clearly not developed to the degree of prominence that it has in the human.

An electronmicrographic comparison of eccrine sweat glands from cat and human shows that the secretory portions are structurally and biochemically identical, but that the duct in the cat is only one tenth the length of the gland, while in man it is about one third to one half (Munger and Brusilow, 1961). Mitochondria are much more prominent in the basal cells of the duct in the human, and the cuticular border of the surface cells of the duct is much thicker. Perhaps, as suggested by Munger and Brusilow, these differences are associated with the fact that sweat secreted by the cat is essentially isotonic with interstitial fluid, while in the human it is hypotonic as a result of ductal reabsorption of

NaCl. These differences are sufficiently fundamental as to imply a major evolutionary development in man with the likelihood that other differences may also differentiate the two species. The appearance of positive SPRs in man together with the contrasts in ductal development suggests a link between the two, but the origin of the electrical differences is probably elsewhere as will be discussed in a later section.

C. Evidence for the Motor Accessory Role of EDA

Results from a number of studies indicate that EDA behaves to an extent as an accessory to skeletal motor activity either present (Starch, 1910; White, 1930; Wenger and Irwin, 1936), or anticipated (Pugh *et al.*, 1966). Darrow and Freeman (1934) maintained that the topographical specificity manifested by the palmar and dorsal surfaces of the hand represented the tendency of the dorsum to respond primarily to muscular activity, the palm to ideational. A later study (Edelberg and Wright, 1964) indicated that motor activity could not explain these differences.

There is, however, one type of activity in which motor behavior is clearly responsible for a type of topographical specificity in the *skin resistance response* (SRR). If two homologous sites on the right and left palms are simultaneously monitored, their SRR amplitudes to stimuli such as loud sounds are usually somewhat different, but generally not more so than 1.5:1 (Fisher, 1958; Obrist, 1963). When the subject flexes one foot strongly, the amplitude ratio shifts in favor of the ipsilateral hand (Culp and Edelberg, 1966). There is also a segmental effect such that with simultaneous monitoring of a hand and an ipsilateral foot, flexing of the contralateral hand shifts the ratio of response amplitudes in favor of the hand. Conversely, when the contralateral foot is flexed, the ratio shifts in favor of the foot.

These data have been pursued further using the SPR (Edelberg and Beaver, 1972, unpublished). In these experiments the SPR was recorded from the little finger of each hand, and the amplitude ratio of the responses to ipsilateral flexion of either thumb was examined. The change in ratio according to the side which was flexed was even more dramatic than in the first study and more consistent. A perceptual-motor task, involving motor activity at very low force, namely the identification of a soft material, using the thumb and forefinger, showed task-related laterality which was just as pronounced (Fig. 1). In most of these experiments, the predominant response was negative. When positive responses were prominent, they too displayed marked laterality. These lateral effects have been demonstrated in the above cases with

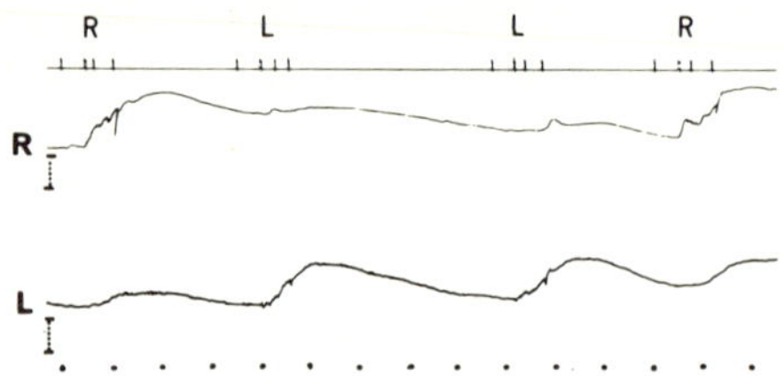

FIG. 1. Simultaneous skin potential tracings from the right and left finger tips. Stimuli are tactile identification tasks performed by either the right or left hand as indicated by the letters on the stimulus trace (R and L). Vertical calibration signals, 1 mV; time marks at 15-second intervals; negative is upward.

strong motor activity alone, and with gentle motor activity coupled with tactual scanning. A recent demonstration (Gildersleeve, Edelberg, and Nichols, 1972, unpublished) has shown a significant though less marked laterality effect in a tactile discrimination task, in which the object is moved across the motionless fingers of either hand. Thus, EDA appears to be regionally associated with activation for tactile behavior in which the motor component is absent, as well as with motor activity in which tactile behavior is absent.

D. CENTRAL NEURAL MECHANISMS FOR THE ELECTRODERMAL RESPONSE

The neurophysiology of EDA has been reviewed by Darrow (1937a), Wang (1957, 1958, 1964), and Bloch (1965), and has been summarized by this author (Edelberg, 1972a). For the present purposes, attention will be given briefly to those areas most likely involved in the adaptive behaviors discussed above.

The first of these is the thermoregulatory control system which includes portions of the prechiasmic, tuberal, and anterolateral hypothalamic areas (Kuno, 1956; Wang, 1964). Integrated with this, but perhaps also functioning independently in the control of EDA, are various limbic structures including the amygdala, hippocampus, and limbic cortex which have connecting pathways to the hypothalamus. They may utilize the same final common path as does the thermoregulatory mechanism.

Excitatory and inhibitory areas have been demonstrated in the premotor cortex, area 6, as well as in other portions of the frontal lobe including the granular cortex (Wang and Lu, 1930; Langworthy and Richter, 1930; Schwartz, 1937; Grueninger et al., 1965; Wilcott, 1969; Wilcott and Bradley, 1970). The fibers from area 6 descend along the pyramidal tracts. These are apparently independent of the hypothalamus, since hypothalamic section does not interfere with responses elicited from area 6, but section of the cerebral peduncles does so (Wang and Lu, 1930). Since other fibers from the premotor area contribute to the coordination of fine motor activity, it is tempting to regard EDA initiated in area 6 also as acting in an accessory role to such motor activity, a view taken by Darrow (1937a). Added to this is the fact that areas of the striopallidum have also been demonstrated to exert a modulating influence upon EDA (Wang, 1964). In view of the part played by this system in the extrapyramidal coordination of motor activity, the likelihood that EDA is serving in a motor accessory capacity becomes even more compelling. The by-passing of the hypothalamus by these fibers suggests that manipulative and thermoregulatory sudomotor activity may be separately controlled, a conclusion which is especially relevant to later discussion.

Modulation of EDA is not only a task of the basal ganglia, but also of the reticular formation, including the midline thalamic as well as the bulbar and mesencephalic areas. The last is excitatory as well as facilitatory. The introduction of the reticular formation as a control area for EDA leads to a consideration of the work of Bloch (1965) on its role in the behavioral aspects of electrodermal activity. Bloch, in a critical appraisal of this area based primarily on observations on the cat, interprets EDR as a reflection of the state of central arousal. He concludes that EDA is essentially the resultant of control by the facilitatory and inhibitory areas of the reticular formation, in a dynamic interaction with each other and with descending inhibitory influences from the cortex. The inhibitory influence of the cortex, however, is seen as itself controlled by ascending influences from the reticular formation, the whole being closely correlated with state of alertness. Bloch sees EDR serving essentially as part of a complex of adjustments in preparation for dealing with a novel situation or an emergency.

Insofar as the brainstem reticular formation has connections with the striopallidum and the cerebellum, and has been demonstrated to exercise considerable control over muscle tonus and muscle reactivity via the gamma efferents, one may postulate that, as in the case of the premotor cortex, reticular modulation of sweat gland activity is a concomitant of skeletal motor control. This system moderates reactivity in a considerably different way than does the premotor area, in that it controls the overall setting of the state of arousal (and of muscle tension) at a level appropriate to the perceived situation rather than for the finely controlled motor behavior occurring in skilled manipulative performance. Electrodermal responses which are largely mediated by reticular activity would seem more likely to be in preparation for locomotion than manipulation. They may also be subject to reticular inhibition in some situations, for example during stress (Harrison, 1964; Mackinnon, 1969).

The conception of neurodermal activity as a concomitant of general arousal places greater emphasis on arousal-linked modulation and less on specific adaptation than does this author. Bloch's points are well supported and may accurately describe electrodermal behavior in the cat, in view of the primitive development of its manipulative faculties. There is little doubt that the reticular formation does regulate the general level of electrodermal responsivity in man (Wang, 1957, 1958). However, the exquisitely subtle requirements of manipulative skill in this species are such that one can expect a greater incidence of motor-linked EDA of cortical origin, in which the quality and amplitude are dictated predominantly by task requirements rather than by level of arousal.

The diencephalic thermoregulatory centers, although associated largely with sweating other than on the extremities, may also play a role in palmar or plantar EDA of emotional origin, possibly in coordination with other limbic structures. Kuno (1956) has argued that sudomotor activity in the cat has mixed thermoregulatory and "mental" components, while in the human, thermoregulatory sweating is confined to nonpalmar, nonplantar areas. If true, one would expect to note differences in the behavior of these areas, reflecting some specificity of neural outflow, as has been indicated in an earlier section. Such difference of neural control might explain the palmar-dorsal response specificity described earlier. However, Wilcott (1963) has demonstrated that under suitable circumstances, palmar areas do participate in thermoregulatory sweating, and nonpalmar areas in emotional sweating.

The above discussion emphasizes the existence of specialized brain areas which tend to elicit EDA in conjunction with fine motor activity, others which function in locomotor activity, and still others in thermoregulatory activity. It is very likely that these specialized controls may, under conditions of serious threat, become diffusely activated to provide the organism (especially man) with a slippery, grasp-eluding body exterior and moist palmar and plantar surfaces for protection against abrasion during flight.

III. Peripheral Physiological Processes

A. RECENT DEVELOPMENTS

Efforts to construct an internally consistent, peripheral model that would account for the diverse array of reported observations as well as mediating the adaptive functions described above have been for the most part frustrating. Several relatively recent developments in this area have been useful in clarifying certain aspects of the nature of the peripheral physiological system underlying EDA. They are not yet a matter of common knowledge, however, and a brief discussion of each may be helpful for the understanding of the subsequent arguments.

B. The Local Potential Response (LPR)

In 1921, Ebbecke described a local decrease in skin resistance in response to such stimuli as pressure, electrical current, heat, etc. (Ebbecke, 1921). This could be demonstrated on various parts of the body but not on the palms, a finding confirmed by Richter (1929). Rein (1929) showed that this response was accompanied by a positive potential shift. The phenomenon was given scant attention, perhaps in large part because of a paper by Lewis and Zotterman (1926–1927) which claimed to show that the response was simply the consequence of damage to the skin. The arguments presented by Lewis and Zotterman appear to be fallacious, however, in large part because they used needle pricks as their principal stimulus and may very well have damaged the epidermis (Edelberg, 1972a, pp. 372–373).

In a recent study (Edelberg, 1973), the local potential response (LPR) was elicited by inflation of a bladder attached to the skin in such a way that it compressed the site at standard pressure or stretched it under standard tension. The local potential response was almost always positive but could on rare occasion be negative. It was readily recorded with a microelectrode from the surface but not when the electrode perforated the epidermis very slightly. It is therefore not of vascular origin. It was found on the palmar surface, though at a reduced amplitude, and could be conspicuously demonstrated on the forearm. Its polarity could be reversed by the local application of Na_2SO_4 (Fig. 2), and its amplitude could be reduced by application of $5\ M$ NaCl. Local responses from the finger were attentuated by 15 minutes of exsanguination, potentiated by short periods of local cooling to $10°C$.

Of special significance was the fact that the LPR could be elicited from the fingernail. The nail plate although seemingly impervious to water, actually can soak up saline and allow registration of potentials from the nail bed. Reflex potential responses can be elicited from such a site (Edelberg, 1965), but resistance decreases can not, and there is some question as to whether these reflex potential responses are of vascular or epidermal origin. When a small electrode (e.g., 3 mm diameter) is mounted in the center of the nail, and the tip of the nail is

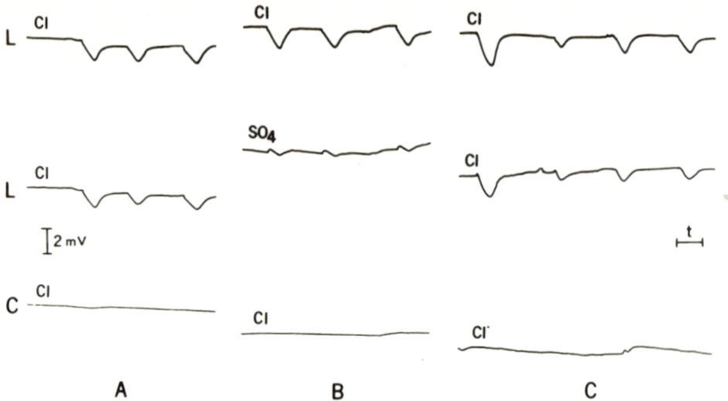

FIG. 2. Effect of 0.5 *M* Na₂SO₄ on LPR. Upper and middle traces are recorded from fingers containing stretch devices. Lower trace is from a site responding only to central impulses. Panel A, all sites in 0.1 *M* NaCl; B, middle site in Na₂SO₄; C, middle site returned to 0.1 *M* NaCl. Time line (t), 10 seconds; negative is upward.

lifted, LPRs of high amplitude may be observed (Fig. 3). Suitable controls showed these were not produced by current leakage to surrounding skin or by volume conduction from natural skin areas. Their occurrence appears to provide strong support for a nonsweat gland origin of the LPR.

Of considerable relevance to the interpretation of the LPR is the study by Shuster (1963) of the effect of local pressure on sweating. He

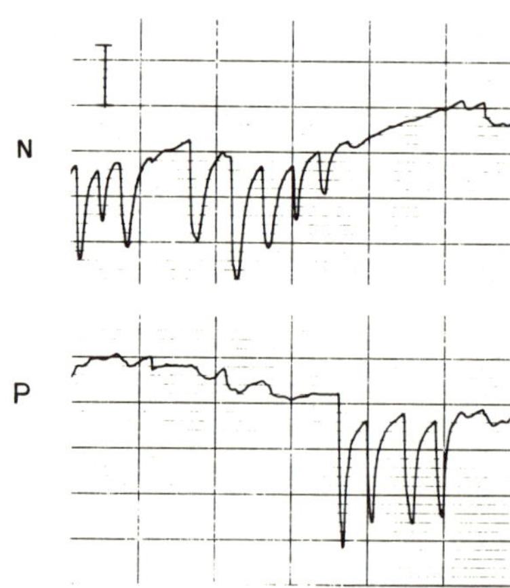

FIG. 3. LPRs obtained from the nail bed (N) by lifting tip of nail (first half of upper trace). Lower trace is a simultaneous recording from the palmar (P) surface of the finger under the nail. In the last half of this trace four LPRs have been elicited by stretch of the skin. Note absence of spread of response between sites. Vertical lines, 30-second intervals; vertical calibration, 5 mV; negative is upward.

found that sweat output could be greatly reduced by pressure on the skin site, a procedure which also elicits the LPR. Control experiments demonstrated that the reduction in sweat output could not be explained by arterial or venous occlusion or by damming back of sweat within the ducts. Since sweating may continue in blocked pores often to the point of rupture (miliaria), he argued that secretion had not been arrested, but rather that an increased rate of sweat *absorption,* caused by the pressure, is the explanation for the reduction in sweat output. Shuster also found that the concentration of NaCl in the residual sweat remained unchanged and concluded that reabsorption of ions as well as of water had been increased.

These findings raise the possibility that the associated LPR may be in some way related to water and ion movement. A simple hypothesis is that the deformation of the skin produces an increase in the water and ion permeability of a selective membrane. Similarities between the LPR and positive SPR suggest that both may originate in the same membrane. Like the LPR, the positive SPR is influenced by surface electrolytes (Edelberg, 1972a), is attenuated by interruption of blood flow (Nakayama and Takagi, 1958; Wilcott, 1958b), and is eliminated by puncture of the epidermis (Edelberg, unpublished data). In addition, the LPR and SPR in a given subject covary in amplitude over time (Fig. 4) and show mutual occlusive effects (Edelberg, 1973). Unlike the LPR, the positive SPR is attenuated at 10°C (Yokota *et al.,* 1959), possibly because of inactivation of nerve endings; their activity is not required for the LPR.

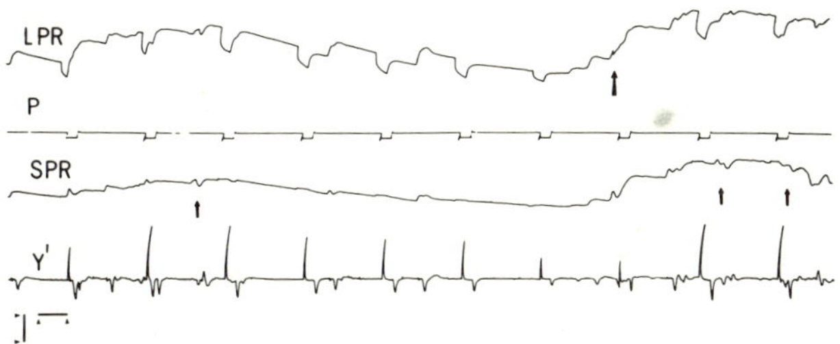

FIG. 4. Covariation of amplitude of LPR and positive SPR as a function of skin potential level. Upper trace is from finger fitted with a compression device, actuated at 30-second intervals for 5 seconds. Second trace, P, shows periods of compression. Third trace, SPR, is similar to LPR recording but without the compression device. Lower trace, Y¹, is the first derivative of the LPR trace; upward spikes are a measure of the amplitude of the fast component of the LPR. Arrows on SPR trace indicate positive responses. Arrow on upper trace shows occlusion of LPR which occurs during a positive component in the SPR. Vertical calibration, 10 mV; horizontal calibration, 10 seconds; negative is upward.

C. The Reabsorption Reflex

If two parallel wires are imbedded in very close proximity in a plastic plate and ground flush with the surface, one obtains a unit useful for measuring the hydration of the skin (Edelberg, 1966). When one places such a unit in contact with the skin without electrode paste and imposes an alternating current between the two wires, the current passes laterally from one electrode to the other along the skin surface rather than penetrating the epidermis. The impedance thus measured varies with the hydration level of the corneum. Usually when an EDR occurs, impedance falls, due to the concomitant evolution of sweat. Often, however, the impedance increases sharply at the onset of the response (Fig. 5).

The relative prevalence of increased hydration or of reduced hydration (reabsorption) is related to the nature of the stimulus rather than to response amplitude. The incidence of absorption responses is greatest with conversation, both with speaking and listening, least with simple physical stimulation by lights or tones. The probability of finding reabsorption responses is associated with a higher incidence of positive SPRs. The conscious cat, which does not produce positive SPRs, also does not manifest reabsorption reflexes (Edelberg and Deckert, unpublished data).

Certain conditions are necessary for the demonstration of the reabsorption phenomenon, one being full ducts and a well-hydrated site, the other an EDR with an appreciable output of sweat. Conceivably, changes in skin hydration, *skin potential level* (SPL), or *skin conductance level* (SCL) could explain the transition when recordings at the

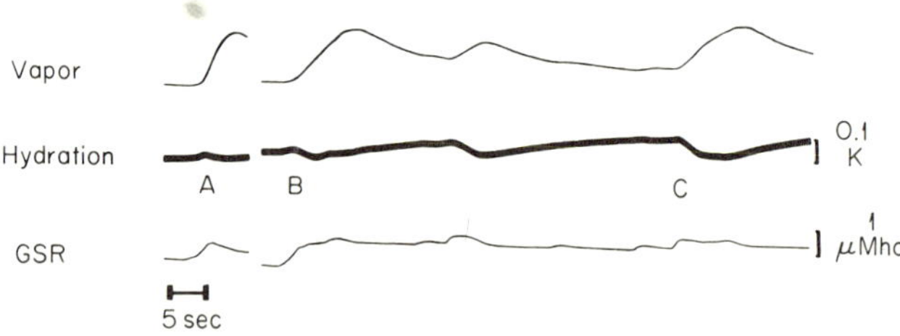

FIG. 5. Absorption responses (middle trace) obtained from finger pad. Upper trace is obtained simultaneously from another finger pad with a dry air flow system. The hydration trace shows some unfiltered residue of the low frequency energizing current applied to the transducer. A 40-second strip of inactive record between responses a and b has been removed. GSR, galvanic skin response. (From Edelberg, 1966. Copyright by the American Psychological Association, and reproduced by permission.)

transducer site change from a process of increasing hydration to one of dehydration in conjunction with the EDR. However, the sudden appearance of reabsorption waves without appreciable change in these electrodermal variables suggests that a mechanism under separate control accounts for the effect. The association of the positive SPR with the absorption phenomenon, and the probable association of the LPR with increased absorption, indicated by Shuster's work, further reinforce the suspicion that these responses represent changes in the same effector.

D. The Mosaic Model and Effects of Hydration

When two adjacent areas at the surface of the skin are at different potentials, a current may be expected to flow between them, even without the application of external electrodes. The potential recorded at the surface will be the resultant of the difference in potential between the two sites and of their respective "internal" resistances. In effect a voltage divider is formed by the two resistance legs. The skin may be regarded as a mosaic structure in which this situation exists; experimental data indicate that the sweat glands are more negative than the adjacent corneum.

The electrical model which describes the behavior of such a system has been presented elsewhere (Edelberg, 1968). Briefly it postulates two parallel sources at different potentials (in fact one of these may be zero) with separate variable internal resistances (Fig. 6). With any change in the internal resistance of either generator, i.e., the sweat gland or epidermis, or of its pathway to the surface, i.e., the sweat duct or corneum, the potential measured at the surface will change even if there

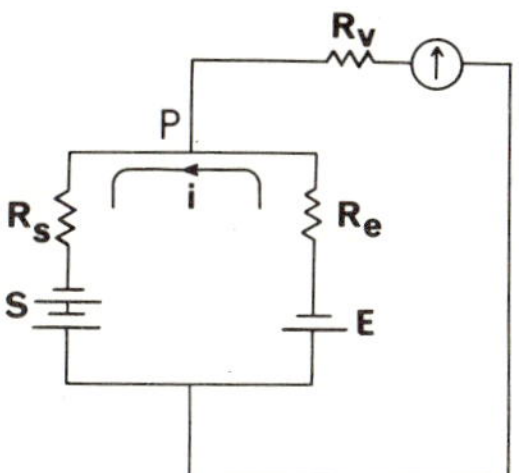

Fig. 6. Circuit representing the contribution of the sweat gland potential, S, and the epidermal potential, E, to the surface potential of the skin, P. Abbreviations: R_s, the combined internal resistance of the sweat gland membrane and sweat duct; R_e, the combined internal resistance of the epidermal membrane and the resistance of the corneum; R_r, the input resistance of the amplifier; i, the internal current (from Edelberg, 1968, by permission of the New York Academy of Sciences, New York).

is no change in the potential of either generator. Since the sweat gland is more negative than the epidermis, drying of the corneum should, by increasing the resistance of the associated leg, cause the surface potential to become more negative. If the corneum is moderately dry, overflow of sweat decreases its resistance and should cause a positive potential swing resembling the positive SPR. The report by Darrow *et al.* (1957) that positive SPRs could be observed only when emission of sweat was in evidence seems relevant. The first prediction was confirmed when the corneum was dehydrated by placing the skin in polyethylene glycol containing saline. Fowles and Venables (1970b) confirmed this effect, and Fowles and Rosenberry (1970) demonstrated that the positive SPR is potentiated by dehydration of the corneum as predicted by the model. Fowles states that in the fully hydrated condition the depression of the positive SPR probably occurs because the passage of sweat into the corneum can not further hydrate a fully hydrated epidermis.

While the evidence is strong that positive potential shifts may be produced as a result of wetting the incompletely hydrated corneum, it is doubtful that this effect can account for positive SPRs at a conventionally prepared electrode site. Consider a layer of electrode paste on the skin surface. When the sweat emerges, it is usually less than 0.1 M; the upper regions of the corneum are equilibrated with the paste, usually 0.05–0.1 M NaCl, often higher. The emerging sweat clearly can not account for an appreciable increase in conductance at the surface.

Suchi (1955) has shown that the observed resistance of wet corneum actually becomes greater as a microelectrode is pushed beneath the surface layer; the resistance at a depth of 250 μ was as much as twice that observed at the surface, due probably to greater lateral spread of current at the surface. This suggests the possibility that the lateral passage of sweat from the duct may produce a significant conductance change in the deeper portions of the corneum which have been partially dried by reabsorption. A question then arises about the speed of this process. Can it account for positive SPRs which commonly reach peak in 1–2 seconds after their onset? In view of the observation by Schulz and her co-workers (1965) that an oil-trapped section of saline in a sweat duct takes 10 minutes to diffuse into the corneum, the transductal diffusion of water appears to be too slow to explain the typical jetlike positive waves which appear as part of the SPR. While exit of sweat from the pore might explain a process of this speed, conditions near the surface are ordinarily such that sweat is not likely to reduce corneal resistance sufficiently to produce positive SPRs of the magnitude observed. If hydration changes do account for positive potential waves, they probably occur below the surface and have a slower time course than "membrane" waves. Slow positive waves taking of the order of 5 seconds to reach peak, have in fact been frequently observed in the records of individuals who at other periods of the run produce positive SPRs of the fast (1- to 2-second) variety.

It should be emphasized that while alteration of the water content or conductivity of the corneum is capable of producing such effects, a change of the *internal resistance of the generator* or of its *membrane potential* may also do so. Thus, an increase in the permeability of the epidermis should cause a positive shift in surface potential in the same way as would occur from wetting of the corneum. This would summate with any attending positive shift in membrane potential.

E. Poral Closure and Self-Regulation of Hydration Level

Peiss and Randal (1957), Brebner and Kerslake (1964), and Sarkany, Shuster, and Stammers (1965) have shown that skin that is soaked in water stops sweating, apparently because hydration of the corneum causes it to swell, occluding the sweat ducts. If the skin is soaked in 15% NaCl, the pores remain open, and sweating is not reduced.

A self-regulating mechanism thus seems to exist such that if sweat is produced faster than its rate of reabsorption or evaporation, it will increase the hydration of the corneum and reduce sweating by poral closure. If the pores are partially closed, the passive rate of reabsorption under an osmotic driving force may exceed the rate of sweat excretion. Hydration will then be reduced; the sweat pores will open a bit, increasing sweat output somewhat, and readjusting corneal hydration to a slightly higher value. With such a mechanism, skin in contact with objects should reach a self-adjusted level of hydration which is at some intermediate value between very dry and very wet. The steady-state level which is reached would be determined by a combination of reabsorption rate and sudorific rate, both of which are presumed to be under neural control.

Poral closure may be a confounding factor in the interpretation of experiments aimed at testing the mosaic model by artificial alteration in corneal hydration. For example, while dehydration increases the resistance of the epidermal limb of the internal circuit and should, therefore, cause an increase in surface negativity, it also causes opening of the pores, which should produce the same effect. An additional complication pointed out by Fowles and Rosenberry (1970) is that the poral closure that occurs at higher levels of hydration may cause stretching of the occluded sweat duct during a response, with a variety of possible consequences. Their point is well taken.

IV. Evidence for Two Different Responding Elements

During the course of a series of studies on the peripheral physiology of the EDR, a number of observations suggested that this reflex probably consisted of more than one component. *These did not necessarily imply that the components were under independent control.* The components did, however, respond differently to various experimental variables. In these experiments two sites under similar conditions were usually observed concurrently while the subject was presented an assortment of stimuli. One of the sites was then exposed to a peripheral change such as temperature or chemical environment, and the results were examined to detect alterations in the ratio of their response amplitudes or base levels. It was noted that the ratio of the responses at the two sites were usually altered by this manipulation, but that the degree of alteration was not consistent for all responses. In each case, efforts were made to explain the phenomenon on the basis of such things as base level or amplitude effects, but such explanations usually failed to account satisfactorily for the result. These various findings will be briefly described.

A. Temperature

When two finger sites were maintained at a surface temperature of 26°C, the ratios of almost all resistance responses were the same (Edelberg, 1963b). When one of them was changed to 37°C, the ratio became variable (Fig. 7). Spontaneous responses became appreciably potentiated at the higher temperature. Larger responses, elicited by deep breaths, largely retained their original relationship.

B. Vasoconstriction

In one study (Edelberg, 1964a), sites on the fingers of the right and left hand were used. Intense vasoconstriction was produced on one hand by cooling, while maintaining the recording site on the same hand at normal skin temperatures by the use of a small heated chamber. Under these conditions, there was no change in base resistance on the cooled hand, but the SRR was markedly reduced. More surprising than this apparent dissociation of response amplitude and base level was the behavior of some subjects whose response amplitude was significantly

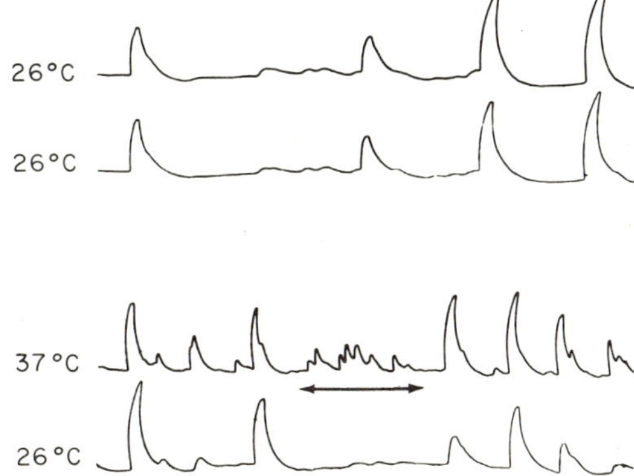

Fig. 7. Differential effect of temperature increase on various resistance responses. In upper traces, both finger sites are at same temperature. In lower traces, one of them has been heated to 37°C. Note disproportionate increase in spontaneous responses above double arrow and in the next large response (from Edelberg, 1963b, by permission of the U.S.A.F. School of Aerospace Medicine, Brook Air Force Base, Texas).

attenuated at the vasoconstricted site, while at the same time their spontaneous electrodermal frequency at this site rose appreciably in comparison with those from the control site. It appeared that a separate effector, responsible for small responses, or perhaps spontaneous responses, was affected differently by vasoconstriction than was that responsible for the larger, elicited responses.

C. Chemical Effects

In another study, Edelberg, Greiner, and Burch (1960) examined the effect of various topically applied electrolytes on the electrodermal system. These generally caused a marked potentiation or attenuation of the EDR according to the ionic species. The effects were sometimes very different for different responses, and they too appeared to vary according to the nature of the stimulus, although again response amplitude may have been the distinguishing feature.

D. High-Current Density

The effects of high-current density (e.g., 100 μA/cm^2 applied for 8 minutes) were examined in another study (Edelberg, unpublished data). Here, as in the other cases, there was a differential effect on various responses possibly according to the nature of the stimulus, but again with changes in amplitude confusing the interpretation.

E. TOPOGRAPHICAL DIFFERENCES

When two dissimilar sites such as the sole and the palm are simultaneously monitored, the relative representation of a given response at the two areas varies considerably as a function of the type of stimulus. These striking differences may be ascribed to differences in function and innervation of the two sites, or to differences in the structure of the two sites, e.g., the thickness of the corneum. The latter is the most conspicuous difference between the two areas.

This observation led to the investigation of similar relations between the palmar (volar) and dorsal surfaces of the finger (Edelberg and Wright, 1964; Mordkoff *et al.*, 1967; Katkin *et al.*, 1967). It was possible to achieve variations in the relative response amplitude of these two sites by utilizing such stimulus differences as alerting for a perceptual task *vs.* attending to the associated perceptual display or even between alerting for a reaction time task and alerting for a perceptual task. It was further demonstrated that the results could not be attributed to amplitude differences (Fig. 8).

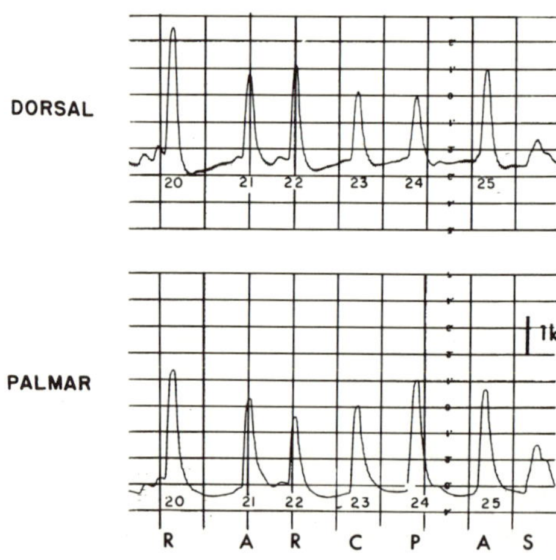

FIG. 8. Variation in relative response amplitudes of skin resistance responses from dorsal and palmar surfaces of the finger. Letters below lower trace denote stimuli: R, reaction time execution; A, alerting for reaction time; R, reaction time execution; C, command for deep breath; P, execution of deep breath; A, alerting for perceptual test; S, perceptual test. Note difference in the ratios for A and R or R and P. Recordings made with condensor coupling, time constant 6 seconds. Vertical lines at 15-second intervals.

The stimulus specificity of the response could be demonstrated as well using, instead of the ratio of amplitudes of the palmar and dorsal resistance responses, the ratio of the palmar sweat response to the palmar resistance response. It was concluded that various stimuli are differentially effective in eliciting predominantly epidermal or predominantly sudomotor responses, and that the ratio of the response amplitudes from two areas with differing concentrations of sweat glands varies accordingly as a function of the type of stimulus. The equally plausible explanation that these effects simply represent differential activation of the palmar or dorsal surfaces, as had been claimed earlier by Darrow and Freeman (1934), was considered an unlikely one in view of the successful discrimination using sweat and resistance responses from the palm alone. It must be pointed out, however, that sweat was recorded from a different finger than was resistance, and it is possible that these results reflected differential innervation to the two sites rather than to their epidermal and sudomotor effectors.

Several additional findings supported the likelihood of the participation of two separate effectors in the EDR. One related to the last topic was Wilcott's (1960) observation that the variations in SRL from palmar and nonpalmar surfaces (including the back of the hand) are unrelated. He concluded, in agreement with Richter (1929), that there are different mechanisms controlling palmar and nonpalmar skin resistance.

Further evidence for the presence of two separate electrodermal effectors was provided by microelectrode recordings of the SRR. It was shown (Edelberg, 1961a) that the SRR may be recorded as well from the epidermis some distance from the sweat gland as from the sweat pore itself, even when such nonsweat gland sites were surgically isolated from the sweat gland. This was probably not due to current leakage, since the two areas behaved oppositely in their polarization response to high-density currents (Edelberg, 1971a).

An interesting observation supporting the two-component concept was found in a study of the effect of skin hydration on skin potentials (Edelberg, 1968). The relative strength of the positive and negative components of the SPR varies considerably, and several investigators have shown that their relative contribution to the response can be changed by altering the stimulus situation (Forbes and Bolles, 1936; Edelberg, 1963a; Loveless and Thetford, 1966; Shmavonian *et al.,* 1968). Again, amplitude differences may account for the apparent specificity. Several of these authors concluded that the two components had independent origins. One finding in the hydration study does point to the occurrence of two parallel, separate processes. Two sites on the

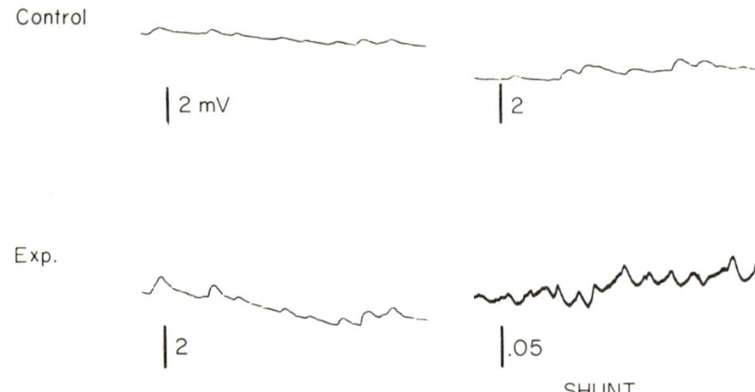

FIG. 9. Inversion of negative skin potential response produced by heavy load-ing. Left panel: both sites recorded with 2 MΩ input impedance. Right panel: one pair (lower trace) shunted with 44 kΩ (subject resistance 402 kΩ) and gain increased fourfold (modified from Edelberg, 1968, by permission of the New York Academy of Sciences, New York).

volar surface of the finger, each referred to a separate reference site may show similar uniphasic negative responses. When one pair is shunted with a resistance equal to about one tenth the measured resistance, the responses of this pair may be changed to the uniphasic positive or biphasic form (Fig. 9). Unless there is an explanation which escapes this author, such a conversion can only occur if two parallel voltage generators of different values are involved in the response. With this assumption, the reversal of response polarity may be predicted from the quantitative expression shown in the publication of that study.

V. Evidence for Two Independent Innervations

There seems to be little question that at least two elements partici-pate in the electrodermal response. A question of even greater relevance to behavioral interpretation is whether these are under independent control. Most of the evidence showing a dissociation in the relative participation of these components does not exclude passive peripheral mechanisms as an explanation. In particular, the effects of differences in initial levels, response amplitude, or differential properties of two compared sites are likely explanations. The existence of palmar-dorsal response specificity seems at least to imply different and independent innervation of these areas, if not of the responding elements, i.e., the sweat gland and epidermis.

One form of comparison which dispenses with the need for con-sidering such alternatives is that in which responses from a *single site* are compared under conditions in which initial conductance, initial potential, and response amplitude are all constant. In this situation, changes in the shape of the response as a function of type of stimulus may be demonstrated. The nature of such findings is the subject of the following discussion.

Variations in Electrodermal Recovery Rate

The observation that reflex absorption responses appear suddenly, and that their relative incidence is related to the nature of the stimulus or activity (Edelberg, 1966), suggested that it may be part of a specific adaptation for certain types of behavior. It appeared reasonable to expect that acceleration of the reabsorption of sweat might be associated with acceleration of recovery of the EDR.

The measurement of electrodermal recovery rate was accomplished by considering the recovery limb of the response as essentially exponential and determining its time constant either by template-matching or by measurement of recovery half-time (Edelberg, 1970). It should be emphasized that this measure is theoretically independent of amplitude and is an intrinsic index of the rate of a recovery process, not simply an expression of the absolute steepness of the recovery slope. Recovery rate was in fact found to vary independently of response amplitude (Edelberg, 1970) or of base conductance (Edelberg, 1972b). It not only increased with the prevalence of reflex reabsorption activity, but also with the incidence of positive SPRs (Fig. 10).

Results demonstrated that the recovery limb could indeed change markedly from one wave to the next, as a function of stimulus change, even though response amplitude, conductance level, and potential level were the same. Rapid recovery is apparently associated with mobilization for goal-oriented behavior and is positively correlated

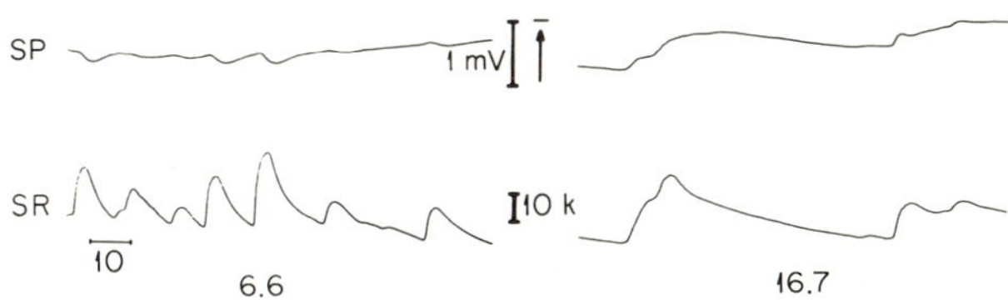

Fig. 10. Relation of EDR rate to polarity of skin potential (SP). Left panel: fast recovery of skin resistance (SR) response with positive SPRs. Right panel: slow recovery with negative SPRs. Numbers under lower trace refer to average time constant in seconds. Time line, 10 seconds.

with level of performance on simple tasks, but it is not a measure of activation per se. Recovery rate is also positively correlated with speed of reaction time (Edelberg, 1971b). The measure has been shown to differentiate schizophrenics from normals (Ax and Bamford, 1970), and to discriminate between responses as a function of anticipation (Furedy, 1972; Lockhart, 1972).

Retardation of recovery rate has been shown to occur in the presence of threatening stimuli, such as threat of shock, or disturbing words in a word-association series (Edelberg, 1971b). The differential effects of task orientation and apprehension on recovery rate imply that a process responsible for controlling electrodermal recovery is responding in a sensitive manner to the behavioral demands of the situation. As such, it probably represents an adaptive process. The significance of these relationships will hopefully be clarified in the treatment of the physiological model.

The relation of electrodermal recovery rate to rate of reabsorption may result from the fact that skin conductance depends upon the level of sweat in the ducts and the wetness of the corneum. The more rapidly these are reduced following a response, the more quickly the increase in conductance is reversed. On the other hand, if an active membrane is associated with the absorption reflex, the faster recovery rate may simply reflect the greater contribution of the fast-recovering membrane response to the total EDR. A recent finding indicates that the membrane component may play an important role. High currents have been shown by Wilcott (1964) to depress the positive SPR which, according to evidence presented here, is thought to be of membrane origin. A follow-up of this work (Edelberg, unpublished data) shows that the imposition of a high voltage, 22.5 V for 4 minutes, induces a marked slowing of electrodermal recovery rate as well, usually about 50%. The interpretation is that the effects of high current upon the positive SPR and upon electrodermal recovery rate represent inactivation of a common structure.

VI. Peripheral Physiological Mechanisms

The previous discussion can serve as a guide in the formulation of a physiological model consistent with a diverse set of observations, here and in the literature. In the following sections several especially significant findings are examined in conjunction with the recent findings discussed above. They lead to the postulation of certain basic characteristics of this model as follows:

1. The Sweat Gland Contributes Increasingly to Surface Negativity As the Ducts Become Filled

Schulz and her co-workers (1965) have measured the potential inside the human sweat gland and found it to be about 20–50 mV more negative than the tissues. With an intraluminal micropipette at the level of the germinating layer, and with the glandular segment and lower duct blocked with oil, they continued to record high negative potentials and concluded that the potential probably arises in the middle or upper part of the duct below the corneum. The negativity of the sweat gland pore with reference to the surrounding corneum has also been noted (Edelberg, 1968). The concentration of sweat glands on the palm is of the order of twice that on the dorsal surface (Krause, 1844), and consistent with this, the palmar surface is about 10–20 mV more negative (Edelberg, 1967). When the site is activated it becomes even more negative (Leiderman and Shapiro, 1964). These observations lead to the conclusion that filling of the sweat gland ducts enhances the negative surface potential, a conclusion that is also consistent with the predictions of the mosaic model.

That the secretory process in the glandular portion of the sweat gland does not give rise to a negative wave, as suggested by Martin and Venables (1966), is indicated by the microelectrode observations of Shaver, Brusilow, and Cooke (1965) on the cat foot pad. With an intraductal micropipette at the level of the germinating layer, they recorded negative SPRs following each sympathetic stimulation, but not when they lowered the electrode deeper into the duct. These results may bear a relation to those of Schulz *et al.* (1965) who found that the origin of the negative intraductal potential was probably in the same general region. The origin of the intraductal negative potential responses poses a dilemma, since the ducts remained full during the observations. Conceivably, they may be a product of epidermal membrane changes.

2. The Fullness of the Sweat Ducts Is a Major Determinant of Skin Conductance Level

Two findings indicate that the fullness of the glands influences conductivity. One is the observation by Thomas and Korr (1957) showing conductance to be directly related to the number of filled sweat glands. Another is the demonstration by Adams of the relation of conductance to the amount of previous stimulation of the sympathetic

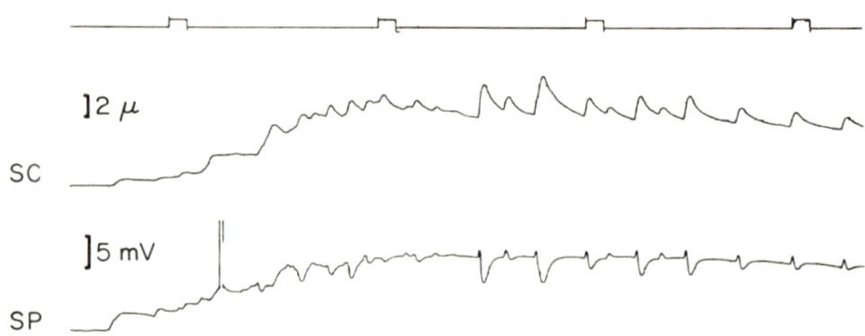

FIG. 11. Simultaneous transition of waveform of skin potential (SP) and skin conductance (SC) responses as skin potential level becomes more negative. Signals on the upper trace are of 5 seconds duration and are at 1-minute intervals. SP negativity increases upward.

supply to the cat foot pad. After stimulation of the sympathetic supply to the pad has continued long enough, the ducts are full, and the increased emission of vapor from the surface becomes measurable (Adams, 1966). Corresponding measurement of electrical conductivity (Adams, 1967) showed that the associated conductance changes may be precisely explained by the increase in the level of sweat in the ducts and the increased hydration of the corneum.

The similarity of conductance and potential responses at low base levels is consistent with this conclusion. When the resting level of potential is very low, the ducts are presumed to be relatively empty. A response of small to moderate size will then cause an elevation of the sweat level in the ducts, without overflow or appreciable lateral loss to the corneum (Adams, 1966). The associated conductance response has a staircase shape, very similar to that of the negative potential response; recovery of both is slow (Fig. 11). Both appear to be reflecting the same condition, namely the level of sweat in the duct. Darrow (1937b), taking a very different view of the situation, stated that this slow recovery was probably due to a "relatively permanent increase in (neurophysiological) activity."

3. *A Selective Labile Membrane Accounts for Part of the Conductance Response and for the Positive Potential Response*

One significant finding is that sweating may be reduced by as much as 70% by arterial occlusion, without any appreciable fall in the SRR (Edelberg, 1964b). A dorsal finger site showing no sweat output may have SRRs equal in amplitude to those from a palmar site which is producing substantial sweat responses. These observations imply that the resistance response, though to some extent undoubtedly reflecting the amount of sweat produced, must be largely dependent upon some other mechanism, presumably a change in the permeability of a membrane.

The involvement of a membrane is further indicated by the fact that bivalent cations such as calcium or zinc may potentiate SRR by as much as 250%, while at the same time reducing skin resistance level (SRL). Even more pertinent to the membrane hypothesis is the fact that these ionic effects depend upon the polarity of the measuring current, the ratio of anodal to cathodal potentiation being typically 1.5:1 (Edelberg *et al.*, 1960), often as high as 2:1 (Edelberg and Burch, 1962). Control experiments showed that the polarity effects can not be due to selective driving of cations or anions into the corneum by the measuring currents. While the potentiating effects of these ions could conceivably be explained by their dehydrating effects upon the corneum, and the consequent opening of sweat pores which have been closed by the control solutions, the explanation for the polarity effect does appear to demand the participation of a selective membrane in the EDR. An additional observation which suggests that the positive SPR is also of membrane origin is the sevenfold increase in the amplitude of the positive SPR, induced by exposure to $1\,M$ $AlCl_3$ (Edelberg, 1972a).

It seems almost certain that these ionic effects can not be due to action on the glandular portion of the sweat unit. Arguments to this effect have been summarized elsewhere (Edelberg, 1972a). One observation of particular relevance to this conclusion is that of Papa and Kligman (1966). They showed that a 3-minute exposure to a current of 500–750 μA drove methylene blue, a cationic dye, into the skin, but that it did not penetrate the sweat duct even as far as the level of the germinating layer. This exposure would be equivalent to 150 minutes at 10 $\mu A/cm^2$, the level used in the author's experiments, which were usually much shorter than this. Although inorganic cations may have a higher mobility, the amount of backward movement due to flushing by sweat secretion during this period of repeated stimulation would easily keep ahead of the iontophoretic migration of the fastest ion. It is, therefore, highly improbable that ions entered the ducts in the earlier electrolyte experiments.

The distinction between conductance responses resulting from ductal filling and those resulting from membrane activation may be seen in Fig. 11. The early steplike increases with slow recovery have already been referred to as examples of the effect of increase in sweat level at the deeper regions of the duct. At higher resting levels, the slow conductance responses still appear but superimposed on them are sharp conductance increases with rapid recovery. It is suggested that these fast conductance responses represent the membrane process. The rapid recovery of the latter responses leads to the conclusion that the fast (membrane) response is not an important contributor to SCL. This does not rule out an influence on SCL from tonic discharge to the membrane.

One common type of potential response, not yet accounted for, is a uniphasic negative wave with fast recovery. These are presumed to be caused by partial ductal filling with rapid reabsorption. The associated positive wave is apparently not intense enough at the surface to carry the response below baseline (Holmquest and Edelberg, 1964).

4. *The Labile Membrane Lies in the Epidermis. Its Reflex Increase in Ion-Permeability Is Also Accompanied by an Increase in Permeability to Water*

Up to this point of development, the model can account for a negative surface potential, for negative SPRs, and for conductance increases, all a function of ductal sweat level. A membrane process accounting for a major share in the conductance response has also been postulated, but little has been said about the nature of the membrane or its effects on surface potentials.

The active membrane is thought to lie in the epidermis. The basis for this conclusion arises in a variety of observations, in particular the marked similarity in the characteristics of the positive SPR and the LPR, that suggest these represent the activity of a common effector. The fact that the LPR is elicited more conspicuously from areas which have few or no sweat glands, such as the forearm or the nail bed, than from the area which has the highest concentration of sweat glands, i.e., the finger tip, implies a nonsweat gland origin. The epidermis, rather than the sweat gland, is a choice candidate. The site of origin of the positive SPR is therefore also tentatively placed in the epidermis.

Activation of this membrane is apparently associated with an increase in permeability to water. When the sweat pores are closed by adequate hydration of the surrounding corneum, the evolution of sweat during the EDR is blocked, so that the nature of the reabsorption process may be better observed. Under these conditions, when positive SPRs occur the sudden reduction of surface hydration which commonly occurs has its onset at almost exactly the same time as that of the positive SPR. The association of the incidence of absorption waves and of positive SPRs, and this close phasic relation between the two, suggest a causal link between them.

While there is not any doubt that sweat is reabsorbed from the corneum, the exact routing of this return flow is uncertain. Optical records of the outpouring of sweat at the surface (Fig. 12) have been obtained (Edelberg, unpublished data) by photoelectric instrumentation of the Netsky prism technique used by Thomas and Korr (1957). These demonstrate what is consistent with microscopic examination, namely that sweat may emerge from the pore and remain standing, or may be quickly withdrawn as if it returned through the pore or its crater. Sweat may be reabsorbed at a rate that keeps up with its rate of excretion so that the record consists of a series of short-lived increases in surface sweat, superimposed on a relatively stable base level (Fig. 12, lower trace). Interestingly, Darrow (1932) observed a similar effect microscopically and noted that it might suggest an active reabsorption process, but then proceeded to discount this conclusion on the basis of other observations.

Whether sweat returns via the duct or via the corneum can not be determined. If it returns to the body via the corneum and germinating layer, it would encounter the barrier layer whose resistance to water is considerable, perhaps too great to account for the rate of reabsorption. The rate of evaporation from the nonsweating human forearm is approximately 0.2–0.8 mg/hr/cm² (Baker and Kligman, 1967; Spruit, 1971). Presumably this would also reflect the rate of reabsorption, and in general agreement with this Adams (1966) has estimated the rate at which water reenters the body from the cat foot pad at 1.38 mg/hr/cm². Compared with this, the evaporative water loss from the palm during sudorific activity is of the order of 5–20 mg/hr/cm² (Adams and Vaughan, 1965).

The comparison of secretory rates with probable reabsorptive rates through a nonsweat gland channel implies the participation of the sweat gland in the reabsorption of sweat, if one is to account for the

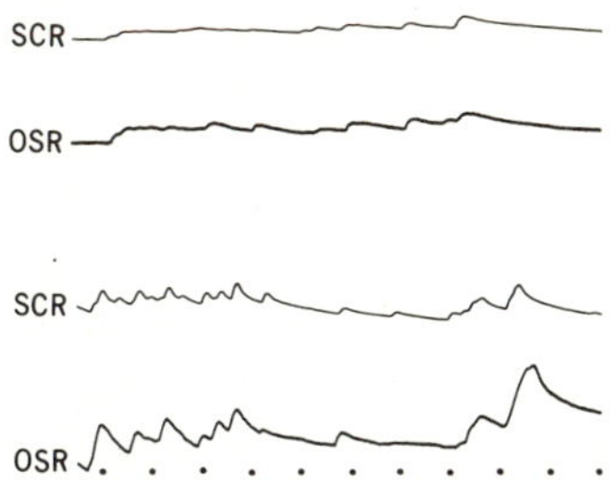

FIG. 12. Comparison of waveform of skin conductance response (SCR) and optical sweat response (OSR) in two different subjects. Upper traces: examples showing slow recovery; lower traces, rapid recovery.

capacity of reabsorption to keep up with secretion. However, this conclusion may be unwarranted. During measurement of insensible evaporative water loss, care is taken to reduce sudomotor activity to a minimum, for example, by local administration of scopolamine (Baker and Kligman, 1967). Under these conditions, tonic and phasic activation of the epidermal membrane would be minimal or absent, and observed rates of water transfer across it may be only a small fraction of that occurring during sweat gland activation, when presumably the membrane is also activated. Moreover, measurements of the water resistance of the corneum have been made by evaporation into a dry atmosphere. It seems entirely possible that this rate is enhanced when the corneum is wet and, therefore, swollen. The situation may be similar to the behavior of a layer of dry mulch which is almost impervious to water until it has had time to become "wet," after which water runs through it readily. Suchi (1955) in a similar vein has suggested that the sweat duct wall in the corneum might be more permeable to water when wet than when dry.

The data on rate of output of sweat have been obtained with the surface exposed to a current of dry air (Adams and Vaughan, 1965) and are presumed to be maximal. On the other hand, reflex reabsorption has been accomplished under conditions in which the corneum is well hydrated (usually by the application of an impermeable plate or prism). This condition is very likely to cause partial occlusion of the pores and reduction in sweat output. It is likely that a well-hydrated site will show less sweating and greater absorption than quantitative data would indicate, and an extraductal route may account for all of the reabsorbed sweat.

An alternative route for the return of sweat is via the corneum until it meets the barrier, then laterally across the sweat duct wall, then down the duct, penetrating the barrier, then outward across the wall into the germinating layer. This layer contains a network of intercellular canaliculi through which even very large molecules move readily (Nordquist et al., 1966). It would finally enter the dermis by diffusing across the dermoepidermal boundary. One could postulate that the site of the control gate is either at the sweat duct wall or at the dermoepidermal boundary, but since evidence already presented implicates a nonsweat gland area, one would be inclined to place the control gate at the dermoepidermal boundary. This route is not too likely if water must reenter the duct at a time when intraductal pressure is high. On the other hand, if the secretory response (or myoepithelial contraction) is actually over in the first second, this may be a likely route. The fact that vapor waves from a dry site last about

5 seconds may reflect a lag due to the hydraulic capacitance of the corneum (Adams, 1966) rather than the actual duration of secretion. Whichever route is taken, whether transductal or transbarrier, the control gate is considered to lie in the epidermis rather than the duct. If sweat crosses the barrier layer via the ductal route, it implies that the control is most likely at the dermoepidermal boundary. If it takes the transbarrier route, the gate may lie anywhere below the corneal barrier.

The membrane in addition to controlling rate of return of water, also appears to change its permeability to ions. The evidence from experiments with electrolytes (Edelberg *et al.,* 1960) supports this view, and in addition one may point to the fact that the major increase in conductance usually occurs after the onset of the positive SPR. Another piece of supporting evidence is Shuster's (1963) demonstration that pressure on the skin increases not only the rate of reabsorption of water but of ions as well.

The avenue of approach of surface ions to the control membrane may be directly through the corneal barrier rather than via the duct. Despite its low *specific* conductivity, the epidermal area is very great as compared with the cross-sectional area of the sweat glands, over 200:1 over the entire body according to Kuno (1956, p. 18). There is considerable evidence, reviewed elsewhere (Edelberg, 1971a), which demonstrates that relatively large ions may migrate from the surface to the granular layer and even through, though not necessarily beyond, the germinating layer.

5. The Positive Potential (Membrane) Change Observed at the Skin Surface Increases As the Sweat Ducts Become Fuller and Hence As Skin Potential Becomes More Negative

One additional requirement of the physiological model is that it account for the fact that positive SPRs do not normally appear until the SPL exceeds a certain level (Fig. 11), and moreover that the higher this level, the larger the amplitude of this response component. The correlation of the amplitude of the positive SPR with the magnitude of the negative skin potential level has been reported by Montagu (1958), Trehub, Tucker, and Cazavelan (1962), and Wilcott (1967a). This observation can easily be explained by supposing that a neural process which initiates the positive response comes into play only as higher levels of SPL, and therefore of activation, are reached. The sequence in Fig. 11 suggests this may be happening, since the first two slowly recovering potential responses are not accompanied by fast-recovering conductance responses. In many other cases, however, fast-recovering conductance responses do occur at low SPL along with uniphasic negative SPRs. This observation, together with that of the covariation of LPR and positive SPR amplitude with SPL (Fig. 4), suggest that for some reason higher negative SPL facilitates the (surface) observation of positive responses of membrane origin.

A likely explanation, a physical one, rests upon the mosaic model of internal circuit currents (Edelberg, 1968) described earlier. Consider first the case of a membrane that changes its conductivity only, the membrane potential remaining constant. Any change in the internal resistance of the membrane, can be observed only if there is another parallel structure serving as the second leg of the voltage divider (Fig. 6). As long as the sweat ducts are not filled to the point at which the epidermal membrane is punctuated by open ducts, the skin will behave as if it is a homogeneous membrane, and any changes in the epidermis will show up as a conductance change without an associated potential response. This is the basal state described by Christie and Venables (1971) in which the observed skin potential is considered to reflect only the epidermal membrane potential, negative with respect to the tissues, but not as negative as when the ducts become filled. In terms of the mosaic model, the above condition would be described as one in which the internal resistance of the sweat duct limb of the circuit is so high that changes in epidermal resistance have a negligible effect upon the division of voltage and hence upon the surface potential.

As the ducts are filled, and the internal resistance of the sweat unit falls, the surface becomes more negative as a consequence of the re-distribution of internal voltages. Concomitantly, the relative resistances of the two elements becomes such that the system is sensitive to a decrease in the internal resistance of the epidermal limb, resulting in a positive shift of surface potential. For example, if the resistance of the (composite) sweat duct were 1 MΩ, and its potential 35 mV, while the resistance of the membrane were 50 kΩ, and its potential 10 mV, a change in membrane resistance to 40 kΩ would alter surface potential by only 0.23 mV. If the resistance of the sweat duct fell to 100 kΩ, as a result of filling, the same membrane change would cause a 1.17 mV shift in surface potential. The latter case would also be associated with a more negative surface resting potential, 18.3 mV as compared with 11.2 mV. It should be appreciated that this discussion pertains to a change in the internal resistance of the membrane, and not of the pathway to the surface produced by hydration. The latter also produces changes, as discussed in another section.

The above can represent only part of the story. If the membrane which is responsible for generating the skin potential response is the same which gives rise to the LPR, as has been argued here, its activation must be associated with a positive shift in the transmembrane potential. The reasoning is that the positive LPR is easily produced from the nail bed which has no sweat glands; the internal circuit model can therefore not be invoked to explain these potential responses on the basis of conductivity changes alone. That conductivity changes occur in this membrane is evident in the local *conductance* responses which are also elicited from the nail bed.

How does one account for the fact that changes in membrane *potential* can be observed at the surface only at higher SPLs? The answer can be found in a reexamination of the internal circuit analysis (Edelberg, 1968). The expression for representation of the surface potential when the measuring instrument has a very high input resistance is:

$$P = E + [R_e/(R_e + R_s)]S - [R_e/(R_e + R_s)]E$$

Where P is the surface potential, E the epidermal potential, S the sweat gland potential, R_e the internal and series resistance of the epidermis, and R_s the internal and series resistance of the sweat gland (Fig. 6).

If R_e and R_s do not change during the response, the change in surface potential, ΔP, for a given change in epidermal potential, ΔE, with no change in sweat gland potential, would be:

$$\Delta P = \Delta E - [R_e/(R_e + R_s)]\Delta E$$

If R_s is very much smaller than R_e, this reduces to:

$$\Delta P = 0$$

If R_s is very much greater than R_e, it reduces to:

$$\Delta P = \Delta E$$

Of considerable importance is the fact that the relative representation of epidermal membrane changes at the skin surface is a function not of the absolute internal resistances but of their ratio.

In the case of the skin, Adams (personal communication) has argued that a zone in the corneum beneath the barrier layer may be especially active in terms of change in its hydration and dehydration. This zone, he believes, is isolated from the surface to an extent by an intermediate barrier. Buettner (1965) has reported evidence for such a barrier. When the skin is at rest, reabsorption would tend to dehydrate this zone, resulting in a high resistance in series with the epidermis. In this condition, with the sweat glands filled only to the level of the germinating layer, the ratio of R_e to R_s is very high and very little, if any, of the change in membrane potential would be reflected at the surface. As sweat rose still further in the ducts, R_s would fall, producing a negative potential shift at the surface. Subsequently, as sweat diffused into the corneum, there would be a slow potential drift, due in part to fall of the sweat level in the ducts and in part to hydration of the corneum, and reduction in R_e. The slow rate of this effect (Fig. 11) implies that it does not account for the usual positive SPR, though overflow from the sweat pore into a dry corneum may do so.

As R_e falls, the ratio of R_e to R_s would become such as to allow a significant portion of any change in membrane potential to appear at the surface. The proportion of such representation would increase as the corneum became more hydrated at its deeper levels, a condition associated with full ducts and hence high negative SPL. As a result of the intermediate barrier, manipulation of surface hydration may have little effect on conditions at the deeper region.

This restraint upon the surface observation of membrane processes could account for the reliable covariation of the amplitudes of LPR and positive SPR seen in Fig. 4. The alternative explanation, that such covariation reflects tonic influences upon the membrane that is their common site of origin, while attractive for many reasons, is more speculative. Even if tonic influences should mediate this effect, the contribution of the internal circuit would have to be taken into account.

A. Peripheral Controls

A range of evidence points to the existence of two components which frequently participate in the same response but which may dissociate to varying extents. It seems that the sweat gland is *always* involved. The activity of the epidermis, however, appears to be highly variable and to determine whether reabsorption occurs very rapidly or slowly, whether conductance responses recover rapidly or slowly, and whether an appreciable positive SPR accompanies the EDR. The nature of the neural controls which permits this spectrum of behavior is at present a matter of speculation.

There are two major requirements, among others, to be met by any postulated system of neural controls. One of these is that there be an arrangement for differential regulation of secretory and epidermal membrane activity, in order to account for the response specificity of EDA indicated by the variation in its recovery rate. Secondly, there must be a provision to account for the relatively stabile delay in any individual between the onset of the conductance response and that of the positive limb of the SPR. Various possibilities that meet these requirements may be considered; at present there does not appear to be a sufficient basis for making a choice, but some are in considerably better agreement with available evidence than are others. Apparent alternative choices may be briefly listed:

1. Separate innervation, centrally time-locked, for the sweat gland and for the membrane; tonic modulation of either element is neither required nor ruled out.

2. A single phasic innervation to both elements with diffusion delay to the epidermal (or ductal) membrane, and with independent tonic modulation of the membrane.

3. A single phasic innervation to the sweat gland alone, with mechanical triggering of the membrane, and with tonic modulation of the membrane alone.

In each case, variation in tonic modulation of the membrane would be seen as affecting the amplitude of its response to a neural burst of any given intensity. The first of these possibilities, with the help of internal circuit currents to explain the effects of SPL on the positive SPR, can account for essentially all findings, and it may be parsimonious to adopt it. However, the supposition that the two controls are independent, though time-locked, while not improbable enough to warrant dismissing it, nevertheless is more contrived than the others. The third possibility is tentatively rejected on the grounds that mechanical triggering by intraductal pressure should cause a variation in the phase relation according to the fullness of the ducts at the onset of the response. The SPL is considered a reliable indicator of duct filling, and the phase lag has been shown to be independent of SPL (Edelberg, unpublished data).

This leaves us with the second possibility as most acceptable, in that it allows independence of control of the two elements, yet makes no requirement for exact central neural time-locking of their discharge. The likelihood of a 1-second added response delay for the positive SPR due to diffusion time is not unrealistic. Of the 1.5 to 2 second latency typically found at the palm, about one third is probably due to peripheral conduction time, since the difference in appearance of the response at the forehead and foot is of the order of 1 second (Bloch, 1965). Bloch concludes that an appreciable portion of the latency is accounted for by delay at the neuroglandular junction. In further support of this, he reports a latency of .77 seconds when the peripheral nerve of the cat is stimulated near the foot pad. Patton (1948) also presents evidence for a long neuroglandular delay in the EDR. With doubling or tripling of diffusion distance from nerve ending to epidermal effector, the longer delay of the positive SPR would be accounted for. It should be remembered, however, that an unknown part of the delay in Bloch's experiment is attributable to the latent period of the sweat gland itself.

The location of the water control gate, since it appears to be under neural control, is probably in the germinating layer. In view of the profusion of canaliculi in this layer, it is probably freely permeable to water throughout, and a gate would likely be at its upper or lower boundary. Nerve fibers have been observed in the epidermis (Arthur and Shelley, 1959). The authors reported finding intraepidermal fibers only on nonpalmar, nonplantar surfaces, but in the discussion section of their paper, Rothman cites work by Yamazaki, demonstrating another type of intraepidermal fiber found only on the palms and soles. It is tempting to hypothesize that these differentially staining fibers reflect different innervation of contact and of noncontact areas. Arthur and Shelley concluded that the nonpalmar, nonplantar fibers were probably sensory. If they are not sensory, it is possible that they control the permeability of the upper cell layers. Since cells near the granular layer are in a degenerative stage, however, it does not seem likely that they would participate in such activities. A more likely site is the dermoepidermal boundary, which is easily accessible to nerve endings and is an active cell layer.

An experiment by Takagi and Nakayama (1959) sheds light on the location of this active membrane. They applied a blistering agent, removed the corneum, and recorded from the exposed area. They observed positive SPRs. Since blisters form *below* the granular layer (Rothman, 1954, pp. 699–707), it is presumed that the origin of these responses must have been at the last remaining barrier, namely the dermoepidermal boundary.

Inhibition of the tonic discharge to the control gate, by reducing tonic and phasic sweat reabsorption, would allow most of the secreted sweat to reach the surface, flooding it and thereby affording the organism a passive type of defense mechanism. The inactivation of the membrane component of the response would attenuate or eliminate the positive SPR and would also retard the recovery rate of the SRR. Slowing of recovery rate in the face of various noxious or threatening situations does in fact occur (Edelberg, 1971b, 1972b; Furedy, 1972).

Even if the above considerations are valid, another determinant of the potential level of the epidermis must be considered, namely electrolyte balance, in particular extracellular potassium and sodium levels. Christie and Venables (1971a, 1971b) have demonstrated that when the concentration of the external electrolyte is controlled, the skin potential reached at basal (inactive) conditions is a function of the internal/external concentration gradient of potassium or of sodium. They attributed this to an effect upon the epidermal potential. Fowles and Venables (1968, 1970a) have also considered the effects of internal electrolytes upon skin potential and have arrived at the conclusion that these influences may be mediated by alteration of the state of the sweat duct, incidental to variation in the rate of reabsorption of sodium. They suggest that this process is controlled by aldosterone level, and therefore subject to the effects of stress-induced adrenocorticotropic hormone (ACTH) release. It is of interest that another hormone, ADH, has recently been implicated in the regulation of sweat secretion (Quatrale and Speir, 1970).

B. Compatibility with Other Observations

The application of this hypothesis to numerous other observations in the literature was tested during its formulation. It may be useful to consider some of these results as they relate to this model.

Wilcott's (1962b) finding of very high intraindividual correlations between positive SPRs and sweat responses are consistent with the model, which assumes both are produced by the same discharge. Other of Wilcott's data (1964) showing a dissociation between sweating, skin potential, and skin resistance are also predicted by the present model. It should be pointed out, however, that Wilcott's (1967a) interpretation of these and other findings has led him to hypothesize an entirely opposite relationship, namely that the epidermal response accounts for the negative SPR, "sweating depolarization" for the positive.

Another observation by Wilcott (1964) is explained rather well by the present working model. He applied high currents to the skin and found that regardless of its direction, SPL became more positive, and positive SPRs were attenuated. Negative SPRs were at the same time potentiated. Since the sweat gland is assumed to account for the negative SPR, potentiation of this component implies that the current was not adversely affecting the sweat gland. In fact, considering the convincing arguments against the sweat gland as a likely route for electrical current flow, the current was probably not even reaching the secretory segment of the sweat gland at appreciable density. The membrane was the more likely target. If the high current tended to depolarize it, it would as a consequence increase its ion permeability, causing a positive shift in surface potential, as well as inactivating the membrane as a responding element. This is consistent with this author's observation (Edelberg, unpublished data) that high current causes a marked slowing of the recovery limb, a result to be expected if the fast-recovering membrane component is eliminated from the combined response.

Wilcott's observations (1958b, 1962a) that the negative SPR is not affected by exsanguination despite the elimination of sweating appears to be at odds with the proposed mechanism for this component of the potential response. Nakayama and Takagi (1958) also reported disappearance of the positive but not the negative SPR by arterial occlusion. A replication of Wilcott's study by this author (Edelberg, unpublished data) reveals that there is an immediate large increase in amplitude of the negative component upon termination of the occlusive episode. The reappearance of the positive wave was delayed some minutes, a finding also reported by Wilcott (1958b). A plausible explanation is that the negative SPR was also attenuated by the interruption of blood flow. The concurrent depression of the epidermal response would reduce the rate of sweat reabsorption as well as the opposing positive deflection, thereby resulting in an *apparent* maintenance of negative SPR amplitude.

Two interrelated observations on the action of $AlCl_3$ may also be consistent with the model, though with some uncertainty. One of these is the finding that topical application of 1 M $AlCl_3$ produces a sevenfold increase in the positive SPR (Edelberg, 1972a) and in the SRR (Edelberg *et al.,* 1960) from the distal segment of the finger. The other is the demonstration by Papa and Kligman (1967) that the antiperspirant effect of $AlCl_3$ is due not to the fact that it closes the sweat pores, but that it so increases the rate of reabsorption of sweat that little reaches the surface. In terms of the present model one would postulate that $AlCl_3$ reduces the discharge threshold of the membrane so that even with small responses and low neural tonicity, discharge tends to be maximal, potentiating positive SPRs, SRRs, and absorption. At a gross level, this seems to fit the requirements for compatibility with the model, but consideration of the possible physicochemical mechanisms by which the necessary ends are achieved injects a considerable element of doubt.

Martin and Venables (1966), in an evaluation of the role of the sweat gland, state that atropine has little effect on SPL. This finding is at odds with the expectations of the present model. The study cited (Venables and Martin, 1966) does show, however, that atropine reduced SPL by about 10 mV, i.e., by about one quarter. In view of the finding (Edelberg, 1968) that the average potential difference between sweat gland and epidermal areas was 11 mV, this does not appear to be inconsistent with present predictions. Moreover, if atropine, in addition to its effect on the sweat gland, also blocks impulses to the epidermis, the contribution of this effect to surface potential would be a negative shift which would in part cancel the effect due to action on the sweat gland. Since atropine blocks all skin conductance and potential responsivity (Martin and Venables, 1966), any innervation of an active epidermal membrane is presumably cholinergic.

A more serious contradiction to the present model is their finding in the same study that neostigmine induced sweating, yet caused a fall in SPL. This, too, may not be serious if we consider the likelihood that neostigmine, being an anticholinesterase, would tend to enhance depolarization of the epidermal membrane, contributing to a positive shift in SPL. Apparently this may outweigh the opposing effect on the sweat gland.

Richter (1926) found that atropine or neural section does not alter the resistance of the back of the hand. This would indicate that tonic discharge does not contribute to SPL, and would also be consistent with Bloch's (1965) conclusion that SCL is determined not by tonic discharge but by the cumulative effects of previous activity. In view of the fact that at low levels of tonic discharge no effect should be expected from these blocking procedures, there remains the question of whether they were accomplished at adequate control levels of tonic discharge to demonstrate its cessation. An added reason to suspect a tonic discharge to the membrane is the observation that the increase in negativity of the palm which occurs during activation is frequently accompanied by a decrease in negativity on various nonpalmar areas (Edelberg and Cook, unpublished data). It is also possible that the tonic discharge influences excitability but not resting conductance.

Another pharmacologic effect to be tested against the proposed model is the temporal difference in the disappearance (and return) of positive and negative SPR components after hyoscyamine blockade (Martin and Venables, 1964). This can be explained by the influence of SPL on the positive SPR. Whether the positive response is of membrane or of hydration origin, this effect should cause it to disappear prior to the cessation of sweat gland activity and to reappear some time after the resumption of sweat gland responses.

The finding by Loveless and Thetford (1966) that the positive SPR habituates faster than the negative is consistent with the model, despite the assumption of a single discharge to both elements. This finding would not require independent central rates of habituation of two separate processes. Rather it may resemble the hyoscyamine sequence. As the sweat response diminishes, SPL presumably reaches the point at which it is too low to allow observation of positive SPRs at the surface. If those authors were actually observing positive SPRs due to hydration of the corneum, the same sequence would be expected. There is some question, however, about which response habituates first, since two subsequent studies have reported results in the opposite direction (Shmavonian *et al.,* 1968; Raskin *et al.,* 1969). Forbes and Bolles (1936), in agreement with Loveless and Thetford, found it was the positive SPR that habituated most readily.

One last observation may be considered in the light of the proposed system. How is the response specificity of palmar *vs.* dorsal sites to be explained? While separate independent neural supplies to the two areas may be postulated, it is still possible to account for this phenomenon within the framework of variations in relative activities of epidermal and sweat gland components. We need only assume that the tonic level may be adjusted rapidly. When a change in epidermal excitability occurs as a result of such regulation, the ratio of subsequent response amplitudes from any two sites having a difference in sweat gland concentration must also change. The changing demands of the task situation can apparently call forth different adaptations; a change in tonic discharge to the dermoepidermal boundary may be one of these.

C. A Critique of the Hydration Model

While the involvement in EDA of a labile membrane, either ductal or epidermal, appears very likely, it is conceivable that the SRR and negative SPR are due to the presecretory process in the glandular membrane (Martin and Venables, 1966), and that other phenomena are explained by the simple effects of ductal filling and hydrating of the corneum. Adams (1967) and Stombaugh and Adams (1970) have taken a well-defended stand in support of a simplified model in which even the presecretory process is ignored, and *all* effects are attributed to filling of the ducts and wetting of the corneum. In view of the rationality of Adams' arguments, it seems profitable to examine the extent to which such a model is tenable.

The evidence pointing to the participation of an active membrane in the electrodermal response rests especially on the effects of various ions. The nature of these effects is suggestive of their action on biological membranes. The potentiating (or attenuating) effect of the various ions used, however, corresponds to their position in the lyophyllic series; aluminum would exert the greatest dehydrating effect on the corneum, potassium among the least. As Peiss and Randall (1957), Brebner and Kerslake (1964), and Sarkany *et al.* (1965) have demonstrated, increasing hydration of the corneum leads to swelling of the keratin ring and closure of the sweat pore. An electrolyte such as KCl which permits corneal hydration would promote poral closure, thereby reducing sweating and perhaps, therefore, the EDR, as found empirically. Conversely the aluminum ion, which dehydrates the corneum, would keep the sweat pores fully open and result in potentiation of any sweat gland contribution to the total response. The aluminum ion can produce a dramatic potentiation of the positive SPR (Edelberg, 1972a), an effect which at first glance seems to imply the involvement of a membrane. The hydration model (Edelberg, 1968) predicts that drying of the corneum should cause larger (though slower) SPRs as sweat diffuses from the duct into the surrounding dehydrated corneum, a prediction which is empirically supported.

A serious objection to the hydration model is seen in the fact that the potentiating effect of aluminum and other ions varies considerably as a function of polarity of current, an occurrence which in biology almost certainly implies the involvement of a membrane. A second objection is the conclusion reached by Lykken, Miller, and Strahan (1966), on the basis of the analysis of electrical transients, that very little of the SRR can be attributed to an ohmic change. Gildemeister (1928) reached a similar conclusion though on a less convincing basis. Yet another observation which appears to demand the involvement of an active membrane is the sudden appearance of a reabsorption reflex, discussed elsewhere in this paper, although even this effect could be explained by postulating the sudden (unlikely) occurrence of poral closure at the observed site.

While the effects of ions on SRR amplitude can conceivably be due to their effect on the hydration of the corneum, two other chemical effects probably can not. One is the attenuating effect of the cationic detergent sodium benzalkonium chloride (Zephiran) in only 0.005 M concentration (Edelberg et al., 1960). Detergents have been recognized for their powerful lytic effect upon biological membrane (Hober et al., 1948). Another chemical factor is pH. This, too, is unlikely to exert its powerful effect by virtue of hydration of the corneum. Even these agents could be supposed to exert a specific hydrating effect upon the swelling properties of the keratin ring around the sweat pore, such that they cause poral closure at lesser degrees of hydration.

If we allow for a considerable sensitivity of the hydration properties of the corneum to the chemical environment, much of the electrical behavior of the skin becomes consistent with a passive hydration model. Probably the two most difficult observations to account for in terms of this model are the reabsorption reflex and the effect of polarity upon the potentiation of SCR by certain cation and anions. Regarding the polarity effect, one may postulate such unusual properties as a differential change in permeability of the corneum to cations and anions when it becomes hydrated. This in effect gives selective membrane characteristics to the corneum; the departure of these properties from the expected characteristics of wet corneum tends to exceed the limits of plausibility.

The hydration model explains, par excellence, the nature of the effects of artificial alteration of the hydration of the skin on skin potential and on SPR (Edelberg, 1968; Fowles and Rosenberry, 1970; Fowles and Venables, 1970b). It also is consistent with numerous other observations, including those of Adams and his co-workers on the relation of conductance changes to sweat production and that of Darrow *et al.* (1957) on the synchrony between the occurrence of the positive SPR and the visual appearance of sweat at the surface. Its compatibility with other findings requires the assumption of such unlikely mechanisms that the arguments take on an aspect of incredibility. Its defense appears tenable only if one also considers the presecretory glandular membrane response as the origin of potential and conductance changes. This membrane could serve to account for those phenomena with which the simple hydration model has such difficulty. The evidence afforded by the intraductal experiments of Shaver *et al.* (1965) and of Schulz *et al.* (1965) tends to discredit such an assumption. Moreover the remote likelihood that the agents which so markedly alter SCR amplitude can do so by reaching the secretory portion of the sweat gland also discourages this stand. It appears that if hydration is to take the place of a ductal or epidermal membrane in explaining experimental observations, it must do so without the help of the secretory membrane, a task which it appears to fall short of accomplishing.

VII. Overview

A. THE SWEAT CIRCUIT MODEL

The foregoing arguments lead to a picture of the cutaneous portion of the neurodermal system, consisting of a sweat gland with a high intraluminal negative potential and an active epidermal membrane, probably located at the dermoepidermal junction. This membrane has an outside negative potential, though not as negative as that of the sweat gland. A single (phasic) neural discharge causes increased secretion by the sweat gland and a delayed increase in the permeability of the membrane. The extent of the permeability increase in the membrane is determined by the tonic discharge level of an independent innervation. It may be essentially absent at times.

The phasic discharge is not accompanied by any appreciable change in the potential (and probably conductance) of the glandular portion of the sweat gland. The rise of sweat in the ducts causes an increase in conductance level of the site, and, due to internal circuit currents, an increase in surface negativity. The discharge of the epidermal membrane is delayed about 1–2 seconds due to additional time required for diffusion of acetylcholine; when it occurs, it produces a positive shift in membrane potential, observable at the surface only if the sweat ducts are filled adequately to hydrate the deeper regions of the corneum. It is accompanied by an increase in permeability to ions and also to water. The former provides a significant contribution to the conductance response. The latter enhances the rate of reabsorption of sweat.

If the tonic discharge to the membrane is low, the EDR may be mainly sudorific. It will be characterized by uniphasic negative SPRs and slow SCR recovery limbs. If the tonic discharge is high, positive SPRs will be prominent (provided the ducts are filled), and SCRs will have rapid recoveries, reflecting the greater contribution of the epidermal membrane. At intermediate tonic levels, the membrane effect may be enough to accelerate recovery of the negative SPR but not sufficient to produce a net positive deflection. The result is a fast recovering negative SPR.

When the corneum is only partially hydrated, diffusion of sweat from the duct may, by increasing corneal conductivity at its deeper levels, cause a different kind of positive deflection due to internal current flow. It is distinguishable from positive membrane responses by the longer duration of build-up, and its slower recovery. If the *surface* of the corneum is dry, i.e., when a "dry" electrode paste or none at all is used, overflow of sweat from the pores may also produce a positive deflection, one which is considerably faster than its deeper counterpart. Returning sweat as well as potential-driven ions probably enter the dermis primarily across the dermoepidermal junction, but it is not certain whether the path is directly across the corneal barrier layer or whether penetration of that zone is made via a short length of the sweat duct.

This concept of peripheral mechanisms is consistent with the major observations reported in the literature. Some of its characteristics seem a bit contrived; too many degrees of freedom are allowed in accounting for various observations. It nevertheless presents an integrated model which can serve usefully as one against which to test future observations, and to be modified where appropriate.

B. The Water Control Gate and Adaptation

The question arises as to the adaptive function of the control gate that regulates water reabsorption. A land-locked animal must conserve water and toward this end is provided with a water-resistant covering. Various requirements, thermoregulatory and mechanical, demand that he be provided with a system for getting water across the barrier into the corneum in a controlled manner. The reabsorption of excess sweat provides him not only with a water economy measure but with a means of more delicate regulation of the adaptive processes. The level of corneal hydration reached would depend on the activity of the gate control, which presumably may be "set" by the CNS in accordance with situational requirements. If the surface is to be used for ambulation, a higher level of hydration may be desired, and reabsorption would be set at a lower level. For a nonaggressive defense, flooding of the surface could be accomplished by complete inhibition of reabsorption, a type of protection which is reminiscent of the emergency discharge of mucous by frog skin (Wilcott, 1967b). For manipulative activity where delicate adjustment of surface moisture is advantageous, a higher reabsorption rate would be adaptive.

These effects could in fact be accomplished without any change in secretory rate. On the other hand, variation in secretion could accomplish the same end without any change in rate of reabsorption. Why then should this added mechanism of control have evolved? One answer seems to be in the finer adjustment made possible by the combined controls over secretion and reabsorption, and in the lesser tendency of the system to overshoot and to oscillate. Examples of dual controls over autonomic effectors are common throughout the body, for example, in the control of pupil size, of heart rate, of stomach motility, or of blood sugar. Another benefit appears to be in the diversity of hydration effects allowed by the two mechanisms, i.e., in the relative wetting of the surface and of the deeper regions of the corneum.

One other advantage is considerably more speculative. Opening of the control gate, either by the local mechanical effect of contact (the LPR mechanism) or by a neural action, would enhance the flux of water through the germinating layer, bringing oxygen to the region and removing wastes. In such a case, the "setting" of the water permeability of the control gate or its discharge by mechanical disturbance may represent an indirect tactile sensitization mechanism and may explain the apparent relation of electrodermal discharge to tactile sensitivity (Edelberg, 1961b).

Acknowledgment

The preparation of this article and much of the research which it covers have been supported in part by Grant MH-19722 and previous grants from the National Institute of Mental Health.

References

Adams, T. (1966). Characteristics of eccrine sweat gland activity in the footpad of the cat. *Journal of Applied Physiology* 21, 1004–1012.

Adams, T. (1967). Skin electrical phenomena as established by sweat gland activity and skin hydraulic capacitance. *Federation Proceedings* 26, 446.

Adams, T., and Hunter, W. S. (1969). Modification of skin mechanical properties by eccrine sweat gland activity. *Journal of Applied Physiology* 26, 417–419.

Adams, T., and Vaughan, J. A. (1965). Human eccrine sweat gland activity and palmar electrical skin resistance. *Journal of Applied Physiology* 20, 980–983.

Adams, T., Morgan, M. L., Hunter, W. S., and Holmes, K. R. (1970). Temperature regulation of the unanesthetized cat during mild cold and severe heat stress. *Journal of Applied Physiology* 29, 852–858.

Arthur, R. P., and Shelley, W. B. (1959). The innervation of human epidermis. *Journal of Investigative Dermatology* 32, 397–411.

Ax, A. F., and Bamford, J. L. (1970). The GSR recovery limb in chronic schizophrenia. *Psychophysiology* 7, 145–147.

Baker, H., and Kligman, A. M. (1967). Measurement of transepidermal water loss by electrical hygrometry. *Archives of Dermatology* 96, 441–452.

Berlyne, D. E. (1966). Curiosity and exploration. *Science* 153, 25–33.

Bloch, V. (1965). Le contrôle central de l'activité électrodermale. (Étude neurophysiologique et psychophysiologique d'un indice sympathique de l'activation réticulaire.) *Journal de Physiologie (Paris)* 57, Supplement 13, 132 pp.

Brebner, D. F., and Kerslake, D. McK. (1964). The time course of the decline in sweating produced by wetting the skin. *Journal of Physiology (London)* 175, 295–302.

Buettner, K. J. K. (1965). The moisture of human skin as affected by water transfer. *Journal of the Society of Cosmetic Chemists* 16, 133–143.

Christie, M. J., and Venables, P. H. (1971a). Effects on "basal" skin potential level of varying the concentration of an external electrolyte. *Journal of Psychosomatic Research* 15, 343–348.

Christie, M. J., and Venables, P. H. (1971b). Sodium and potassium electrolytes and "basal" skin potential levels in male and female subjects. *Japanese Journal of Physiology* 21, 659–668.

Culp, W. C., and Edelberg, R. (1966). Regional response specificity in the electrodermal reflex. *Perceptual and Motor Skills* 23, 623–627.

Darrow, C. W. (1932). The relation of the galvanic skin reflex recovery curve to reactivity, resistance level, and perspiration. *Journal of General Psychology* 7, 261–271.

Darrow, C. W. (1936). The galvanic skin reflex (sweating) and blood pressure as preparatory and facilitative functions. *Psychological Bulletin* 33, 73–94.

Darrow, C. W. (1937a). Neural mechanisms controlling the palmar galvanic skin reflex and palmar sweating. *Archives of Neurology and Psychiatry* 37, 641–663.

Darrow, C. W. (1937b). The equation of the galvanic skin reflex curve: I. The dynamics of reaction in relation to excitation background. *Journal of General Psychology* 16, 285–309.

Darrow, C. W., and Freeman, G. L. (1934). Palmar skin-resistance changes contrasted with non-palmar changes, and rate of insensible weight loss. *Journal of Experimental Psychology* **17**, 739–748.

Darrow, C. W., Wilcott, R. C., Siegel, A., Wilson, J., Watanabe, K., and Vieth, R. (1957). The mechanism of diphasic skin potential response. *Electroencephalography and Clinical Neurophysiology* **9**, 169.

Ebbecke, U. (1921). Die lokale galvanische Reaction der Haut. Über die Beziehung zwischen lokaler Reizung und elektrischer Leitfähigkeit. *Pflüger's Archiv für die Gesamte Physiologie des Menschen und der Tiere* **190**, 230–269.

Edelberg, R. (1961a). Microelectrode study of the galvanic skin response. *Federation Proceedings, Federation of American Societies for Experimental Biology* **20**, 326.

Edelberg, R. (1961b). The relationship between the galvanic skin response, vasoconstriction and tactile sensitivity. *Journal of Experimental Psychology* **62**, 187–195.

Edelberg, R. (1963a). Electrophysiologic characteristics and interpretation of skin potentials. *U.S.A.F. School of Aerospace Medicine Technical Documentary Report* **TDR-63-95.**

Edelberg, R. (1963b). Influence of cooling of adjacent areas on GSR and base resistance of an isothermal site. *U.S.A.F. School of Aerospace Medicine Technical Documentary Report* **TDR-63-70.**

Edelberg, R. (1964a). Effect of vasoconstriction on galvanic skin response amplitude. *Journal of Applied Physiology* **19**, 427–430.

Edelberg, R. (1964b). Independence of galvanic skin response amplitude and sweat production. *Journal of Investigative Dermatology* **42**, 443–448.

Edelberg, R. (1965). Electrodermal responses from the fingernail: An enigma. *Annual Meeting, Society for Psychophysiological Research, 5th, Houston.*

Edelberg, R. (1966). Response of cutaneous water barrier to ideational stimulation: A GSR component. *Journal of Comparative and Physiological Psychology* **61**, 28–33.

Edelberg, R. (1967). Electrical properties of the skin. *In* "Methods in Psychophysiology" (C. C. Brown, ed.), Ch. 1. Williams & Wilkins, Baltimore, Maryland.

Edelberg, R. (1968). Biopotentials from the skin surface: the hydration effect. *Annals of the New York Academy of Sciences* **148**, 252–262.

Edelberg, R. (1970). The information content of the recovery limb of the electrodermal response. *Psychophysiology* **6**, 527–539.

Edelberg, R. (1971a). Electrical properties of the skin. *In* "Biophysical Properties of the Skin" (H. R. Elden, ed.), Ch. 15. Wiley, New York.

Edelberg, R. (1971b). The relation of slow electrodermal recovery rate to protective behavior. *Annual Meeting, Society for Psychophysiological Research, 11th, St. Louis.*

Edelberg, R. (1972a). Electrical activity of the skin. *In* "Handbook of Psychophysiology" (N. Greenfield and R. Sternbach, eds.), Ch. 9. Holt, New York.

Edelberg, R. (1972b). Electrodermal recovery rate, goal-orientation, and aversion. *Psychophysiology* **9**, 512–520.

Edelberg, R. (1973). The local electrical response of the skin to deformation. *Journal of Applied Physiology* **34**, 334–340.

Edelberg, R., and Beaver, W. (1972). Laterality of the skin potential response to tactual and motor activity. Unpublished manuscript.

Edelberg, R., and Burch, N. R. (1962). Skin resistance and galvanic skin response. Influence of surface variables and methodological implications. *Archives of General Psychiatry* **7**, 163–169.

Edelberg, R., and Wright, D. J. (1964). Two GSR effector organs and their stimulus specificity. *Psychophysiology* **1**, 39–47.

Edelberg, R., Greiner, T., and Burch, N. R. (1960). Some membrane properties of the effector in the galvanic skin response. *Journal of Applied Physiology* **15**, 691–696.

Fisher, S. (1958). Body image and asymmetry of body reactivity. *Journal of Abnormal and Social Psychology* **57**, 292–298.

Forbes, T. W., and Bolles, M. M. (1936). Correlation of the response potentials of the skin with "exciting" and "nonexciting" stimuli. *Journal of Psychology* **2**, 273–285.

Fowles, D. C., and Rosenberry, R. (1970). The effects of epidermal hydration on the positive skin potential response and on prestimulus skin potential level. *Annual Meeting, Midwestern Psychological Association, 42nd, Cincinnati.*

Fowles, D. C., and Venables, P. H. (1968). Endocrine factors in palmar skin potential. *Psychonomic Science* **10**, 387–388.

Fowles, D. C., and Venables, P. H. (1970a). The effects of epidermal hydration and sodium reabsorption on palmar skin potential. *Psychological Bulletin* **73**, 363–378.

Fowles, D. C., and Venables, P. H. (1970b). The reduction of palmar skin potential by epidermal hydration. *Psychophysiology* **7**, 254–261.

Fujimori, B. (1955). Studies on the galvanic skin response using the current and potential methods. *Japanese Journal of Physiology* **5**, 394–405.

Furedy, J. J. (1972). Electrodermal recovery time as a supra sensitive autonomic index of anticipated intensity of threatened shock. *Psychophysiology* **9**, 281–282.

Gildemeister, M. (1928). Über elektrischen Widerstand, Kapazität und Polarisation der Haut, II. Menschliche Haut. *Pflüger's Archiv für die Gesamte Physiologie des Menschen und der Tiere* **219**, 89–110.

Gildersleeve, K. R., Edelberg, R., and Nichols, S. (1972). Factors influencing the lateral asymmetry of the electrodermal response. Unpublished manuscript.

Grueninger, W. E., Kimble, D. P., Grueninger, J., and Levine, S. (1965). GSR and corticosteroid response in monkeys with bilateral frontal ablations. *Neuropsychologia* **3**, 205–216.

Harrison, J. (1964). The behavior of the palmar sweat glands in stress. *Journal of Psychosomatic Research* **8**, 187–191.

Hober, R., Langston, M., Strausser, H., and Macey, R. (1948). Studies on the physiological effects of non-polar-polar organic electrolytes. II. The influence of detergents upon the potentiometric reaction and the contractility of nerve and muscle. *Journal of General Physiology* **32**, 111–120.

Holmquest, D., and Edelberg, R. (1964). Problems in the analysis of the endosomatic galvanic skin response. *Psychophysiology* **1**, 48–54.

Katkin, E. S., Weintraub, G. S., and Yasser, A. M. (1967). Stimulus specificity of epidermal and sweat gland contributions to GSR. *Journal of Comparative and Physiological Psychology* **64**, 186–190.

Krause, C. F. (1844). "Wagners Handworterbuch der Physiologie," Vol. 2, p. 131. Quoted by Kuno (1956).

Kuno, Y. (1956). "Human Perspiration." Thomas, Springfield, Illinois.

Lacey, J. I. (1959). Psychophysiological approaches to the evaluation of a psychotherapeutic process and outcome. *Research in Psychotherapy, American Psychological Association Conference, Washington, D. C.*

Langworthy, O. R., and Richter, C. P. (1930). The influence of efferent cerebral pathways upon the sympathetic nervous system. *Brain* **53**, 178–193.

Leiderman, P. H., and Shapiro, D. (1964). Studies on the galvanic skin potential level: some behavioral correlates. *Journal of Psychosomatic Research* **7**, 277–281.

Lewis, T., and Zotterman, Y. (1926–1927). Vascular reactions of the human skin to injury: VIII. The resistance of the human skin to constant currents, in relation to injury and vascular response. *Journal of Physiology (London)* **62**, 280–288.

Lloyd, D. P. C. (1961). Action potential and secretory potential of sweat glands. *Proceedings of the National Academy of Sciences. U. S.* **47**, 351–358.

Lockhart, R. A. (1972). Interrelations between amplitude, latency, recruitment and the Edelberg recovery measure for the galvanic skin response. *Psychophysiology* **9**, 437–442.

Loveless, E., and Thetford, P. E. (1966). Interpretation and conditioning of the positive and negative components of the skin potential response. *Psychological Record* **16**, 357–360.

Lykken, D. T., Miller, R. D., and Strahan, R. F. (1966). GSR and polarization capacity of the skin. *Psychonomic Science* **4**, 355–356.

McCleary, R. A. (1950). The nature of the galvanic skin response. *Psychological Bulletin* **47**, 97–117.

Mackinnon, P. C. B. (1969). The palmar anhidrotic response to stress in schizophrenic patients and in control groups. *Journal of Psychiatric Research* **7**, 1–8.

Martin, I., and Venables, P. H. (1964). The contribution of sweat gland activity to measures of palmar skin conductance and potential. *Annual Meeting, Society for Psychophysiological Research, 4th, Washington, D. C.*

Martin, I., and Venables, P. H. (1966). Mechanisms of palmar skin resistance and skin potential. *Psychological Bulletin* **65**, 347–357.

Montagu, J. D. (1958). The psycho-galvanic reflex: a comparison of A.C. skin resistance and skin potential changes. *Journal of Neurology, Neurosurgery and Psychiatry* **21**, 119–128.

Montagu, J. D., and Coles, E. M. (1966). Mechanism and measurement of the galvanic skin response. *Psychological Bulletin* **65**, 261–279.

Mordkoff, A. M., Edelberg, R., and Ustick, M. (1967). The differential conditionability of two components of the skin conductance response. *Psychophysiology* **4**, 40–47.

Munger, B. L., and Brusilow, S. W. (1961). An electron microscopic study of eccrine sweat glands of the cat foot and toe pads: evidence for ductal reabsorption in the human. *Journal of Biophysical and Biochemical Cytology* **11**, 403–417.

Nakayama, T., and Takagi, K. (1958). Two components involved in galvanic skin response. *Japanese Journal of Physiology* **8**, 21–30.

Nordquist, R. E., Olson, R. L., and Everett, M. A. (1966). The transport, uptake, and storage of ferritin in human epidermis. *Archives of Dermatology* **94**, 482–490.

Obrist, P. A. (1963). Skin resistance levels and galvanic skin response: unilateral differences. *Science* 139, 227–228.

Papa, C. M., and Kligman, A. M. (1966). Sweat pore patterns. *Journal of Investigative Dermatology* 46, 193–197.

Papa, C. M., and Kligman, A. M. (1967). Mechanisms of eccrine anidrosis. II. The antiperspirant effect of aluminum salts. *Journal of Investigative Dermatology* 49, 139–145.

Patton, H. D. (1948). Secretory innervation of the cat's foot pad. *Journal of Neurophysiology* 11, 217–227.

Peiss, C. N., and Randall, W. C. (1957). The effect of vapor impermeable gloves on evaporation and sweat suppression in the hand. *Journal of Investigative Dermatology* 28, 443–448.

Pugh, L. A., Oldroyd, C. A., Ray, T. S., and Clark, M. L. (1966). Muscular effort and electrodermal responses. *Journal of Experimental Psychology* 71, 241–248.

Quatrale, R. P., and Speir, E. H. (1970). The effect of ADH on eccrine sweating in the rat. *Journal of Investigative Dermatology* 55, 344–349.

Raskin, D. C., Kotses, H., and Bever, J. (1969). Autonomic indicators of orienting and defensive reflexes. *Journal of Experimental Psychology* 80, 423–433.

Rein, H. (1929). Die elektrophysiologie der haut. *In* "Handbuch der Haut und Geschlechtskrankheiten" (J. Jadassohn, ed.), Vol. 1, pp. 43–91. Springer-Verlag, Berlin and New York.

Richter, C. P. (1926). The significance of changes in the electrical resistance of the body during sleep. *Proceedings of the National Academy of Sciences, U. S.* 12, 214–222.

Richter, C. P. (1929). Physiological factors involved in the electric resistance of the skin. *American Journal of Physiology* 88, 596–615.

Rothman, S. (1954). "Physiology and Biochemistry of the Skin." Univ. of Chicago Press, Chicago, Illinois.

Sarkany, I., Shuster, S., and Stammers, M. C. (1965). Occlusion of the sweat pore by hydration. *British Journal of Dermatology* 77, 101–104.

Schulz, I., Ullrich, K. J., Frömter, E., Holzgreve, H., Frick, A., and Hegel, U. (1965). Mikropunktion und electrische Potentialmessung an Schweissdrusen des Menschen. *Pflüger's Archiv für die Gesamte Physiologie des Menschen und der Tiere* 284, 360–372.

Schwartz, H. G. (1934). Reflex activity within the sympathetic nervous system. *American Journal of Physiology* 109, 593–604.

Schwartz, H. G. (1937). Effect of experimental lesions of the cortex on the "psychogalvanic reflex" in the cat. *Archives of Neurology and Psychiatry* 38, 308–320.

Shaver, B. A., Jr., Brusilow, S. W., and Cooke, R. E. (1962). Origin of the galvanic skin response. *Proceedings of the Society for Experimental Biology and Medicine* 110, 559–564.

Shaver, B. A., Jr., Brusilow, S. W., and Cooke, R. E. (1965). Electrophysiology of the sweat gland: Intraductal potential changes during secretion. *Bulletin of the Johns Hopkins Hospital* 116, 100–109.

Shmavonian, B. M., Miller, L. H., and Cohen, S. I. (1968). Differences among age and sex groups in electrodermal conditioning. *Psychophysiology* 5, 119–131.

Shock, N. W., and Coombs, C. H. (1937). Changes in skin resistance and affective tone. *American Journal of Psychology* **49**, 611–620.

Shuster, S. (1963). Graded sweat-duct occlusion; technique for studying sweat-gland function. *Clinical Science* **20**, 89–95.

Spruit, D. (1971). The interference of some substances with the water vapor loss of human skin. *Dermatologica* **142**, 89–92.

Starch, D. (1910). Mental processes and concomitant galvanometric changes. *Psychological Review* **17**, 19–36.

Stombaugh, D. P., and Adams, T. (1970). Skin potential and conductance in the footpad of the cat as functions of eccrine sweat gland activity and epidermal hydration. *Federation Proceedings, Federation of American Societies for Experimental Biology* **29**, 794.

Suchi, T. (1955). Experiments on electrical resistance of the human epidermis. *Japanese Journal of Physiology* **5**, 75–80.

Takagi, K., and Nakayama, T. (1959). Peripheral effector mechanism of galvanic skin reflex. *Japanese Journal of Physiology* **9**, 1–7.

Thomas, P. E., and Korr, I. M. (1957). Relationship between sweat gland activity and electrical resistance of the skin. *Journal of Applied Physiology* **10**, 505–510.

Trehub, A., Tucker, I., and Cazavelan, J. (1962). Epidermal b-waves and changes in basal potentials of the skin. *American Journal of Psychology* **75**, 140–143.

Venables, P. H., and Martin, I. (1966). The relation of palmar sweat gland activity to level of skin potential and conductance. *Psychophysiology* **3**, 302–311.

Venables, P. H., and Martin, I. (1967). Skin resistance and skin potential. *In* "A Manual of Psychophysiological Methods" (P. H. Venables and I. Martin, eds.), Ch. 2. Wiley, New York.

Wang, G. H. (1957). The galvanic skin reflex: A review of old and recent works from a physiologic point of view. *American Journal of Physical Medicine* **36**, 295–320.

Wang, G. H. (1958). The galvanic skin reflex: A review of old and recent works from a physiologic point of view. *American Journal of Physical Medicine* **37**, 35–57.

Wang, G. H. (1964). "The Neural Control of Sweating." Univ. of Wisconsin Press, Madison, Wisconsin.

Wang, G. H., and Lu, T. W. (1930). Galvanic skin reflex induced in the cat by stimulation of the motor area of the cerebral cortex. *Chinese Journal of Physiology* **4**, 303–324.

Wenger, M. A., and Irwin, O. C. (1936). Fluctuations in skin resistance of infants and adults and their relation to muscular processes. *University of Iowa Studies in Child Welfare* **12**, 143–179.

White, M. M. (1930). Relation of bodily tension to electrical resistance. *Journal of Experimental Psychology* **13**, 267–277.

Wilcott, R. C. (1958a). Correlation of skin resistance and potential. *Journal of Comparative and Physiological Psychology* **51**, 691–696.

Wilcott, R. C. (1958b). Effects of local blood removal on the skin resistance and potential. *Journal of Comparative and Physiological Psychology* **51**, 295–300.

Wilcott, R. C. (1960). A comparison of palmar and non-palmar skin conductance. *Journal of Comparative and Physiological Psychology* **53**, 38–41.

Wilcott, R. C. (1962a). Effects of exsanguination on sweating and skin potential responses. *Journal of Comparative and Physiological Psychology* **55**, 1136–1137.

Wilcott, R. C. (1962b). Palmar skin sweating vs palmar skin resistance and skin potential. *Journal of Comparative and Physiological Psychology* **55**, 327–331.

Wilcott, R. C. (1963). Effects of high environmental temperature on sweating and skin resistance. *Journal of Comparative and Physiological Psychology* **56**, 778–782.

Wilcott, R. C. (1964). The partial independence of skin potential and skin resistance from sweating. *Psychophysiology* **1**, 55–66.

Wilcott, R. C. (1965). A comparative study of the skin potential, skin resistance, and sweating of the cat's foot pad. *Psychophysiology* **2**, 62–71.

Wilcott, R. C. (1966). Adaptive value of arousal sweating and the epidermal mechanism related to skin potential and skin resistance. *Psychophysiology* **2**, 249–262.

Wilcott, R. C. (1967a). Arousal sweating and electrodermal phenomena. *Psychological Bulletin* **67**, 58–72.

Wilcott, R. C. (1967b). Skin potential response of the frog. *Journal of Comparative and Physiological Psychology* **63**, 214–219.

Wilcott, R. C. (1969). Electrical stimulation of the anterior cortex and skin-potential responses in the cat. *Journal of Comparative and Physiological Psychology* **69**, 465–472.

Wilcott, R. C., and Bradley, H. H. (1970). Low-frequency electrical stimulation of the cat's anterior cortex and inhibition of skin potential responses. *Journal of Comparative and Physiological Psychology* **72**, 351–355.

Yokota, T., Takahashi, T., Kondo, M., and Fujimori, B. (1959). Studies on the diphasic wave form of the galvanic skin reflex. *Electroencephalography and Clinical Neurophysiology* **11**, 687–696.

The Adipose Tissue System and Food Intake

Robert A. Liebelt, Cassius B. Bordelon,[1] and
Annabel G. Liebelt

*Departments of Cell and Molecular Biology and Medicine,
Medical College of Georgia, Augusta, Georgia*

I. Introduction

"Obesity results from overeating." This widely accepted truism implies that excess lipid accumulation in adipose tissue reflects a food intake in excess of the body's energy requirements. This concept has resulted in focusing cardinal attention on factors controlling food intake, and in assigning a passive role to the adipose tissue mass of the body by considering it a mere storage compartment of the lipid resulting from unnecessarily ingested calories. This attitude in part can be traced back to the long-held idea of Flemming who in 1871 suggested that adipose tissue is nothing more than the nonspecific accumulation of excess lipids in the loose connective tissue cells pervading

[1] Present address: Department of Anatomy, Baylor College of Medicine, Houston, Texas.

211

the entire body (Flemming, 1871). However, subsequent data and thinking have now questioned this conclusion, resulting in the elevation of adipose tissue to the status of a highly specialized tissue which, in the minds of some, deserves the dignity of being considered a full-fledged, organ-type complex. This newly found elevation of adipose tissue to a structural complex capable of responding to and perhaps even initiating regulatory-type stimuli in the control of lipid deposition and mobilization raises the question as to the possible interdigitating roles of adipose tissue function and food intake regulation. The existence of such a functional relationship has been suggested (Hervey, 1969; Kennedy, 1953; Lepkovsky, 1973), but the supporting data remain scanty and inconclusive. Thus, it would appear timely to reexamine this enigma. Therefore the emphasis of our studies has been directed to the question "Does a feedback mechanism exist between adipose tissue and regulatory mechanisms for food intake located in the central nervous system?" Both topics namely "adipose tissue" and "food intake regulation" have been exhaustively reviewed in two of the "Handbooks of Physiology" (Renold and Cahill, 1965; Code, 1967), and therefore it would be presumptuous on our part to attempt to once again review the literature as pertains to the objectives of this presentation. Although our own work will serve as the basis for the development of certain concepts and ideas, it becomes almost needless to say that reports of numerous investigators have influenced our thinking and approach to this problem in spite of our citing only specific works.

II. Origin and Evolution of the "Fat Organ Concept"

The recent selection of adipose tissue as a specific topic covered by a total of 93 authors in one of the "Handbooks of Physiology" (Renold and Cahill, 1965) perhaps best reflects the culmination of the efforts and thoughts of numerous investigators who have attempted to overcome the 100-year-old attitude that adipose tissue is nothing more than a nonspecific accumulation of lipids in loose connective tissue cellular elements by providing evidence favoring the specialized nature of adipose tissue. During this span of time at least three major contributions began to focus attention on the specialized nature of adipose tissue: Wassermann (1926) concluded that the fat lobule represents a distinct anatomical structure arising from a primitive organ made up of a complex of mesenchymal cells and capillaries which, upon being filled with lipid, can be designated a fat organ. Actually, several investigators prior to Wassermann including Toldt (1888), Hammar (1895), and Maximow (1927) essentially agreed that adipose tissue cells were specialized cells differentiating from undifferentiated mesenchymal cells about blood vessels and challenged Flemming's conclusion that adipose tissue represented the accumulation of lipids in ordinary loose connective tissue cells. But Wassermann extended these findings by recognizing the similarity of the embryological development of adipose tissue and that of hematopoietic tissue and the reticuloendothelial system in particular, and added a functional dimension to the specialized nature of adipose tissue (Wassermann, 1965).

Another contribution was that of Wertheimer and Shapiro (1948) who correlated the data from their laboratory and from those of numerous other investigators, especially those of Schoenheimer and Rittenberg (1935), concerning the dynamic turnover rates of lipids in adipose tissue to dispel any notion that adipose tissue was metabolically inert.

Still another major contribution was the continued efforts of Hausberger (1938) who showed that undifferentiated tissue from regions committed to the formation of "white fat" depots differentiates into adipose tissue when transplanted to other sites. This biological finding plus the quantitative morphological demonstration of adipose tissue having an abundant blood supply (Gersh and Still, 1945) as well as a specific nerve supply (Boecke, 1933) tended to finalize the concept of adipose tissue as being a fat organ. It should be noted in passing, however, that the matter of innervation of white adipose tissue is being reexamined, since myelinated or nonmyelinated nerve fibers are only rarely seen with the electron microscope in white adipose tissue, and those encountered are some distance from the fat cells in the intercellular matrix (Napolitano, 1965). Also the use of a fluorescence technique for localization of catecholamines has demonstrated innervation of only the vasculature of the white adipose tissue (Wirsén, 1965a,b). Thus the mechanisms of neurogenic stimuli on fat organ physiology remain unclear.

Hausberger *et al.* (1954) also deserve credit for carrying out a series of both *in vivo* and *in vitro* biochemical studies in which they took into account the compartmentalization of adipose tissue into the lipid portion and lipid-free component (cellular and intercellular constituents). Thus, by relating the biochemical activity of adipose tissue to the lipid-free mass as contrasted to wet weight (including lipid), he and his colleagues provided evidence that the metabolic characteristics of adipose tissue in many instances manifested levels of biochemical activity comparable to those of liver and muscle.

Extension of the fat organ concept to man has been evidenced by the description of several specific anatomical sites containing adipose tissue in both the embryonic and adult man (Tedischi, 1946; Wassermann, 1965). The easily observed sex differences in "fat" distribution in man also supports this contention. Further support is derived from the use of certain anatomic sites of the body surface to determine degrees of obesity in man with the use of skin calipers (Keys and Brozek, 1953).

Many investigators have undertaken a biochemical analysis of specific facets of adipose tissue (Renold and Cahill, 1965). An area proving particularly fruitful concerns the system mediated through 3′,5′-cyclic adenosine monophosphate (AMP) which regulates the lipolytic activity of adipose tissue. Utilizing an approach of working with isolated "fat cells," the direct effects of various chemical compounds including hormones on the adipocyte can be analyzed (Rodbell, 1964). The continuing application of many of the newer techniques of cellular and molecular biology will undoubtedly extend our understanding of the fat organ concept. It is upon this background of morphological, physiological, and biochemical analyses that our own studies have evolved.

III. White Fat vs. Brown Fat

The "fat organ concept" engenders some confusion concerning the morphological and functional attributes of adipose tissue when no functional distinction is made between white and brown adipose tissue, since there is a tendency to interchange the functional attributes of these two types of adipose tissue. It has long been a source of debate (Johansson, 1959) whether white and brown adipose tissue are indeed discrete entities or merely interconvertible forms of the same tissue. Morphologically the "signet ring" appearance of the white fat cell differentiates it unmistakably from the multiloculated, centrally placed nucleus of the brown fat cell. Similarly, the yellowish-white appearance of white fat contrasts sharply with the light to dark brown appearance of brown fat. White adipose tissue constitutes the bulk of adipose tissue and is ubiquitously distributed throughout the organism. Brown adipose tissue is more restrictively distributed being found predominantly in the interscapular region of all newborn mammals as well as of certain adult mammals including the mouse and rat (Rasmussen, 1922; Sleter, 1969).

Biochemical studies have revealed that brown fat has an exceedingly high metabolic rate as compared to white adipose tissue. Some authors including Smith (1961) have concluded that brown adipose tissue is itself a site of heat production. This attribute is in agreement with the recently advanced hypothesis that brown adipose tissue serves a thermoregulatory function, especially in hibernating animals.

In spite of these differences between the two types of adipose tissue, there are several similarities that support the conclusion of Wertheimer and Shapiro (1948) that "brown fat tissue may be looked upon as adipose tissue that did not develop beyond its embryonic state." Favoring the "embryonic" nature of brown fat is the multilocular stage during white fat differentiation, the apparent replacement of brown fat cells by unilocular white fat cells with aging, and the experimental conversion of multilocular brown fat cells to unilocular cells by high fat or carbohydrate diets or by denervation (Hull, 1966). However, the recent distinction between the ultrastructural arrangement of the mitochondria found in white and brown fat cells has permitted the suggestion that unilocular cells in brown fat regions differ ultrastructurally from those in white fat regions (Hull, 1966). Furthermore, this has led to the speculation that the presence of unilocular cells in predominantly brown fat areas and the replacement of multilocular by presumably white fat cells may indicate brown fat cell replacement by hyperplasia of white adipose tissue rather than a transformation of brown to white fat (Hull, 1966). Thus, it would appear to be premature at this time to consider functional attributes of brown adipose tissue to be identical to those of white adipose tissue as encompassed in the "fat organ concept."

IV. Physiological Implication of the "Fat Organ Concept"

A. CHICK EMBRYO

Our initial studies in this field reemphasized the implications of Wassermann's "fat organ concept" as manifested at the organismal level of organization. Utilizing the chick embryo and subsequently the adult chicken, we were able to demonstrate (Liebelt and Eastlick, 1952) that localized masses of adipose tissue or fat depots developed consistently in 16 specific anatomical sites at relatively specific times of development and persisted throughout the adult life of the bird. In the adult bird, an allometric growth relationship exists between the lipid-free component (cellular plus intercellular matrix) of a specific fat depot and body weight, similar to that found for other organs (von Bertalanffy, 1960). On the other hand, the lipid content of this same fat depot showed a relationship to body weight that suggested independence of the lipid from the lipid-free components of adipose tissue. The lipid-free or cellular complex appeared to reflect a more stable type of development as compared to the lipid component of a given fat organ, since the latter fluctuated with the nutritional status of the host more readily. Subsequent investigations have been carried out on the biochemical characteristics of these same specific fat depots in the developing chick embryo (Feldman *et al.*, 1962a,b). All of these data support the concept that adipose tissue is distributed throughout the chick body as discrete anatomical structures which have the morphological and functional attributes of individual organs. Subsequently, similar findings were reported for other species of birds (King and Farner, 1965; McGreal and Farner, 1956).

B. Inbred Mouse

Numerous investigators have noted or taken advantage of the constant appearance of adipose tissue at definite body locations in a variety of embryonic and adult mammals. The discreteness in size and shape and the specificity of localization of the testicular (epididymal), parametrial, and pararenal fat depots in rodents has resulted in the preferential use of these structures for numerous physiological and biochemical investigations on adipose tissue (Renold and Cahill, 1965).

In an attempt to investigate the interrelationships between genetic, sex, hormonal, and nutritional factors in the development and functional characteristics of adipose tissue, we selected inbred strains of mice as the experimental model system. Two specific fat depots (Liebelt, 1959), the inguinal fat organs (IFO) and the gonadal fat organs (GFO), were concentrated on because (*1*) these fat organs persist at these sites throughout the lifespan of the animal, (*2*) the IFO represents a subcutaneous fat depot, whereas the GFO represents an internal structure, (*3*) these fat organs can be easily excised, and (*4*) there is a structural symmetry in that little differences in weight (3–5%) between right and left fat organs of either type can be found.

Two important qualifications, however, must be made regarding these two fat depots: (*1*) the IFO is invaded by the mammary gland ductile system during normal development and (*2*) the GFO in the female is the parametrial fat depot and not the fat depot surrounding the ovary. Thus any condition that causes mammary gland stimulation or regression (such as pregnancy or postpartum changes) precludes the use of IFO in studying changes in lipid, water, and lipid-free mass, and the anatomical disposition of the female GFO requires precise and careful dissection because of an extensive blood supply derived from the reproductive organs and of somewhat vague boundaries in extremely obese animals.

The growth characteristics of the GFO and IFO were originally studied in NH/Ki and CBA/Ki mice of both sexes, between the ages of 5 and 365 days and, subsequently, in eight additional strains (BALB/c/Ki, DBA/2/Ki, C3H/Ki, A/Ki, Af/Ki, C57Bl/Ki, AKR/Ki and YBR/Ki).[2] The IFO and GFO of each strain were studied with respect to changes in (1) lipid content, (2) water content, and (3) lipid-free material (cellular and intercellular constituents).

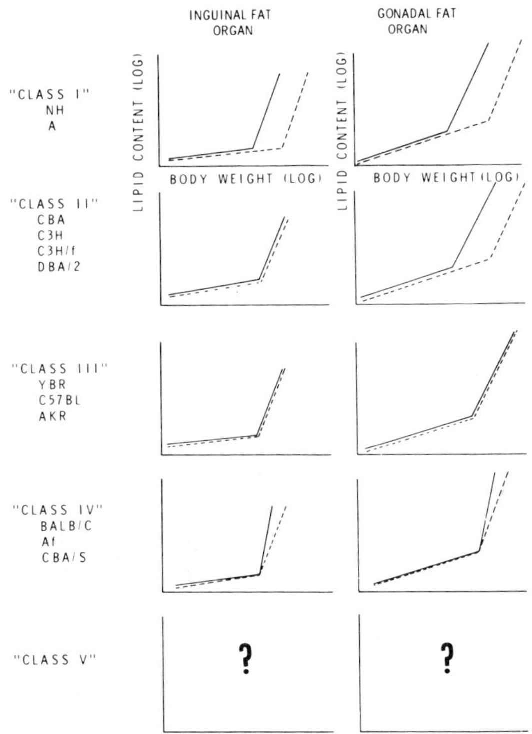

FIG. 1. A diagrammatic representation of the "classes" of patterns of lipid deposition related to sex differences between lipid content of inguinal and gonadal fat organs and body weight. "Class V" represents the existence of possible other types of patterns as additional strains of mice are studied (from Liebelt and Liebelt, 1969).

[2] Staats, J., ed. (1969). Inbred strains of mice. No. 6. Companion issue to *Mouse Newsletter* No. 41, July, 104–107. Jackson Laboratory, Bar Harbor, Maine.

Several basic observations were obtained from these studies. First, the growth of the lipid-free component of either fat organ follows an allometric pattern similar to that of other body organs and appears to be independent of lipid deposition within the fat organ during normal growth. Normal growth should be emphasized because in later discussions on the behavior of the fat organs during excessive deposition of lipid such as in goldthioglucose-induced obesity, the lipid-free component shows significant changes as the obesity progresses. Secondly, the water content of the fat organs is directly related to its lipid-free component and is not significantly influenced by the lipid content of the fat organ. Finally and perhaps of greatest significance was the finding of the important role of genetic factors and sex differences in fat organ physiology as reflected by lipid content. The patterns of lipid deposition in these two fat organs in the various strains could be divided into four different classes (Fig. 1): Class I—A sex difference in both IFO and GFO; Class II—a sex difference in GFO only; Class III—no sex difference in either IFO or GFO; Class IV—a tendency toward a sex difference in IFO and GFO or possibly an intermediate state between Classes I and III (Liebelt and Liebelt, 1969).

The question arose as to whether or not these patterns of lipid deposition were expressions of genetically determined factors. Appropriate genetic studies showed that F_1 hybrid mice of NH (Class I) and CBA (Class II) parentage were of the Class II type, while F_1 hybrids of BALB/c (Class IV) with CBA (Class II) parentage manifested Class IV patterns (Fig. 2). Additional genetic studies as to the segregation of the patterns in F_2 populations as well as in backcross type of studies are still in progress. The findings to date demonstrated that these patterns of lipid deposition are in part under the control of genetically determined factors which characterize a given strain of mouse.

These findings raised the question as to whether the genetic differences in patterns of lipid deposition were extrinsic or intrinsic to the fat organ *per se*. This question could be answered easily by the use of the parent-to-F_1 hybrid grafting technique in inbred mice, assuming that "free grafts" of adipose tissue would be accepted by the F_1 hybrid host and become physiologically functional. To date, the literature has recorded success of fat organ autografts in rats (Hausberger, 1955) and man (Woodruff, 1960), and we subsequently demonstrated the functional incorporation of adipose tissue grafts in the mouse's ear (Liebelt, 1963; Liebelt *et al.*, 1965).

"Free grafts" of adipose tissue from genetically "obese" NH mice and from genetically "lean" DBA/2 mice were implanted in the

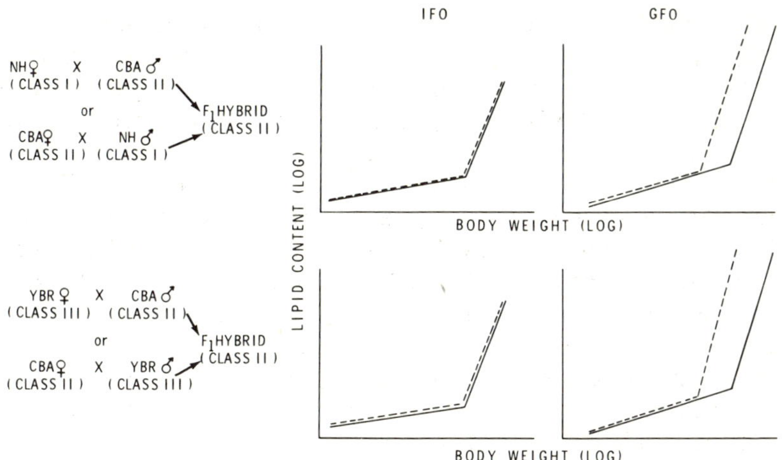

FIG. 2. A diagrammatic presentation of examples of genetic expression in the
F_1 hybrids of parents with different patterns of lipid deposition in inguinal (IFO)
and gonadal (GFO) fat organs as compared to body weight. Solid line is male;
dashed line is female.

right and left ear, respectively, of a single F_1 hybrid host. In effect
these two genetically distinct adipose tissues were exposed to an identical physiological environment in terms of ingested calories, hormonal
milieu, and energy expenditure. In spite of this common environment, the
two adipose tissues reflected their parental origin in that the grafts derived from the NH parent deposited a significantly greater amount of
lipid than did those from the DBA/2 parent. *Thus, the genetic basis or
"site of gene action" for the differences in quantities of lipid content
between the two strains appears to be localized within the adipose
tissue per se.*

The importance of genetic determinants in the problem of obesity
has been described (Mayer, 1953), and experiments determining the
site of gene action deserve attention. Hausberger (1959) concluded
that the obesity in the obese-hyperglycemic strain of mice was associated
with some systemic factor rather than with adipose tissue *per se.* This
is in contrast to our studies which suggest that the "obesity" observed
in the NH strain is related to some factor intrinsic to the adipose tissue
complex. However, a degree of caution must be exercised in interpreting the results at hand, for although the increased lipid deposition in
NH mice could be associated with an unique physiological mechanism
within the adipose tissue, it could also reflect a difference in vascularization potential or cellular growth potential of transplanted NH as compared to DBA/2 adipose tissue. Recently, we have found (Liebelt

et al., unpublished studies) that the fatty acid composition, as determined by gas-liquid chromatography, of the lipids obtained from IFO and GFO and ear grafts in CBA mice differ as to the palmitic (C16) and palmitoleic (C16-1) fatty acid contents. The mean C16 value in IFO and GFO was 19.2% as compared to a mean of 13% in the ear grafts; the C16-1 value was 6.45% and 14.9%, respectively. Thus, the question of physiological "normalcy" of the ear grafts of adipose tissue obviously must be considered in analyzing data obtained by this transplantation technique. Nevertheless, if a feedback type relationship does indeed exist between the adipose tissue system and the centrally located neurogenic mechanisms controlling food intake, then the importance of regulatory mechanisms intrinsic to adipose tissue *per se* becomes of increasing significance in attempting to understand the regulation of food intake.

Two troublesome questions arise from some of the above findings: First, to what extent does the lipid content of IFO and GFO reflect the lipid content of the entire "adipose tissue system," and how does the lipid content relate to the patterns of lipid deposition? Secondly, do all strains of mice have a relatively comparable amount of lipid stored for any given body weight, and do the patterns depicted merely reflect a difference in distribution of the lipid in the various fat depots?

We have to date completed studies related to these two questions in only four strains of mice (NH, CBA, BALB/c, and YBR), each representing one of the four classes of patterns of lipid deposition. In both sexes of all four strains, a direct relationship exists between the lipid content of IFO and total body lipid content. A similar direct relationship between GFO and total body lipid content in both sexes was found in the NH, BALB/c, and YBR strains of mice. However, there was a sex difference in the relationship between lipid content of the GFO and total body lipid content of male and female CBA mice, since for a given amount of body lipid the GFO of the CBA female contains approximately twice as much lipid as does that of the male. A similar sex difference has been described in guinea pigs in which the male stored more lipid in the internal depots than did females (Pitts, 1956). This relationship between the lipid content of IFO and GFO and total body lipid content is of physiological significance in that it suggests that lipid deposition proceeds in an orderly manner with respect to these specific sites.

Several investigators have taken advantage of this relationship from a practical point of view, namely using the lipid content of a given fat depot as an index of total body lipid content (Babineau and Page,

1955; Hull, 1960). But it also has been found, in rats at least, that the ratio of depot lipid to body lipid is age-dependent, decreasing with increasing age (Peckham *et al.,* 1962).

The total body lipid content represented different percentages of the body weight in the four strains. At a given body weight of 25 gm, the total body lipid content constituted approximately 35% vs. 20% in females and males, respectively of the NH strain as compared to 18% and 12% in CBA mice, 16% and 12% in BALB/c mice, and 10% in both sexes of YBR mice. Thus, it would appear that the patterns of lipid deposition are not reflections of a redistribution of similar body lipid contents among the various fat depots.

In an attempt to further study the effects of genetic factors on the development of inguinal and gonadal fat organs, (NH × CBA) F_1 and (CBA × NH) F_1 hybrids were used to evaluate the influence of both maternal and paternal genetics on patterns of lipid deposition in the offspring. It will be recalled that the NH strain represents a Class I type and CBA strain represents a Class II type. The lipid content of the IFO in the two reciprocal hybrid combinations showed the same developmental pattern as that observed in the CBA parent. The developmental pattern of the GFO was similar to both the NH and CBA parents as expected, since they are similar in the two classes. Of importance, though, was the amount of lipid deposited within the two fat organs in both F_1 hybrid combinations. Namely, it exceeded that normally found in CBA mice. It should be recalled that the NH strain of mouse becomes "obese" at approximately 6 months of age (30–35% of body weight represented by lipid), and both F_1 hybrid combination also attained an "obese state" at 8 months of age (35–40% of body weight represented by lipid). On the other hand a CBA mouse of similar age and body weight has only approximately 15% of the body weight existing as lipid. It would appear that while the pattern of development of the IFO and ostensibly the GFO in the F_1 hybrid mice is related to the genetic influence of the CBA parent, the quantitative difference in total body lipid content reflects the influence of the NH parent(s). A similar type of finding was obtained in a F_1 hybrid combination between CBA mice (Class II) and YBR mice (Class III). The F_1 hybrid offsprings were of the Class II type. A unique feature was that the "yellow" (CBA × YBR) F_1 hybrids were "obese," whereas the "brown" littermates were "lean." In spite of the differences in lipid content between the IFO and GFO of the "obese" and "lean" animals, the Class II pattern of lipid deposition prevailed in all (CBA × YBR) F_1 hybrids (Fig. 3). It has tentatively been proposed that at least two distinct genetically controlled mecha-

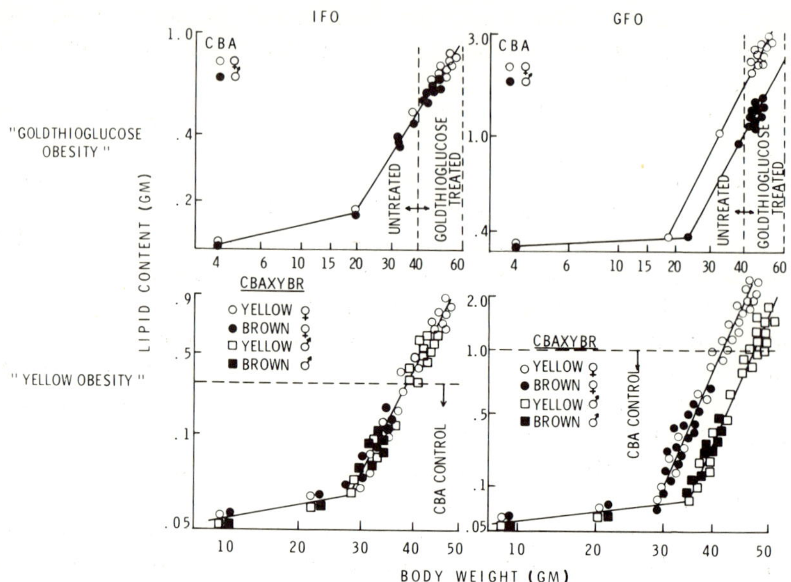

FIG. 3. Influence of superimposition of excessive lipid deposition as manifested in "goldthioglucose obesity" and "yellow obesity" on patterns of lipid deposition in inguinal (IFO) and gonadal (GFO) fat organs.

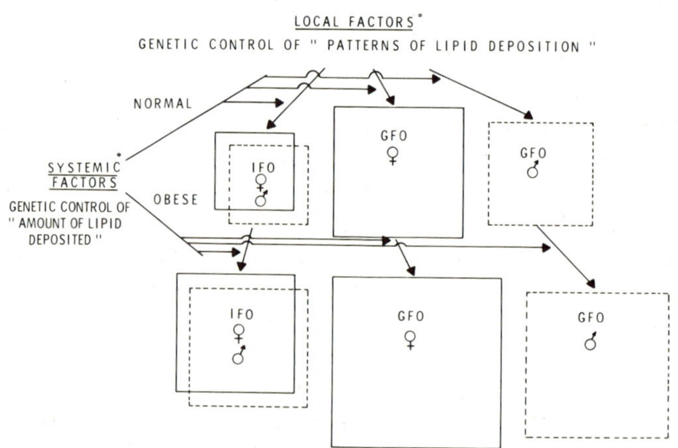

FIG. 4. A diagrammatic presentation of a working hypothesis related to the genetic control of "local" and "systemic" factors responsible for lipid deposition in inguinal (IFO) and gonadal (GFO) fat organs (from Liebelt and Liebelt, 1969). Factors to be considered. Local: (a) cell number; (b) vascular pattern; (c) innervation pattern; (d) cell metabolism. Systemic: (a) autoregulatory mechanisms; (b) hormonal; (c) neurogenic; (d) dietary.

nisms determined lipid content of the IFO and GFO: (*1*) the pattern of lipid deposition (rate) and (*2*) the amount of lipid deposited (Liebelt and Liebelt, 1969). A working hypothesis regarding these phenomena has been proposed (Fig. 4).

C. The Rat

Although the rat has been used extensively in studies concerned with food intake regulation and the biochemistry of adipose tissue, unfortunately relatively few studies have directed their attention to a systematic analysis of the fat organ concept in this commonly used laboratory animal. The data available point toward numerous similarities between the mouse and the rat in that specific fat depots of the latter including the inguinal, perirenal, and genital increase in proportion to body weight (Reed *et al.*, 1930; Hausberger and Gujob, 1937; Wislicki and Hermann-Hollander, 1966). Recently it has been shown that age, diet, and sex influence the rate of lipid deposition in seven fat depots of Osborne Mendel rats (Schemmel *et al.*, 1970a). The increasing availability of inbred strains of rats has also provided the opportunity to study the role of genetic factors in lipid deposition (Schemmel *et al.*, 1970b). The possibilities of using the rat to study the interrelationships between the adipose tissue mass and food intake regulation are numerous.

V. Response of the Fat Organs to Excessive Lipid Deposition in Experimentally Obese Mice

In the course of our studies it became important to determine to what extent the patterns of lipid deposition and the relationship of the lipid content in IFO and GFO to total body lipid content were altered by pathophysiological states in which excessive lipid deposition was superimposed upon these genetically controlled mechanisms operating during normal growth and development.

These studies were greatly facilitated by the original discovery of Brecher and Waxler (1949) that a single injection of goldthioglucose (GTG) produced a massive obesity in a certain percentage of injected mice. Later it was shown that the observed obesity was associated with the development of localized areas of destruction within the ventromedial region of the hypothalamus resulting in the development of hyperphagia (Liebelt and Perry, 1967). This observation not only provided us with a tool for study of the response of IFO and GFO to increased lipid deposition, but also provided a means for studying the effects of changes in fat organ characteristics on food intake regulation as mediated through those control mechanisms which are localized to the ventromedial region of the hypothalamus.

In the course of surveying the responsiveness of various inbred strains of mice in our laboratory to GTG, it was concluded that genetic factors were extremely important. The CBA/Ki mouse proved to be the strain of choice for our projected studies, since nearly 100% of these mice when injected with a single injection of GTG responded with a uniform and consistent weight gain leading to an obese state. This was in contrast to the variations and inconsistency of weight gain observed in other strains of mice and sublines of CBA mice from other sources. Thus, an experimental animal model was available to study the effects of progressive deposition of lipids in IFO and GFO upon the patterns and amounts of lipid that are characteristic of this strain during normal growth and development.

A striking contrast in the amount and rate but not in the Class II type pattern of lipid deposition in IFO and GFO following the administration of GTG (Fig. 3) was observed in CBA/Ki mice with the GFO depositing lipid at a more rapid rate than IFO (Liebelt *et al.*, 1965). This demonstrated that the "individuality" of these two fat organs in terms of rates and amounts of lipid deposition seen during normal development prevailed during the development of the GTG-induced obesity, and suggested that these genetically controlled phenomena manifested as differences in rates of lipid deposition between sexes were intact as excess lipid deposition proceeded.

As one could have predicted on the basis of the above that the genetic relationship between IFO and GFO lipid content to total body lipid content also persisted in the GTG-obese animals. This finding suggests the basic regulatory mechanisms were intact but functioning at a new "set point."

The establishment of a "set point" at some period during development as pertains to the determination of certain quantities of total body lipid content deserves mentioning. It has been shown in experimental animals that the body weight and body lipid content attained in adult life can be influenced by the size of the litter from which a given animal was obtained (Kennedy, 1957; MacDowell *et al.*, 1936; Parkes, 1926, 1929; Widdowson, 1965). The effect of litter size is essentially one of finding animals obtained from large litters neither attain the body weight nor body lipid content of animals derived from small litters at ages of 20–40 weeks, in spite of being on an *ad libitum* diet. It is assumed that those animals from larger litters did not receive as much milk during the suckling period as compared to those from small litters, and thus the level of nutrition during the early development stages brings about the establishment of a certain setting of a "set point" regulating body mass which is maintained throughout the normal life of the animal. We have carried out similar studies in mice with somewhat dissimilar results (McBurney, 1964). Using the BALB/c strain of mouse, the small nursing litter consisted of three pups and the large nursing litter, six pups. Animals from both sized litters and of both sexes were killed at weanling age (25 days) and at 120 days of age. Unexpectedly there were no significant differences in the body weights when comparing the two different sized litters at weanling and 120 days of age. Males and females of both sized litters attained approximately the same body weight by weanling age. However, the males of the small litter group showed the characteristic sex difference in increased body weight as compared to the female at 120 days, but there was no sex difference in body weight among animals from the large litter group. On the other hand, the lipid index (IFO + GFO lipid content) for weanling males and females of the small litter group was 59.8 ± 1.2 and 57.9 ± 1.5 mg respectively, whereas the weanling males and females of the large litter group showed an index of 58.5 ± 0.9 and 45.5 ± 1.8 mg, respectively. The males of the small litter group at 120 days had a lipid index of 238 ± 2.1 mg as compared to 269 ± 3.1 mg in the females. This was contrasted to a lipid index of 148 ± 3.2 and 183 ± 2.9 mg in the males and females, respectively in the large litter group at 120 days. The size of nursing litters also influenced heart and kidney weight at 120 days of age of a given mouse. *Although these data will be published elsewhere in more detail, it is sufficient to say that early nutrition during the nursing period of development can apparently establish a certain "set point" control level for specific components of the body mass, namely, adipose tissue.* It remains to be determined how food intake regulation is influenced by the manipulation of litter size.

The one observation suggesting a change in IFO and GFO responsiveness during development of the GTG-induced obesity was the difference in proportionality of the percent of lipid in IFO and GFO as related to total body lipid content. Whereas in both males and females the IFO accommodated approximately 6% of the total lipid content in both normal and obese mice, the GFO accommodated a strikingly higher percent of total body lipid content in both obese males (22.5% *vs.* 13.7%) and females (28.2% *vs.* 16.1%). A study was designed to answer the question as to whether the lipid-storing capacity of either IFO or GFO is responsible for this sex-dependent difference. CBA/Ki males and females ranging in age from 2 to 9 months were injected with the obesity-inducing dose of GTG (0.4 mg/gm body weight). Animals of increasingly older ages were selected so as the preinjection level of lipid content in IFO and GFO reflected an increasing proportion of the potential lipid-storing capacity of each fat depot. Superimposition of GTG-obesity revealed that the IFO does appear to have a ceiling on lipid deposition at approximately 0.5 grams, whereas a similar capacity could not be defined for the GFO. Thus, the differential potential of the two fat organs for accommodating the total body lipids could be accounted for by the IFO reaching its maximum capacity at 6% of total body lipid content (TBLC), with continued lipid deposition being accommodated in the seemingly limitless expansion of the GFO. In spite of this shift in deposition sites, the TBLC remained proportional to GFO as well as IFO lipid content. This suggested some form of interaction between IFO and GFO mediated on a systemic basis.

In ascertaining the basis for the differences in lipid-storing capacity of IFO and GFO, we studied the changes in cell size and lipid-free mass of IFO and GFO during GTG-obesity in CBA/Ki mice (Liebelt, 1963; Liebelt et al., 1965). It was found that the mean size of the fat cells increased rapidly up to approximately 40 days after injection and then remained relatively constant for the remainder of the study (110 days post-GTG injection). The lipid content of the IFO and GFO showed a similar type of pattern in that it increased rapidly and then continued to increase at a slower rate. On the other hand, the lipid-free component did not show a significant increase in weight until approximately 80 days after GTG injection. These results are consistent with earlier studies in the guinea pig (Pitts, 1956) which concluded that increased lipid deposition occurred initially in existing fat cells. The additional feature of our study is the suggestion that when the existing fat cells are "saturated," then new fat cells are formed to accommodate the increasing lipid content. Although our results do not permit us to conclude that adipose tissue underwent a hyperplasia during the development of GTG-induced obesity, several investigators have shown that the DNA content of specific fat depots of the rat increases with excessive lipid deposition (Peckham et al., 1962). Recently it has been concluded utilizing a technique of counting and sizing isolated fat cells that human obesity is accompanied by an increase in the number of adipocytes (Hirsch and Knittle, 1970). However, the obesity that follows the destruction of the ventromedial region of the hypothalamus of the rat appears to come about exclusively by an increase in adipose cell size (Hirsch and Han, 1969). Although mitotic activity has been demonstrated in adipose tissue utilizing the method of autoradiography (Hellman and Hellerstrom, 1961; Zingg et al., 1962), it remains to be demonstrated which cell type(s) undergoes mitotic division during hyperplasia of the fat organ. This remains one of the key problems in discussing the biology of the fat organs as pertains to obesity, especially as it relates to the neoplastic-like state of the adipose tissue mass in obese individuals. It is conceivable that continued stimulation of the adipose tissue mass through some mechanism associated with excessive food intake could initiate a neoplastic transformation and progressive increase in the cellular component of the adipose tissue mass.

VI. Autoregulation of the Adipose Tissue Mass

Any attempt to establish the existence of feedback mechanisms between adipose tissue and food intake requires support for the concept that the anatomically dispersed fat organs are in some manner functionally integrated into a unitary adipose tissue mass. The idea that anatomically dispersed tissue of a similar type can be integrated into a functional whole is not new since myeloid tissue functions within the body as an integrated unit as proposed in the erythron concept (Wintrobe, 1961). The integration of the numerous bones of the skeleton into a functional osseous mass concerned with regulating calcium levels in the body via the parathormone and thyrocalcitonin secretions represents another example. Perhaps a similar type of integrative relationship will be found for the muscle mass of the organism (Cahill, 1970). A study of the embryological development of adipose tissue permitted Wassermann to conclude that this tissue should be included with the blood-forming organs as a system of specific organs instrumental in the synthesis and release of lipids (Wassermann, 1958). Unfortunately, experimental data supporting the idea of an integrated system of adipose tissue are meager. Recently, advantage was taken of a rather simple technique in the mouse of transplanting pieces of syngeneic adipose tissue into intact hosts and those surgically deficient in adipose tissue (Liebelt, 1963). The rationale for this approach stems from the observations which indicate that the organism somehow exerts a close control over the growth of a particular tissue, so that the mass of that tissue is in proportion to the size of the organism as a whole (Poole, 1966). The persistence of this regulatory control in adult animals is revealed in part by the compensatory growth of remaining portions of a partially removed organ system, e.g., liver restoration (or regeneration) following subtotal hepatectomy (Bucher, 1963) and enlargement of the remaining kidney following unilateral nephrectomy (Williams, 1961).

The technique of transplantation of syngeneic tissues provides another approach to understanding the nature of these growth-regulating mechanisms. The principal assumption one must make is that superimposing normal syngeneic tissue upon an intact, adult host with a homeostatically regulated total organ mass should result in either a successful graft with compensatory reduction in size of the *in situ* organ, or an unsuccessful graft due to the inability of the host to incorporate excessive tissue mass as the result of some "inhibitory factor." However, in the latter case by this line of reasoning the graft should be successful in a syngeneic host in which a deficit for that particular tissue has been produced. These principles have been demonstrated with several tissues including the ovary and spleen in intact and ovariectomized or splenectomized hosts, respectively. Thus, a syngeneic ovary implanted into an intact female host will atrophy over a period of weeks, whereas identical ovarian tissue remains viable and even hormonally functional when implanted into an ovariectomized host (Krohn, 1959). Similarly, isogeneic splenic tissue remains viable and increases in mass when placed in a splenectomized host, whereas it atrophies in an intact host (Metcalf, 1964).

Applying this technique and rationale to the question of autoregulation of adipose tissue mass it was found that syngeneic grafts of adipose tissue showed evidence of necrosis or lack of vascularization in intact, adult hosts between 2 and 9 months after transplantation (Liebelt *et al.*, 1968). However, upon surgical removal of one or more fat depots to produce a deficit in the total adipose tissue mass, the number of viable adipose tissue grafts increase in similar genetic hosts during a comparable period (Fig. 5). It was concluded from this study that the anatomically dispersed fat organs appear to be under some form of autoregulation and integrated into a total adipose tissue mass (Fig. 6) and, hence, the basis for referring to the "adipose tissue system." Evidence that this growth-regulating mechanism is prevalent during the development of GTG obesity in adult mice is suggested by additional findings that

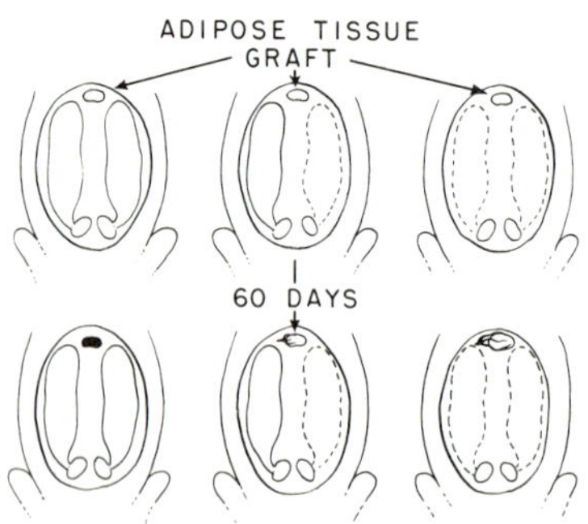

FIG. 5. A diagrammatic summary depicting the atrophy of syngeneic grafts of adipose tissue in intact hosts and the increasing vascularity and size of grafts in hosts with one or both gonadal fat organs surgically removed.

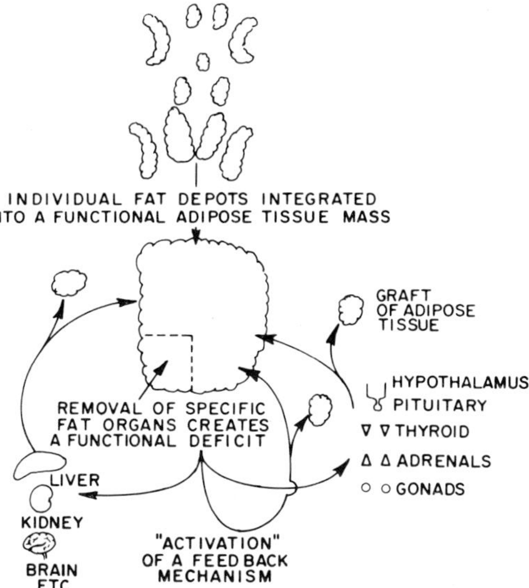

FIG. 6. A diagram depicting a working hypothesis for the possible mechanisms responsible for the integration (autoregulation) of the various fat depots of the body into an "adipose tissue system."

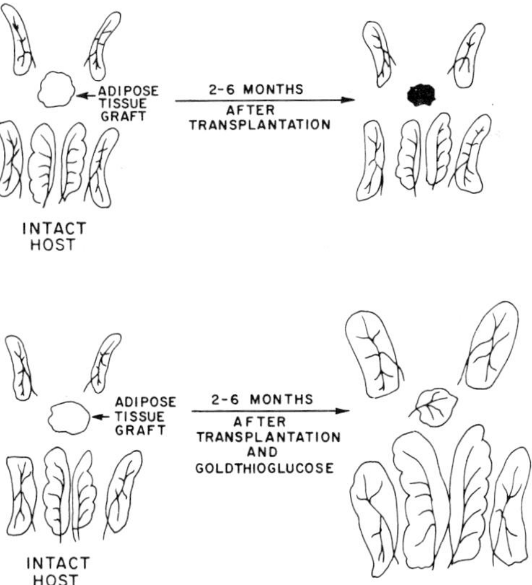

FIG. 7. A diagrammatic depiction demonstrating successful incorporation of syngeneic grafts of adipose tissue into the expanding adipose tissue mass during the development of goldthioglucose-induced obesity in intact CBA/Ki mice. This is in contrast to unsuccessful adipose tissue grafts (black) in normal, intact CBA mice.

syngeneic grafts are successful in intact hosts during the dynamic phases of weight gain and increased lipid deposition, but they are unsuccessful in intact hosts that are in the static phase of weight gain and lipid deposition at the time the syngeneic grafts are transplanted (Fig. 7).

The results of these transplantation studies, coupled with the findings of how the lipid content of IFO and GFO reflect the total body lipid content, provide encouragement for considering the anatomically dispersed fat depots as being systemically integrated into a functional adipose tissue mass. Whether humoral factors similar to erythropoietin (Gordon, 1959) or leukopoietins (Bierman, 1964), which are considered to play important integrative roles in hematopoiesis, or hormonal factors, known to influence lipid deposition or mobilization, represent the critical factors in regulating the adipose tissue mass will await further study.

VII. Food Intake Regulation in Goldthioglucose-Treated Mice

The uniquely uniform and consistent responsiveness of the CBA/Ki mice to the obesity-inducing effects of GTG has provided us with an opportunity to analyze in some detail the localization and destruction of certain areas of the brain following GTG, and in turn the localization at least in part of control mechanisms in this area of the brain that are associated with several physiological and behavioral modalities (Liebelt and Perry, 1967). There seems little doubt that the consistency with which localized lesions in the hypothalamus can be produced in some strains of mice following a single injection of GTG suggests an important role for this compound in future physiological investigations. Although the main interest in GTG has centered on the obesity and hyperphagia that develops with the hypothalamic lesions, lesions produced by GTG in this same area of the brain have been associated with endocrine dysfunction, ulcerogenesis, and possibly emotionality depending upon the strain of mouse used and dose of GTG administered (Liebelt and Perry, 1967). Unlike the placement of electrolytic lesions in selected areas of the brain, GTG-induced lesions are limited in a utilitarian sense in that they localize to specific sites as determined in part by the physiological state of the animal. Another limitation of this agent is that the lesions are not confined to the ventromedial region of the hypothalamus, but areas of destruction can also be found in the area postrema, subfornical, and preoptic areas in animals bearing GTG-induced ventromedial lesions. However, the size of the lesions in both the hypothalamic and extrahypothalamic sites can be regulated in part by dose, genetics, sex, and age of the mouse, making it possible to produce animals with defined but altered physiological states for investigation purposes. Although this topic has been reviewed recently (Liebelt and Perry, 1967), the present discussion will focus upon the hyperphagia and obesity occurring in several strains of mice following a single injection of GTG.

As noted above, the extent of hypothalamic destruction was found within morphological and functional limits related to the amount of GTG injected. Obviously measurements of the acute lesions induced by GTG within 2–3 days postinjection precluded any critical study relating degree of damage to food intake and weight gain. Thus, it became necessary to develop a technique that would permit assessment of the degree of hypothalamic damage some 30–60 days after GTG, when postnecrotic scar formation and shrinkage have taken place and sufficient time has elapsed for the obesity to develop.

Using a Zeiss Integrating Ocular and in later studies a planimeter on tracings obtained from 50-μ-thick serial sections through the hypothalamus, it was possible to estimate the area of the ventromedial nu-

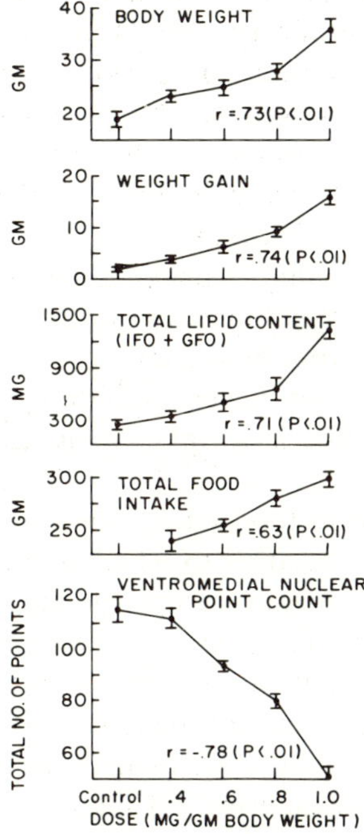

FIG. 8. The quantitative relationships between amount of goldthioglucose injected into Balb/c mice and body weight, weight gain, lipid content of inguinal (IFO) and gonadal (GFO) fat depots, total food intake, and ventromedial nuclear point count.

cleus in each section and thus the cumulative areas representing the volume of this nuclear complex (McBurney *et al.,* 1965). An inverse relationship was found by this method between dose of GTG administered 60 days prior to obtaining the brains and the remaining ventromedial nuclear complex. Several inherent difficulties in any method of this type must be recognized, including tissue changes associated with fixation and sectioning, shrinkage, and scar formation during the healing process, and the problem of estimating the exact boundaries of the nuclear complex for counting purposes. Nevertheless, increases in lesion size, food intake, weight gain, and lipid content of IFO and GFO were directly proportional to the dose of GTG injected and proportional inversely to the residual volume of the ventromedial nucleus (Figs. 8 and 9).

On the basis of these studies we proposed the existence of some form of quantitative representation of neural elements involved in food intake regulation existing in the mouse hypothalamus. The implications of this suggestion has some bearing on the studies described below.

The uniform response of CBA/Ki mice has also permitted food intake studies (Liebelt and Perry, 1967) to be carried out during the immediate postinjection period, the period of rapid increase in weight gain (dynamic phase), as well as the period when body weight plateaued (static phase). Characteristically, the food intake pattern occasionally shows a sharp decrease in food intake during the immediate postinjection period for 2–3 days; this is followed by a gradual increase in daily food intake, reaching a peak in approximately 2 weeks, and then by a gradual return to preinjection levels in another 2-week period (Fig. 10). Interestingly, food intake levels return to normal preinjection levels in treated males, but never quite return to baseline levels in females. This sex difference is a rather consistent finding and warrants further study.

This transient increase in food intake suggested an adaptation mechanism. The question was raised as to whether this change in food intake was indeed permanent. To explore this matter, CBA/Ki mice that had been obese as a result of a GTG injection 4 months earlier were starved for varying periods of time then returned to ad libitum feedings (Liebelt and Perry, 1967). The transient increase in food intake was again demonstrated suggesting that a permanent alteration was involved in food intake regulation mechanisms. Of interest was the observation that the animals upon refeeding plateaued at essentially the same body weight at which they had plateaued prior to starvation, and the same type of pattern was seen in nontreated control mice when starved and then refed. This finely regulated relationship between food intake and

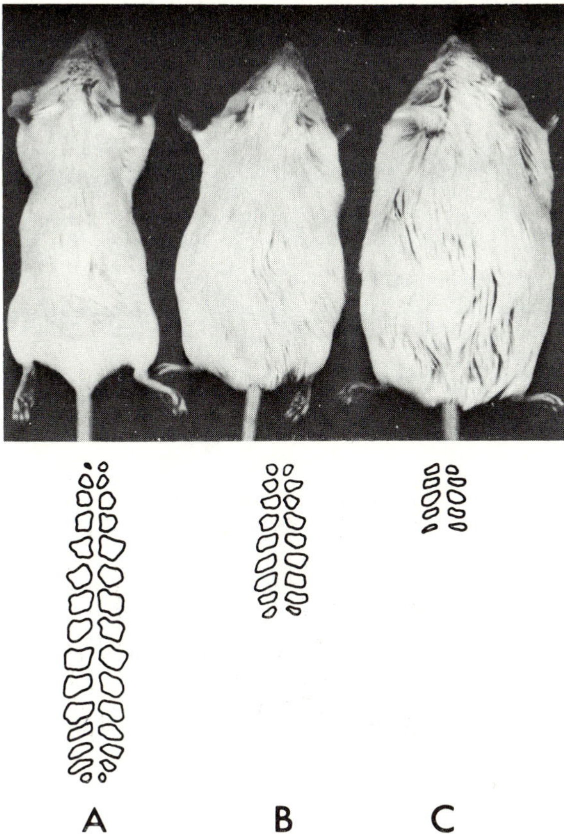

FIG. 9. Comparison of body size in control (A), moderately obese (B), and extremely obese (C) Balb/c mice following single injection of 0, 0.6, and 0.8 mg per gram body weight of goldthioglucose, respectively, and respective tracings of intact and "residual" ventromedial nuclear complexes obtained from serial sections of hypothalamus at 60 days postinjection.

body weight suggested that these alterations found in the GTG-treated mice are quantitative rather than qualitative and reflected the establishment of a new "set point" in terms of food intake, energy expenditure, and adipose tissue mass. On the basis of these findings, the possibility presented itself that the transient hyperphagia and stabilization of body weight and in turn body lipid content were all interrelated through some type of feedback mechanism, that is in simple terms, as the fat cells began to fill and distend with lipid due to the excess caloric intake, inhibitory signals emanating from the fat organs brought about a diminution in food intake. This is the same type of concept as that embodied

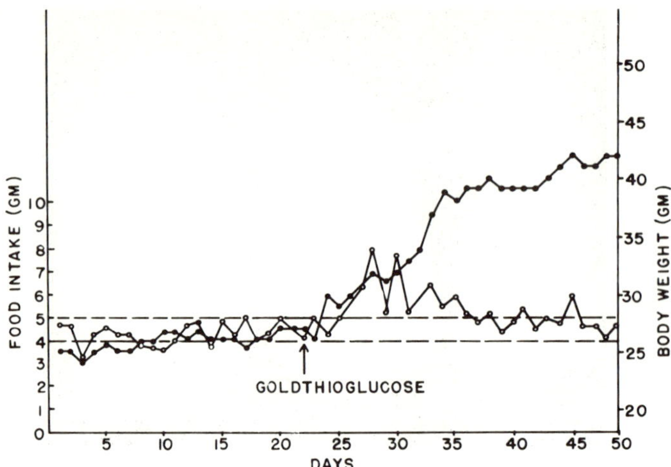

FIG. 10. Changes in food intake and body weight following a single injection of goldthioglucose in CBA/Ki mice. ● Body weight; ○ food intake.

in the Hering-Breuer reflex involving the distention and collapse of the pulmonary alveoli.

This rather simplistic type of reasoning initiated several studies concerned with the physiological effects of surgical removal of specific fat depots in food intake as described in the next section. For if such a relationship indeed existed, the deficiency in the fat organ mass would manifest itself in some alteration in food intake.

VIII. Surgical Removal of Specific Fat Organs and Food Intake

Since the lipid content of GFO accounts for 20–25% of the total body lipids in GTG obese CBA/Ki mice, it was assumed that removal of this fat organ would reduce the lipid-storing potential significantly resulting in a shunting of the excess calories in the form of lipid to the remaining depots and in turn having them reach their saturation level more rapidly. If the filling of the fat depot did in fact tend to suppress food intake, then one would expect the "peak" of the transient hyperphagia to occur earlier in the deficient animal as compared to the intact animal following GTG. Actually, no difference was seen in either the overall pattern of food intake or increase in body weight. Additional studies revealed that in animals deficient in GFO when treated with GTG, the IFO undergoes a "compensatory hypertrophy" indicating that no single specific fat organ is critical in the relationship between food intake regulation, weight gain, and fat organ activity; rather, the "total mass" of adipose tissue distributed throughout the body would have to be considered in any type of postulated regulatory mechanism (Liebelt *et al.*, 1965).

In spite of the similar types of overall patterns of food intake and body weight gain in GFO-deficient and intact CBA/Ki mice treated with GTG, a closer examination of the daily food intake and gain in body weight suggested some differences in the rate at which animals lacking their GFOs gained weight as compared to the sham-operated and intact animals. A study was carried out in which the amount of food eaten, the number of days required, and the number of grams of food necessary to gain 1 gm in body weight were all calculated on the basis of an increase of 17 gm in body weight. A 17 gm increase in body weight was rather arbitrarily elected because it represented the attainment of a selected body weight during the rapid increase following GTG. The results of this study indicated that males and females lacking their GFO eat significantly less food after GTG and yet in a significantly shorter period of time attain a 17 gm increase in body weight as compared to sham-operated and intact groups (Liebelt *et al.*, 1965). In turn, calculations demonstrated that the GFO-deficient animals required approximately 11 gm of food to gain each gram in body weight as opposed to the 15 gm of food required for a 1 gm increase in body weight in the sham-operated and intact groups. These data suggested to us that the removal of the GFO prior to the development of GTG-induced obesity creates an alteration in metabolic activity of the animal in terms of a more effective conversion of ingested food into deposited lipids. The possibility was considered that perhaps the removal of GFO prior to the injection of GTG resulted in metabolic changes in the host that were manifested in quantitative differences in degree of damage to the hypothalamus, and that larger or smaller lesions accounted for the differences in "efficiency" in converting ingested food deposited lipid. This consideration was prompted by a series of studies demonstrating that changes in glucose metabolism as influenced by either a diabetic state or the administration of insulin could prevent or enhance the development of hypothalamic lesions following the injection of GTG (Debons *et al.*, 1968, 1969).

A study has been completed in which GFOs were removed prior to GTG and 7 days after GTG. No significant difference was noted between the two groups; both groups showed a more efficient utilization of food as expressed by increased lipid deposition following GTG as compared to intact and sham-operated animals. Thus it would appear that the removal of a given portion of the adipose tissue mass in some unknown manner brings about a physiological change that, during the development of GTG-induced obesity, results in more rapid and efficient means of lipid deposition. However, this "efficiency state" is not a permanent one; rather, there is a gradual reversion to that of the non-operated animal state as the increase in lipid deposition proceeds (Liebelt *et al.*, 1965).

Another question was posed, namely, what is the effect of removal of GFO on food intake in "chronically obese" mice previously treated with GTG? Thus would disruption of the postulated new "set point" relative to total adipose tissue mass by surgical removal of GFO initiate an increase in food intake to reestablish the level of lipid content commensurate with the induced state of obesity? CBA/S mice that had received a single injection of GTG (0.65 mg/gm body weight) approximately 6 months earlier were placed in individual cages after having been housed with four to six animals per cage. All animals showed a 2 to 8 gm weight loss during the first 2 weeks after separation into individual cages. In general, the majority of animals remained at their new body weight during the third week of the study. Pairs of animals were then matched on the basis of similar body weights and food intake during a 15-day period prior to surgery. Both members were subjected to identical surgical procedures, but only one member had both GFO removed. In spite of variation and certain discrepancies between body weight changes and lipid content of IFO, all partners that had GFO removed ate more food during the 33-day period following surgery than did the sham-operated partner (Liebelt *et al.*, 1965).

The above studies on GFO ablation failed to demonstrate conclusively any feedback relationship between food intake regulatory mechanisms and the functional state of the adipose tissue mass. One could explain the discrepancies by postulating the existence of two separate regulatory mechanisms: (*1*) the quantitative regulation of food intake associated with the degree of damage of the hypothalamus and (*2*) the amount of lipid eventually deposited in the adipose tissue mass as a function of the metabolic state of this tissue complex. It was at this point that another approach to the problem presented itself, namely a study of the effects of GTG in animals which already are obese.

IX. Effects of Goldthioglucose-Induced Obesity in Genetically Obese Mice

Following our findings suggesting that a quantitative representation of neural elements in the ventromedial region of the hypothalamus is involved in food intake regulation, we found a report in the literature suggesting that the basis for the characteristic "yellow obesity" in mice was an alteration in some neuroendocrine mechanism, since certain nuclear complexes of the hypothalamus were smaller in the "yellow obese" mice than in the "brown lean" littermates (Silberberg and Silberberg, 1957). We then carried out a study using our point-count method and later the planimeter method to measure the "volume" of the ventromedial nuclear complexes in both "yellow obese" (CBA × YBR) F_1 hybrids and "brown lean" littermates. No differences were found in the nuclear volumes between the "yellow" and "brown" animals using these quantitative methods.

It then became of interest to determine the effects of GTG on weight gain, lipid deposition, and food intake in both the "yellow obese" and "brown lean" mice. Several investigators have inquired as to whether forced-fed (Cohn and Joseph, 1959) or insulin-induced (Hoebel and Teitelbaum, 1966) "obese" rats maintain some form of body weight regulation especially after superimposition of hypothalamic lesions in the ventromedial region. The results of the latter study permitted a conclusion that some stimulus correlated with obesity controls food intake, probably by activating cells in the ventromedial hypothalamus. Forced-fed cockerels which become obese stop eating in 7–10 days after cessation of the forced feeding, but return to normal feeding patterns as the lipid content in the fat depots return to control levels (Lepkovsky and Furuta, 1971). The development of obesity in the brown (lean) littermates following GTG had already been described, but the effects of hypothalamic damage on animals already obese remained to be determined. Both "obese" (approximately 50 gm in body weight) and "lean" (approximately 34 gm in body weight) F_1 hybrids were used in this study. All of the yellow mice showed an initial weight loss ranging from 3 to 15 gm when placed in individual cages to permit recording of individual food intake as was seen in the chronically obese GTG mice when placed in individual cages. We arbitrarily selected only those obese animals that showed a weight loss of 5 gm or less for the study. This phenomenon certainly deserves closer consideration in interpreting data obtained from studies of this type. All (CBA × YBR) F_1 hybrid animals (yellow and brown) were injected with GTG. The presence of the CBA genetics in the host provided the uniform susceptibility to lesion production. Whereas the "brown" littermates showed a characteristic increase in body weight (34.9 ± 0.1 to 43.0 ± 2.0 gm), lipid content of IFO plus GFO (1.1 ± 0.07 to 2.8 ± 0.21 gm) and food intake for a 30-day period after injection of GTG (147.3 ± 0.9 to 176.8 ± 7.6 gm), the "yellow" littermates also showed increases in these three parameters but at a lesser magnitude. Body weight increased from 43.1 ± 0.2 to 45.6 ± 0.2 gm, lipid content (IFO plus GFO) 2.2 ±

0.06 to 3.0 ± 0.16 gm, and food intake for the 30-day period from 161.5 ± 5.3 to 177.5 ± 1.2 gm (Liebelt *et al.,* 1965). In spite of these differences, the degree of hypothalamic damage as based on the residual volume of the ventromedial nuclear complex was the same in both the "obese" and "lean" mice. It would be of interest and importance to develop conditions under which the initial weight loss seen in the obese mice when placed in individual cages could be prevented, as this may account for some of the slight increases seen in these three parameters in the obese mice. Nevertheless, we were impressed that the quantitative representation of neural elements in the hypothalamus associated with the regulatory influences of food intake and lipid deposition did not appear to be independent of regulatory influences originating from areas peripheral to the hypothalamus. The degree to which the potential lipid-storing capacity of any fat organ is filled and which, in turn, reflects the total lipid content of the animal, should be considered as one possible source of these peripheral regulatory influences acting upon hypothalamic centers.

X. Anorexia and Lipid Mobilization in Tumor-Bearing Mice

Most of these aforementioned studies tend to focus attention on the "afferent limb" of a postulated feedback mechanism between food intake regulation and adipose tissue function, that is presentation of appropriate metabolic substances to the adipose tissue for lipid deposition. However, data pertaining to the "efferent limb," that is, the influence of the functional state of the fat depot on food intake, are just as rare.

We have two bits of data that suggest that the levels of blood lipids derived from adipose tissue indeed influence food intake. One is concerned with the effects of adrenalectomy on body weight of "spontaneously" obese mice (Liebelt, 1963; Liebelt *et al.,* 1965). In this study NH mice or their F_1 hybrids weighing 40–55 gm were bilaterally adrenalectomized and maintained on deoxycorticosterone trimethyl acetate. Characteristically these animals showed a significant loss in body weight due primarily to decrease in body lipid content during a 7- to 14-day postoperative period. Of interest was the fact that these animals maintained this reduced body weight and remained in healthy condition for periods up to 6 months. Other strains of mice showed the same weight loss but gradually returned to the preoperative body weight. We were able to demonstrate that the unique feature of the NH strain was failure to develop accessory adrenal cortical tissue following adrenalectomy. The other strains did develop accessory adrenal tissue which was correlated with the return to preoperative body weight. Of interest to the present discussion is that in both strains during the period of rapid weight loss there was a striking decrease in food intake that showed its lowest level approximately 5 days after surgery. Initially we ascribed this to the surgical trauma. But repeated sham operations including ovariectomy and gonadectomy did not produce this food intake pattern. A simple analysis of the blood lipid levels showed a hyperlipemia reaching a peak in approximately 4 days after surgery, thus suggesting a possible relationship between the hyperlipemia and the decreased food intake.

The second bits of data were found in a study concerned with a tumor-host relationship utilizing two transplanted tumors in GTG obese and genetically obese mouse hosts. Anorexia and cachexia are observed in certain cancer patients as well as experimental animals bearing certain transplanted tumors (Begg, 1958; Mider, 1955). A series of studies were undertaken in which CBA and (C57Bl × CBA) F_1 hybrids were used as recipients for a subcutaneous implant of a transplantable CBA stomach tumor (CBA # 2663). Both untreated and GTG obese animals were used, and daily food intake and body weights were recorded before and after transplantation of the tumor. The animals were autopsied when the tumor reached a size of approximately 1.5 cm. The results of this study showed that in spite of a 46–49% lipid loss in the IFO and a 46–55% lipid loss in GFO of untreated males and females bearing CBA # 2663 stomach tumor, there was no change in total body weight (carcass weight plus tumor weight) or food intake. On the other hand, GTG obese hosts bearing the same tumor showed a striking decrease in total body weight and, most interesting, a reduction in food intake to almost zero.

Although another transplantable tumor (C57Bl fibrosarcoma) caused a similar degree of reduction in IFO and GFO lipid content in GTG obese (C57Bl × CBA) F_1 hybrids, there was no significant reduction in total body weight or, more importantly, of food intake. However, an important difference between the two tumor systems was found in the rate of lipid mobilization. Obese mice bearing the stomach tumor lost approximately 44 mg/day of lipid from IFO and GFO combined as compared to 19 mg/day lost from these same two fat depots in the same genetic host bearing the C57Bl fibrosarcoma. A further comparison between the genetically obese and lean (CBA × YBR) F_1 hybrids bearing the CBA # 2663 stomach tumor indicated that the percent lipid loss in IFO and GFO fat depots was essentially the same in both lean and obese hosts. However, the absolute amount lost was much greater in the obese than in the lean. This was of great interest because during this period of lipid mobilization food intake was greatly reduced in the obese hosts and remained essentially normal in the lean hosts.

It was concluded from these various studies that the mobilization of lipids from the fat depots brought about a reduction in food intake in either GTG obese or in genetically obese mice as a result of the rate at which lipids were mobilized and of the amount available for mobilization (Liebelt *et al.*, 1971). As a working hypothesis, it was proposed that the tumor is producing a humoral substance capable of depleting fat cells (Fig. 11). It was further suggested that an elevation of blood lipid levels associated with the mobilization of depot lipids acts upon the "feeding centers" of the hypothalamus and brings about a suppression in food intake. Evidence available to support the former proposal is well documented in the literature, namely, the hyperlipemia associated with the growth of transplanted tumors in rats and mice (Begg, 1958; Mider, 1955). In one particular study in mice, it has been shown that an acute lipid loss and increased acetate-^{14}C incorporation in body fat can also be evoked by a nonviable preparation of the Krebs-2 transplanted tumor (Costa and Holland, 1962). The question may be raised as to why a suppression of food intake was not observed in nonobese hosts bearing the same tumors and showing a relatively marked lipid mobilization. The sensitivity of our measuring technique may have been an important factor. At the present, it would appear that the combination of an obese host with excessive amounts of stored lipids plus the fast-growing CBA stomach tumor greatly "magnifies" the entire phenomenon so that our measuring techniques can detect the ensuing events. Hopefully, more sensitive methods and techniques of measuring food intake can be brought to bear on this problem in the future.

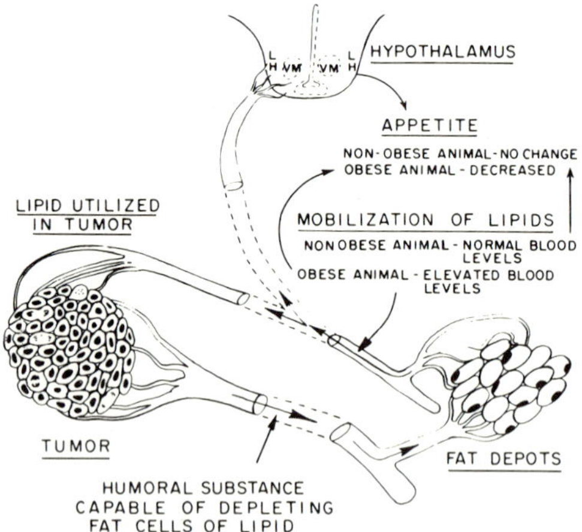

Fig. 11. A diagrammatic depiction of a working hypothesis to account for the changes in body lipid content and food intake in normal and experimentally obese mice bearing a spontaneous or transplanted neoplasm.

In recent studies concerned with documentation of several aspects of the proposed working hypothesis, several bits of unpublished data are available. First, it is now possible to grow CBA # 2663 stomach tumor cells in tissue culture (Liebelt *et al.,* 1973). After the tenth passage in tissue culture, these cells, when injected subcutaneously into appropriate test mice, grow and continue to produce lipid depletion of the IFO and GFO. Thus, it would appear that multiple tissue culture passage has no deleterious effects on the ability of these cells to produce the hypothetical lipid-mobilizing substance. With the successful adaptation of these cells to a monolayer culture, the next objective is to determine if these cells are actively secreting such a factor into the media. Should this be the case, it may become possible to isolate and characterize this potentially significant lipid mobilizing factor.

The second series of studies have been directed to an analysis of the blood lipids by gas-liquid chromatography in tumor-bearing hosts as well as normal animals in relation to food intake patterns. Analysis of blood lipids in GTG obese and GTG obese tumor bearers (CBA # 2663 stomach tumor) were compatible with the above hypothesis. Every lipid fraction of the neutral lipids studied was significantly increased in both male and female tumor bearers (Gehring, 1970). The females, however, had significant increases in only the triglyceride fractions, and in the males the significant increases were limited to the steroid and steroid C-18 and C-20 ester fractions. However, these sex differences may have been only reflections of the differences in total amount of lipid stored in the two sexes. The anorexia seen in GTG obese tumor-bearing mice was correlatable with increased blood lipid levels.

Following up this study in nonobese, nontumor-bearing mice, neutral plasma lipids were analyzed in 24-hour fasted animals, animals just entering into a feeding phase at 8:00 p.m., and animals during a nonfeeding phase (12:00 noon) as pertains to a 24-hour period. The "physiologically hungry" (8:00 p.m.) mice were relatively plasma-depleted of esterified fatty acids and steroids in both sexes as compared to the "physiologically anorexic" mice at 12:00 noon.

The high levels of plasma lipids in the tumor-bearing animals were compatible with the hypothesis that the stomach tumor was elaborating some type of adipokinetic substance (Lipsett, 1954). A saline homogenate of the CBA stomach tumor was injected into 24-hour fasted CBA/Ki mice and the neutral plasma lipids analyzed. It was found that those animals treated with the homogenate showed a significant rise in steroid ester levels as compared to animals injected with homogenates of other tumors, saline, and untreated animals. Thus, although the data are still incomplete, the two major components of the proposed working hypothesis appear to exist in the CBA # 2663 tumor-host system.

Namely, this tumor apparently elaborates some type of "lipid-mobilizing" substance which causes an increase in the neutral plasma lipids presumably for utilization by the tumor but which incidently is presumably monitored by hypothalamic control centers which inhibit food intake. However, the need for more precise measurements of these phenomena becomes obvious before definitive conclusions can be reached.

XI. Discussion

In spite of the absence of conclusive evidence that a functional link-up exists between food intake regulation and the metabolic state of the adipose tissue mass of the body, the data available at the present time certainly tend to encourage one to explore this possibility in attempting to understand the regulation of body mass in general and lipid content of adipose tissue in particular.

Actually the "lipostatic theory" of food intake regulation considers the amount of lipid present in the body as an important factor in the mechanisms involved in a closed-loop regulatory system for energy balance. Thus, in effect, the lipostatic theory suggests that the quantity of fat in the body is physiologically regulated. But the theory offers no explanation as to how this is done or how the information is transmitted to the hypothalamus (Kennedy, 1953). Recently, Hervey (1969) has suggested a tentative mechanism for the sensing facet of a lipostatic system. He suggested that a specific hormone may provide the body with a means of measuring the amount of stored lipid by means of the dilution principle. The latter requires a tracer which is soluble in both plasma and lipid and has a high partition coefficient in favor of lipid. Because steroids generally have the necessary solubility properties, and because the central regulation of food intake responds to steroids as shown experimentally, Hervey considered it possible that the physiological tracer is a steroid. Others are in basic agreement with this concept, although definitive studies, including food intake measurements, are lacking. The maintenance of a relatively constant body weight despite variation in caloric intake and energy expenditure suggests that body mass is probably controlled by a homeostatic mechanism which regulates the metabolism of adipose tissue (Kekwick and Pawan, 1969).

Our own studies, backtracking from investigations originally directed toward the biology of the fat depots and the central regulating mechanisms of food intake have also oriented us toward the concept of the existence of a humorally mediated substance(s) that integrates the anatomically dispersed fat depots into a functional adipose tissue mass. This in turn presumably regulates the ingestion of food whose calories are subsequently utilized to maintain a constancy in body mass in the adult animal.

The influence of various types of hormones including steroids, catecholamines, thyroxine, insulin, as well as various pituitary hormones on adipose tissue physiology has been well documented (Rudman *et al.,* 1965). Recently we found (Liebelt *et al.,* unpublished studies) that the presence of testicular androgens suppresses food intake in males treated with GTG and also tends to rechannel any GTG-induced weight gain away from lipid deposition and toward protein anabolism. Furthermore, these studies indicated that the sex differences seen in food intake and lipid deposition in mice with lesions in the hypothalamus were not due to an active effect of estrogen, as suggested by Cox *et al.* (1969) in rats with hypothalamic lesions but rather to the presence or absence of androgens. However, no sex differences in the rate of weight gain were found in animals receiving hypothalamic knife cuts, since normal males typically gained more rapidly than normal females, and the lesion-induced rate of weight gain appeared to replace rather than be summative to the normal rate of weight gain peculiar to each sex (Gold, 1970). Unfortunately in both of these studies only body weight was used as a criterion for increased body mass, making it impossible to state at this time whether the increases in body weight reflected any sex-dependent preference for deposition of lipid.

Hausberger and Hausberger (1966) have recently carried out studies in castration-induced obesity in mice which again focused attention on the important role of gonadal and adrenal steroids in regulation of lipid deposition. Developmental aspects of hormonal control of eating and weight gain are gradually attracting interest. Several lines of evidence indicate that in the prepubertal female regulation of both these functions may differ qualitatively from those in the sexually mature female (Wade and Zucker, 1970). The sex difference evident in lipid deposition in man as well as in many domestic and experimental animals has not been explored in any great depth, even though it might reveal some important clues to our understanding of energy regulation.

Another area of apparent importance in food intake regulation is the role of prolactin. It is well documented in the literature that the lactating rats nursing litters of various sizes show an increase in food intake paralleling the increase in litter size (Kumaresan and Turner, 1968). Some investigators concluded that the number of suckling pups affects the rate of secretion of those anterior pituitary hormones concerned with the growth and maintenance of the mammary gland (Ota and Yokoyama, 1967a). Although some investigators including Cross (1961) have emphasized that the neural stimulation of appetite by suckling is the major factor in inducing enhanced food intake and body growth in lactating rats, others believe that a humoral factor plays a more significant role in this phenomenon (Ota and Yokoyama, 1967b). Recently we have reported that virgin mice bearing pituitary isografts placed beneath the kidney capsule manifested an increase in food intake and lipid deposition (Briggs *et al.*, 1968). Pituitary glands removed from hypothalamic influences, and thus presumably removed from the prolactin-inhibitory factor (Meites and Nicoll, 1966) continue to secrete prolactin and/or growth hormone. This raises questions regarding the levels of prolactin and/or growth hormone to be found in mice with GTG-induced hypothalamic lesions. Recently, GTG-induced hypothalamic lesions have been associated with an increase in mouse pituitary prolactin content (Sinha and Vander Laan, 1971).

The role of growth hormone in influencing body lipid content has been the subject of several investigators. It has been suggested that the obesity observed in rats following placement of electrolytic lesions in the hypothalamus is related to an absolute or relative deficiency in growth hormone secretion (Bernardis and Skelton, 1967; Han, 1967). However, we have recently shown that hypothalamic knife cuts can result in the development of obesity regardless of whether there is a decrease, no change, or an increase in linear growth (Palka *et al.*, 1972). This suggests that obesity and growth hormone secretion can be dissociated. Such a concept is in agreement with previously reported findings that animals with varying sized hypothalamic lesions develop a decrease in plasma growth hormone levels, but increases in plasma insulin levels and in carcass fat (Bernardis and Frohman, 1970).

Although the above findings would strongly suggest that an important role is played by the hypothalamic-pituitary axis in the physiological activity of adipose tissue, some conflicting data remain concerning the role of the pituitary in hypothalamic obesity. Hetherington and Ranson (1942) showed that total hypophysectomy of rats 1 week following electrolytic lesions of the hypothalamus failed to impede the appearance of an adiposity as pronounced as that found in lesioned animals with intact pituitaries. Animals that had been hypophysectomized for longer periods of time also become obese following hypothalamic lesions (Hetherington, 1944). It was therefore concluded that hypothalamic lesions do not cause excessive lipid deposition by inducing an abnormal balance in pituitary secretions. Their findings were confirmed at a later date by Kennedy (1958). On the other hand, it has been reported that hypophysectomy prevented the development of obesity in mice which received GTG (Redding *et al.*, 1966). Unfortunately these authors only reported body weight and carried out no histological analysis of the hypothalamus. We have examined the effects of GTG in CBA/Ki mice following hypophysectomy and found that removal of the pituitary prevents any increase in body weight after GTG, despite the development of characteristic GTG-induced hypothalamic lesions. However, we also found that whereas hypophysectomy prevented an increase in lipid content of GTG-treated female mice with definite hypothalamic lesions, the rate of increase although not the total amount of lipid deposition in similarly treated males was not inhibited. It would thus appear that the role of neuroendocrine mechanisms in any postulated relationship between adipose tissue system and food intake must be examined more thoroughly, possibly in more than one species.

Of course the hypothetical humoral factor considered responsible for the interaction between the adipose tissue system and food intake regulation need not be one of the classically defined hormones. Lipid-mobilizing substances have been prepared from the urine of fasting rabbits (Weil and Stetten, 1947), rats (Stevenson *et al.*, 1964) and man (Chalmers *et al.*, 1960), and more recently the lipolytic activity of certain brain extracts has been described (Hollett, 1968). The lipid mobilizing capacity of a factor obtained from porcine hypothalamus could in great measure but not completely be accounted for by adreno-corticotropic hormone (ACTH) and/or its analogs with adrenocortico-tropic activity (Redding and Schally, 1970). Thus it is conceivable that there exists a humoral agent serving as the afferent limb which either directly or indirectly regulates adipose tissue, with some adipose tissue constituent such as a steroid serving as the efferent limb as proposed by Hervey (1969). Further support for the existence of a "circulating factor" influencing food intake regulation in the rat comes from the parabiotic experiments of Hervey (1969) in which one of the parabionts had an electrolytic lesion placed in the ventromedial region of the hypothalamus and the other remained intact. Although food intake was not measured, but, rather, changes in body weight, it was suggested that a factor passed across the anastomotic connection from the lesioned to the unlesioned parabiont causing a suppression of food intake in the latter. Unfortunately other investigators (Han *et al.*, 1963) have been unable to confirm this observation in rats, indicating the need for additional investigation. Yet "obese" and "lean" mice of the obese-hyperglycemic strain when placed in parabiosis tended to support Hervey's findings (Coleman and Hummel, 1969). Another study demonstrated that blood obtained from a recently fed rat would impart an inhibition of food intake when injected into a "hungry" control (Davis *et al.*, 1967). It will be of importance to determine the nature of this blood-borne factor. Still another piece of evidence, albeit indirect in nature, comes from the study showing changes in the fatty acid composition of adipose tissue obtained from animals with two types of experimental obesity as compared to non-obese controls (Haessler and Crawford, 1965). The depot fat from the obese animals also released fatty acids poorly when incubated *in vitro*. Both these findings suggested the possibility of a metabolic defect in the adipose tissue of the obese animals. Parabiosis of these genetically obese with genetically lean mice failed to reveal any evidence of a circulating regulatory substance responsible for changes in depot fat composition. However, a defective adipose tissue responsiveness to a circulating factor would have to be considered. In any event, from these selected examples it appears that the characterization of a "lipid-regulating factor" in the blood may be imminent but certainly will require further efforts.

The importance of the gastrointestinal tract in regulation of food intake is well-documented. Recently, Lepkovsky (1973) has proposed a concept which implicates the adipose tissue system in the role of regulating the rate of absorption of food calories from the small intestine. Essentially, the hypothesis holds that when depot lipid content is below a postulated set-point, there is a mandatory diversion of food calories to the depots by an increased rate in absorption.

The recent description of Widdowson (1970) of the "harmony of growth" justifies a note of caution as to focusing all attention on any one body system, in this instance the adipose tissue system, when attempting to understand the interrelationships between food intake, energy expenditures, and body composition. However, the dissecting out and characterization of the functional and organizational components of the adipose tissue system as pertains to the regulation of food intake should be encouraged. Hopefully it will then become possible to integrate these expected findings along with those from the already relatively well-defined body systems, e.g., nervous, digestive, endocrine, etc., and in particular the often neglected osseous and muscular systems. Thus, in effect, attempts to define the "internal ecosystem" of the organism, i.e., the interaction of the constituent body systems with ingested nutrients, will provide a clearer perspective of the integrative workings involved in food intake regulation.

Acknowledgments

Original studies described in this paper were supported by grants AM-15822 and GM-1503 from The National Institutes of Health and The American Cancer Society. The generous contribution of goldthioglucose by the Schering Corporation is gratefully appreciated. We wish to thank Dr. L. Delmonte for her assistance in reading this manuscript.

References

Babineau, L.-M., and Page, E. (1955). On body fat and body water in rats. *Canadian Journal of Biochemistry and Physiology* 33, 970–979.

Begg, R. W. (1958). Tumor-host relations. *Advances in Cancer Research* 1, 1–30.

Bernardis, L., and Frohman, L. (1970). Effect of lesion size in the ventromedial hypothalamus on growth hormone and insulin levels in weanling rats. *Neuroendocrinology* 6, 319–328.

Bernardis, L., and Skelton, F. (1967). Growth and obesity in male rats after placement of ventromedial hypothalamic lesions at four different ages. *Journal of Endocrinology* 38, 351–352.

Bierman, H. R. (1964). Characteristics of Leukopoietin G in animals and man. *Annals of the New York Academy of Sciences* 113, 753–765.

Boecke, J. (1933). Über die innervation Fettzelle. *Zeitschrift für Mikroskopisch-Anatomische Forschung* 33, 233.

Brecher, G., and Waxler, S. (1949). Obesity in albino mice due to a single injection of goldthioglucose. *Proceedings of the Society for Experimental Biology and Medicine* 70, 498–500.

Briggs, R., Liebelt, A., and Liebelt, R. (1968). Systemic effects of hypophysial isografts in female inbred mice. *Journal of the National Cancer Institute* 40, 1227–1244.

Bucher, N. L. R. (1963). Regeneration of mammalian liver. *International Review of Cytology* 15, 245–300.

Cahill, G. (1970). Starvation in man. *New England Journal of Medicine* 282, 668–675.

Chalmers, T., Pawan, G., and Kekwick, A. (1960). Fat mobilizing activity of human urine extract. *American Journal of Clinical Nutrition* 8, 728–732.

Code, C. F., ed. (1967). "Handbook of Physiology, Sect. 6: Alimentary Canal, Vol. I: Food and Water Intake." Amer. Physiol. Soc., Washington, D. C.

Cohn, C., and Joseph, D. (1959). Changes in body composition attendant on force feeding. *American Journal of Physiology* 196, 965–968.

Coleman, D., and Hummel, K. (1969). Effects of parabiosis of normal with genetically diabetic mice. *American Journal of Physiology* 217, 1298–1304.

Costa, G., and Holland, J. (1962). Effects of Krebs-2 carcinoma on lipide metabolism of male Swiss mice. *Cancer Research* 22, 1081–1083.

Cox, V., Kakolewski, J., and Valenstein, E. (1969). Sex differences in hyperphagia and obesity. *Journal of Comparative and Physiological Psychology* 67, 320–326.

Cross, B. (1961). Neural control of lactation. *In* "Milk: The Mammary Gland and its Secretion" (S. K. Kon and A. T. Cowie, eds.), Vol. 1, pp. 229–277. Academic Press, New York.

Davis, J., Gallagher, R., and Ladove, R. (1967). Food intake controlled by a blood factor. *Science* 156, 1247–1248.

Debons, A., Krimsky, I., Likuski, H., From, A., and Cloutier, R. J. (1968). Goldthioglucose damage to the satiety center: inhibition in diabetes. *American Journal of Physiology* 214, 652–658.

Debons, A., Krimsky, I., From, A., and Cloutier, R. J. (1969). Rapid effects of insulin on the hypothalamic satiety center. *American Journal of Physiology* 217, 1114–1118.

Feldman, G., Churchwell, L., Culp, T., Doyle, F., and Jonsson, H. (1962a). Lipid content of the subcutaneous fat organs of the chick embryo. *Poultry Science* 41, 1232–1240.

Feldman, G., Doyle, F., Lawler, M., Rodgers, R., and Churchwell, L. (1962b). Enzymatic activity of the developing subcutaneous fat organs of the chick. *Poultry Science* **41**, 1423–1428.

Flemming, W. (1871). Über Bildung und Ruckbiloung der Fettzelle in Bindegewebe. *Archiv. für Mikroskopische Anatomie* **7**, 321.

Gehring, G. (1970). Tumor-host relations: Effects of goldthioglucose and 2663 stomach carcinoma on plasma neutral lipids in CBA/Ki mice. M.S. Thesis. Baylor College of Medicine, Houston, Texas.

Gersh, I., and Still, M. A. (1945). Blood vessels in fat tissue. Relation to problems of gas exchange. *Journal of Experimental Medicine* **81**, 219–231.

Gold, R. (1970). Hypothalamic hyperphagia: Males get just as fat as females. *Journal of Comparative and Physiological Psychology* **71**, 347–356.

Gordon, A. (1959). Hemopoietine. *Physiological Review* **39**, 1–40.

Haessler, H., and Crawford, J. (1965). Alterations in the fatty acid composition of depot fat associated with obesity. *Annals of the New York Academy of Sciences* **131**, 476–484.

Hammar, J. A. (1895). Zur Kenntnis Des Fettgewebes. *Archiv. für Mikroskopische Anatomie* **45**, 512–514.

Han, P. W. (1967). Hypothalamic obesity in rats without hyperphagia. *Transactions of the New York Academy of Sciences* **30**, 229–243.

Han, P. W., Mu, J., and Lepkovsky, S. (1963). Food intake in parabiotic rats. *American Journal of Physiology* **205**, 1139–1143.

Hausberger, F. X. (1938). Über die Wachstuns und Entwichlungs fahigkeit Transplantie to Fettgeweheheimlager von Ratten. *Virchows Archiv. für Pathologische Anatomie und Physiologie und für Klinische Medizin* **302**, 640–656.

Hausberger, F. X. (1955). Quantitative studies on the development of autotransplants of immature adipose tissue of rats. *Anatomical Record* **122**, 507–516.

Hausberger, F. X. (1959). Behavior of transplanted adipose tissue of hereditarily obese mice. *Anatomical Record* **135**, 109–113.

Hausberger, F. X., and Gujob, O. (1937). Uber die veränderungen des gehaltes an fett-wasser-, glykogen-, and trochen sub tanz im wachsenden fettgewebe junger ratten. *Naunyn-Schmiedebergs Archiv. für Experimentelle Pathologie und Pharmakologie* **187**, 647–654.

Hausberger, F. X., and Hausberger, B. (1966). Castration-induced obesity in mice. *Acta Endocrinologica (Copenhagen)* **53**, 571–583.

Hausberger, F. X., Milstein, S. W., and Rutman, R. J. (1954). The influence of insulin on glucose utilization in adipose and hepatic tissues *in vitro*. *Journal of Biological Chemistry* **208**, 431–438.

Hellman, B., and Hellerstrom, C. (1961). Cell renewal in the white and brown fat tissue of the rat. *Acta Pathologica et Microbiologica Scandinavica* **51**, 347–353.

Hervey, G. R. (1969). Regulation of energy balance. *Nature (London)* **222**, 629–631.

Hetherington, A. (1944). Production of hypothalamic obesity in rats already displaying chronic hypopituitarism. *American Journal of Physiology* **140**, 89–92.

Hetherington, A., and Ranson, S. (1942). Effect of early hypophysectomy on hypothalamic obesity. *Endocrinology* **31**, 30–34.

Hirsch, J., and Han, P. W. (1969). Cellularity of rat adipose tissue: Effects of growth, starvation and obesity. *Journal of Lipid Research* **10**, 77–82.

Hirsch, J., and Knittle, J. (1970). Cellularity of obese and non-obese human adipose tissue. *Federation Proceeding, Federation of American Societies for Experimental Biology* **29**, 1516–1521.

Hoebel, B., and Teitelbaum, P. (1966). Weight regulation in normal and hypothalamic hyperphagic rats. *Journal of Comparative and Physiological Psychology* **61**, 189–193.

Hollett, C. (1968). Tentative identification of lipid mobilizing substance from the calf mid-brain. *Biochemical and Biophysical Research Communications* **32**, 48–55.

Hull, D. (1966). The structure and function of brown adipose tissue. *British Medical Bulletin* **22**, 92–96.

Hull, P. (1960). Genetic relations between carcass fat and body weight in mice. *Journal of Agricultural Science* **55**, 317–321.

Johansson, B. (1959). Brown fat: A review. *Metabolism, Clinical and Experimental* **8**, 221–239.

Kekwick, A., and Pawan, G. (1969). Body weight, food and energy. *Lancet* **1**, 822–825.

Kennedy, G. C. (1953). The role of depot fat in the hypothalamic control of food intake in the rat. *Proceedings of the Royal Society, Series B* **140**, 578–582.

Kennedy, G. C. (1957). The development with age of hypothalamic restraint upon the appetite of the rat. *Journal of Endocrinology* **16**, 9–17.

Kennedy, G. C. (1958). Effect of increased appetite and insulin on growth in the hypophysectomized rat. *Journal of Endocrinology* **17**, 161–166.

Keys, A., and Brozek, J. (1953). Body fat in adult man. *Physiological Reviews* **33**, 245–325.

King, J., and Farner, D. (1965). Studies of fat deposition in migratory birds. *Annals of the New York Academy of Sciences* **131**, 422–440.

Krohn, P. L. (1959). Transplantation of endocrine glands. *In* "Transplantation of Tissues" (L. A. Peer, ed.), Vol. II, pp. 401–469. Williams & Wilkins, Baltimore, Maryland.

Kumaresan, P., and Turner, C. W. (1968). Effects of pregnancy on feed consumption and mammary gland growth in rats. *Proceedings of the Society for Experimental Biology and Medicine* **129**, 957–960.

Lepkovsky, S., and Furuta, F. (1971). The role of homeostasis in adipose tissues upon regulation of food intake in white leghorn cockerels. *Poultry Science* **50**, 573–579.

Lepkovsky, S. (1973). Newer concepts in the regulation of food intake. *American Journal of Clinical Nutrition* **26**, 271–284.

Liebelt, R. A. (1959). Postnatal development of two types of fat depots in the NH and CBA inbred strains of mice. *American Journal of Anatomy* **105**, 197–218.

Liebelt, R. A. (1963). Response of adipose tissue in experimental obesity as influenced by genetic hormonal and neurogenic factors. *Annals of the New York Academy of Sciences* **110**, 723–748.

Liebelt, R. A., and Eastlick, H. L. (1952). The organ-like nature of the subcutaneous fat bodies in the chicken. *Poultry Science* **33**, 169–179.

Liebelt, R. A., and Liebelt, A. G. (1969). Regulation of lipid content in two specific fat depots of the mouse. *Proceedings of the International Congress of Nutrition, 8th, Prague, Excerpta Medica Intern. Cong. Ser. No. 213*, pp. 271–273.

Liebelt, R. A., and Perry, J. H. (1967). Action of goldthioglucose on the central nervous system. *In* "Handbook of Physiology, Sect. 6: Alimentary Canal" (C. F. Code, ed.), Vol. 1, pp. 271–285. Amer. Physiol. Soc., Washington, D. C.

Liebelt, R. A., Ichinoe, S., and Nicholson, N. (1965). Regulatory influences of adipose tissue on food intake and body weight. *Annals of the New York Academy of Sciences* 131, 559–582.

Liebelt, R. A., Vismara, L., and Liebelt, A. G. (1968). Autoregulation of adipose tissue mass in mouse. *Proceedings of the Society for Experimental Biology and Medicine* 127, 458–462.

Liebelt, R. A., Liebelt, A. G., and Johnston, H. M. (1971). Lipid mobilization and food intake in experimentally obese mice bearing transplanted tumors. *Proceedings of the Society for Experimental Biology and Medicine* 138, 482–490.

Liebelt, R. A., Gehring, G., Schuster, G., and Liebelt, A. (1973). Paraneoplastic syndromes in experimental model systems. *Annals of the New York Academy of Sciences* (in press).

Lipsett, M. (1954). Humoral syndromes associated with non-endocrine tumors. *Annals of Internal Medicine* 61, 733–738.

McBurney, P. L. (1964). Quantitative relationships between food intake and ventromedial nuclear size. M.S. Thesis. Baylor Univ., Waco, Texas.

McBurney, P. L., Liebelt, R. A., and Perry, J. H. (1965). Quantitative relationships between food intake lipid deposition and hypothalamic damage in goldthioglucose obesity. *Texas Reports in Biology and Medicine* 23, 737–752.

MacDowell, E., Gates, W., and MacDowell, C. (1936). Influence of the quantity of nutrition upon growth of suckling mouse. *Journal of General Physiology* 13, 529–545.

McGreal, R., and Farner, D. (1956). Premigratory fat deposition in the Gambel White-Crowned Sparrow. *Northwest Science* 30, 12–23.

Maximow, A. (1927). Bindegewebe und Blutbildande Gewebe. *Handbuch der Mikroskopische Anatomie des Menschen* 12, Part 1, 292.

Mayer, J. (1953). Genetic, traumatic and environmental factors in the etiology of obesity. *Physiological Reviews* 33, 472–508.

Meites, J., and Nicoll, C. (1966). Adenohypophysis-prolactin. *Annual Review of Physiology* 28, 57–88.

Metcalf, D. (1964). Restricted growth capacity of multiple spleen grafts. *Transplantation* 2, 387–392.

Mider, G. (1955). Some tumor-host relationships. *Proceedings of the Canadian Cancer Research Conference* 1, 120–130.

Napolitano, L. (1965). Observations on the fine structure of adipose cells. *Annals of the New York Academy of Sciences* 131, 34–42.

Ota, K., and Yokoyama, A. (1967a). Body weight and food consumption of lactating rats nursing various sizes of litters. *Journal of Endocrinology* 38, 263–268.

Ota, K., and Yokoyama, A. (1967b). Body weight and food consumption of lactating rats: Effects of ovariectomy and of arrest and resumption of suckling. *Journal of Endocrinology* 38, 251–261.

Palka, Y., Liebelt, R., and Critchlow, V. (1971). Obesity and increased growth following partial or complete isolation of ventromedial hypothalamus. *Physiology & Behavior* **7**, 187–194.

Parkes, A. S. (1926). Growth of young mice according to size of litter. *Annals of Applied Biology* **13**, 374–394.

Parkes, A. S. (1929). Note on the growth of young mice suckled by rats. *Annals of Applied Biology* **16**, 171–173.

Peckham, S., Entenman, C., and Carroll, H. (1962). Influence of hypercaloric diet on gross body and adipose tissue composition in the rat. *Journal of Nutrition* **77**, 187–197.

Pitts, G. C. (1956). Body fat accumulation in the guinea pig. *American Journal of Physiology* **185**, 41–48.

Poole, B. (1966). The stimulus to hypertrophic growth. *Advances in Morphogenesis* **5**, 93–129.

Rasmussen, H. T. (1922). The glandular status of brown multilocular adipose tissue. *Endocrinology* **6**, 760–770.

Redding, T., and Schally, A. (1970). Lipid mobilizing factor from the hypothalamus. *Metabolism, Clinical and Experimental* **19**, 641–652.

Redding, T., Bowers, C., and Schally, A. (1966). Effects of hypophysectomy on hypothalamic obesity in CBA mice. *Proceedings of the Society for Experimental Biology and Medicine* **121**, 726–729.

Reed, L., Yamaguchi, F., Anderson, W., and Mendel, L. (1930). Factors influencing the distribution and character of adipose tissue in the rat. *Journal of Biological Chemistry* **87**, 147–155.

Renold, A., and Cahill, G. F., eds. (1965). "Handbook of Physiology, Sect. 5: Adipose Tissue." Amer. Physiol. Soc., Washington, D. C.

Rodbell, M. (1964). Metabolism of isolated fat cells. I. Effects of hormones on glucose metabolism and lipolysis. *Journal of Biological Chemistry* **239**, 375–380.

Rudman, D., Girolamo, M., Malken, M., and Garcia, L. (1965). The adipokinetic property of hypophyseal peptides and catecholamines: A problem in comparative endocrinology. *In* "Handbook of Physiology, Sect. 5: Adipose Tissue" (A. Renold and G. F. Cahill, eds.), pp. 533–547. Amer. Physiol. Soc., Washington, D. C.

Schemmel, R., Mickelsen, O., and Mostosky, V. (1970a). Influence of body weight, age, diet and sex on fat depots in rats. *Anatomical Record* **166**, 437–446.

Schemmel, R., Mickelsen, O., and Gill, J. (1970b). Dietary obesity in rats: Body weight and body fat accretion in seven strains of rats. *Journal of Nutrition* **100**, 1041–1048.

Schoenheimer, R., and Rittenberg, D. (1935). Deuterium as an indicator in the study of intermediary metabolism. III. Role of fat tissue. *Journal of Biological Chemistry* **111**, 175–181.

Silberberg, M., and Silberberg, R. (1957). Neuroendocrine system and obesity: Studies in "yellow mice." *Journal of the Mount Sinai Hospital, New York* **24**, 1207–1213.

Sinha, Y. N., and Vander Laan, W. P. (1971). Effects of goldthioglucose and bipiperidyl mustard on pituitary prolactin and growth hormone content of C3H mice. *Proceedings of the Society for Experimental Biology and Medicine* **136**, 830–833.

Sleter, E. R. (1969). Fine structure of brown adipose tissue. *Laboratory Investigation* 21, 246–258.

Smith, R. E. (1961). Thermogenic activity of the hibernating gland in the cold-acclimated rat. *Physiologist* 4, 113–118.

Stevenson, J. A. F., Cox, B., and Salauka, A. (1964). A fat mobilizing and anorectic substance in the urine of fasting rats. *Proceedings of the Society for Experimental Biology Medicine* 115, 424–429.

Tedischi, C. G. (1946). Systemic multicentric lipoblastosis. *Archives of Pathology* 42, 320–337.

Toldt, C. (1888). "Lehrbuck der Gewebelehre." Stuttgart.

von Bertalanffy, F. (1960). Principles and theory of growth. *In* "Fundamental Aspects of Normal and Malignant Growth" (W. Nowinski, ed.), pp. 137–259. Elsevier, Amsterdam.

Wade, G., and Zucher, I. (1970). Development of hormonal control over food intake and body weight in female rats. *Journal of Comparative and Physiological Psychology* 70, 213–220.

Wassermann, F. (1926). Die Fettorgane des Menschen. Entwichlung, Bau and Systematische Stellung des Sogenannten Fettgewebes. *Zeitschrift für Zellforschung und Mikroskopische Anatomie* 3, 235–329.

Wassermann, F. (1958). In Discussion: Action of insulin and cortisone on adipose tissue. *Diabetes* 7, 211–220.

Wassermann, F. (1965). Development of adipose tissue. *In* "Handbook of Physiology, Sect. 5: Adipose Tissue" (A. Renold and G. F. Cahill, eds.), pp. 87–100. Amer. Physiol. Soc., Washington, D. C.

Weil, R., and Stetten, De W. (1947). The urinary excretion of fat mobilizing agent. *Journal of Biological Chemistry* 168, 129–132.

Wertheimer, E., and Shapiro, B. (1948). The physiology of adipose tissue. *Physiological Reviews* 28, 451–464.

Widdowson, E. (1965). Factors affecting the growth rate of laboratory animals. *Cosmetic Toxicology* 3, 721–733.

Widdowson, E. (1970). Harmony of growth. *Lancet* 1, 901–905.

Williams, G. E. G. (1961). Some aspects of compensatory hyperplasia of the kidney. *British Journal of Experimental Pathology* 42, 386–396.

Wintrobe, M. (1961). "Clinical Hematology." Lea & Febiger, Philadelphia, Pennsylvania.

Wirsén, C. (1965a). Distribution of adrenergic nerve fibers in brown and white adipose tissue. *In* "Handbook of Physiology, Sect. 5: Adipose Tissue" (A. Renold and G. F. Cahill, eds.), pp. 197–199. Amer. Physiol. Soc., Washington, D. C.

Wirsén, C. (1965b). Studies in lipid mobilization. *Acta Physiologica Scandinavica, Supplementum* 252, 1–46.

Wislicki, L., and Hermann-Hollander, E. (1966). Distribution of brown and pararenal fat in rats of various weights. *Israel Journal of Medical Sciences* 2, 192–195.

Woodruff, M. (1960). "Transplantation of Tissues and Organs," pp. 280–284. Thomas, Springfield, Illinois.

Zingg, W. A., Angel, A., and Steinberg, M. D. (1962). Studies on the number and volume of fat cells. *Canadian Journal of Biochemistry and Physiology* 40, 437–442.

Neurophysiological Analysis of Mating Behavior Responses as Hormone-Sensitive Reflexes

Donald Pfaff, Catherine Lewis, Carol Diakow,
and Melvyn Keiner
*Rockefeller University,
New York, New York*

I. Introduction

Mating behavior in rodents shows a striking and well-documented dependence on steroid sex hormone levels (see reviews by Beach, 1948; Young, 1961; Phoenix *et al.*, 1967). Therefore, endocrinological approaches have facilitated the analysis of mating responses. These approaches have included removing the source of the hormone, replacing the hormone by injection, implanting it locally in the brain, and studying the distribution of radioactively labeled hormones. Moreover, mating behavior of rodents is easily elicited in the laboratory and has an obvious biological importance. Finally, its sensory-motor aspects appear more stereotyped than many other behaviors. For all of these reasons, mating behavior is an attractive subject for neurophysiological analysis.

The striking effects of sex hormones on rodent mating behavior open the way to a logical experimental strategy for the physiological study of mating behavior mechanisms. Such a strategy can be put in the form of three research problems:

1. Determine if and where sex hormones are taken up in brain tissue.

2. Search for and characterize phyiological effects of hormones in brain tissue.

3. Understand how the detailed neurophysiological effects of sex hormones are related to their effects on mating behavior.

The organization of this article reflects this research strategy.

II. Localization of Cells Concentrating Steroid Sex Hormones in the Rat Brain

A large body of data from several laboratories shows that a limbic-hypothalamic system of cells concentrates estradiol (and, to a smaller extent, testosterone) more highly than any other brain region.

Early experiments using scintillation counting of dissected brain regions after systemic injection of radioactive estradiol found higher uptake in the hypothalamus than in such regions as cerebral cortex, especially at times one hour or longer after injection (Eisenfeld and Axelrod, 1965, 1966; Kato and Villee, 1967a,b). These data have been confirmed (McGuire and Lisk, 1968, 1969; Green *et al.*, 1969). In particular, when a larger number of finely dissected brain regions is studied, estradiol is seen to be highly concentrated not only in the hypothalamus, but also in the preoptic area, septum, amygdala, and to a lesser extent, hippocampus (McEwen and Pfaff, 1970). In regions of highest uptake, estradiol is concentrated by cell nuclei (Zigmond and McEwen, 1970; Chader and Villee, 1970).

Another property expected of physiologically significant hormone binding is that a limited number of "receptor" molecules would account for the hormone concentration by neurons in particular parts of the brain. Because of the limited capacity of any given number of such molecules, preinjection of nonradioactive hormone should be able to flood a significant proportion of binding sites, preventing radioactive hormone from occupying them. In fact, preinjection of nonradioactive estradiol does show such "binding site competition" with radioactive estradiol in regions of the brain showing high estradiol uptake, notably the hypothalamus, preoptic area, and amygdala (Eisenfeld and Axelrod, 1965, 1966; Kato and Villee, 1967b; McEwen and Pfaff, 1970).

Cells from a brain region dissected as a unit for the purpose of scintillation counting usually comprise a heterogeneous population on both anatomical and functional grounds. Therefore, a technique such as autoradiography, in which labeled cells can be detected individually, can be used to advantage. Autoradiographic studies of tritiated estradiol uptake in the female rat brain have revealed a limbic-hypothalamic system of estradiol-concentrating cells which agrees with and adds anatomical detail to the results of scintillation counting experiments.

In the most recent series of experiments in our laboratory (Pfaff, 1972; Pfaff and Keiner, 1972, 1973), we have prepared autoradiograms from frozen brain tissue by cutting frozen sections in the cryostat in the darkroom and mounting the unfixed, unembedded sections directly from the cryostat knife onto emulsion-coated slides (modified from Anderson and Greenwald, 1969). This approach yielded series of autoradiographic maps of estradiol-concentrating cells as are shown in Fig. 1. Peak concentrations of labeled cells were seen in the lateral septum, the diagonal band of Broca, the medial preoptic area, and medial anterior hypothalamus, nucleus of the stria terminalis, cortical and medial amygdaloid nuclei, arcuate and ventromedial nuclei of the hypothalamus, the ventral premamillary nucleus, and the lateral portion of the central gray (Fig. 1). Somewhat lower concentrations of labeled cells were seen in the ventral hippocampus. In other regions of the brain, such as the cerebral cortex, cerebellum, or lower brainstem, occasional labeled cells were seen, but these few cells were not found in regular, well-defined loci from section to section or from rat to rat and were usually less intensely labeled. The basic limbic-hypothalamic distribution of estradiol-concentrating cells confirms the conclusions based on an earlier series of autoradiograms which used a different technical approach (Pfaff, 1968a) and agrees with scintillation counting results (McEwen and Pfaff, 1970).

In the preoptic area and anterior hypothalamus, sites of peak estradiol uptake overlap with sites in which implanted estrogen facilitates female sex behavior in rats (Lisk, 1962, 1967) and cats (Michael, 1965). In general, locations with the highest numbers of estradiol-concentrating cells show good anatomical correspondence to preoptic and hypothalamic regions implicated in reproductive function (pituitary or behavior control) by results of implantation and lesion studies (Sawyer, 1960; Lisk, 1967). This correspondence suggests that concentration of estradiol by neurons in the phylogenetically old limbic-hypothalamic system is correlated with functional estradiol effects related to reproduction.

The distribution of labeled cells across brain structures following systemic injections of tritiated testosterone matches closely the pattern of uptake of radioactive estradiol (Pfaff, 1968b; McEwen *et al.*,

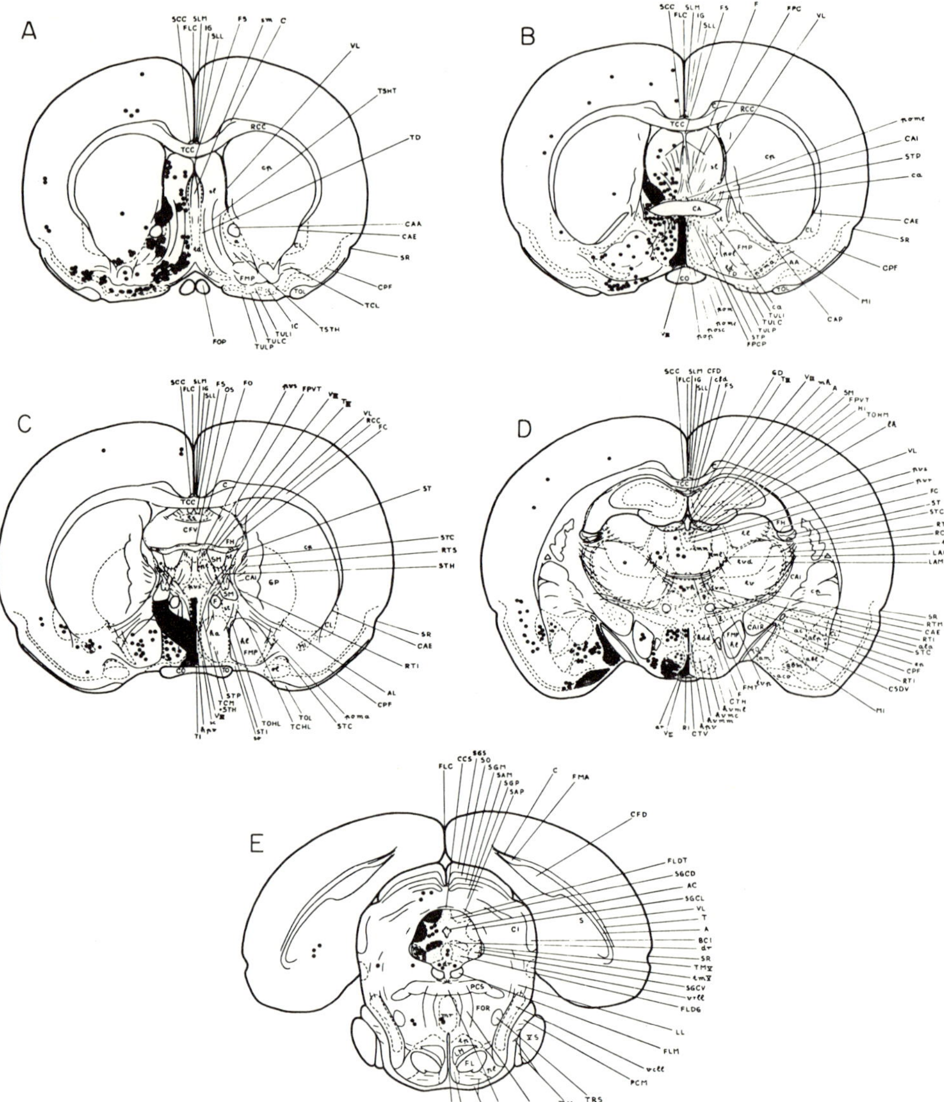

FIG. 1. Maps showing locations of estradiol-concentrating cells in the brain of an ovariectomized female rat. Two hours after intraperitoneal injection of estradiol-³H, each of nine females was sacrificed, and the brain quickly frozen. Autoradiograms were prepared by directly mounting unfixed, unembedded frozen sections from the cryostat knife in the darkroom onto emulsion-coated slides. The maps shown were selected from a representative female brain, at levels which include some of the regions of highest estradiol concentration. Locations of estra-

1970a,b). For both hormones, peak uptake is seen in the limbic-hypothalamic system of cells described above, with quantitatively less uptake in other brain regions. Within the limbic-hypothalamic system, best testosterone uptake appeared in somewhat more anterior basal forebrain structures, compared to the distribution of estradiol-concentrating cells (Pfaff, 1968b). Also, in scintillation-counting experiments, testosterone was concentrated somewhat less than estradiol from the blood and showed less specific uptake in the preoptic area and hypothalamus (McEwen *et al.*, 1970a,b). Cells in the brain regions which concentrate both estradiol and testosterone cannot be thought of as nonspecific accumulators of steroids, since radioactive corticosterone, an adrenal steroid hormone, has been shown both by cell fractionation (McEwen *et al.*, 1969, 1970c) and autoradiographic (Gerlach and McEwen, 1972) methods to be concentrated most highly in the hippocampus and relatively poorly by preoptic-hypothalamic sex steroid target cells.

The overall topography of estradiol concentration in the rat brain is similar for females and males, and this is also the case for testosterone (Pfaff, 1968b; McEwen and Pfaff, 1970; McEwen *et al.*, 1970a,b). However, concentration of estradiol in the anterior hypothalamus specifically appears to be quantitatively higher in control females compared to males or neonatally androgenized females (McEwen and Pfaff, 1970). Studied autoradiographically (Zigmond and Pfaff, unpublished data), this quantitative sex difference appears to be greatest in particular cell groups, rather than being spread equally throughout the anterior hypothalamus.

III. Electrophysiological Effects of Sex Hormones on Single-Unit Activity in the Rat Brain

A. Proof That Effects Exist

Kawakami and Sawyer (1959a,b) measured EEG arousal and after-reaction patterns of wave activity in the cerebral cortex of female rabbits and showed definitively that electrical activity of the brain can

---

diol-concentrating cells are plotted on the left side of drawings from the rat brain atlas of König and Klippel (1963), while the right side is reserved for anatomical abbreviations. Section A is from König and Klippel's Fig. 16; B from Fig. 19; C from Fig. 25; D from Fig. 33; and E from Fig. 54. Each dot on the left side of the drawings shows the position of an estradiol-concentrating cell. Where many dots would overlap, that area is filled in with solid black (from Pfaff, 1972b; Pfaff and Keiner, 1972).

be altered by gonadal steroid injection. More recently, attempts have been made to measure effects of gonadal steroids on the firing of single neurons, particularly at sites of peak steroid uptake. Beyer and Sawyer (1969) have reviewed some of this work.

Progesterone was the first substance for which single unit effects were reported. Barraclough and Cross (1963) showed that progesterone could affect the responses of single units in the lateral hypothalamus of anesthetized female rats. The existence of a progesterone effect has been confirmed (Ramirez *et al.*, 1967; Komisaruk *et al.*, 1967; Beyer *et al.*, 1967; Lincoln, 1969b). Likewise, estradiol effects have been reported on responses to peripheral stimuli by hypothalamic and mesencephalic units in female rats (Lincoln and Cross, 1967; Kawakami and Kubo, 1971) and cats (Alcaraz *et al.*, 1969; Beyer, 1972). Finally, testosterone injections in castrated male rats influence the resting discharge and responses of neurons in the preoptic region and also in other areas of the brain (Pfaff and Pfaffmann, 1969a).

B. Attempts to Interpret Effects in Terms of Behavior

Although it is widely agreed that progesterone affects neuronal activity, there has been some disagreement about the extent to which it has specific effects on stimuli related to reproduction. Some authors have tended to emphasize the fact that some hypothalamic cells show selective responses to sex-related stimuli, and that progesterone may affect responses to such stimuli without affecting responses to other stimuli (Barraclough and Cross, 1963; Haller and Barraclough, 1970). Other authors have found that under certain conditions progesterone can decrease neuronal responses to *any* arousing stimulus, and that it also affects cortical EEG responses to such stimuli (Komisaruk *et al.*, 1967; Lincoln, 1969b). Similar questions arise regarding effects of testosterone. It is possible to detect testosterone effects on single-unit responses to stimuli which have no obvious relation to reproduction (Pfaff and Pfaffmann, 1969a). Also, we found that testosterone alters resting discharge rates and responsivity of mesencephalic reticular formation units and alters the cortical EEG in some preparations. However, the occurrence of single-unit effects of testosterone in reticular formation tended to be correlated with effects in the EEG, while preoptic unit effects tended to occur independently of EEG effects (Pfaff and Pfaffmann, 1969a).

Discussion about the specificity of the progesterone effect has raised the general question: Which electrophysiological functions are affected by each sex hormone and which are not? Progress toward answering this question can be illustrated by experiments with testosterone. Testosterone altered resting discharge rates of some neurons in the preoptic area, and also either increased the absolute magnitudes of response or reversed the direction of response to individual odor stimuli by some units (Pfaff and Pfaffmann, 1969a). However, when neurons were tested with several odor stimuli before and after testosterone injection, the *relative* response magnitudes of the neuron to the different odors remained the same before and after hormone treatment; the most powerful odor stimulant before injection still gave the best responses after injection, the weakest stimulant also remained weakest, and so forth. Also, during recording from an individual unit, if response direction to one odorant was reversed following testosterone, it was also reversed for all the other odorants used. These findings with acute testosterone injections were supported by comparisons between normal and castrated male rats. First, we defined a measure of differential responsiveness of individual neurons to different odors (Pfaff and Pfaffmann, 1969b). Using the differential response measure, we found a sharpening of coding for female urine odors by neurons in the preoptic area. This sharpening occurred equally well in normal and castrated male rats (Pfaff and Gregory, 1971a). Thus, both with acute testosterone injections and with normal–castrate comparisons, it appears that coding of olfactory stimuli by preoptic area neurons is not androgen sensitive.

High correlations between changes in unit firing rate and changes in the cortical EEG have been observed for some cells in the hypothalamus and preoptic area of urethane-anesthetized rats (Komisaruk *et al.*, 1967; Ramirez *et al.*, 1967; Lincoln, 1969a,b; Pfaff and Pfaffmann, 1969a). This correlation is androgen-sensitive; we found that a higher proportion of preoptic neurons in normal than in castrated male rats showed significant correlations to the cortical EEG (Pfaff and Gregory, 1971b). The higher proportion in normal males resulted from the larger number of neurons showing EEG correlation similar to that of reticular formation cells (Schlag and Balvin, 1963), that is, increasing firing rate during EEG "activation."

This testosterone effect on relation of units to the EEG, and the pattern of results with single-unit responses to odors, summarized above, suggested a comparison between electrophysiological measures of testosterone effects and behavioral effects of androgens in male rats (Table IA). Essential to this comparison is the notion of how a single unit participates in the coding (or "neural identification") of odors— i.e., by responding differently to different odors. Using a measure of differential response by single units, olfactory coding of odors by

TABLE I
SPECULATIVE COMPARISONS BETWEEN HORMONE-SENSITIVE AND
HORMONE-INSENSITIVE BEHAVIORAL AND
ELECTROPHYSIOLOGICAL FUNCTIONS
IN RATS

A. Effects of androgenic hormones on responses to female rat odors by male rats: IS EACH MEASURE AFFECTED BY TESTOSTERONE?

	Behavioral results	Electrophysiological results
Identification of olfactory stimuli	Detection and discrimination of female urine odors NO (Carr and Caul, 1962; Carr *et al.*, 1962)	Olfactory coding by *differential* responses of preoptic neurons NO (Pfaff and Gregory, 1971a)
Motivationally dependent behavioral activation by olfactory stimuli	Preference for estrous female odors YES (LeMagnen, 1952; Carr *et al.*, 1965, 1966; Pfaff and Pfaffmann, 1969b)	? Candidates for basis of motivational effects: Resting neuronal discharge and *absolute* response magnitude of preoptic neurons (Pfaff and Pfaffmann, 1969a); Relation to EEG (Pfaff and Gregory, 1971b)

B. Effects of adrenal hormones on responses of rats to salt: IS EACH MEASURE AFFECTED BY ADRENALECTOMY?

Identification of salt solutions	Salt taste threshold measurements NO (Carr, 1952; Harriman and MacLeod, 1953)	Chorda tympani nerve responses to salt NO (Pfaffmann and Bare, 1950)
Motivational dependent response to salt ("salt hunger")	Preference for salt YES (Richter, 1936)	?

preoptic neurons was not affected by testicular androgens. Neither is the behavioral identification of sex odors affected by androgenic hormones (Carr and Caul, 1962; Carr *et al.*, 1962). Thus, it seems possible that the coding of responses to female rat odors by preoptic neurons in male rats, which is androgen-insensitive, corresponds to the behavioral detection and discrimination of female rat odors by male rats, which also is not affected by testicular androgens. In contrast, behavioral *preferences* for female rat odors *are* androgen sensitive (see Table IA). Candidates for the electrophysiological correlate of this testosterone effect presently would include preoptic neuronal resting discharge, absolute magnitude of the responses of preoptic neurons to odors, and relation of single-unit firing to the cortical EEG.

This speculative formulation may gain some credence from the similar alignment of experimental results on adrenalectomy and salt hunger (Table IB). Adrenalectomy affects neither behavioral detection thresholds for salt (Carr, 1952; Harriman and MacLeod, 1953) nor peripheral taste nerve responses to salt (Pfaffmann and Bare, 1950): detection and peripheral stimulus coding functions seem insensitive to mineralocorticoids. However, rats show a striking increase in preference for salt solutions after adrenalectomy (Richter, 1936). The electrophysiological correlate for this behavioral preference function is unknown.

The analyses presented here are attempts to link electrophysiological effects of sex hormones to behavioral effects by examining various properties of single-unit activity after hormone manipulation. Other approaches to correlation with behavior would include chronic recording, as can be achieved with telemetry (Pfaff *et al.*, 1971). Most of the examples above come from experiments with testosterone. Similar attempts with estrogen to relate electrophysiological to behavioral effects have been made by comparing estrogen effects on responses to sex-related and "control" stimuli, during recording from hypothalamic units in female rats (Lincoln and Cross, 1967) or mesencephalic units in female cats (Alcaraz *et al.*, 1969). However, for both testosterone and estradiol, a systematic approach to the interpretation of sex hormone effects on single units must involve identifying with neurophysiological methods the neural circuits in which hormone-sensitive cells participate, in order to show the relation of these cells to mating behavior control circuits.

IV. Analysis of Lordosis in the Female Rat as a Hormone-Sensitive Reflex

To discern the meaning of an individual neuron's concentration of, and response to a steroid hormone, it is necessary to specify some of its other physiological characteristics. Rather than merely recording its histological location, we must be able to determine what its relations are with other neurons, that is, to describe its participation in certain neural circuits. Instead of choosing such circuits for study arbitrarily, we have selected a more rational approach to the study of hormone-sensitive neurons: to describe how they participate in circuits controlling mating behavior. Toward this end we are attempting to iden-

TABLE II

STEPS IN THE IDENTIFICATION OF NEURAL CIRCUITS CONTROLLING
MATING BEHAVIOR REFLEXES

Description of reflex
    A. Detailed description of behavioral elements (analysis of movie films, X-rays)
    B. Description of muscles causing response
    C. Analysis of sensory input (experimental interference with stimuli from male; experimental imitation of stimuli from male)

Neural determinants of reflex
    D. Reflexes in the spinal female
    E. Supraspinal neural circuits controlling mating reflexes
    F. Location of estradiol-sensitive neurons in lordosis-control circuits

tify the circuits which mediate mating behavior. When this is done it may be possible to see how hormone-induced changes in hormone-sensitive neurons cause hormone-induced changes in mating behavior.

Our strategy for the identification of neural circuits mediating mating behavior is presented in Table II. The first three steps, analysis of the behavioral elements and of their motor and sensory components, constitute a "reflexological" description of mating responses. A precise description of this sort facilitates the last three steps—analyses of the neural bases for mating reflexes.

Description of portions of a mating behavior sequence as reflexes need only imply that well-defined sets of stimuli from the mating partner and other sources are known to determine well-defined constellations of muscular responses.

We have focused on the most striking reflex in the female rat's mating behavior, lordosis, for three reasons. First, in quantitative terms, the uptake of radioactive estradiol in the female rat brain appears to be more specific than the uptake of radioactive testosterone in the male rat's brain (McEwen and Pfaff, 1970; McEwen *et al.*, 1970a,b; Zigmond and McEwen, 1970). Second, the effect of estradiol on lordosis in the female rat is the strongest, most specific hormone-behavior link we have found in rats (Pfaff, 1970b, 1972a). Estradiol stimulates feminine behavior directly, rather than requiring pituitary hormones as intermediates (Pfaff, 1970a). Third, the lordosis reflex appears to have a simple enough topography to submit to neurophysiological analysis.

A. DESCRIPTION OF THE BEHAVIOR BY FILM ANALYSIS

In many previous studies of estrogenic effects on female behavior, lordosis could be used more or less as an indicator of estrus. As such it could almost be treated as a unitary event. However, identifying the neural circuits underlying lordosis poses a problem of analyzing motor control. In these terms it is obvious that describing individual sensory and motor elements of the lordosis reflex would facilitate further study.

We have used color moving picture films of mating encounters between normal male rats and estrous female rats, taken from the side (Pfaff, 1971) and from below the mating pair, to analyze frame-by-frame the impact of the male on the female and her lordosis response. Figure 2 shows traced outline drawings from single frames of movies to illustrate a few of the main events in the idealized lordosis reflex. Although these particular drawings were taken from only two mating encounters, their main features are typical of large numbers of mating sequences which include lordosis by estrogen-progesterone primed receptive females and intromission by large, sexually experienced vigorous male rats. At the end of a fast "darting" sequence the female comes abruptly to a halt. The male, following her, mounts from the rear, contacting her flanks (and sometimes her thighs) with his forepaws and front legs, and often contacting her back with his nose and chin (Fig. 2A). Holding onto her, he "walks up" with his rear legs (Fig. 2B) until his lower abdomen and pelvis are pressing over and around the female's rump and tailbase, and his rear legs may also be pressing against the back of her rear legs and hips. The male then begins thrusting his pelvic region against the female. In a rapid series of repetitive thrusts, the initial thrusts may be well in back of the vaginal region or off to the side (Fig. 2C). Before and during these initial thrusts the female has begun to extend her legs and raise her tailbase. Subsequent thrusts of the male's penis may be better directed toward the vaginal region (Fig. 2D), culminating in thrusts right at the vaginal opening (Fig. 2E) and eventual penile insertion into the vagina ("intromission") (Fig. 2F). By the time the penis has reached the vagina the female has elevated her rump so far, due both to rear leg extension and to vertebral dorsiflexion of the rump and tailbase, that the male can bend his hindquarters underneath, even to the point that during intromission the back of his body obscures the view of her genital region from below (Fig. 2F). Directly after intromission the male dismounts with a backward springing movement, leaving the female in the lordosis posture: legs extended, and vertebral column dorsiflexed so that head, rump, and tailbase are raised while the thorax is lowered (Fig. 2G).

The order of events during lordosis can be described objectively by recording on special score sheets (a) the frame numbers in which the onsets and offsets of discrete events occur, and (b) the values in each frame of continuous variables such as angles or positions of body

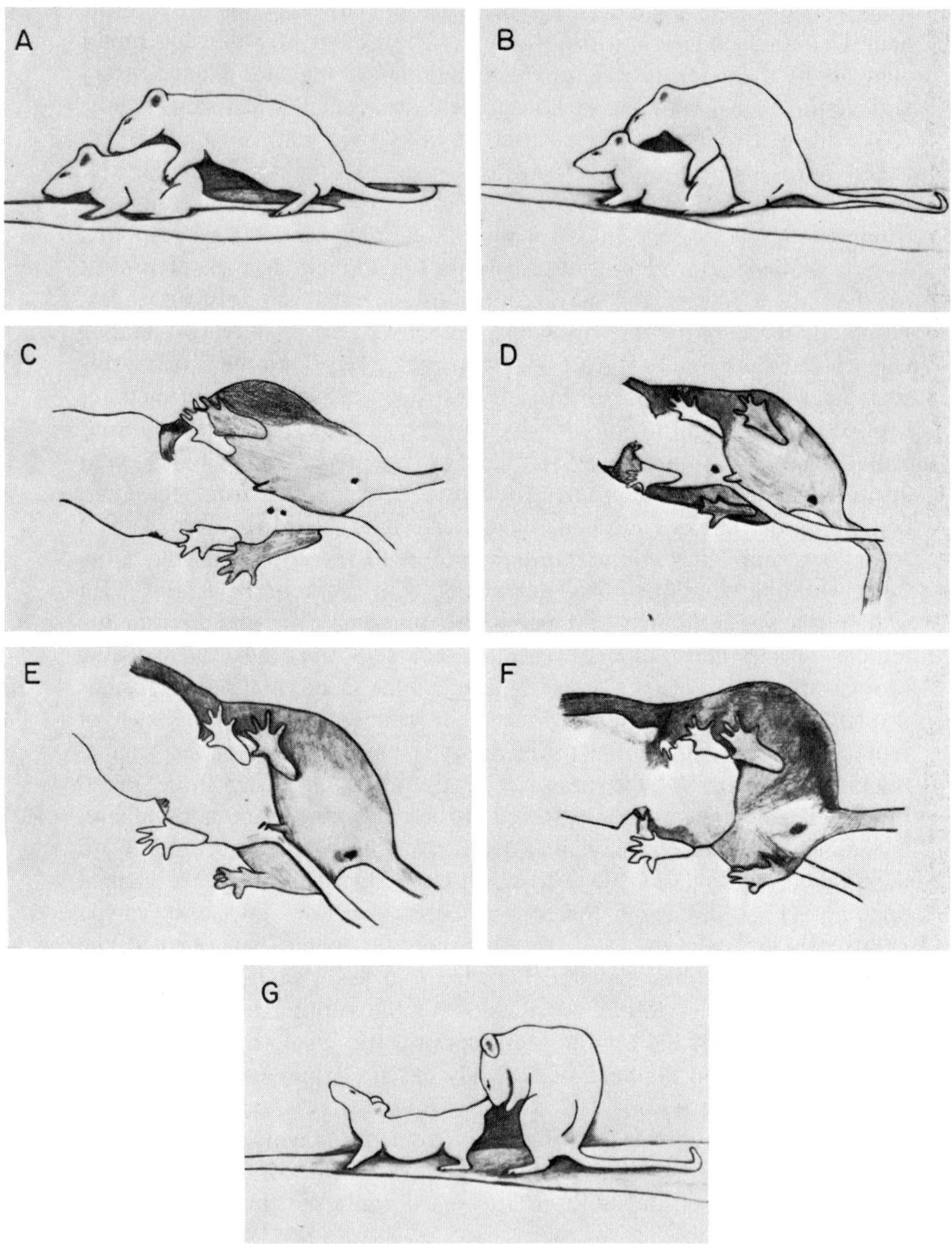

FIG. 2. Traced outline drawings from single frames of movie films of mating encounters between male and female rats. Parts A, B, and G were taken from

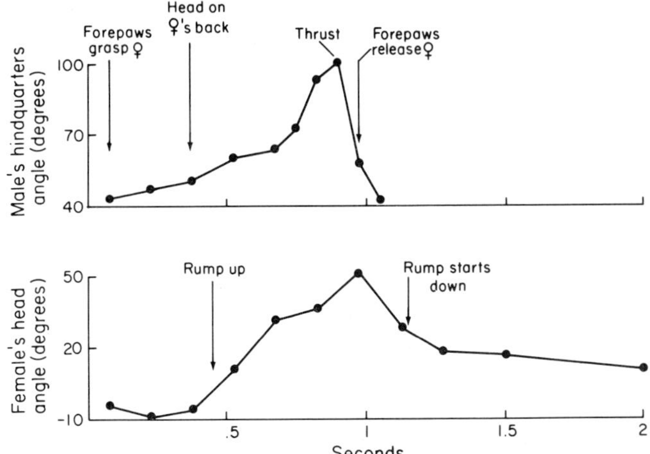

FIG. 3. Graph of a mating encounter between a vigorous, sexually experienced male and estrous female rat. Upper plot refers to the male's behavior; lower to female's. In all angular measurements, 0° is horizontal, and 90° is vertical. Data were transcribed from special score sheets for frame-by-frame analyses of color movie films. A total of 55 lordoses were analyzed in this way. The early occurrence of initial rump and tailbase elevation by the female was a typical feature of her lordosis reflex (from Pfaff, 1971).

parts. We have analyzed lordosis in this way in films taken from the side (Pfaff, 1971), measuring the angle of the male's hindquarters and the angle of the female's nasal bone with respect to horizontal. The encounter graphed in Fig. 3, between a very aggressive male and a highly receptive female, is typical except for the absence of repetitive thrusting before the male's penile insertion. A constant feature of these graphs was that the first detectable rump and tailbase elevation (due to leg extension and to vertebral dorsiflexion) occurred well before penile insertion.

Preliminary data from an X-ray cinematographic analysis of lordosis (obtained with the help of Dr. F. Jenkins, of Columbia University) support the view obtained with conventional movie analysis. The

the side (cf. Stone and Ferguson, 1940). Parts C, D, E, and F were taken from below (cf. Beach and Rabedeau, 1959; Bermant, 1965), and in these frames the body of the male is shaded while the female is not. Part A represents the first point at which the male touches the female, and the succeeding pictures are in chronological order, ending (G) just after the male's dismount. The male rats used for these observations were large, sexually experienced and vigorous, while the females were ovariectomized and brought into estrus with large priming doses of estradiol benzoate and progesterone. See text for further description.

lordotic reflex responses to somatic stimuli from the male consist of leg extension and vertebral dorsiflexion and can precede penile insertion into the vagina.

These observations from movie film analyses (from the side and below) and X-ray pictures of lordosis have been used to establish the appearance and order of events in Fig. 10.

B. Muscular Basis of Lordosis

Perhaps the most unique element of the lordosis reflex is the vertebral column dorsiflexion, characterized by head, rump, and tailbase elevation, and thorax lowering. We have begun to study the muscular basis of this movement.

Muscles which extend ("dorsiflex") the vertebral column have been described in the dog (Miller *et al.*, 1964, pp. 162–194) and the cat (Reighard and Jennings, 1935, pp. 123–138). These are overlapping and partially fused longitudinal systems of epaxial spinal muscles which lie dorsal and dorsolateral to the vertebral column. Among them, the longissimus system and the multifidus spinae have an especially strong extensor action on the rump and tailbase.

In the rat, we have observed that applying electrical pulse stimuli directly to the corresponding longitudinal muscle systems, lying dorsal and dorsolateral to the vertebral column, causes extension (dorsiflexion) of the spinal column. Stimulating muscles located caudally causes rump and tail elevation, while stimulating more anterior in this muscle system causes thorax depression. We have not yet established the exact degree of correspondence between individual muscle names in the rat and those in the cat or dog. However, it seems clear that motor neurons controlling the longissimus and related epaxial muscle systems must be involved in executing the lordosis reflex.

C. Analysis of Sensory Requirements for Lordosis

1. Review of Stimuli Applied by the Male

Contact between the sexually experienced male rat and estrous female rat during mating encounters may be divided roughly into three parts, on the basis of film analysis. First, the male's forepaws and head contact the female's flanks and back. Second, the male's pelvis region and penis contact the female's tailbase region, groin, and perivaginal areas. Finally, during intromission, the female receives intravaginal stimulation. We have attempted to discover which among these stimuli are necessary for lordosis by removing them selectively (Section IV,C,2, below), and which are sufficient by imitating them selectively (Section IV,C,3, below).

2. Attempts to Prevent Selected Stimuli

In a series of experiments, subcutaneous injections of procaine in certain regions of the skin of female rats affected not only the mating behavior of the female but also that of the male.

During initial experiments, ovariectomized females brought into estrus by estradiol and progesterone treatment were injected subcutaneously with procaine throughout the flank, back, and perineal (perivaginal) regions. Our attempt was to anesthetize locally in each female almost all of the area contacted by the male's paws, head, and pelvis. This treatment significantly lowered the females' lordosis quotient (i.e., the percentage of mounts by the male on which the female does lordosis) (Fig. 4). Surprisingly, the performance of intromission in

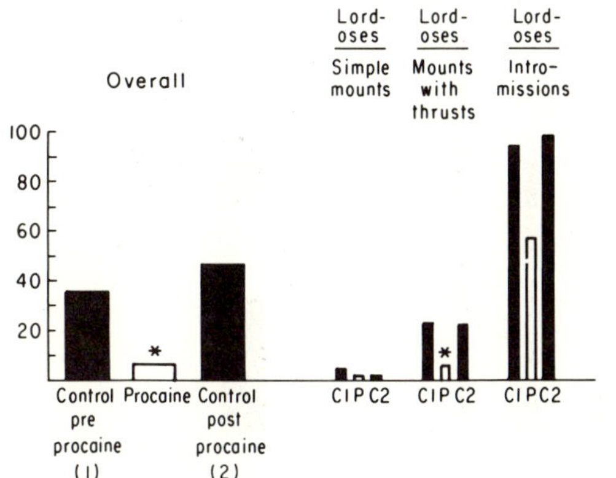

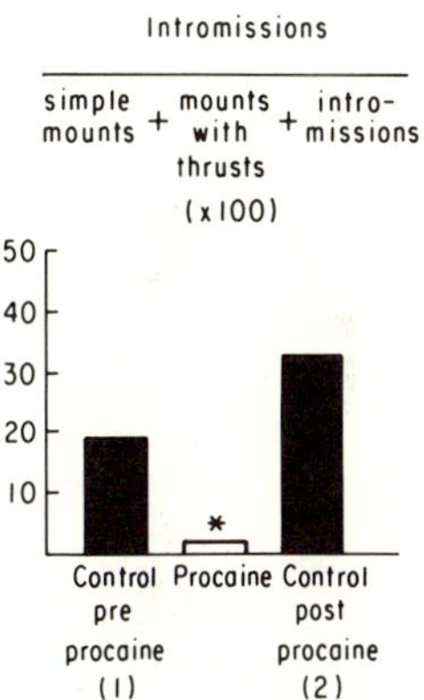

FIG. 4. Effects of subcutaneous procaine injections in the flank, back, and perivaginal regions of *female* rats on lordosis quotient of the female and on the performance of intromission by the male. In the middle of the figure, the overall lordosis quotient is broken down into separate parts showing the females' lordotic responses to simple mounts, mounts with thrusts, and intromissions. Results for each of the six females were averaged, and then the data were averaged across females. Each animal served as its own pre-procaine control (six 8-minute tests) and post-procaine control (one test), and the "procaine" results are averaged across two tests. Females had been ovariectomized and brought into heat with 6 μg estradiol benzoate 2 days before and .5 mg progesterone 4 hours before each test. C1, control before procaine; C2, control after procaine; P, procaine; *, $p < .02$.

the males was also lowered. A significantly decreased proportion of their total number of responses toward the female resulted in intromission. This combination of effects can be understood by assuming that early in each mating encounter the female's response to a somatic stimulus from the male in the procaine-affected area has two important functions. First, it is part of her reflex progression toward a lordosis posture and, if prevented, lordosis is interfered with. Second, it is important for allowing the male's reflex progression toward intromission, and if prevented, intromission is interfered with. Further experiments using superficial cutaneous denervation are required to verify that the procaine effect on the female is purely sensory, and that underlying muscles are not affected directly.

The effect of local anesthesia in the female on the behavior of the female and male can be documented further by breaking down the overall lordosis quotient into separate parts showing the responses of females to simple mounts, mounts with thrusts and intromissions (Fig.

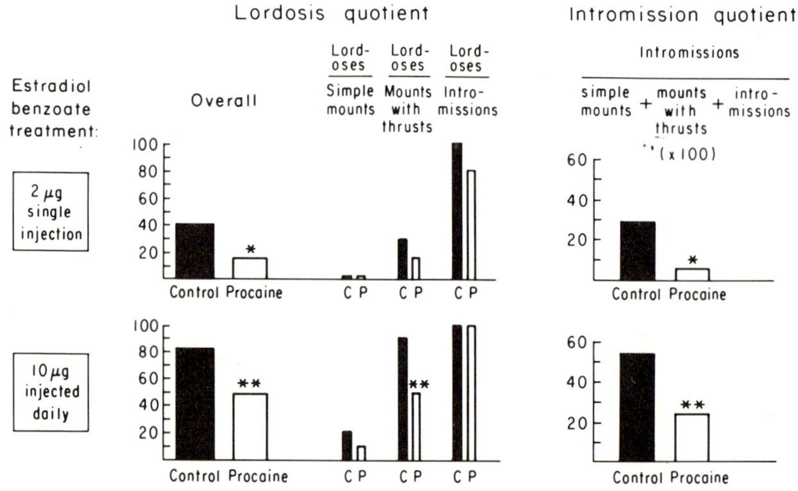

FIG. 5. Effects of subcutaneous procaine injections in the perivaginal and tailbase areas of the *female* rat's pelvis, on lordosis quotient of the female and on intromission by the male. In the middle of the figure the overall average lordosis quotient is broken down into separate parts showing the females' average lordotic responses to simple mounts, mounts with thrusts, and intromissions. Females ($N = 12$) were ovariectomized and tested following either single 2 μg or daily 10 μg estradiol benzoate regimes followed by .5 mg progesterone on the morning of test day. The control condition was subcutaneous injection of physiological saline rather than procaine. Each female was used in both pelvic procaine and control conditions, and in flank-abdomen-back procaine and control conditions (Fig. 6), and the experiment was counterbalanced for order. Each test was 8 minutes long and was started 5–9 minutes after procaine or control (physiological saline) injections. C, control; P, procaine; *, $p < .05$; **, $p < .005$.

4). Before procaine treatment, about 20% of the responses of males resulted in intromission, and virtually all of those intromissions accompanied lordosis. When procaine prevented the females' responses to some of the initial somatic stimuli from the male, lordosis and intromission were prevented during some of the mating encounters. This "moves" each such encounter from the intromission-with-lordosis category to the "thrust-without-lordosis" category, significantly decreasing the intromission quotient and the ratio of lordoses/mounts-with-thrusts (Fig. 4).

In order to see if the effect of the overall procaine treatment of the female (Fig. 4) was due primarily to anesthesia in a more restricted area on her skin, the overall treatment was divided into two parts. First, the female's pelvic region was anesthetized by subcutaneous injections of procaine around the clitoris, vagina, and tailbase. This treatment lowered the lordosis quotient in ovariectomized female rats given either relatively low (2 μg) or relatively high (10 μg daily) estradiol treatments followed by progesterone, and also lowered the males' intromission quotient under either condition (Fig. 5). Second, the female's flanks, lateral edges of the abdomen, and the back around the lower edge of the ribcage were injected subcutaneously with procaine. This "flank-abdomen-back" treatment had minimal effects on the female rat (appearing only during the high-estrogen regime) and no significant effects on the males' frequency of intromission (Fig. 6).

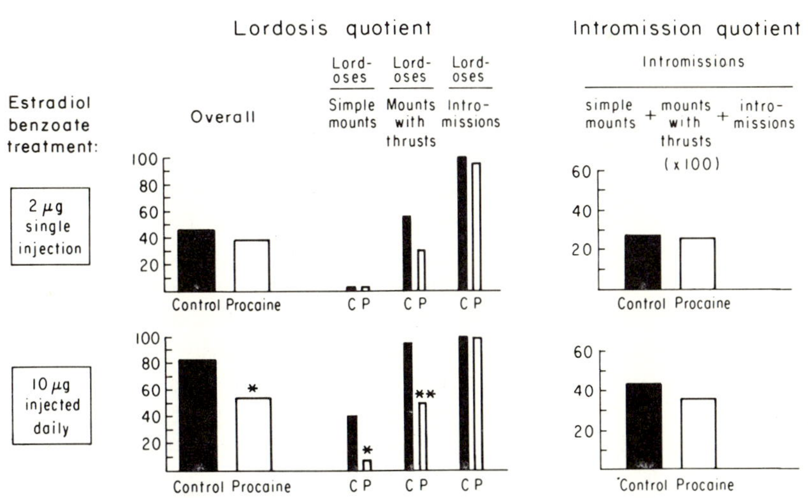

FIG. 6. Effects of subcutaneous injections of procaine in the flank, lateral abdomen, and back regions of the *female* rat, on lordosis by the female and intromission by the male. Other experimental conditions and calculations identical to those in Fig. 5. C, control; P, procaine; *, $p < .05$; **, $p < .005$.

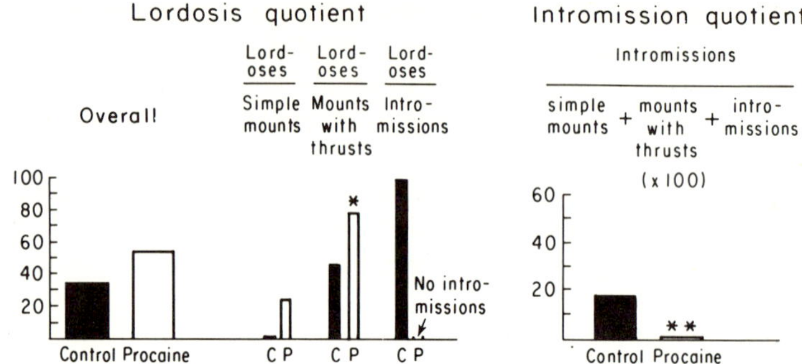

FIG. 7. Effects of subcutaneous procaine injections around the base of the penis of *male* rats on intromission by the male and lordosis by the female. Intromissions were prevented by the penile procaine treatment, but lordoses were not. In the middle of the figure, the overall average lordosis quotient is broken down into separate parts showing the females' average lordotic responses to simple mounts, mounts with thrusts, and intromissions. Males were eight experienced maters; the 12 females used were ovariectomized and brought into estrus with estradiol and progesterone. The males were not injected in the control condition. Each animal was used both in "procaine" (one test) and control (one test) conditions, counterbalanced for order. Each test was 8 minutes long, beginning 6 minutes after procaine injection. C, control; P, procaine; *, $p < .05$; **, $p < .001$.

Thus, the more important stimuli to the female for producing the effect shown in Fig. 4 apparently came from the male's impact on the perivaginal and tailbase regions.

Finally, procaine was injected subcutaneously around the base of the penis of the male rats used in these experiments to prevent intromission (Carlsson and Larsson, 1964; Adler and Bermant, 1966; Sachs and Barfield, 1970), thus preventing intravaginal stimulation due to penile insertion. This treatment did effectively prevent intromission without preventing mounting. However, it failed to lower the lordosis quotient of the female rats (Fig. 7). The ineffectiveness of experimentally induced loss of intromission in lowering lordosis quotient fits with four other lines of evidence suggesting that deep intravaginal stimulation from the penis is not necessary for lordosis. First, in normal sequences of encounters between vigorous male rats and estrous female rats, lordosis often occurs during mounts which do not result in intromission (Fig. 8). Second, in studying the order of events during lordosis it is clear that the legs are extended and the rump and tailbase raised significantly *before* the male's deep intromittory thrust is achieved (Figs. 3 and 10). Third, artificial stimulation without vaginal probing is sufficient to cause lordosis (see Section IV,C,3, below).

Finally, Ball (1934) showed that female rats can perform lordosis in response to the male after surgical removal of the vagina.

The relation of lordosis to intromission, and some of the data above, can be discussed from one point of view using the data in Fig. 8. In many experimental situations involving sexually experienced male rats and estrous female rats, lordosis and intromission tend to co-occur: either they are both present or both absent on any individual mating encounter. Is this correlation due to intromission causing lordosis, or lordosis causing intromission? The data in Fig. 8 indicate that lordosis may occur quite often without intromission, while intromission hardly ever occurs without lordosis. Correspondingly, the evidence summarized above shows that intromission (penile insertion deep into the vagina) is not a necessary cause of lordosis (Fig. 7), while anesthetizing the female's pelvic region with procaine in such a way as to interfere with lordosis also interfered with intromission (Figs. 4 and 5). This suggests that some aspect of the female's early response to stimulation in the pelvic region from the male is important both for her lordosis and for his intromission. Such a causal relationship would produce the nonrandom distribution shown in Fig. 8.

In summary, the procaine experiments indicate that stimulation from the male on the pelvic area of the female is important for producing lordosis, that intravaginal stimulation from deep penile insertion is not important, and that flank and back stimulation may be important at least in the highly (10 μg/day) estrogenized female rat.

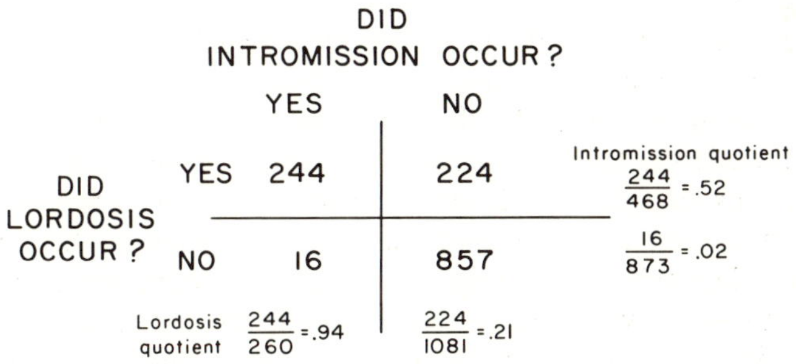

FIG. 8. Relation between the occurrence of lordosis and intromission in series of encounters between sexually vigorous male rats and receptive female rats (ovariectomized, and brought into estrus with 6 μg estradiol benzoate + 0.5 mg progesterone). Data were generated by six pairs of male and female rats during six 8-minute tests per pair. Each mount was scored for presence or absence of lordosis and intromission, and counts as one datum in this figure (total number of mounts = 1341). While lordosis often occurred without intromission, intromission hardly ever occurred without lordosis. χ^2 test, $p < .001$.

3. Attempts to Mimic Selected Stimuli

In order to discover which stimuli are sufficient for lordosis, we have attempted to substitute manual stimuli applied by the experimenter for certain parts of the male rat's stimulation of the female. Used carefully, this approach can yield an index of receptivity which agrees well with the female's responses to the male rat (Ball, 1937; Blandau *et al.*, 1941; Adler and Bell, 1969). However, caution is required, because during functional conditions such as constant estrus (Adler and Bell, 1969), the agreement among these indices may break down, and, when cervical probing is included among the manual stimuli, females may show lordosis after ovariectomy or during diestrus when they are not responsive to male rats (Komisaruk and Diakow, in preparation). Nevertheless, manual stimulation should help to "dissect" experimentally the stimulus array provided by the male rat, particularly when it yields results consistent with those of other techniques.

We have found that light scratching on the flanks and back of female rats (ovariectomized, and brought into estrus with 30 μg estradiol and .5 mg progesterone) causes rear leg extension or abduction, and stiffening of the tail (Diakow *et al.*, 1973). Likewise, light tickling of the perineal and ventral tailbase regions caused leg extension and tail elevation, especially if combined with light scratching on the flanks and back. None of these stimuli involved exerting much pressure downward on the back or upward from beneath the pubic bone. Also, none of these stimuli regularly caused lordosis, i.e., marked vertebral dorsiflexion including active dorsiflexion of the rump.

When to the combined flank and perineal (perivaginal) stimuli there was added a component of pressure, lordosis, including dorsiflexion of the rump, often occurred. In this stimulus the first and fourth (ring) fingers palpated the flanks and back while the second and third fingers curved in back of and underneath the pubic bone (in a forked position with one finger on either side of the tailbase), so that the finger tips ended on either side of the vagina and clitoris. With the hand in this position, pressure was exerted by pushing upward with the second and third fingers from below the female's pubic bone, and downward with the lowest row of knuckles onto the female's lumbar region and across the back. It is significant that the male rat would not be able to apply this stimulus, which involves pressure from below the genital region, until he could get his pelvic region below the female's hindquarters, i.e., until she had raised her rump and tailbase using a combination of leg extension and tailbase elevation.

The minimal stimulus sufficient to trigger lordosis reliably in our estrogenized female rats covered virtually all of the flank, back, tailbase,

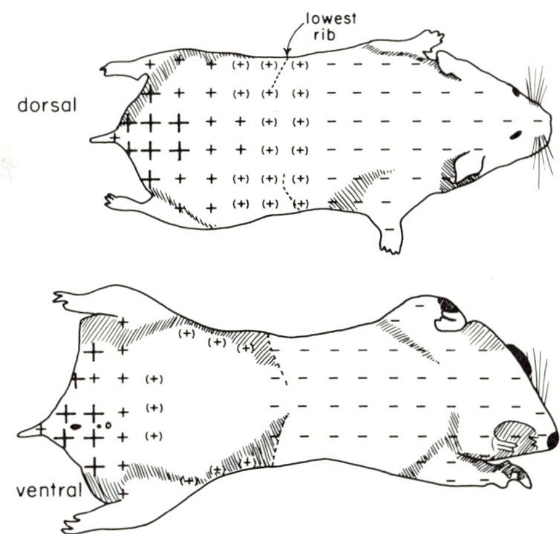

FIG. 9. Individual points on the skin of female hamsters from which lordosis could be elicited by the pressure of one finger of the experimenter or by rubbing against the direction of hair growth. The hamsters selected for testing were in intense estrus, 2–4 hours after the onset of darkness in their light cycle. The figure shows a composite map, in which all seven hamsters showed the same basic distribution of sensitive points. Lordosis was scored according to the female's elevation of her tail and rump and prolonged immobility after cessation of stimulation (from Pfaff and Lewis, in preparation). $+$, strongest lordoses; +, lordosis; (+), weaker, less reliable lordosis, better with bilateral stimulation; −, no lordosis.

and perivaginal skin areas contacted by the male rat during his mounts and pelvic thrusts. Interestingly, the same skin areas are active in triggering lordosis by manual stimulation of naturally estrous female hamsters (Fig. 9) (Pfaff and Lewis, in preparation). Seven female hamsters were selected for intense estrus from 2 to 4 hours after the onset of darkness in their light cycle, and after preliminary handling, were tested by lightly pressing with one finger in certain skin areas, or by rubbing selected areas against the direction of hair growth. While female rats required pressure stimuli over virtually *all* of the flank-back-pelvic skin area contacted by the male, female hamsters' lordoses were often triggered by relatively light stimuli at *single points* within this area, especially if these points were in the groin or perineal regions (Fig. 9).

4. "Sequential Reflex" Model of Lordosis

The data above can be summarized in a graphic description of lordosis in the female rat (Fig. 10), which may also stimulate further research

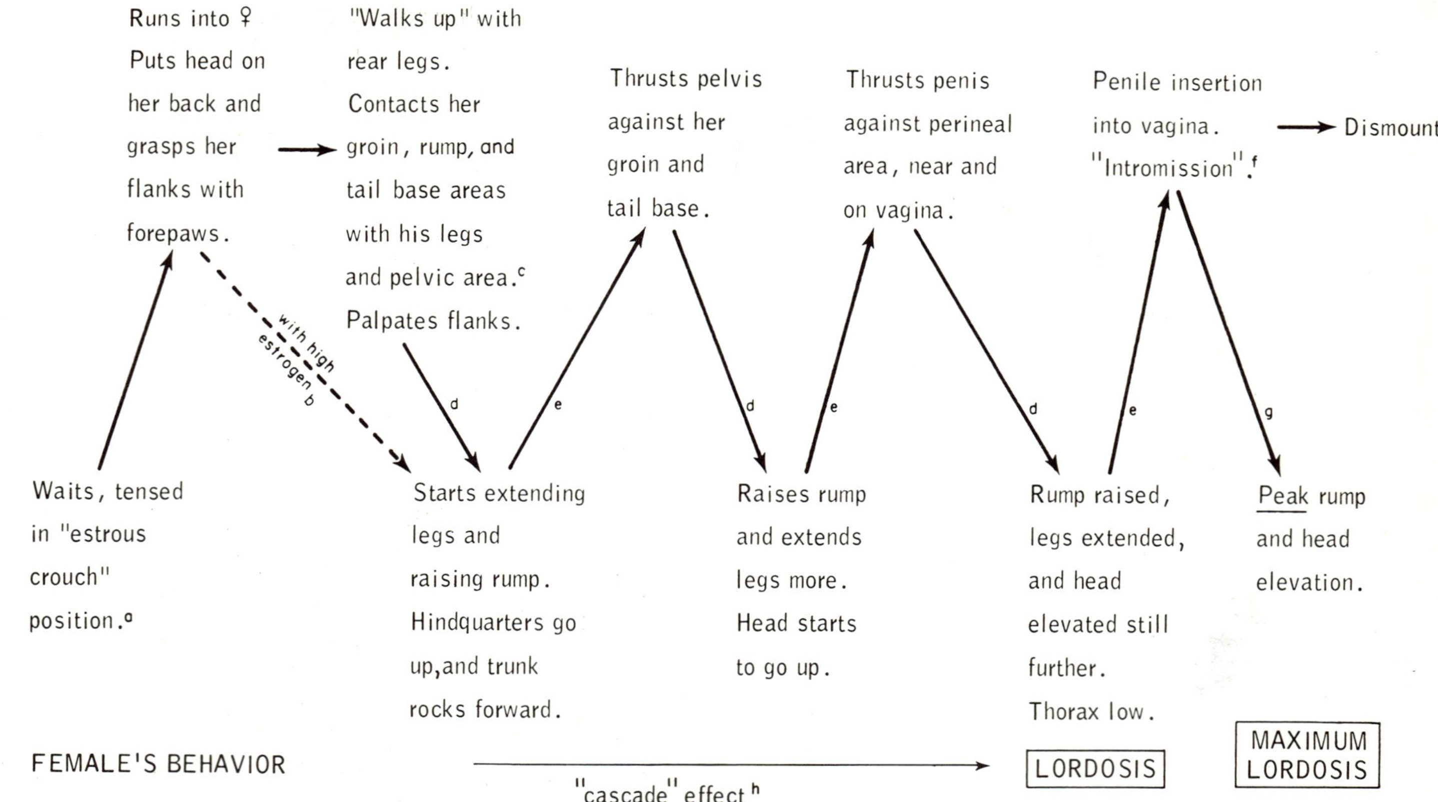

MALE'S BEHAVIOR
Runs into ♀
Puts head on
her back and
grasps her
flanks with
forepaws.
"Walks up" with
rear legs.
Contacts her
groin, rump, and
tail base areas
with his legs
and pelvic area.c
Palpates flanks.
Thrusts pelvis
against her
groin and
tail base.
Thrusts penis
against perineal
area, near and
on vagina.
Penile insertion
into vagina.
"Intromission".f
Dismount
with high estrogen b
d
e
d
e
d
e
g
Waits, tensed
in "estrous
crouch"
position.a
Starts extending
legs and
raising rump.
Hindquarters go
up, and trunk
rocks forward.
Raises rump
and extends
legs more.
Head starts
to go up.
Rump raised,
legs extended,
and head
elevated still
further.
Thorax low.
Peak rump
and head
elevation.
FEMALE'S BEHAVIOR
"cascade" effect h
LORDOSIS
MAXIMUM LORDOSIS

FIG. 10. "Sequential reflex" model of lordosis reflex in the female rat. Time is from left to right. Male's behavior above; female's, below. The appearance and order of events in this schematic summary were derived from film and X-ray descriptions of lordosis (Section IV,A). Hypothesized functional relations between events, indicated by heavy arrows, were inferred from procaine experiments (Section IV,C,2) and manual stimulation observations (Section IV,C,3). See text for running description of events represented in model. *Notes referring to evidence for "sequential-reflex model of lordosis in rat": a,* Female is usually in an "estrous crouch" position at the end of a darting run. It can be argued (Fig. 11, annotation *d*; and see text) that the sudden halt of darting runs, resulting in this posture, facilitates contact with the male, support of his weight, and initiation of the lordosis reflex. *b,* "Flank-abdomen-back" procaine lowered the lordosis quotient only in rats with high estrogen levels (see text, Section IV,C,2). Therefore, either (*a*) it was harder to achieve complete flank and back anesthesia, (*b*) flank stimulation's role in triggering lordosis is less direct and constant than the role of pelvic stimuli, or (*c*) it does not play a crucial and unique role in triggering lordosis. In manual stimulation tests (text, Section IV,C,3) and informal observations, flank stimuli alone rarely elicit lordosis. *c,* X-ray and movie film analysis of pictures taken from the side and below show that the male's pelvis, legs, and abdomen initially contact the female's dorsal hindquarters and the side of her tailbase, not her ventral side. Manual stimulation shows that light flank and groin stimulation is adequate to produce leg extension and tailbase elevation in the female (from Diakow *et al.,* 1973). *d,* Treatment of the female's pelvic area with procaine interfered with lordosis, presumably by interfering with the female's response to stimuli on the pelvic area of her skin from the male (text, Section IV,C,2). This procaine treatment appears to break the sequence of responses in which the male's pelvic region advances closer to the perineal area, and his penis thrusts progressively closer to the outer lip of the vagina. Manual stimulation of the same skin region of the female (the tailbase and perivaginal region) causes leg extension and tail elevation (from Diakow *et al.,* 1973). Thus the female's response to the male's stimulation there can allow his subsequent thrusts closer to the vagina. The number of stages shown in this progression (Fig. 10) has been portrayed large enough to represent the events recognizable in film and X-ray analysis. Further research may reveal a larger number of stages of male–female reflex interaction. *e,* The "pelvic procaine" treatment which lowered lordosis quotients also reduced intromission frequency (see text, Section IV,C,2). Therefore, the female's responses to pelvic stimuli determine subsequent behavior by the male. In particular, the leg extension and tailbase elevation response which the female rat shows to light pelvic area stimulation (Diakow *et al.,* 1973) would allow the male's hindquarters to get beneath her hindquarters and apply the upward pressure which is sufficient to elicit a full lordosis posture. *f,* In film analysis, it can be seen that intromission follows lordosis rather than preceding it. Secondly, lordosis sometimes occurs on mounts-with-thrusts that do not include intromission (Fig. 8). In manual stimulation tests, flank, rump, and perineal pressure can cause lordosis without intravaginal stimulation (Diakow *et al.,* 1973). Lordosis can also occur with the vagina surgically removed (Ball, 1934; Kaufman, 1953) or sewed shut (Hard and Larsson, 1968). Finally, penile anesthesia which prevents intromission does not lower lordosis quotients (text, Section IV,C,2 and Fig. 7). Thus, intromission and consequent deep vaginal stimulation may inten-

on this response. The *appearance* and *sequence* of events in the model come from the film analyses and X-ray pictures of lordosis, described in Section IV,A, above. The arrows in the model represent hypothetical (causal) *functional relations* between events, inferred from procaine experiments (Section IV,C,2) and observations with manual stimulation (Section IV,C,3).

In this model, the male is conceived of as stimulating first the flank and back of the female (with his paws and head), then the region of the tailbase and groin (with his pelvic region), then the perineal area eventually touching the outer vaginal lip (with his penis), and finally the deep intravaginal epithelium (during intromission). From the manual stimulation results (Section IV,C,3) and from film observations it appears that the female extends her legs and raises her tailbase in response to flank stimuli combined with stimuli from the male's first impact in the tailbase and groin area. This response in turn allows the male's thrusting pelvis greater access to the groin and perineal area, thus intensifying the cutaneous stimulation which, as the manual stimulation evidence shows, causes the female to raise her hindquarters. When she has raised her rump high enough for the male to bend his pelvis underneath, he can exert pressure upward by thrusting on the perineal area. This achieves the stimulation which, in the manual stimulation experiment, was sufficient to trigger lordosis (overall vertebral dorsiflexion, with the legs already extended) in the receptive female rat.

Pelvic procaine treatment of the female, diminishing her response to the male's stimulation in the tailbase-groin-perineal area, breaks the chain of causal relations, thus interfering with lordosis and, therefore, with intromission. Procaine treatment of the female's flanks did not break the chain of events entirely (except for an effect on lordosis in highly estrogenized females), and therefore it is either harder to achieve complete flank anesthesia or flank stimuli do not play as crucial and unique a role in triggering lordosis. Penile procaine treat-

---

sify lordosis but do not primarily cause lordosis. *g*, In movie films it can be seen that intromission causes an exaggeration of the already evident lordosis posture (Pfaff, 1971), and the lordosis posture is held longer if intromission occurs (Kuehn and Beach, 1963). *h*, Each response by the female allows the male hindquarters to approach closer to the vaginal area thereby, in turn, to apply stimuli for a still more extreme response by the female. In particular, the female's initial rump elevation eventually allows the male's pelvis to get beneath her pubic bone and apply an upward pressure on the perineal area. Such a pressure stimulus greatly facilitates lordosis in manual stimulation tests (from Diakow *et al.*, 1973).

ment of the male, preventing intromission, did not interfere with lordosis. This, coupled with the film observation that a moderate (though not maximal) lordosis posture has been achieved before insertion of the penis, clearly places intromission *after* lordosis in the chain of events. That is, reflex movements eventuating in maximal lordosis posture have been initiated and reached at least a moderate stage of completion before the penis enters the vagina.

In this description, two main concepts stand out. First, the female's reflex responses to stimuli early in the sequence allow the male to apply subsequent stimuli necessary, in turn, for her subsequent responses. Thus, lordosis would actually be a sequence of reflexes programmed in the female to match adaptively a corresponding sequence programmed in the male. This "cascade" of reflexes could function as a reproductive isolating mechanism, helping to ensure that only conspecifics endocrinologically competent to reproduce would finish the mating behavior sequence. Second, the female's lordosis reflex is conceived as being a normal prerequisite for intromission, rather than the reverse. The number of stages in the reflex sequence (Fig. 10) has been selected large enough to portray recognizable events discretely; with further research a larger number of steps may be identified. However, the present combination of film observations, procaine experiments, and manual stimulation experiments proves that successful mating depends on matched series of reflexes in both the male and the female rat.

5. Synchronization of Male's and Female's Behavior

The coordination and synchrony of the male and female rat's responses with each other during the mount-lordosis encounter may be but a brief (2 or 3 seconds) segment of a much longer chain of synchronized male and female behavior patterns (Fig. 11). Although, for the purpose of neurophysiological analysis, the lordosis reflex itself was chosen for intensive study, this does not deny the existence of a complex train of intertwined behavioral events during at least a 2-day period. The description in Fig. 11 is not an exhaustive representation of male-female mating relations. Rather, it is intended to illustrate how the lordosis encounter fits into a biologically adaptive series of events. At least part of the behavioral coordination between male and female rat can be ascribed to secretions of the appropriate gonadal steroids in each.

Increasing estrogen levels, as are required for ovulation and behavioral receptivity, lead to increased locomotor activity (Richter, 1933; Wang, 1923; Pfaff and Spencer, unpublished observations) under labo-

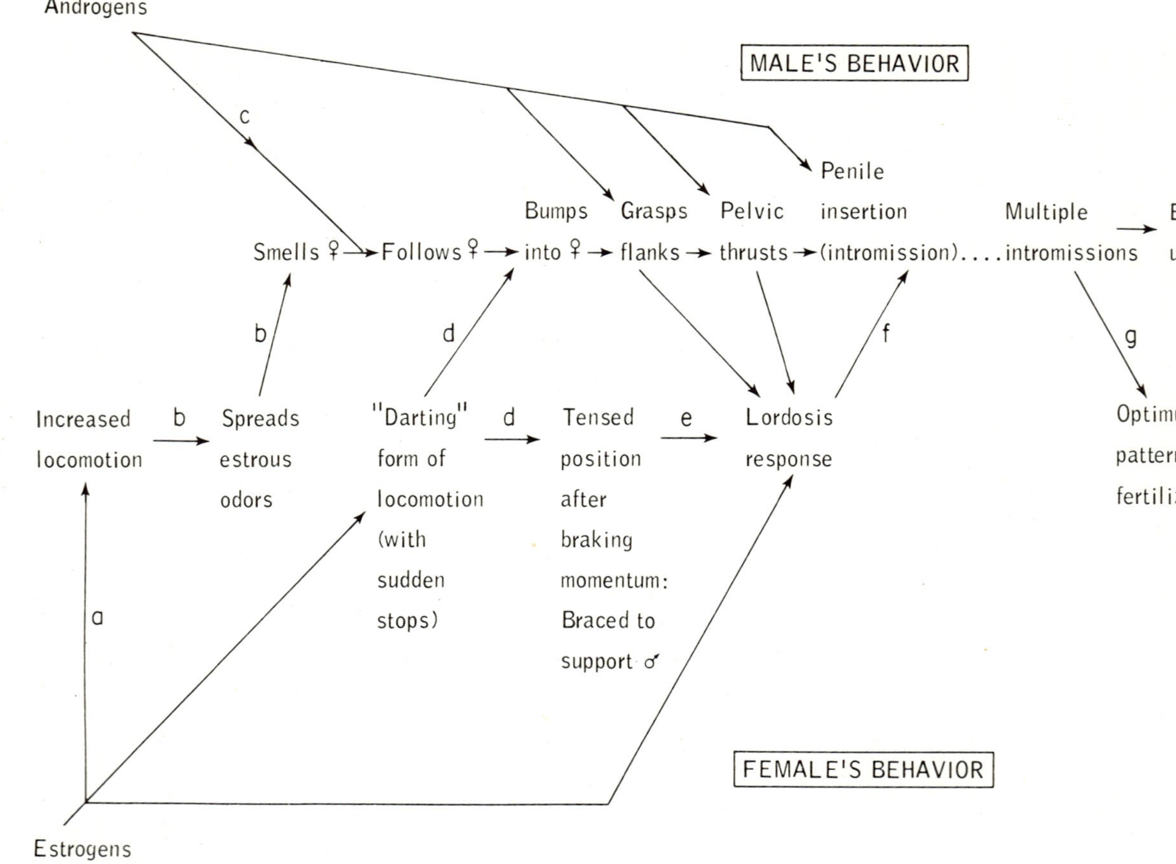

Androgens
MALE'S BEHAVIOR
c
Penile insertion
Bumps Grasps Pelvic
Smells ♀ → Follows ♀ → into ♀ → flanks → thrusts → (intromission)....intromissions
Multiple
Ejac-ulation
b
d
f
g
Increased locomotion
b
Spreads estrous odors
"Darting" d form of locomotion (with sudden stops)
Tensed e position after braking momentum: Braced to support ♂
Lordosis response
Optimum pattern for fertilization
a
Estrogens (and progesterone)
FEMALE'S BEHAVIOR

ratory conditions. In wild rats under seminatural conditions, Calhoun (1963) observed that on the night before ovulation and behavioral receptivity, females toured their quarter-acre enclosure dragging their genital region on the ground in a manner that appeared to be effective in laying a trail of sex odor, especially since males followed and rolled in the apparent trail (see annotation *b* in Fig. 11). Laboratory male rats with normal levels of testicular androgens display intense interest in estrous female sex odors (LeMagnen, 1952; Carr *et al.*, 1965, 1966; Pfaff and Pfaffmann, 1969b). Accordingly, when the wild female rat emerges from her burrow on the night of ovulation, several sexually aroused males may be ready to follow her (Calhoun, 1963). Since the males sniff and investigate her anogenital region, they primarily approach her from behind. In this context, the darting form of locomotion typical of estrous female rats, involving numerous sudden starts, fast dashes with bilaterally synchronized movements, and sudden stops,

---

FIG. 11. Schematic flow chart of events in rat mating behavior, giving partial account of how endocrine secretions and behavioral determinants synchronize behavior of male and female to ensure reproduction. Time reads from left to right. Odor-spreading behavior of female (far left) may occur on the night before ovulation, while most of events on right occur on the night of ovulation. See text for running description of the behavioral synchrony. *Notes referring to evidence for adaptive synchrony of male and female rat mating behavior patterns: a,* Richter (1933); Wang (1923); Pfaff and Spencer (unpublished observations). *b,* Calhoun (1963) observed proestrous females rubbing their genital region on the ground during extended tours of their large enclosure, and male rats were seen to follow and roll in their trails. *c,* LeMagnen (1952), Carr *et al.* (1965, 1966) and Pfaff and Pfaffmann (1969b) have shown that the male rat's attraction to estrous female rat odors depends on androgen levels. *d,* "Darting" locomotion usually is terminated in a sudden halt with the female in an "estrous crouch" position. This may be adaptive, for three reasons. The sudden stop facilitates the male's running into the female from behind. Second, the tense posture seems to facilitate the female's lordosis response (see note *e*). Finally, the crouching posture which results from braking the forward momentum of the darting run may represent an adaptive preparation for withstanding the subsequent forward and downward force of the male's mount. This force is great enough that, in successive movie frames, the entire male–female assembly can be seen sliding forward across the cage floor, with a 200-gm female supporting a 500-gm male. *e,* From results of manual stimulation experiments (Ball, 1937; Diakow *et al.*, 1973), it appears that the muscularly tensed female rat (as seen at the end of a "dart") may perform lordosis more readily than females not tensed in this way. *f,* The female's lordosis reflex allows intromission by the male (see text Sections IV,C,2–C,4 and Fig. 10). *g,* The male's requirement of multiple intromissions for ejaculation, and his subsequent inactivity during a postejaculatory interval both improve chances of fertilization and implantation of the eggs (from Adler, 1968, 1969; Adler and Zoloth, 1970; Wilson *et al.*, 1965).

appears adaptive in three respects (see annotation *d* in Fig. 11). First, the sudden stops, with the male following from the rear, raise the chances that he will bump into the female from the proper direction for mounting. Second, the sudden stops appear to leave the female momentarily in a state of muscular tension in the "estrous crouch" posture: this tension, although poorly defined and not objectively measured, seems to facilitate the lordosis reflex during manual stimulation tests (Ball, 1937; Diakow *et al.*, 1973). Third, since the "dart" involves locomotor movements more bilaterally synchronized than the strict left-right alternations of normal running, its sudden halt puts the female in a bilaterally balanced posture resultant from braking the forward and downward momentum of the dart. This posture would seem an adaptive preparation for supporting the weight of the forward-going male. The forward and downward forces the male can exert are dramatized by seeing on film that the entire male–female assembly sometimes slides forward across the substrate following impact, with the female supporting part or all of the male's weight, which often is more than twice her own. Therefore, a posture which is in fact a position braced against forces in the same direction would appear to be ideal.

When the female stops at the end of a dart, the male grasps her flanks and thrusts with his pelvis and penis. This complex of stimuli triggers her lordosis and allows his penile insertion (intromission) (annotation *f* in Fig. 11). The male rat (*a*) requires several intromissions for ejaculation, and (*b*) is then sexually unresponsive during a postejaculatory interval. Both of these behavioral patterns of the male facilitate fertilization and implantation of the fertilized eggs (Adler, 1968, 1969; Adler and Zoloth, 1970; Wilson *et al.*, 1965).

At several points in this series of events, gonadal steroids are required for the appropriate behavioral responses to occur (Fig. 11). In the case of the male, testicular androgens are required for maximal attraction to the female's odor and for effective mounting and pelvic thrusting to achieve intromission once the female is reached. In the case of the female, ovarian secretions cause the estrous odor, trigger the increased amount and peculiar form of locomotion to spread it, cause the "darting" form of locomotion on the night of ovulation; and are required for the lordosis response to the male when he finally mounts. Thus, as documented by Feder (1971; Feder and Wade, 1973; Joslyn *et al.*, 1971), the same overall gonadal hormonal conditions which facilitate secondary sex organ growth and are correlated with gametogenesis help ensure, through (neural) behavioral mechanisms, that male and female rats endocrinologically competent for reproduction will in fact come together and mate.

D. Studies with Spinal Rats

In preliminary studies with female rats spinally transected at low thoracic levels, we have been unable to elicit reflexes which closely resemble the complete lordosis response. Spinal females were tested weekly with a variety of stimuli on the hindquarters, beginning 2 months and longer after transection to help ensure recovery of reflexes from spinal shock. Light cutaneous stimulation at the side of the tailbase often caused ipsilateral tail deflection, and very strong genital stimuli (pinching of the clitoris or probing the vaginal cervix) caused phasic rump elevations in some females. Among the responses we have seen in spinal females, these have been the most reminiscent of elements of lordosis. None of the responses in six ovariectomized spinal females thus far have been altered significantly by estradiol (10 μg/day) and progesterone (.5 mg) injections. These observations are similar to those made previously by Hart (1969), and suggest that supraspinal pathways are necessary (a) for the complete elaboration of the lordosis reflex, and (b) to account for the hormonal sensitivity of the lordosis reflex.

If we can confirm our conclusions in high-thoracic spinal female rats showing maximal spinal reflex activity, then the overall picture concerning female rats will differ markedly from that with female dogs (Hart, 1970) and male rats (Hart, 1967; Hart and Haugen, 1968). In both of the latter preparations, gonadal steroid treatment has been reported to influence genital reflexes mediated by the spinal cord. In spinal female cats, Bard (1940) observed that anestrous animals displayed sexual reflexes such as treading, tail deviation, and pelvic dorsiflexion, as well as estrous animals, while Maes (1939) and Hart (1971) were able to detect estrogen effects on these reflexes.

E. Supraspinal Effects on Axial Muscles and Rear Legs

Both the results with spinal rats, and the need to relate estrogen-concentrating hormone-sensitive neurons to reflex mechanisms of lordosis, directed attention toward supraspinal control of lordosis movements. We have attacked this problem by exploring the brain of female rats lightly anesthetized with halothane, using stimulating electrodes to try to trigger muscle movements that resemble elements of lordosis (Pfaff and Lewis, in preparation). This strategy is similar to that followed by MacLean (MacLean and Ploog, 1962; MacLean *et al.*, 1963) for studying penile erection in monkeys, and by Rothballer's (1966) and other groups (Beyer *et al.*, 1962a,b; Tindal *et al.*, 1967, 1969; Tindal and Knaggs, 1971) for studying the control of posterior pituitary secretions. By using 85 rats, yielding about 250 electrode penetrations and 2000 electrode points (stimulating at each millimeter of depth), we explored virtually the entire brain from the lower medulla to the basal forebrain at the level of the preoptic area, excepting the cortical and cerebellar surfaces. The female's head was held stereotaxically, and her body was propped into an imitation of the "estrous crouch" position by holding her trunk with rubber bands and taping her rear feet. Stimulating probes were small concentric bipolar electrodes, and the stimuli were trains of pulses 50 per second, .8 msec, with train durations manually set usually at between 2 and 5 seconds long and peak current levels at 300 μA or less. Animals were used without reference to their stage in the estrus cycle.

During experiments, any skeletal movement stimulated was noted along with the position of the electrode. To analyze the results, certain movements which appeared to be elements of the lordosis reflex, or to use the same muscle groups as lordosis elements, were plotted as coded points on a standard series of transverse rat brain sections. Each point yielding such a movement was placed at the histologically verified location of the stimulating electrode. Figure 12 represents 6 of the 13 brain levels used to code results for tail, tailbase, and rump movements. Such movements should depend on the same epaxial muscles, stretched longitudinally dorsolateral and dorsal to the vertebral column, which are important for lordosis. Indeed, some of the stimulated movements looked like exact replications of elements of the lordosis reflex.

Electrode points yielding bilateral extension of the rear legs gave a series of maps similar to those in Fig. 12.

At lower and middle medullary levels (sections including inferior olive and seventh nerve nucleus) points successful in stimulating rump and tail movements were clustered in the ventrolateral brainstem (A and B in Fig. 12). At pontine levels more points were found more dorsally, such that at the level where the fourth ventricle narrows to the cerebral aqueduct many points were found near the ventricle. At the levels of the inferior and superior colliculi (C and D), some points were clustered near the ventrolateral edge of the brainstem, but many more were found around the lateral and dorsolateral edges of the central gray. As the cerebral aqueduct descends into the third ventricle (E), electrode positions for stimulating tail and rump movements also descended, remaining near the ventricle and the habenulointerpeduncular tract. Points yielding clear rump and tail movements were somewhat rarer in the basal forebrain region. However, those found were primarily in the hypothalamus or amygdala. At the preoptic level (F), successful points were found in and near regions of estradiol-concentrating neurons (Fig. 12).

Two main concepts serve to organize (or "account for") the vast majority of points from which tail, tailbase, and rump movements could be stimulated. First, the distribution of points from the lower medulla through the pons and mesencephalon show close correspondence to anatomical projections from the anterolateral columns of the spinal cord. The latter projections have been described in cats and monkeys by Nauta and his colleagues (Nauta and Kuypers, 1958; Mehler *et al.*, 1960) and by others (Anderson and Berry, 1959; Goldberg and Moore, 1967), and can be referred to as spinoreticular projections rather than a spinothalamic path, since most fibers do not reach the thalamus. A brief description of these brainstem projections would be that they travel in a rostral direction radiating diffusely at medullary and lower pontine levels from their primary ventrolateral brainstem position. At levels of the inferior and superior colliculi, although many fibers are still traveling near the lateral and ventrolateral brainstem border, a significant number have moved medially to positions lateral to the central gray.

The anterolateral columns are well known to contain major somatosensory afferent paths. Thus, as well as providing an anatomical organizing principle for the stimulation points in the lower brainstem and mesencephalon, the anterolateral column and its brainstem projections provide pathways which could carry appropriate somatosensory information consequent to stimulation by the male rat. Even the stimulation points which are anterior of the monosynaptic projections from the anterolateral cord may fit into the same concept of a primitive somatosensory pathway. In experimental anatomical studies, central gray lesions caused degeneration following the ventricle ventrally into the hypothalamus, in a manner similar to the stimulation points in Fig. 12 (Hamilton and Skultety, 1970; Chi, 1970). Moreover, fibers passing through the lateral posterior hypothalamus have been reported to travel rostrally in the medial forebrain bundle and terminate anterior to the preoptic area (Guillery, 1957). Therefore, although it is not proved that our stimulation effects are due to the stimulation of afferent paths, there is topographical correspondence between these stimulation points and known somatosensory anatomical projections from the spinal cord to the lower brainstem and central gray, and from the central gray into the basal forebrain. Whether or not these projections carry essential information from the male rat's stimulation of the female remains to be studied by lesion and electrical recording methods.

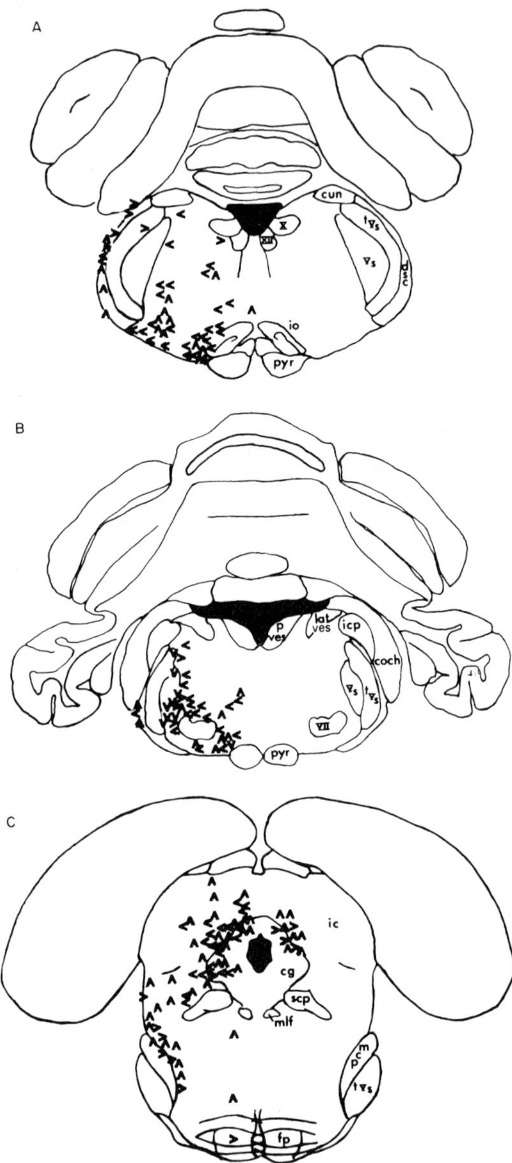

FIG. 12. Six of the maps representing points in the female rat brain from which tail, tailbase, and rump movements could be stimulated. Distribution of points for these movements in the lower brainstem and mesencephalon matches anatomical projections from the anterolateral columns of the spinal cord (Nauta and Kuypers, 1958). Around the central gray and in the preoptic area, the stimulation points intersect with regions of estradiol-concentrating neurons (from

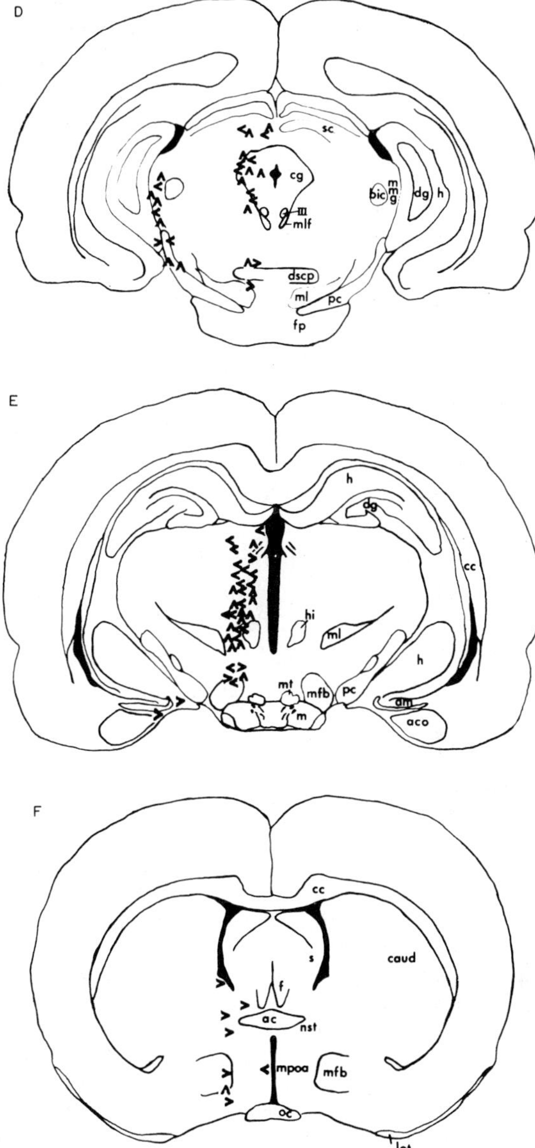

Pfaff, 1972b; Pfaff and Keiner, 1972; see also Fig. 1). See text for details of
procedure. *Symbols* (plotted, for convenience, only on the left side of brain
drawings): <, movement of tail, tailbase, or rump to the side ipsilateral to
the stimulating electrodes; >, movement to contralateral side; ∧, elevation of
tail, tailbase, or rump. In the drawing of the inferior colliculus level, because
of the large number of symbols, some had to be plotted on the right, and for

A second main feature of the stimulation results is the overlap between the distribution of tail and rump stimulation points and the regions containing peak numbers of estradiol-concentrating neurons. In the central gray and in the preoptic area this coincidence or contiguity is most obvious. Some overlap also occurred in the amygdala and hypothalamus.

The purpose of exploring the female rat brain with stimulating electrodes was to discover neural structures controlling elements of the lordosis reflex. However, four qualifications should be placed on the identification of the points plotted in Fig. 12 as a "lordosis pathway." The first qualification is that the experiments were conducted in anesthetized animals using artificial electrical stimulation. Thus, work with awake, free-moving rats using both electrical stimulation and recording techniques would be required to study the activity of the same anatomical points during natural lordosis. Secondly, since Fig. 12 shows only a distribution of individually identified anatomical points, it is only an inference to call part of the distribution a "pathway." Further work with anesthetized preparations, in which one point in the distribution could be electrically stimulated while single-unit activity at another point was being recorded, would help to describe the connections within the distribution. For both of these reasons it can be concluded only that we have described a "potential pathway" for control of some lordosislike movements.

A third qualification concerns the relation between the movements stimulated and pain responses. The question arises partly because of the overlap between the distributions of "successful" stimulation points and

---

these symbols only, arrows pointed to right denote ipsilateral movements. *Abbreviations:* ac, anterior commissure; aco, cortical amygdaloid nucleus; am, medial amygdaloid nucleus; bic, brachium of the inferior colliculus; caud, caudate-putamen; cc, corpus callosum; cg, central gray; coch, ventral cochlear nucleus; cun, cuneate nucleus; dg, dentate gyrus of the hippocampus; dsc, dorsal spinocerebellar tract; dscp, decussation of the superior cerebellar peduncle; f, fornix; fp, fronto-pontine fibers; h, hippocampus (Ammon's horn); hi, habenulo-interpeduncular tract; ic, inferior colliculus; icp, inferior cerebellar peduncle; io, inferior olive; lat ves, lateral vestibular nucleus; lot, lateral olfactory tract; m, mammillary bodies; mcp, middle cerebellar peduncle; mfb, medial forebrain bundle; ml, medial lemniscus; mlf, medial longitudinal fasciculus; mmg, magnocellular medial geniculate body; mpoa, medial preoptic area; mt, mammillothalamic tract; nst, nucleus of the stria terminalis; oc, optic chiasm; pc, cerebral peduncle; p.ves, principal vestibular nucleus; pyr, pyramidal tract; s, septum; sc, superior colliculus; scp, superior cerebellar peduncle; III, nucleus of the oculomotor nerve; Vs, nucleus of spinal rad., trigeminal nerve; tVs, spinal radiation of the trigeminal nerve; VII, nucleus of the facial nerve; X, dorsal motor nucleus of the vagus nerve; XII, nucleus of the hypoglossal nerve.

spinal somatosensory input. Also, the responses plotted in Fig. 12 were often accompanied by other movements, such as breathing changes or forepaw or face movements. Moreover, it was occasionally (though rarely) possible to trigger tail, trunk, or hindleg movements somewhat like those plotted in Fig. 12 with severely "painful" peripheral stimuli especially around the rear half of the body. However, for several reasons it is unlikely that the tail, rump, and rear leg movements reported above were merely pain responses in an artifactual sense. First, in several preparations it was possible to demonstrate obvious examples of lordoticlike responses to electrical stimulation of the brain, while there were minimal or no responses to strong painful stimuli (either peripheral stimuli such as pinches or electrical stimulation of dura). Second, in some preparations where pain responses to peripheral skin pinches were present, the responses took a much different form than tail and leg responses to electrical stimulation of the brain. Third, it is possible to get additional information by comparison to the female hamster. It has been possible in several anesthetized hamster preparations to electrically stimulate tail raising from the preoptic area. In these preparations, lightly anesthetized hamsters responded to a variety of painful stimuli (except those in the genital area) with tail *lowering* (tucking it between the legs). Since lordosis in the hamster, as in the rat, involves raising the tailbase, these observations dissociate a brain-stimulated lordoticlike response (at an anatomical point also included in the rat's "potential pathway" for lordosis) from pain responses.

Two further considerations on the relation of lordosis stimulation to pain involve the actual physiological role of strong somatosensory input in the initiation of sexual responses. In moving picture analyses of rat mating behavior, it appears that the male rat does, in fact, apply strong somatosensory stimuli to a wide area of the female rat's body. His head presses on her ribcage; his paws palpate her flanks and abdomen; his pelvic area, rear legs, and penis thrust at her rump, groin, and genital areas; and she is supporting some (if not all) of his weight, which is often twice her own. The onset of all these stimuli is sudden and need only last a second or two to elicit her lordosis response. In light of these natural stimulus conditions, it is possible that abrupt electrical stimulation of somatosensory pathways such as the spinoreticular tracts provide a partial imitation of the neural excitation caused by the male rat. Secondly, in the male rat, painful or otherwise arousing stimuli can stimulate sexual performance (Barfield and Sachs, 1968; Larsson, 1963; Caggiula and Eibergen, 1969). In the estrous female rat it is evident that the normal sequence of "darting" locomotions ending in the estrous crouch involves a high degree of muscular tension which must be accompanied by a state of "arousal." During manual stimulation of lordosis, in fact, we have noticed that a muscularly tensed ("aroused") female may be more likely to show lordosis to artificial skin stimuli. Thus, there may be a normal role for nonspecific brainstem ("arousing") excitation in the triggering of the lordosis reflex.

The last qualification concerning a possible "lordosis pathway" is that electrical brain stimulation in the anesthetized female rat never triggered a complete lordosis response. Rather, we observed movements of tail, rump, and rear legs, which looked like excellent copies of elements of the lordosis movement. Bilateral rear leg extension and tailbase or rump elevation do seem to occur in their most striking form during lordosis, but also could be implicated in other reflex patterns. Therefore, if the "potential pathways" discovered in these experiments are related to lordosis control, there is still a possibility that the same neurons could be used, in different patterns, for the control of other reflexes.

F. Model of Estrogenic Control over Lordosis

Classical ideas regarding the actions of sex hormones on mating behavior in mammals emphasize that sex hormones may alter the state of neurons in circuits controlling mating responses (Beach, 1948, pp. 255–275). Sex hormones have not been thought actually to create neural circuits in the adult where none existed before. Bard's (1940) ability to elicit sexual reflexes in brain-transected anestrous cats demonstrated the presence of reflex circuits in the absence of adequate hormone levels. Also, the commonly observed ability of an occasional diestrous or ovariectomized female rat to show a lordosis response (although rarely) supports the same point, and suggests that in some as yet undefined manner estrogens and progesterone activate circuits for mating behavior rather than creating them.

Hierarchical models of neural control systems have abounded in neurology, neurophysiology, and physiological psychology. One long-standing hierarchical model for the control of mating behavior states that rostrally placed neural centers control caudally placed sexual reflex circuits, primarily by inhibiting them, and that sex hormones can act on sex behavior by releasing the lower reflexive mechanisms from inhibition (Beach, 1967). The release of clasping responses by hindbrain transections in male frogs (Hutchison and Poynton, 1963), and the exaggeration of lordosis in female rats after decortication (Beach, 1943), both support this possibility. These and other theoretical and experimental contributions are consistent with a hierarchical view of neural and hormonal control over sex behavior. In such a view, which can be used to summarize some of our experimental findings, actions of sex hormones on neurons at basal forebrain and mesencephalic loci alter the downstream effects of those neurons on lower brainstem and spinal reflex circuits, and in doing so permit sex responses to occur.

In Fig. 13, a working model for the control of the lordosis reflex by estrogen-sensitive neurons is presented. Somatosensory stimuli (particularly in the pelvic region) are conceived as triggering the lordosis response according to the mechanism illustrated in Fig. 10. Since the

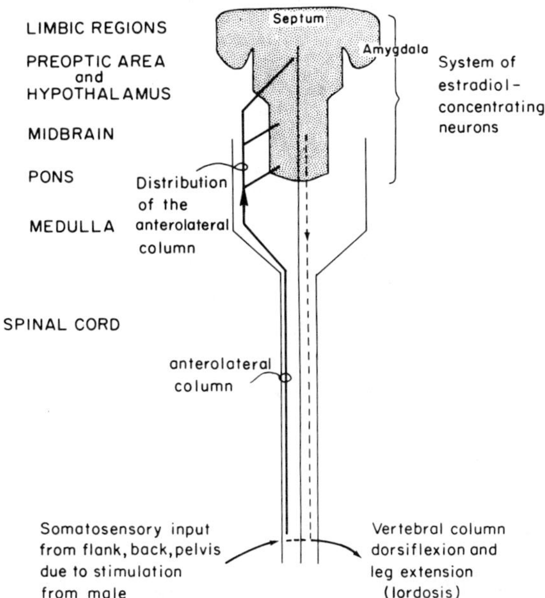

FIG. 13. Working model of minimal circuit by which estrogens facilitate the lordosis reflex in female rats. At the bottom of the figure, sensory and motor elements of the lordosis reflex are represented. Since spinal rats exhibit neither a complete nor an estrogen-sensitive lordosis response to manual stimuli, a supraspinal control loop must exist. The model represents the afferent side of this loop as running in the anterolateral column of the spinal cord. At the lateral borders of the central gray the known distribution from this pathway (Nauta and Kuypers, 1958) intersects with the known distribution of estradiol-concentrating neurons (Pfaff, 1972b; Pfaff and Keiner, 1972; see also Fig. 1), represented here by the speckled region. Stimulation points for eliciting tail and rump movements follow the lower brainstem distribution of the anterolateral column, and intersect with the region of estradiol-concentrating neurons not only at the central gray but also in the preoptic area (Fig. 12). The descending limb of the supraspinal control loop is not specified. The model indicates that estrogens could influence the lordosis reflex by acting at the intersections between the distribution of estradiol-concentrating neurons and the supraspinal control pathway defined, thus far, by electrical stimulation results.

full response is not obtainable in spinal preparations, and since we have not detected estrogen-sensitive hindquarters responses in these preparations, a supraspinal control loop must be assumed. Somatosensory pathways in the anterolateral columns of the spinal cord, and their brainstem projections, are hypothesized to participate on the afferent side of this control loop because (*a*) the distribution of our electrical stimulation points matches anatomical projections from the anterolateral column, and (*b*) modalities of sensation known to be represented in these pathways would be appropriate to signal the stimuli coming from the impact of the male rat on the female. Whether the electrical stimulation results reported above are due exclusively to stimulating a sensory pathway is a question for further research. If the effects seen thus far are purely sensory in nature, the location of the motor side of the control loop remains to be discovered. Finally, an important feature of the electrical stimulation results, and of this model, is the intersection between pathways related to elements of the lordosis response and the regions containing peak numbers of estradiol-concentrating neurons (Figs. 1, 12, and 13). These intersections have been shown above to occur primarily at the lateral borders of the central gray and in the preoptic area. It is primarily at such intersections where estrogens, acting through their effects on estradiol-concentrating neurons, might affect the properties of supraspinal circuits controlling lordosis.

V. Summary

1. Estradiol is concentrated by a system of neurons reliably found in certain limbic structures (notably the septum and corticomedial amygdala), in the medial preoptic area, the medial hypothalamus, and around the lateral borders of the central gray. The basic distribution of estradiol-concentrating neurons in this phylogenetically old limbic-hypothalamic system has been described in this laboratory using two different autoradiographic approaches, and both agree with the results of scintillation counting of finely dissected brain regions after estradiol-^{3}H injection. Brain regions which show peak uptake of radioactive estradiol in female rats also tend to show the best uptake of radioactive testosterone in male rats.

2. Testosterone affects the single-unit activity of neurons in the preoptic area of castrated male rats. Work in other laboratories has also shown that electrophysiological activity of single neurons in female rats can be affected by estrogens and progesterone. Considering the spectrum of electrophysiological functions which have been tested for hormone-sensitivity—taking into account resting discharge, absolute magnitude

of response to stimuli, questions of stimulus coding, and relations to the cortical EEG—makes it possible to form hypotheses concerning the nature of the effect of testosterone (and other hormones) on the basal forebrain.

3. To discern the physiological and behavioral meaning of concentration by single neurons of steroid sex hormones and their effect on the electrophysiological activity of single neurons, it is necessary to know how hormone-sensitive cells participate in the neural circuits which control mating behavior responses. By way of identifying neural circuits controlling the lordosis reflex in the female rat we have: (*a*) used movie film analysis to describe sensory and motor elements of lordosis, (*b*) found that the vertebral dorsiflexion of lordosis can be caused by stimulating deep epaxial muscles of the back located dorsolateral and dorsal to the vertebral column; (*c*) found that lordosis is dependent on stimulation applied by the male rat to the pelvic region of the female. Her response to this stimulation permits him to apply subsequent stimuli leading to lordosis, and subsequently to intromission. Thus, successful mating is proven to depend on an interrelated sequence of reflexes in the male and female rat; (*d*) spinal females with transections at the low thoracic level have not shown the complete lordosis reflex and have not thus far displayed estrogen-sensitive hindquarters responses; (*e*) electrical stimulation of supraspinal points can elicit tail, tailbase, and rump movements, some of which resemble elements of the lordosis reflex. The distribution of such stimulation points in the lower brainstem matches the anatomical projections of the anterolateral columns of the spinal cord and, at higher levels, intersects with regions of estradiol-concentrating neurons. Following these observations, we hypothesize that somatosensory stimulation from the male rat critical for lordosis influences activity of neurons in the anterolateral columns of the spinal cord and their distribution in the brainstem reticular formation. We suggest that it is at least at the intersections between this primitive ascending reticular system (as revealed by the electrical stimulation experiments) and the distribution of estrogen-concentrating neurons that estradiol exerts its powerful influence over the lordosis reflex.

References

Adler, N. T. (1968). Effects of the male's copulatory behavior in the initiation of pregnancy in the female rat. *Anatomical Record* **160**, 305.

Adler, N. T. (1969). Effects of the male's copulatory behavior on successful pregnancy of the female rat. *Journal of Comparative and Physiological Psychology* **69**, 613–622.

Adler, N. T., and Bell, D. (1969). Constant estrus in rats: vaginal, reflexive and behavioral changes. *Physiology & Behavior* 4, 151–153.

Adler, N. T., and Bermant, G. (1966). Sexual behavior of male rats: effects of reduced sensory feedback. *Journal of Comparative and Physiological Psychology* 61, 240–243.

Adler, N. T., and Zoloth, S. R. (1970). Copulatory behavior can inhibit pregnancy in female rats. *Science* 168, 1480–1482.

Alcaraz, M., Guzmán-Flores, C., Salas, M., and Beyer, C. (1969). Effect of estrogen on the responsitivity of hypothalamic and mesencephalic neurons in the female cat. *Brain Research* 15, 439–446.

Anderson, C. H., and Greenwald, G. S. (1969). Autoradiographic analysis of estradiol uptake in the brain and pituitary of the female rat. *Endocrinology* 85, 1160–1165.

Anderson, F. D., and Berry, C. M. (1959). Degeneration studies of long ascending fiber systems in the cat brain stem. *Journal of Comparative Neurology* 111, 195–229.

Ball, J. (1934). Sex behavior of the rat after removal of the uterus and vagina. *Journal of Comparative and Physiological Psychology* 18, 419–422.

Ball, J. (1937). A test for measuring sexual excitability in the female rat. *Comparative Psychology Monographs* 14, 1–37.

Bard, P. (1940). The hypothalamus and sexual behavior. *Research Publications, Association for Research in Nervous and Mental Disease* 20, 551–579.

Barfield, R. D., and Sachs, B. D. (1968). Sexual behavior: stimulation by painful electrical shock to skin in male rats. *Science* 161, 392–395.

Barraclough, C., and Cross, B. (1963). Unit activity in the hypothalamus of the cyclic female rat: Effect of genital stimuli and progesterone. *Journal of Endocrinology* 26, 339–359.

Beach, F. A. (1943). Effects of injury to the cerebral cortex upon the display of masculine and feminine mating behavior by female rats. *Journal of Comparative Psychology* 36, 169–198.

Beach, F. A. (1948). "Hormones and Behavior." Cooper Square Publ., New York.

Beach, F. A. (1967). Cerebral and hormonal control of reflexive mechanisms involved in copulatory behavior. *Physiological Reviews* 47, 289–316.

Beach, F. A., and Rabedeau, R. G. (1959). Sexual exhaustion and recovery in the male hamster. *Journal of Comparative and Physiological Psychology* 52, 56–61.

Bermant, G. (1965). Rat sexual behavior: Photographic analysis of the intromission response. *Psychonomic Science* 2, 65–66.

Beyer, C. (1972). Effect of estrogen on brain stem neuronal responsivity in the cat. *In* "Steroid Hormones and Brain Function" (C. H. Sawyer, and R. A. Gorski, eds.), pp. 121–126. Univ. of California Press, Berkeley.

Beyer, C., and Sawyer, C. H. (1969). Hypothalamic unit activity related to control of the pituitary gland. *In* "Frontiers in Neuroendocrinology" (W. F. Ganong, and L. Martini, eds.), pp. 255–287. Oxford Univ. Press, London and New York.

Beyer, C., Mena, F., Pacheco, P., and Alcaraz, M. (1962a). Blockage of lactation by brain-stem lesions in the cat. *American Journal of Physiology* 202, 465–468.

Beyer, C., Tindal, J. S., and Sawyer, C. H. (1962b). Electrophysiological study of projections from mesencephalic central gray matter to forebrain in the rabbit. *Experimental Neurology* 6, 435–450.

Beyer, C., Ramirez, V. D., Whitmoyer, D. E., and Sawyer, C. H. (1967). Effects of hormones on the electrical activity of the brain in the rat and rabbit. *Experimental Neurology* 18, 313–326.

Blandau, R. J., Boling, R. J., and Young, W. C. (1941). The length of heat in the albino rat as determined by the copulatory response. *Anatomical Record* 79, 453–463.

Caggiula, A. R., and Eibergen, R. (1969). Copulation of virgin male rats evoked by painful peripheral stimulation. *Journal of Comparative and Physiological Psychology* 69, 414–419.

Calhoun, J. B. (1963). "The Ecology and Sociology of the Norway Rat." U. S. Dep. Health, Educ. Welfare, Pub. Health Serv., Bethesda, Maryland.

Carlsson, S. G., and Larsson, K. (1964). Mating in male rats after local anesthetization of the glans penis. *Zeitschrift für Tierpsychologie* 21, 854–856.

Carr, W. J. (1952). The effect of adrenalectomy upon the NaCl taste threshold in rat. *Journal of Comparative and Physiological Psychology* 45, 377–380.

Carr, W. J., and Caul, W. F. (1962). The effect of castration in the rat upon the discrimination of sex odors. *Animal Behavior* 10, 20–27.

Carr, W. J., Solberg, B., and Pfaffmann, C. (1962). The olfactory threshold for estrous female urine in normal and castrated male rats. *Journal of Comparative and Physiological Psychology* 55, 415–417.

Carr, W. J., Loeb, L. S., and Dissinger, M. L. (1965). Responses of rats to sex odors. *Journal of Comparative and Physiological Psychology* 59, 370–377.

Carr, W. J., Loeb, L. S., and Wylie, N. R. (1966). Responses to feminine odors in normal and castrated male rats. *Journal of Comparative and Physiological Psychology* 62, 336–338.

Chader, G. J., and Villee, C. A. (1970). Uptake of oestradiol by the rabbit hypothalamus. *Biochemical Journal* 118, 93–97.

Chi, C. C. (1970). An experimental silver study of the ascending projections of the central gray substance and adjacent tegmentum in the rat with observations in the cat. *Journal of Comparative Neurology* 139, 259–272.

Diakow, C., Pfaff, D., and Komisaruk, B. (1973). Sensory and hormonal interactions in eliciting lordosis. *Federation Proceedings, Federation of American Societies for Experimental Biology* (in press).

Eisenfeld, A. J., and Axelrod, J. (1965). Selectivity of estrogen distribution in tissues. *Journal of Pharmacology and Experimental Therapeutics* 150, 469–475.

Eisenfeld, A. J., and Axelrod, J. (1966). Effect of steroid hormones, ovariectomy, estrogen pretreatment, sex and immaturity on the distribution of ^{3}H-estradiol. *Endocrinology* 79, 38–42.

Feder, H. (1971). Estrous cycles and reproductive cycles. *American Psychological Association Meeting, Washington, D. C.*

Feder, H., and Wade, G. N. (1973). Integrative actions of perinatal hormones on neural tissues mediating adult sexual behavior. *In* "The Neurosciences" (F. O. Schmitt, ed.), Vol. 3. M.I.T. Press, Cambridge, Massachusetts.

Gerlach, J. L., and McEwen, B. S. (1972). Rat brain binds adrenal steroid hormone: Radioautography of hippocampus with corticosterone. *Science* 175, 1133–1136.

Goldberg, J. M., and Moore, R. Y. (1967). Ascending projections of the lateral lemniscus in the cat and monkey. *Journal of Comparative Neurology* 129, 143–156.

Green, R., Luttge, W. G., and Whalen, R. E. (1969). Uptake and retention of tritiated estradiol in brain and peripheral tissues of male, female and neonatally androgenized female rats. *Endocrinology* **85**, 373–378.

Guillery, R. W. (1957). Degeneration in the hypothalamic connexions of the albino rat. *Journal of Anatomy* **91**, 91–115.

Haller, E. W., and Barraclough, C. A. (1970). Alterations in unit activity of hypothalamic ventromedial nuclei by stimuli which affect gonadotropic hormone secretion. *Experimental Neurology* **29**, 111–120.

Hamilton, B. L., and Skultety, M. (1970). Efferent connections of the periaqueductal gray matter in the cat. *Journal of Comparative Neurology* **139**, 105–114.

Hard, E., and Larsson, K. (1968). Effects of mounts without intromission upon sexual behaviour in male rats. *Animal Behavior* **16**, 538–540.

Harriman, A. E., and MacLeod, R. B. (1953). Discriminative thresholds of salt for normal and adrenalectomized rats. *American Journal of Psychology* **66**, 465–471.

Hart, B. L. (1967). Testosterone regulation of sexual reflexes in spinal male rats. *Science* **155**, 1283–1284.

Hart, B. L. (1969). Gonadal hormones and sexual reflexes in the female rat. *Hormones and Behavior* **1**, 65–71.

Hart, B. L. (1970). Mating behavior in the female dog and the effects of estrogen on sexual reflexes. *Hormones and Behavior* **1**, 93–104.

Hart, B. L. (1971). Facilitation by estrogen of sexual reflexes in female cats. *Physiology & Behavior* **7**, 675–678.

Hart, B. L., and Haugen, C. M. (1968). Activation of sexual reflexes in male rats by spinal implantation of testosterone. *Physiology & Behavior* **3**, 735–738.

Hutchison, J. B., and Poynton, J. C. (1963). A neurological study of the clasp reflex in *Xenopus laevis* (Daudin). *Behavior* **22**, 41–63.

Joslyn, W. D., Feder, H. H., and Goy, R. W. (1971). Estrogen conditioning and progesterone facilitation of lordosis in guinea pigs. *Physiology & Behavior* **7**, 477–482.

Kato, J., and Villee, C. A. (1967a). Preferential uptake of estradiol by the anterior hypothalamus of the rat. *Endocrinology* **80**, 567–575.

Kato, J., and Villee, C. A. (1967b). Factors affecting uptake of estradiol-6,7-^{3}H by the hypophysis and hypothalamus. *Endocrinology* **80**, 1133–1138.

Kaufman, R. S. (1953). Effects of preventing intromission upon sexual behavior of rats. *Journal of Comparative and Physiological Psychology* **46**, 209–211.

Kawakami, M., and Kubo, K. (1971). Neuro-correlate of limbic-hypothalamo-pituitary-gonadal axis in the rat: Change in limbic-hypothalamic unit activity induced by vaginal and electrical stimulation. *Neuroendocrinology* **7**, 65–89.

Kawakami, M., and Sawyer, C. H. (1959a). Induction of behavioral and electroencephalographic changes in the rabbit by hormone administration of brain stimulation. *Endocrinology* **65**, 631–643.

Kawakami, M., and Sawyer, C. H. (1959b). Neuroendocrine correlates of changes in brain activity thresholds by sex steroids and pituitary hormones. *Endocrinology* **65**, 652–668.

König, J., and Klippel, R. A. (1963). "The Rat Brain." Williams & Wilkins, Baltimore, Maryland.

Komisaruk, B. R., McDonald, P. G., Whitmoyer, D. I., and Sawyer, C. H.

(1967). Effects of progesterone and sensory stimulation of EEG and neuronal activity in the rat. *Experimental Neurology* 19, 494–507.

Kuehn, R. E., and Beach, F. A. (1963). Quantitative measurement of sexual receptivity in female rats. *Behaviour* 21, 282–299.

Larsson, K. (1963). Non-specific stimulation and sexual behaviour in the male rat. *Behaviour* 20, 110–114.

LeMagnen, J. (1952). Les phénomènes olfacto-sexuels chez le rat blanc. *Archives des Sciences Physiologiques* 6, 295–331.

Lincoln, D. W. (1969a). Correlation of unit activity in the hypothalamus with EEG patterns associated with the sleep cycle. *Experimental Neurology* 24, 1–18.

Lincoln, D. W. (1969b). Effects of progesterone on the electrical activity of the forebrain. *Journal of Endocrinology* 45, 585–596.

Lincoln, D. W., and Cross, B. (1967). Effect of oestrogen on the responsiveness of neurones in the hypothalamus, septum and preoptic area of rats with light-induced persistent oestrus. *Journal of Endocrinology* 37, 191–203.

Lisk, R. D. (1962). Dencephalic placement of estradiol and sexual receptivity in the female rat. *American Journal of Physiology* 203, 493–496.

Lisk, R. D. (1967). Sexual behavior: hormonal control. *In* "Neuroendocrinology" (L. Martini and W. F. Ganong, eds.), Vol. 2, pp. 197–239. Academic Press, New York.

McEwen, B. S., and Pfaff, D. W. (1970). Factors influencing sex hormone uptake by rat brain regions. I. Effects of neonatal treatment, hypophysectomy and competing steroid on estradiol uptake. *Brain Research* 21, 1–16.

McEwen, B. S., Weiss, J. M., and Schwartz, L. S. (1969). Uptake of corticosterone by rat brain and its concentration by certain limbic structures. *Brain Research* 16, 227–241.

McEwen, B. S., Pfaff, D. W., and Zigmond, R. E. (1970a). Factors influencing sex hormone uptake by rat brain regions. II. Effects of neonatal treatment and hypophysectomy on testosterone uptake. *Brain Research* 21, 17–28.

McEwen, B. S., Pfaff, D. W., and Zigmond, R. E. (1970b). Factors influencing sex hormone uptake by rat brain regions. III. Effects of competing steroids on testosterone uptake. *Brain Research* 21, 29–38.

McEwen, B. S., Weiss, J. M., and Schwartz, L. S. (1970c). Retention of corticosterone by cell nuclei from brain regions of adrenalectomized rats. *Brain Research* 17, 471–482.

McGuire, J. L., and Lisk, R. D. (1968). Estrogen receptors in the intact rat. *Proceedings of the National Academy of Sciences, U. S.* 61, 497–503.

McGuire, J. L., and Lisk, R. D. (1969). Localization of estrogen receptors in the rat hypothalamus. *Neuroendocrinology* 4, 289–295.

MacLean, P. D., and Ploog, D. W. (1962). Cerebral representation of penile erection. *Journal of Neurophysiology* 25, 29–55.

MacLean, P. D., Denniston, R. H., and Dua, S. (1963). Further studies on cerebral representation of penile erection: caudal thalamus, midbrain, and pons. *Journal of Neurophysiology* 26, 273–293.

Maes, J. P. (1939). Neural mechanisms of sexual behaviour in the female cat. *Nature (London)* 144, 598–599.

Mehler, W. R., Feferman, M. E., and Nauta, W. J. H. (1960). Ascending axon degeneration following anterolateral cordotomy. An experimental study in the monkey. *Brain* 83, 718–750.

Michael, R. P. (1965). Oestrogens in the central nervous system. *British Medical Bulletin* **21**, 87–90.

Miller, M. E., Christensen, G. C., and Evans, H. E. (1964). "Anatomy of the Dog." Saunders, Philadelphia, Pennsylvania.

Nauta, W. J. H., and Kuypers, H. G. J. M. (1958). Some ascending pathways in the brain stem reticular formation. *In* "Reticular Formation of the Brain" (H. H. Jasper *et al.*, eds.), pp. 3–30. Little, Brown, Boston, Massachusetts.

Pfaff, D. W. (1968a). Uptake of estradiol-17B-H^3 in the female rat brain. An autoradiographic study. *Endocrinology* **82**, 1149–1155.

Pfaff, D. W. (1968b). Autoradiographic localization of radioactivity in rat brain after injection of tritiated sex hormones. *Science* **161**, 1355–1356.

Pfaff, D. W. (1970a). Mating behavior of hypophysectomized rats. *Journal of Comparative and Physiological Psychology* **72**, 45–50.

Pfaff, D. W. (1970b). Nature of sex hormone effects on rat sex behavior: Specificity of effects and individual patterns of response. *Journal of Comparative and Physiological Psychology* **73**, 349–358.

Pfaff, D. W. (1971). Movie analysis of female rat mating behavior. *Eastern Psychological Association Meeting, New York,* p. 10.

Pfaff, D. W. (1972a). Steroid sex hormones in the rat brain: Specificity of uptake and physiological effects. *In* "Steroid Hormones and Brain Function" (C. H. Sawyer and R. A. Gorski, eds.), pp. 103–112. Univ. of California Press, Berkeley.

Pfaff, D. W. (1972b). Interactions of steroid sex hormones with brain tissue: Studies of uptake and physiological effects. *In* "The Regulation of Mammalian Reproduction" (S. Segal, ed.), pp. 5–22. Thomas, Springfield, Illinois.

Pfaff, D. W., and Gregory, E. (1971a). Olfactory coding in olfactory bulb and medial forebrain bundle of normal and castrated male rats. *Journal of Neurophysiology* **34**, 208–216.

Pfaff, D. W., and Gregory, E. (1971b). Correlation between preoptic area unit activity and the cortical EEG: Difference between normal and castrated male rats. *Electroencephalography and Clinical Neurophysiology* **31**, 223–230.

Pfaff, D. W., and Keiner, M. (1972). Estradiol-concentrating cells in the rat amygdala as part of a limbic-hypothalamic hormone-sensitive system. *In* "The Neurobiology of the Amygdala" (B. Eleftheriou, ed.), pp. 775–785. Plenum, New York.

Pfaff, D. W., and Keiner, M. (1973). Atlas of estradiol-concentrating cells in the central nervous system of the female rat. *Journal of Comparative Neurology* (in press).

Pfaff, D. W., and Pfaffmann, C. (1969a). Olfactory and hormonal influences on the basal forebrain of the male rat. *Brain Research* **15**, 137–156.

Pfaff, D. W., and Pfaffmann, C. (1969b). Behavioral and electrophysiological responses of male rats to female rat urine odors. *In* "Olfaction and Taste" (C. Pfaffmann, ed.), pp. 258–267. Rockefeller Univ. Press, New York.

Pfaff, D. W., Silva, M. T. A., and Weiss, J. M. (1971). Telemetered recording of hormone effects on hippocampal neurons. *Science* **172**, 394–395.

Pfaffmann, C., and Bare, J. K. (1950). Gustatory nerve discharges in normal and adrenalectomized rats. *Journal of Comparative and Physiological Psychology* **43**, 320–324.

Phoenix, C. H., Goy, R. W., and Young, W. C. (1967). Sexual behavior: general aspects. *In* "Neuroendocrinology" (L. Martini and W. F. Ganong, eds.), Vol. 2, pp. 163–196. Academic Press, New York.

Ramirez, V. D., Komisaruk, B. R., Whitmoyer, D. I., and Sawyer, C. H. (1967). Effects of hormones and vaginal stimulation on the EEG and hypothalamic units in rats. *American Journal of Physiology* **212**, 1376–1384.

Reighard, J., and Jennings, H. S. (1935). "Anatomy of the Cat," 3rd Ed. Holt, New York.

Richter, C. P. (1933). The effect of early gonadectomy on the gross body activity of rats. *Endocrinology* **17**, 445–448.

Richter, C. P. (1936). Increased salt appetite in adrenalectomized rats. *American Journal of Physiology* **115**, 155–161.

Rothballer, A. B. (1966). Pathways of secretion and regulation of posterior pituitary factors. *Research Publications, Association for Research in Nervous and Mental Disease* **43**, 86–131.

Sachs, B. D., and Barfield, R. J. (1970). Temporal patterning of sexual behavior in the male rat. *Journal of Comparative and Physiological Psychology* **73**, 359–364.

Sawyer, C. H. (1960). Reproductive behavior. *In* "Handbook of Physiology, Sect. 1: Neurophysiology" (J. Field, H. W. Magoun, and V. E. Hall, eds.), Vol. II, pp. 1225–1240. Amer. Physiol. Soc., Washington, D. C.

Schlag, J., and Balvin, R. (1963). Background activity in the cerebral cortex and reticular formation in relation with the electroencephalogram. *Experimental Neurology* **8**, 203–216.

Stone, C. P., and Ferguson, L. W. (1940). Temporal relationships in the copulatory acts of adult male rats. *Journal of Comparative Psychology* **30**, 419–433.

Tindal, J. S., and Knaggs, G. S. (1971). Determination of the detailed hypothalamic route of the milk-ejection reflex in the guinea-pig. *Journal of Endocrinology* **50**, 135–152.

Tindal, J. S., Knaggs, G. S., and Turvey, A. (1967). The afferent path of the milk-ejection reflex in the brain of the guinea-pig. *Journal of Endocrinology* **38**, 337–349.

Tindal, J. S., Knaggs, G. S., and Turvey, A. (1969). The afferent path of the milk-ejection reflex in the brain of the rabbit. *Journal of Endocrinology* **43**, 663–671.

Wang, G. H. (1923). The relation between spontaneous activity and oestrous cycle in the white rat. *Comparative Psychology Monographs* **2**, No. 6.

Wilson, J. R., Adler, N. T., and Le Boeuf, B. (1965). The effects of intromission frequency on successful pregnancy in the female rat. *Proceedings of the National Academy of Sciences, U. S.* **53**, 1392–1395.

Young, W. C. (1961). The hormones and mating behavior. *In* "Sex and Internal Secretions" (W. C. Young, ed.), pp. 1173–1239. Williams & Wilkins, Baltimore, Maryland.

Zigmond, R. E., and McEwen, B. S. (1970). Selective retention of estradiol by cell nuclei in specific brain regions of the ovariectomized rat. *Journal of Neurochemistry* **17**, 889–899.

Adrenal Hormones and Emotional Behavior

Gerard P. Smith

*Department of Psychiatry, Cornell University Medical College,
and Edward W. Bourne Behavioral Research Laboratory,
New York Hospital, Westchester Division,
White Plains, New York*

"... And it is always advisable to perceive clearly our ignorance."
Charles Darwin, "The Expression of the Emotions in Man and Animals"

I. Introduction

In 1916, Karl Lashley wrote,

> Discovery of the importance of internal secretions for physiological psychology is leading to a widespread interest in the conditions governing secretion. The difficulties of studying the activity of the ductless glands in man are at present almost insurmountable and their relation to the nervous mechanism and to the changing habit systems of the individual must be judged largely from the conditions in other animals or from analogy with such glands as can be studied directly in man (Lashley, 1916).

In the past 25 years colorimetric, fluorometric, radiochemical, and immunological techniques placed the measurement of most major hormones within experimental reach. This review seeks to answer the question, "Given techniques to measure hormones, how much have we learned of 'their relation to the nervous mechanism and to the changing habit systems of the individual'?" My answer to this broad question will come from scrutinizing the restricted ground occupied by the adrenal glucocorticoids and adrenal catecholamines. This strategy was shaped by the frequent measurement of these hormones in physiological and behavioral contexts.

Adrenal glucocorticoids and catecholamines will be discussed in the following sequence: First, the control of hormonal secretion will be outlined. Second, the sensitivity and reliability of the hormones as emotional respondents will be assessed. Third, the evidence that these hormones are part of the mechanism of emotional behavior will be reviewed.

II. Physiological Control of Adrenal Hormone Secretion

A. ADRENAL CATECHOLAMINES[1]

1. Secretion and Circulation

The catecholamine cells of the adrenal medulla are directly innervated by preganglionic sympathetic neurons whose cell bodies are in the lateral horn of spinal cord segments T_8 to T_{11} (sometimes from T_5 through L_1). The terminals of these neurons form a cholinergic synapse of the nicotinic type on the catecholamine cells (Fig. 1). The catecholamine cells synthesize and store mostly epinephrine in rat, monkey, and man, but approximately equal amounts of epinephrine and norepinephrine in the cat (Malmejac, 1964). Quantal release of acetylcholine from the synaptic neural terminals increases the membrane permeability of the catecholamine cell to calcium. Calcium influx is correlated with the release of catecholamine from its intracellular granular storage form into the veins draining the adrenal medulla (Douglas, 1968). The mechanism of catecholamine release is exocytosis (Smith *et al.*, 1973).[2]

The other source of circulating catecholamines is the postganglionic adrenergic neurons. When activated, these neurons release norepinephrine; most of the released norepinphrine is transported back across the membrane of the adrenergic neurons or is inactivated by methylation

---

[1] Consideration of central catecholamine neurons as respondents or mechanisms of emotion behavior is outside the scope of this review.

[2] The release of catecholamines from sympathetic nerves and adrenal medullary cells is under very active investigation. The interested reader could begin with the proceedings of the Bayer-Symposium II (Schumann and Kroneberg, 1970).

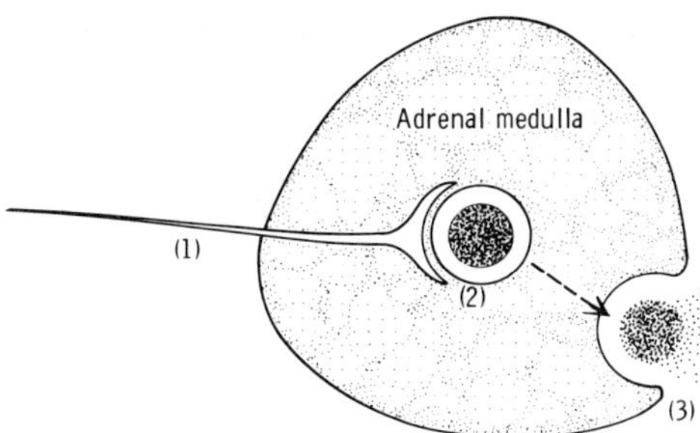

FIG. 1. Schematic of the major events in the secretion of catecholamines from the adrenal medulla. The splanchnic nerves (1) are activated in the lateral columns of the lower thoracic spinal cord. Splanchnic nerve activation releases acetylcholine into the synaptic cleft near a chromaffin cell containing catecholamines in a complex granular storage form (2). Acetylcholine increases the permeability of the chromaffin cell to ionized calcium. The influx of calcium ions is associated with the release of catecholamines from the granular storage form into the venous effluent by exocytosis (3). (There are no real anatomic relationships in this schematic.)

of a hydroxyl group on the catechol structure in the tissue surrounding the synapse by a reaction catalyzed by catechol-*O*-methyltransferase (COMT, Axelrod, 1965). A small fraction of the norepinephrine diffuses unchanged from the synaptic terminals into the blood. Thus, circulating epinephrine is from the adrenal medulla, and most of the circulating norepinephrine is from adrenergic neurons. Some norepinephrine may also come from adrenal medullary cells.

Measurement of circulating catecholamines is difficult because the usual concentrations (epinephrine = .07 ng/ml, norepinephrine = .35 ng/ml) are near the limit of sensitivity of the fluorometric method (Vendsalu, 1960). Measurement is complicated further by the very short initial half-life (10–30 seconds) of injected catecholamine (Axelrod *et al.*, 1959).

2. Urinary Excretion

Most of the data relating catecholamines to behavior consists of measurements of urinary excretion of epinephrine and norepinephrine.[3]

[3] Measurement of catecholamine metabolites in the urine is frequently performed, but the relationship of these metabolites to recently released and physiologically active catecholamines is always ambiguous. Furthermore, the extensive network of brain catecholamine neurons contributes to the catecholamine metabolites in the urine. Brain catecholamine neurons do not contribute to plasma or urinary epinephrine and norepinephrine, however, because there is a barrier to the movement of epinephrine or norepinephrine from brain extracellular fluid or cerebrospinal fluid into blood.

Measurements of urinary excretion are easier than that of plasma concentration, because the concentration of catecholamines is higher in the urine.

Unfortunately the relationship between the release of catecholamines from the adrenal medulla and the urinary excretion of epinephrine (or norepinephrine) is not fixed. There are several reasons for this variability:

1. Only a very small fraction (6% or less) of released catecholamine is found unchanged in the urine (Axelrod, 1965; von Euler and Luft, 1951; von Euler *et al.,* 1954). Most released catecholamines are metabolized by *O*-methylation or oxidative deamination (Axelrod, 1965).

2. Clearance of plasma catecholamine by the kidney is not complete. Approximately 60% of the catecholamine presented to the nephrons is excreted by a combination of filtration and secretion (Rennick and Yoss, 1962).

3. The amount of catecholamine presented to the kidney is the product of plasma concentration of catecholamine and renal blood flow. It is well known that renal blood flow is easily decreased by activation of renal sympathetic nerves (Rushmer *et al.,* 1961). Since the renal nerves and adrenal medulla are activated simultaneously during a variety of emotional and psychological disturbances, it is probable that the presentation of catecholamine to the kidneys is decreased by the fall of renal blood flow, and thus urinary excretion of catecholamines decreases relative to adrenal secretion.

3. Summary

Adrenal medullary secretion of epinephrine and norepinephrine is controlled directly by the central nervous system through the splanchnic nerves. Thus adrenal catecholamine secretion follows activity of the lateral (sympathetic) horn of the lower thoracic spinal cord. To estimate catecholamine secretion, changes of plasma concentration or urinary excretion of catecholamines have been measured. Plasma or urinary epinephrine comes entirely from the adrenal medulla, but plasma or urinary norepinephrine comes predominantly from synaptic terminals of postganglionic sympathetic neurons. Changes of plasma catecholamines should accurately reflect changes of catecholamine secretion, but the low concentration and short half-life of catecholamines in plasma makes accurate measurement difficult. Although measurement of urinary excretion of catecholamines is technically easier, catecholamine metabolism and incomplete renal clearance produce varying relationships between the urinary excretion and the secretion of catecholamines.

B. Adrenal Glucocorticoids[4]

1. Humoral Control and Circadian Rhythm

Control of the secretion of adrenal glucocorticoids is more complex than the control of adrenal catecholamines because two humoral factors mediate central neural influences to the adrenal cortex (Fig. 2). Let us begin with the fact that extracts of the hypothalamic median eminence region are able to stimulate the adenohypophysis *in vivo* or *in vitro* to release adrenocorticotropin (ACTH) (McCann and Porter, 1969). The activity of the median eminence extracts has been named corticotropin-releasing factor (CRF). CRF is probably produced by neurons in the basal hypothalamus because lesions there block CRF

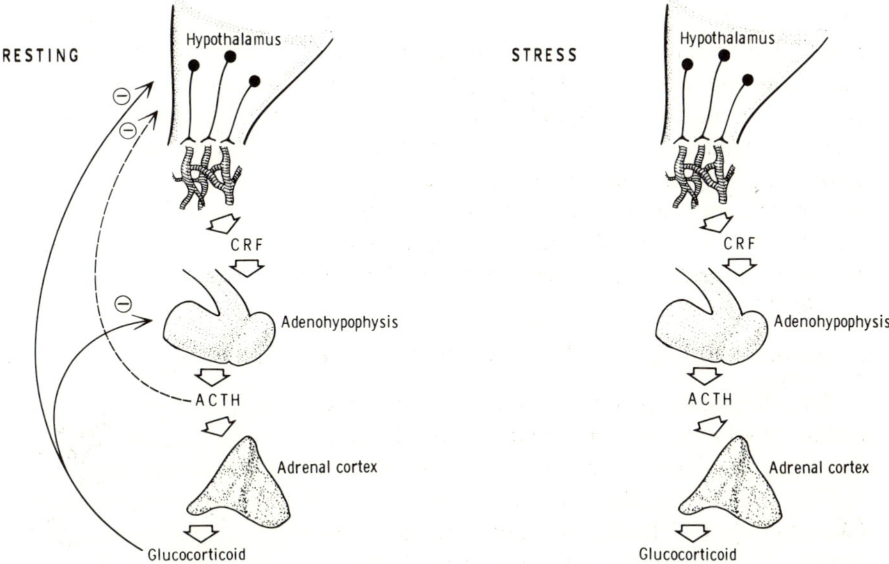

FIG. 2. Schematic of the adrenocortical system. Control of adrenal corticoid secretion is initiated by the activity of hypothalamic neurons which release a peptide called corticotropin-releasing factor (CRF) into the hypophysial portal vessels. CRF stimulates the release of ACTH from the adenohypophysis. ACTH stimulates corticoid secretion from the adrenal cortex. During resting conditions (left panel), there is evidence that the corticoids feedback to inhibit CRF release and ACTH release (solid lines). There is also the possibility that ACTH inhibits CRF release (dotted line). None of these feedback effects have been demonstrated during emotional stress (right panel).

[4] In this review, glucocorticoids refer to the principal adrenocortical hormone which has glucocorticoid action in a given species. In man, monkey, dog, and cat, it is hydrocortisone; in the rat and mouse, it is corticosterone.

release, and electrical stimulation increases CRF release. When these CRF neurons are stimulated by hypothalamic afferents from various brain areas (Raisman and Field, 1971) or by humoral stimuli, they release CRF into the capillaries of the median eminence. CRF then flows through the hypophysial portal system and is distributed through the sinusoids in the adenohypophysis to the cells which secrete ACTH. ACTH reaches the zona fasciculata and reticularis of the adrenal cortex through the systemic circulation. By a chemical sequence not yet understood (Liddle, 1969), ACTH stimulates the synthesis and release of glucocorticoids.

When the activity of this neuroendocrine system is studied by measuring plasma corticoids in samples obtained at frequent intervals throughout 1 day, a marked circadian rhythm is observed. In primates, approximately one-half of the day's cortisol is produced from 4 a.m. to 9 a.m. Plasma corticoids begin to decline in the afternoon and reach their nadir in the period from 9 p.m. to 4 a.m. The rhythm is linked to the activity pattern of the individual. In man, Liddle and co-workers induced a rhythm that was complete within 12 hours when they arranged two 12-hour rest–activity periods within 1 day (Liddle, 1969). The peak and nadir of the circadian rhythm in the rat is reversed from that in man: plasma corticosterone peaks about 4 p.m. and its nadir is about 4 a.m. The temporal shift of the corticoid rhythm follows the nocturnal activity pattern characteristic of the rat.

2. Relationship of ACTH to Adrenal Corticoid Secretion

The circadian corticoid rhythm in rat and man expresses the circadian rhythm of ACTH (Sydnor and Sayers, 1954; Ney *et al.*, 1963). Berson and Yalow (1968) used their sensitive radioimmunoassay for ACTH to compare the concentrations of ACTH with the concentrations of corticoids (17 hydroxycorticosteroids, 17-OHCS) in plasma samples obtained at 30-minute intervals throughout a 24-hour period (Fig. 3). Their results confirmed that the period of highest concentration of ACTH and 17-OHCS was usually from 4 a.m. to noon; the period of lowest concentration of ACTH and 17-OHCS was usually from 8 p.m. to 4 a.m. (Fig. 3). A stunning and unexpected aspect of their results, however, was the frequency and range of changes in the concentration of ACTH. The fluctuations in ACTH were not only large, but they were not always accompanied by the predicted change in plasma 17-OHCS (see subjects Wa. on 1/11, St. on 11/4, Ke. on 1/6). Furthermore, a given concentration of ACTH was associated with various concentrations of 17-OHCS at different points during the 24-

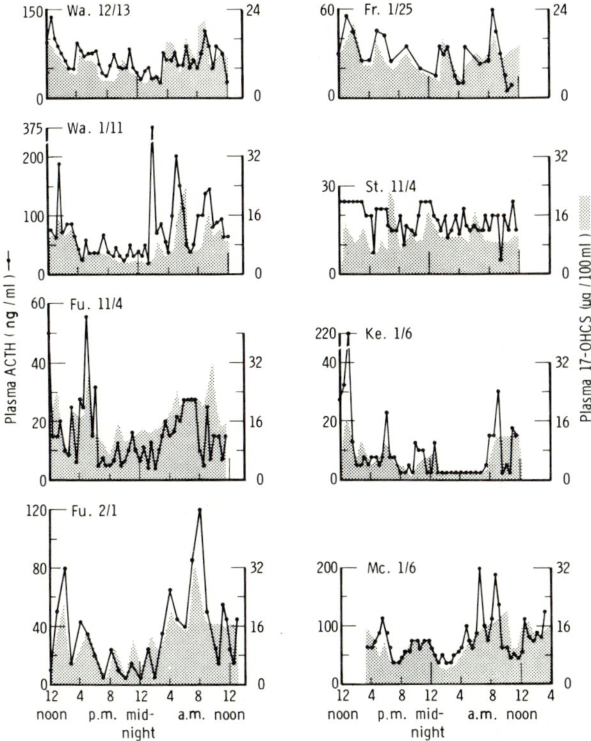

FIG. 3. Simultaneous measurements of plasma immunoreactive ACTH and plasma 17-OHCS throughout the day in six normal human subjects. Note the frequent spikes of high ACTH which are not always reflected by changes of 17-OHCS (redrawn from Berson and Yalow, 1968).

hours in the same subject as well as with various concentrations of 17-OHCS in different subjects. These important data of Berson and Yalow, documenting the frequent dissociations between plasma ACTH and 17-OHCS, cap a decade of investigation into the relationship between pituitary ACTH secretion and corticoid secretion by the adrenal cortex. The possible reasons for a dissociation between concentration of ACTH and concentration of corticoid in a plasma sample are:

1. The response of the human adrenal *in vivo* or the dog adrenal *in vitro* to increasing concentrations of ACTH is rectilinear (Ney *et al.,* 1963; Urquhart, 1965). The maximal adrenocortical output is elicited by approximately 3 mU of ACTH per 100 ml of plasma. This relationship holds for relatively short durations of ACTH stimulation (minutes to 2 or 3 hours). For longer periods of ACTH stimulation, a fixed dose of ACTH elicits a glucocorticoid response that is directly

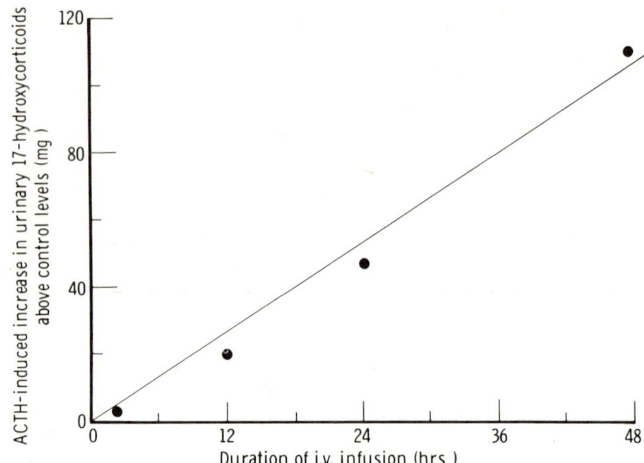

FIG. 4. The same dose of ACTH (32 USP units X-5229/infusion) was infused intravenously into a single patient (R. D., Gout), over different periods of time. When the increase of urinary corticoids above control was calculated, it was clear that the corticoid-stimulating effect of a fixed dose of ACTH was directly related to the duration of the infusion up to 48 hours (redrawn from Liddle *et al.*, 1954).

related to the *duration* of the ACTH stimulation (Liddle *et al.*, 1954): a dose of ACTH infused over 24 hours produced more than twice as much glucocorticoid than the same dose produced when ACTH was infused for 12 hours (Fig. 4).

2. Adrenal blood flow and concentration of ACTH interact, so that with concentrations of ACTH which elicit less than the maximal adrenocortical response, the amount of ACTH (blood flow × concentration) delivered to the adrenal determines the response of the rat or dog adrenal (Urquhart, 1965; Porter and Klaiber, 1965).

3. The response of the human adrenal cortex to maximal stimulation with ACTH varies during a 24-hour period. The glucocorticoid response was significantly less when ACTH was infused for the period lasting from midnight to 8 a.m. than when ACTH was infused during the late morning, afternoon, or evening (Perkoff *et al.*, 1959, Fig. 5). The glucocorticoid response to the infusion of ACTH from midnight to 8 a.m. became equal to the responses to identical infusions during the day or evening when the midnight to 8 a.m. infusion was preceded by a 6-hour infusion of ACTH in a dose that elicited a submaximal response (Fig. 5). These data are evidence that the intensity of ACTH stimulation in the preceding 7–12 hours affects the maximal response of the adrenal cortex elicited by larger doses of ACTH. From this work and that of Nugent *et al.* (1959), it is clear that the intensity of preceding ACTH stimulation affects the glucocorticoid response to a

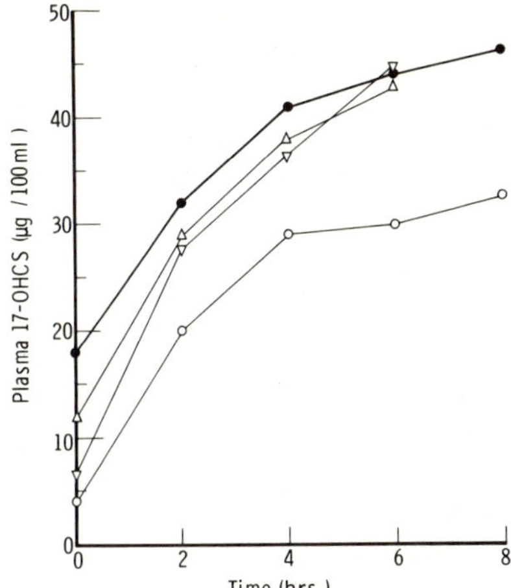

FIG. 5. Each curve represents the plasma corticoid response to maximal ACTH stimulation. The lowest curve connecting the open circles was the corticoid response during the night (12 midnight to 8 a.m.). During half of the night period and during the preceding 6 hours, endogenous corticoid and ACTH secretion was low. If a small, subthreshold dose (.5 U) of ACTH was infused i.v. from 5 p.m. to 11 p.m., the corticoid response (closed circles) to the maximal ACTH stimulation applied during the night (12 midnight to 8 a.m.) was now no different than the maximal corticoid response at earlier periods during the day [triangles (8 a.m. to 2 p.m.) and inverted triangles (4 p.m. to 10 p.m.)]. This is evidence that the corticoid response to ACTH depends upon the recent history of ACTH stimulation of the adrenal cortex (redrawn from Perkoff *et al.*, 1959).

maximal dose of ACTH. Unfortunately, it is just as clear that the "intensity of ACTH stimulation" is a gloss for the complex summation of the amount of ACTH delivered to the adrenal and the temporal pattern of delivery. The data of Berson and Yalow (1968) provide the kind of information that is required to measure the intensity of ACTH stimulation and to analyze the extent to which a glucocorticoid response to ACTH has been affected by the recent history of ACTH stimulation. At this time, the data of Berson and Yalow stand alone. The reports of a radioimmunoassay for rat ACTH (Rees *et al.*, 1971) and a bioassay equal in sensitivity to the radioimmunoassay of Berson and Yalow (Sayers *et al.*, 1971) suggests that more data will be available soon.

4. There is a marked difference in the time it takes ACTH or cortisol to leave the plasma after secretion stops: the half-life ($t_{1/2}$) of ACTH is 25 minutes in man (Berson and Yalow, 1968) and less than 5 minutes in rats (Matsuyama *et al.*, 1972); the $t_{1/2}$ of cortisol is approximately 60 minutes (Hellman *et al.*, 1970).

Of the several reasons for a dissociation of ACTH from plasma 17-OHCS in the samples analyzed by Berson and Yalow (see Fig. 3), concentrations of ACTH above that which should produce a maximal response (about 220 pg/ml is equivalent to 3 mU/100 ml) were present in only two samples. The amount of ACTH delivered and the pattern of ACTH delivery in the hours preceding a given pulse of ACTH secretion probably account for many of the dissociations of ACTH from plasma 17-OHCS. I believe you can be certain that ACTH secretion has increased recently when the plasma 17-OHCS concentration increases abruptly. You can *not,* however, be certain of the magnitude of the increase of ACTH by measuring the increase of plasma 17-OHCS.

The marked fluctuations ("pulsing") of plasma 17-OHCS present in the data of Berson and Yalow (1968) were also observed by Hellman and his colleagues (1970) in their detailed study of a young man. They drew attention to the correlation between marked ACTH and glucocorticoid secretion in the morning hours prior to arising and the frequent presence of rapid-eye-movement (REM) sleep. They also calculated that under the leisurely conditions of the research ward, the adrenal cortex was activated by ACTH for only 6 of 24 hours.

3. Negative Feedback

In addition to the circadian rhythm and frequent "pulsing" of ACTH and corticoids, the control of corticoid secretion is also complicated by a negative feedback effect of corticoids on ACTH secretion.[5] Since the classic observation of Ingle *et al.* (1938), an enormous amount of ink has been spilled on this negative feedback effect of glucocorticoids. Three questions dominated the research:

1. Do exogenous glucocorticoids inhibit ACTH secretion at the brain or at the adenohypophysis?

2. Do exogenous glucocorticoids inhibit ACTH secretion within minutes or hours?

3. Do physiological changes in endogenous glucocorticoids inhibit ACTH secretion?

Not one of these questions has been answered unambiguously. Kendall

---

[5] The reader is warned that there is the possibility that endogenous ACTH can inhibit its own secretion. Evidence for this suggestion has been reviewed (Motta *et al.,* 1969). Availability of sensitive assays for ACTH will facilitate investigation of this proposal. I shall also assume that this "short-loop" negative feedback is trivial during behavioral excitement lasting a relatively short time (see Fig. 2).

(1971) has provided a good review of our ignorance. The aspect of negative feedback which bears directly on the status of ACTH or glucocorticoids as respondents or mechanisms of behavior is the possibility that changes of endogenous glucocorticoids can inhibit ACTH secretion in response to stimuli which occur in the subsequent hour. Although there are experimental data for this possibility (Dallman and Yates, 1968; McHugh and Smith, 1967), most of the evidence is against the hypothesis (Yates *et al.,* 1969; Liddle, 1969). Furthermore, I have not found any investigation of negative feedback in a behavioral experiment, although severely depressed patients appear to be less sensitive to negative feedback than normal subjects (Stokes, 1972). In evaluating ACTH or glucocorticoids as respondents or mechanisms of behavior, I shall assume that negative feedback by endogenous glucocorticoids is trivial (Fig. 2).

4. Summary

In contrast to the direct neural control of the secretion of catecholamines, the secretion of adrenal corticoids is controlled indirectly by a neuroendocrine system which begins in brain and affects the adrenal cortex through the sequential release of CRF and ACTH. The relationship between corticoid secretion and ACTH concentration is variable. Although the secretion of adrenal corticoids can decrease the secretion of CRF or ACTH under some conditions, this negative feedback effect does not seem to operate during emotional stress or behavioral excitement.

III. Adrenal Hormones as Emotional Respondents

A. ADRENAL CATECHOLAMINES

1. Urinary Excretion

In 1954, von Euler and Lundberg introduced the measurement of the output of urinary catecholamines as an emotional respondent (von Euler and Lundberg, 1954). They studied military pilots and passengers during ground activity and during flight. Flight elicited a large increase of epinephrine excretion in passengers and pilots; pilots also had a marked increase of norepinephrine (Table I). When passengers were studied on a night before flight, epinephrine excretion was higher than on a routine night, but the excretion of both catecholamines was lower than during daytime activity (Table I). Thus, von Euler and Lundberg demonstrated high catecholamine excretion during the stress

TABLE I

MEAN URINARY EPINEPHRINE AND NOREPINEPHRINE EXCRETION ($\pm$SE, ng/min)
IN PASSENGERS FOR WHOM FLIGHT WAS A NOVELTY AND IN
PILOTS FOR WHOM FLIGHT WAS A VIGILANCE TASK[a]

	Ground day		Flight day	
	Epinephrine	Nor-epinephrine	Epinephrine	Nor-epinephrine
Passengers	6.7 ± 0.98	24 ± 3.9	24 ± 3.5	27 ± 4.4
Pilots	5.2 ± 1.05	19 ± 3.1	19 ± 3.8	39 ± 4.3
	Routine night		Night before flight	
	Epinephrine	Nor-epinephrine	Epinephrine	Nor-epinephrine
Passengers	2.2 ± 0.65	11 ± 2.5	5.1 ± 0.66	13 ± 1.9

[a] Note that during the day of the flight, epinephrine excretion increased in passengers, and both epinephrine and norepinephrine increased in pilots. Passengers also had a significant increase of epinephrine excretion on the night before flight (from von Euler and Lundberg, 1954).

of flight, differential excretion of norepinephrine in passengers and pilots, higher catecholamine excretion during the day than at night, and increased epinephrine excretion in passengers during the night before a flight stress. This initial study raised several important questions which have encompassed most of the subsequent work.

Catecholamine excretion is higher in the day than at night because the waking state is characterized by upright posture which demands sympathetically mediated cardiovascular adjustments (von Euler *et al.*, 1955; Elmadjian *et al.*, 1957).

The observation that catecholamine excretion increased during or prior to flight stress was quickly confirmed in such diverse stressful situations as hockey games (Elmadjian *et al.*, 1957), psychiatric illnesses (Curtis *et al.*, 1960), or oral examinations (Bogdonoff *et al.*, 1960). All subsequent studies (see reviews by von Euler, 1964; Mason, 1968b; Frankenhaeuser, 1971) are consistent with the statement that increased catecholamine excretion is a respondent of stress.

2. Correlation of Catecholamine Excretion with Specific Emotions

There is no consensus, however, on the interpretation of the differential excretion of norepinephrine and epinephrine which has been frequently observed. Elmadjian and his colleagues (1957) reported three

patterns of catecholamine excretion: first, large increases of norepinephrine and slight increases of epinephrine in professional players during
a hockey game; second, slight increases of norepinephrine and large
increases of epinephrine in psychiatric patients during a diagnostic
interview; and, third, large increases of *both* norepinephrine and
epinephrine during intense display of a variety of emotions. Since
exercise without marked emotional involvement produced only slight
increases in norepinephrine excretion, Elmadjian *et al.* concluded that
the patterns of catecholamine excretion were linked to *specific* emotional states. In an attempt to support this conclusion, they rated 10
psychiatric patients for motor activity and "hostility reactions" and
correlated these behavioral ratings with catecholamine excretion. There
was a tendency for norepinephrine and epinephrine excretion to be
high when the patients were very active or aggressive (see Elmadjian
et al., 1957, Fig. 2, p. 616).

The measurement of differential excretion of catecholamines was
welcomed by those psychophysiologists like Ax (1953) and Funkenstein (1956) who had predicted such differential excretion of catecholamines from different patterns of cardiovascular responses. Ax had
suggested that cardiovascular responses during fear resembled the
responses induced by epinephrine, while the cardiovascular responses
during anger resembled the responses induced by a combined injection
of norepinephrine and epinephrine. Similarly, Funkenstein had argued
that anger ("Anger Out") was associated with a norepinephrinelike
cardiovascular response to mecholyl, while anxiety ("Anger-In") was
associated with an epinephrinelike cardiovascular response.

Further support for specific patterns of catecholamine excretion
linked with specific emotional states appeared in studies of a heterogeneous group of subjects by Silverman *et al.* (1961), but they noted
that the correlation of anxiety with epinephrine excretion or the correlation of anger with norepinephrine was not always observed.

The correlation between anxiety, moderate depression, and mixed
states, and patterns of catecholamine excretion was not convincing
in the report of Curtis *et al.* (1960). Mendelson *et al.* (1960) reported
that 10 subjects increased catecholamine excretion during sensory deprivation. They identified five patterns of catecholamine excretion in
their 10 subjects and could not correlate the pattern of excretion with
behavioral measures.

At this time, Mason and his colleagues reported one of the few
experiments in which plasma epinephrine and norepinephrine were
measured. During a variety of instrumental conditioning tasks performed by rhesus monkeys, Mason *et al.* (1961) noted that plasma

norepinephrine usually increased, but plasma epinephrine increased markedly only in uncertain or novel conditions. Similar data were reported by Bogdonoff *et al.* (1960) in their measurements of the catecholamine excretion of medical students during an oral examination. The degree of general emotional upset covaried with the excretion of epinephrine, but not of norepinephrine.

Frankenhaeuser *et al.* (1962) provided a strong experimental demonstration supporting Mason's observation. Frankenhaeuser *et al.* (1962) made a careful psychophysiological study of four young men undergoing repeated trials of centrifugation. Urinary excretion of both catecholamines was increased on the first trial (Fig. 6). With repeated centrifugation, excretion of norepinephrine remained high, but excretion of epinephrine decreased markedly. Subjective stress reactions obtained by the method of ratio estimation also decreased with repeated centrifugation. In this situation, subjective stress and excretion of epinephrine habituated, but norepinephrine excretion did not. Frankenhaeuser concluded that epinephrine excretion was related primarily to the mental stress of novelty, while norepinephrine excretion was related to the cardiovascular adjustments elicited by centrifugation. The authors put it well: "The *expected G-loads* were higher than the *actual G-loads.*"

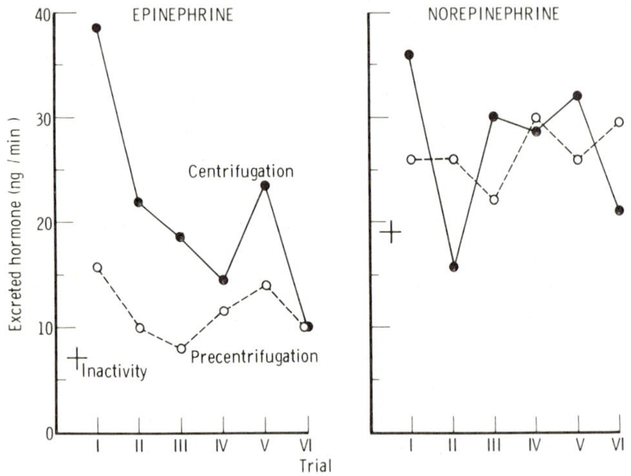

FIG. 6. Mean urinary epinephrine and norepinephrine excretion of four human subjects before (open circles) and during (closed circles) six successive trials in a human centrifuge. + Denotes mean urinary excretion of epinephrine and norepinephrine during a control period of inactivity. Note that the increased excretion of epinephrine habituates, but the increased excretion of norepinephrine does not (redrawn from Frankenhaeuser *et al.*, 1962).

In later experiments, Frankenhaeuser and her colleagues have provided impressive evidence that epinephrine excretion is a reliable respondent of strong emotional arousal, but norepinephrine excretion is not (see review by Frankenhaeuser, 1971).

3. Relation of Epinephrine Excretion to Intensity of Emotional Arousal

Since no experimental data consistently contradict Frankenhaeuser's view, let us review the characteristics of epinephrine excretion to determine its usefulness as a respondent for emotional arousal.

Epinephrine excretion can increase over a 10-fold range. Under resting conditions, epinephrine excretion is reasonably stable when measured at weekly intervals (Patkai and Frankenhaeuser, 1964), but excretion becomes more variable during stress (Frankenhaeuser and Patkai, 1965).

Although the possibility that epinephrine excretion was a respondent for *specific* emotional states was pursued in the initial studies (see above), the work of the past decade did not support that hypothesis. Certainly Levi's observations that epinephrine excretion increased markedly during exciting or erotic films which elicited pleasurable emotions (Levi, 1967) strongly favors the idea that epinephrine excretion reflects the intensity, but not the names, of emotional states.

If epinephrine excretion is related to the intensity of emotional states, how sensitively do changes in epinephrine excretion reflect changes in emotional intensity as reported by subjects or inferred from their behavior? This question of sensitivity is the crucial test of a respondent because it bears directly on *the* psychosomatic problem—the relationship between psychic and physiological measurements.

Bogdonoff *et al.* (1960) found that mean epinephrine excretion increased significantly as students' reports of affective excitement during an examination increased from minimal to moderate or from moderate to marked.

In their study of habituation to gravitational stress (see above), Frankenhaeuser *et al.* (1962) observed that the intensity of subjective reactions measured by ratio estimation were highly correlated with mean epinephrine excretion (Fig. 7).

Frankenhaeuser *et al.* (1965) tried to demonstrate this same correlation in the simpler situation of subjects receiving electrical shocks of varying intensities to the fingers. Subjective unpleasantness (the authors' term) measured by ratio estimation only changed at the highest shock intensity. Epinephrine excretion did not change significantly across the

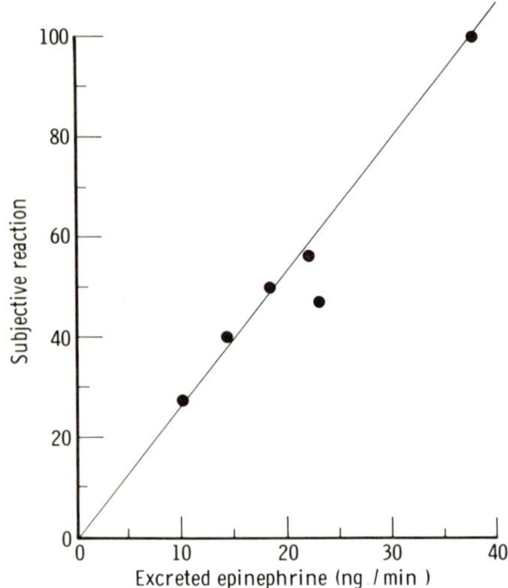

FIG. 7. Subjective reactions to stress of human centrifugation (in percent of stress during first trial) was plotted against the urinary excretion of epinephrine. Data were from the same four subjects and six trials depicted in Fig. 6. Each point corresponds to one trial. The linear correlation has never been replicated in other subjects under different kinds of stress (redrawn from Frankenhaeuser *et al.,* 1962).

range of shock intensities. Thus, this experiment failed to demonstrate that subjective unpleasantness and epinephrine excretion covaried. The possibility that this experiment failed because it used peripheral electric shocks to elicit emotional arousal rather than more usual psychic stimuli was tested in four subsequent experiments by Frankenhaeuser and her colleagues (Patkai *et al.,* 1967; Frankenhaeuser *et al.,* 1967, 1968; Frankenhaeuser and Rissler, 1970). Using a variety of tasks which involved some form of psychological conflict to elicit changes in ratio estimates of emotional arousal (stress and irritation) and changes in epinephrine excretion, Frankenhaeuser's group failed to demonstrate that subjective stress correlated with epinephrine excretion across a broad range of estimates of subjective stress. With a sufficiently large change of stress, epinephrine excretion *usually* increased, but the increment did not covary with increments in subjective stress. The single exception is the correlation found during habituation to gravitational stress discussed above (Frankenhaeuser *et al.,* 1962).

4. Summary

The result of nearly 20 years work on catecholamines as emotional respondents is that epinephrine excretion increases when there is a large change of emotional intensity, but epinephrine excretion is not sensitive to moderate changes of emotional intensity reported by the method of ratio estimation or as predicted from the intensity of electric shock (Mason, 1968a; Frankenhaeuser, 1971). This insensitivity limits the usefulness of catecholamine excretion as a quantitative emotional respondent. Further limitations on epinephrine excretion as an emotional respondent are probably seasonal (Johansson *et al.*, 1969), and definite individual (Frankenhaeuser and Patkai, 1965) differences in epinephrine excretion, and the physiologic fact that the epinephrine *excreted* is less than 6% of the epinephrine *secreted* (see Section II,A,2). The interesting suggestion from early work that patterns of norepinephrine and epinephrine excretion were linked to specific emotional states has not been supported by most recent experiments.

B. ADRENAL GLUCOCORTICOIDS

1. Corticoids and Psychological Stimuli

Psychological stimuli, especially those associated with fear, anxiety, or avoidance behavior, frequently drive the adrenocortical system at nearly maximal rate (Mason, 1968a, 1971; Mason *et al.*, 1968a). Although most psychological stimuli for increasing corticoids are judged noxious and avoided if possible, the appetitive behavior and reward of intracranial self-stimulation have appeared to be important exceptions.

Self-stimulation is associated with large increases of corticoids in rats (Uretsky *et al.*, 1966) and monkeys (McHugh *et al.*, 1966). Interpretation of these data is treacherous, however, because electrical stimulation of the medial forebrain bundle may activate separate neural systems for positive reinforcement and for ACTH release. This would spuriously link the reward of self-stimulation with increases of corticoids. Three results favor such an experimental artifact. First, Slusher (1965) demonstrated that adrenalectomy did not produce any immediate effects on self-stimulation in rats. Second, Uretsky *et al.* (1966) elicited the same increase of plasma corticoids by stimulating electrodes in rats under anesthesia as self-stimulation of these same electrodes elicited. Third, in an experiment just completed, Natelson, Stokes, Root, and I observed that monkeys can self-stimulate at high rates (>3000 lever presses per hour) without eliciting an increase of plasma corticoids.

Since corticoids do not increase necessarily during self-stimulation, and since corticoids do not increase during lever pressing for food reward (Mason *et al.*, 1957), no available evidence supports the idea that corticoids reflect the intensity of appetitive behavior or reward.

2. *Relation of Corticoids to Intensity of Noxious Stimuli*

The assumption that plasma or urinary corticoids reflects the *intensity* of noxious stimuli underlies the interpretation of most experiments which use corticoids as emotional respondents. Despite its frequent use and theoretical importance, Ader, Friedman, and their colleagues have reported the only systematic study of this assumption in a series of papers analyzing the plasma corticosterone response to foot shock or environmental change.

When Friedman *et al.* (1967) varied the intensity of foot shock from .2 to 4.0 mA, plasma corticosterone increased significantly with only 2.0 or 4.0 mA shocks (Fig. 8). The increase was slight (6.5 μg/ 100 ml), and approximately half of the increase was observed in animals transferred to the experimental chamber, but not shocked. When the duration of shock was varied from 30 to 240 seconds, the peak plasma corticosterone response was highest for 120 and 240 seconds of shock, but the difference between mean peak responses to 30 seconds and to 240 seconds was only 6 μg/100 ml. These results demonstrate that the plasma corticosterone response reflects the difference of strength or duration of foot shock at the extremes of the range of parameters tested. The relatively small difference in .plasma corti-

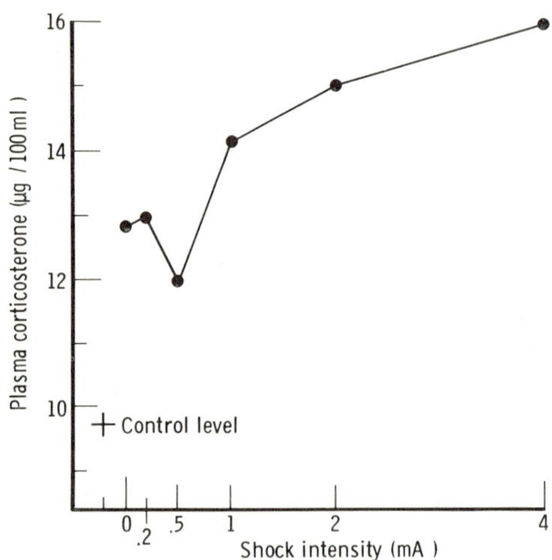

FIG. 8. Plasma corticosterone in rats plotted as a function of the intensity of electric foot shock. Note that the increase of plasma corticosterone to a 4-fold increase of current intensity was very slight and was less than the increase of corticosterone elicited by moving the rats from their cages (+ control level) to the shock box (redrawn from Friedman *et al.*, 1967).

costerone between the maximum and minimum stimulus, however, makes the corticosterone response an insensitive respondent for differentiating intensities of shock (current × duration) that lie between threshold and maximum (Fig. 8). The authors' failure to find a significant interaction between current strength and duration of shock on plasma corticosterone is further evidence that plasma corticosterone does not adequately reflect the differences of intensity (current × duration) of foot shock above threshold.

Ader and Friedman (1968) attempted a similar analysis of the plasma corticosterone response produced by transfer to the experimental cage for durations of 5, 15, 60, 120, and 240 seconds. The plasma corticosterone response was greatest after 240 seconds in the experimental cage (Fig. 9). The response to 240 seconds was significantly larger than the corticosterone response to 5 seconds in the experimental cage, but it was not larger than the corticosterone responses to 15, 60, or 120 seconds. The same relative corticosterone responses occurred when animals were transferred to the experimental cage at the trough of the circadian adrenocortical rhythm as when transfer occurred at the "peak" rhythm (Fig. 9). These results confirm

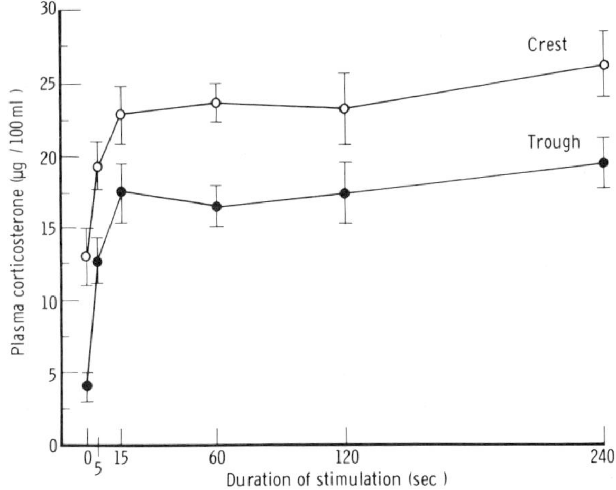

FIG. 9. Plasma corticosterone in rats 15 minutes after varying durations of foot shock. The line connecting open circles denotes corticosterone responses from rats tested at the crest of their circadian adrenocortical rhythm. The line connecting closed circles denotes responses from rats tested at the trough of their rhythm. Durations of foot shock of 15 seconds or more elicit the same corticosterone response. Note that the *change* of corticosterone for a single duration of foot shock is greater in rats tested at the trough of their rhythm. All values are mean ±SE (redrawn from Ader and Friedman, 1968).

the conclusion drawn from their study of foot shock: the plasma corticosterone response differentiates minimal and maximal durations (intensities) of environmental change, but corticosterone responses fail to reflect differences of intensity that occur between threshold and maximum.

Plasma corticosterone responses not only fail to reflect differences of intensity of foot shock or environmental change, but plasma corticosterone also failed to reflect the presumed difference of stimulus intensity obtained by combining environmental change and foot shock (Friedman and Ader, 1967).

3. Which Parameter of Plasma Corticoids Is Best Respondent?

In the course of these investigations Ader and Friedman raised the important methodological question: "Which parameter of plasma corticosterone should be used as a respondent?" (Ader *et al.*, 1967). The force of this question can be appreciated by examining Fig. 10. In comparing plasma corticosterone responses to 5 seconds or 3 minutes of environmental change, should the respondent measure be peak absolute

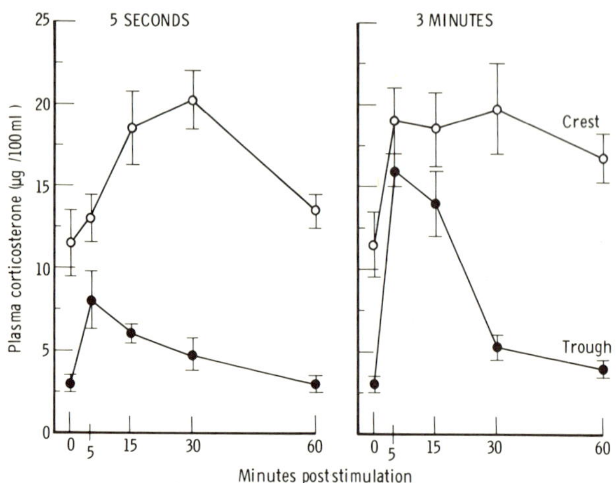

FIG. 10. Plasma corticosterone of rats at varying intervals after receiving 5 seconds or 3 minutes of environmental change. Lines connecting open or closed circles denote responses from rats tested at the crest or trough of their adrenocortical rhythm, respectively. The different shapes of the curves of corticosterone response emphasized the difficulty of choosing the best parameter of corticosterone as an emotional respondent. The curves also indicated the importance of the time of sampling after the emotional stimulus, and at what point in the circadian rhythm the emotional stimulus occurred (redrawn from Ader and Friedman, 1968).

value, peak change from control, duration of response, or the area under the curve of the response? Furthermore, the values of these parameters differ if the same environmental change occurs at the trough or at the peak of the circadian adrenocortical rhythm.

Natelson, Stokes, and I have recently completed an experiment which bears on the same problem. We investigated which parameter of plasma corticoids correlated best with the intensity (current) of electrical stimulation of lateral hypothalamus. The study was performed in monkeys adapted to chronic restraint in primate chairs and living within enclosed booths. Two intensities of current were used. Low intensity was the current required to elicit reliably a just noticeable difference in behavior (alerting). High intensity was Low current multiplied by a factor of 4. Lateral hypothalamic stimulation with High current always elicited marked behavioral excitement.

Using the experimental design of 1 hour of brain stimulation followed by an experimental hour of Low, High, or Sham stimulation, plasma 17-OHCS were highest during High stimulation (Fig. 11). Table II shows that either mean change or peak change of plasma corticoids significantly differentiated Sham, Low, and High stimulation under our experimental conditions. Absolute value of plasma 17-OHCS was not a reliable respondent because control values varied over a wide range despite considerable effort to maintain the conditions of

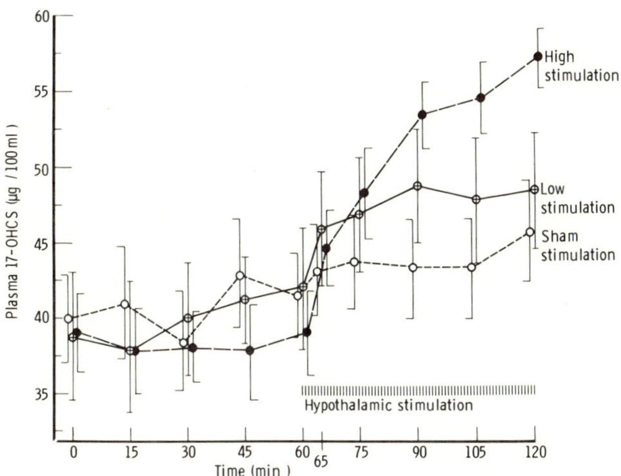

FIG. 11. Mean plasma 17-OHCS ($\pm$SE) at intervals during a control hour and an hour of Sham, Low (0.2–0.8 mA), or High (Low intensity multiplied by 4) hypothalamic stimulation in 11 unanesthetized rhesus monkeys. The plasma 17-OHCS response to Low stimulation was significantly greater than the response to Sham, but it was less than the response to High stimulation.

these experiments constant (range of mean control 17-OHCS: 14.2–77.7 μg/100 ml, $n = 85$). Such a wide range of control values made it impossible to compare absolute values of plasma 17-OHCS during different conditions (Sham, Low, or High) of hypothalamic stimulation.

Although mean change or peak change of 17-OHCS reliably differentiated intensities of hypothalamic stimulation which operationally differed by a factor of 4, the 17-OHCS response to High was only double the 17-OHCS response to Low. There are two reasons for believing that a 2-fold difference is an accurate measure of the respondent range of plasma 17-OHCS in the monkey:

1. The peak change of 17-OHCS to High (20.2 ± 2.3 μg/100 ml, $n = 11$) was maximal because it did not differ from the maximal peak change produced by infusions of 10 U of ACTH (16.4 ± 1.8 μg/100 ml, $n = 6$, $p > 0.05$) under the same experimental conditions.

2. Hypothalamic stimulation with current below threshold for behavioral change failed to increase plasma 17-OHCS in monkeys under similar conditions in an earlier experiment by Hall and Smith (1969). These results in the monkey are consistent with those observed in the rat, and they emphasize that the narrow range of corticoid response limits the ability of any parameter of plasma corticoids to reflect a wide range of intensity of adequate stimuli.

There is another aspect of these hypothalamic experiments of Natelson *et al.* (1973) that is pertinent. Hypothalamic stimulation elicited defense reactions of varying intensity in different animals. Using a scoring technique which ranged from -3.0 (apparently asleep) to $+10.5$ (most excited appearance observed in these experiments), we scored the behavioral excitement elicited by hypothalamic stimulation at

TABLE II

EITHER MEAN CHANGE OR PEAK CHANGE OF PLASMA CORTICOIDS
DIFFERENTIATED THE CORTICOID RESPONSES TO 1 HOUR OF
INTERMITTENT HYPOTHALAMIC ELECTRICAL STIMULATION OF
SHAM, LOW, OR HIGH INTENSITY IN 11 UNANESTHETIZED
RHESUS MONKEYS ADAPTED TO CHAIR RESTRAINT[a]

Parameter of 17-OHCS (μg/100 ml)	Intensity of hypothalamic stimulation		
	Sham	Low	High
Mean change	2.8 ± 1.9	7.2 ± 1.7	13.8 ± 1.7
Peak change	8.6 ± 1.9	12.6 ± 2.1	20.2 ± 2.3

[a] Low intensity (0.2–0.8 mA) produced a just noticeable difference of behavior. High intensity was Low intensity multiplied by a factor of 4. High intensity produced marked behavioral excitement.

the same experimental intervals used for sampling blood for plasma 17-OHCS. This permitted us to correlate the change of behavioral score for excitement with the simultaneous change of plasma 17-OHCS during Sham, Low, or High intensity stimulation (Fig. 12). High stimulation always produced higher behavioral scores than Low stimulation, but High stimulation did not always increase 17-OHCS more. The two monkeys (S-22 and B-3) with the largest increases of behavioral score did not have the largest increases of plasma 17-OHCS (Fig. 12). The two monkeys (1/8 and S-24) with the smallest increases of behavioral score did not have significant increases of plasma 17-OHCS (Fig. 12). Changes of behavioral score between these extremes were associated with increases of plasma 17-OHCS which varied over a 5-fold range (Fig. 12).

The failure to observe a consistent relationship between changes of behavioral score and 17-OHCS during hypothalamic stimulation was probably not an artifact of electrical stimulation, because changes of behavioral score in the same seven monkeys during control periods prior to stimulation were not correlated with change or absolute values of plasma 17-OHCS.

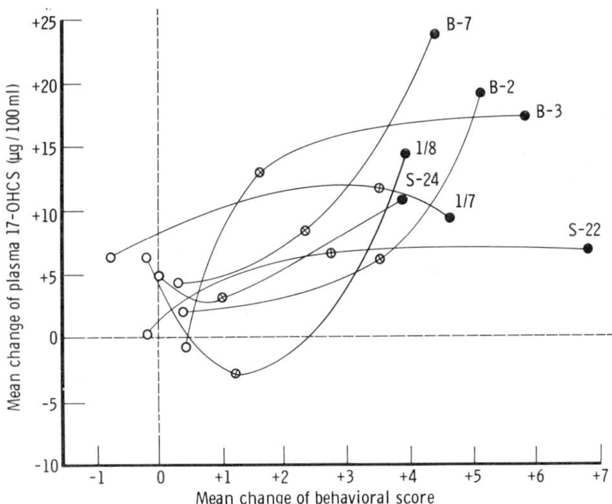

FIG. 12. Mean change of plasma 17-OHCS plotted as a function of mean change of behavioral score for excitement during Sham (open circles), Low (encircled cross), and High (closed circles) hypothalamic stimulation in seven rhesus monkeys. Large changes of behavioral score for excitement were not accompanied by a significant change of plasma 17-OHCS (monkeys S-22, B-3, and 1/7). Note the wide range of changes of plasma 17-OHCS for changes of behavioral score between +1 and +4.

Failure to find a consistent relationship between behavioral score and plasma 17-OHCS may reflect distortions introduced by the experimental conditions of chair restraint, brain stimulation, and the use of an arbitrary technique to score behavioral excitement. On the other hand, failure to find tight linkage between intensity of behavioral excitement and increase of plasma 17-OHCS in this simple, nonsocial situation challenges the traditional assumption that plasma 17-OHCS are respondents that sensitively differentiate the intensity of central emotional states which are inferred from behavioral measures, global clinical judgments, or clinical interviews (see Section III,B,5). At the present time no data refute this challenge.

4. Factors Affecting Corticoid Responses in Animals

We have seen that the use of corticoids as an emotional respondent is limited by the narrow range of response (Sections II,B,2 and Section III,B,3), ambiguity concerning the appropriate parameter of a corticoid response (Section III,B,3), and several experimental failures to demonstrate that plasma corticoids sensitively reflect differences of intensity of noxious stimuli or behavioral excitement (Section III,B,2 and 3). We now review evidence that the corticoid response to an adequate stimulus is shaped by the history of the organism. Levine (1962) observed higher and more sustained corticoid responses to electric shock in adult rats that had been handled in infancy than in nonhandled rats. Handled rats also have lower plasma corticosterone 15 minutes after termination of electric shock than nonhandled rats (Haltmeyer et al., 1967). When placed in a novel environment, handled rats have a smaller corticoid response (Ader and Grota, 1969; Levine, 1967).

The effect of social isolation of monkeys during infancy is apparently not so powerful. Meyer and Bowman (1972) found no difference between monkeys totally or partially isolated as infants and monkeys reared in the jungle in the resting plasma corticoid concentration, the maximal concentration after ACTH, or the concentration of corticoid after venesection or chair restraint for 2 hours. Rose et al. (1969) confirmed the observation that monkeys raised alone had a normal corticoid response to chair restraint, but in contrast to normal monkeys, social isolates did not increase corticoids during a period of adult social isolation.

Adult social experience can also affect corticoid responses. In their study of groups of caged rhesus monkeys, Sassenrath et al. (1969) demonstrated that monkeys which *received* aggressive behaviors frequently had a significantly increased corticoid response to a test dose of ACTH. This increased sensitivity of the adrenal cortex to ACTH was probably the result of chronically increased stimulation with endogenous ACTH (see Section II,B,2) as a result of receiving frequent threats and attacks. There are also marked individual differences which may be the result of developmental or adult experience. Levine *et al.* (1970) reported that monkeys judged highly aggressive (by response to human confrontation) had higher urinary corticoid responses to the experimental cage, and to training and performance of a free-operant avoidance task than monkeys judged less aggressive.

Finally, the conditioning history of an animal can have a dramatic effect on the corticoid response. For example, monkeys required to perform a free-operant avoidance task for 72 hours at weekly intervals have a marked corticoid response initially, but after the twentieth week, monkeys had no corticoid response during avoidance (Brady, 1964).

5. Corticoids as a Respondent in Man

It is likely that corticoid responses in man are also affected by a variety of psychologic, developmental, and experiential factors. Poe *et al.* (1970) reported that 17-OHCS responses of soldiers to basic training were influenced significantly by body weight and some psychological characteristics revealed by the MMPI test. The magnitude of the 17-OHCS response of students to an oral examination was negatively correlated with degree of muscularity (Bridges and Jones, 1968). Such factors are only now beginning to receive the experimental attention they deserve, and most of the human studies using corticoids as an emotional respondent have ignored them.

One of the most thoughtful papers concerned with plasma corticoids as respondents in human emotions came from Mason's group at Walter Reed Hospital in 1957 (Price *et al.*, 1957). They studied patients prior to thoracic or cardiac surgery with psychiatric interviews, psychological test responses, and measurements of plasma and urinary corticoids. On the day prior to surgery mean plasma corticoids were significantly elevated (17.7 μg/100 ml; normal = 12 μg/100 ml). Increases in plasma corticoids did not correlate with specific emotions or with how anxious the patient appeared, but did correlate with what the authors called distress-involvement. By this term they meant the clinical judgment of the "extent to which a patient made active emotional participation with his environment." Their summary still reads well: "The major conclusion suggested by our findings is that the response of the pituitary-adrenocortical system is related to emotional processes, and further, that it is probably not associated with a single specific emotional state, such as anxiety or fear, but rather, is associated with a number of emotional states that have the relatively undifferentiated component of distress-involvement."

The words "involvement" or "emotional participation" direct our attention to the subject's perception of the physical or social stress stimuli. For a subject, his distress is what he perceives. This is an important insight, but it has proven to be difficult to refine or quantify. In a series of papers, Mason and his students (Mason, 1968b) argued that individual differences in 17-OHCS responses to intuitively distressful situations (e.g., parents of a hospitalized leukemic child, soldiers in combat) reflect the use of psychological defense mechanisms, particularly denial, that prevent realistic perception and appraisal. When the defense fails, the 17-OHCS increase. Without a measure of perception or of defense mechanisms other than 17-OHCS, there is a great danger of circularity in this argument which attempts to relate emotional involvement, defense mechanisms, and 17-OHCS.

In 1958 Persky and his colleagues reported a study that is often quoted as demonstrating a linear relationship between increases of 17-OHCS and increases of affect. They measured plasma corticoids before and after a stress interview (Persky *et al.*, 1958). The stress interviews produced relatively small changes in affect ratings, but the authors reported that changes in affect were associated with *less decrease* of plasma corticoid over the 90-minute test period. (Note that there was not an absolute increase of plasma corticoids.) The authors claimed that the small, inferred increases in plasma corticoids correlated linearly and significantly with changes in affect rating, but none of their correlation coefficients for individual subjects were statistically significant (their Table 6). This paper is a good example of a small phenomenon analyzed to death.

Among the numerous human investigations (Mason, 1968b), the measurement of corticoids in depression is pertinent to the discussion of corticoids as an emotional respondent because depression varies in clinical intensity. Gibbons and McHugh (1962) noted that patients judged to be severely depressed by interview and appearance had higher plasma corticoids than mildly depressed patients. As severely depressed patients improved, their plasma corticoids frequently decreased, but this did not always occur. Furthermore, these workers frequently observed both increases and decreases in the plasma corticoid level without a change in clinical rating of severity. Subsequent work (for review, see

Sachar, 1967; Stokes, 1972) has confirmed these results in severely depressed patients and has found variable and small corticoid changes in mild depression.

Recently, Sachar *et al.* (1970) claimed to have delineated a small core of symptoms within the syndrome of depression which correlated with the change in cortisol production better than global clinical judgments of depression. This provocative claim requires independent confirmation because it promises a quantification of emotional intensity in depression. Such a reliable scoring of emotional intensity would facilitate an analysis of corticoids as a respondent in human psychological and clinical studies that could be compared to the results obtained by Natelson *et al.* during defense reactions in monkeys (Section III,B,3). Sachar *et al.* (1970) have not commented on this possibility in their work, but they have emphasized that cortisol production correlates best with core symptoms reflecting emotional turmoil and have argued that increased corticoids are not part of the depressive illness itself (whatever that is). It is important to recognize that this view is an echo of that published by Mason and his colleagues 15 years ago (Price *et al.,* 1957).

6. Summary

Psychological stimuli can drive the adrenocortical system at nearly maximal rate. The perception of the stimulus is important: stimuli judged noxious and avoided, if possible, are effective stimulants of corticoids; stimuli judged rewarding and approached, if possible, are not. Since perception is crucial, it is not surprising that the corticoid response of an organism to an explicit stimulus is shaped by the developmental, social, or conditioning history of the organism.

Although plasma corticoids respond to psychological stimuli, the range of response is narrow (about 2-fold), and the appropriate parameter of response (absolute value, mean change, peak change, etc.) to be used as a respondent is not established. The major limitation on the use of corticoids as respondents, however, is that no parameter of corticoid response sensitively reflects different intensities of physical stimuli or emotional excitement between threshold and maximal emotional stimulation.

There is another problem. Relationship between the concentration of ACTH and the adrenocortical response depends on blood flow and the exposure of the adrenal gland to ACTH in the preceding 8 hours. Thus, the same concentration of ACTH which should be closely related to hypothalamic activity of CRF neurons and, perhaps, to emotional excitement, can produce quite different adrenocortical responses. Until ACTH and corticoids are measured simultaneously as emotional respondents, we will not know how often the absolute concentration or the change of plasma corticoids has misled investigators in the longitudinal studies of individual cases or in the comparison of individuals or groups.

IV. Adrenal Hormones as Mechanisms of Emotional Behavior

A. Adrenal Catecholamines

1. Cannon's Theory of Peripheral Emergency Functions

From the classic studies of Cannon (1915) and his students emerged "the general thesis that the bodily changes which attend great excitement are directed towards efficiency in physical struggle." Epinephrine, released from the adrenal medulla, was a cornerstone of this view. Epinephrine performed emergency functions in behavior by increasing blood glucose, hastening blood coagulation, increasing the number of red blood cells, and decreasing muscular fatigue. These emergency functions of epinephrine permitted efficient behavior but did not affect behavioral functions directly. Epinephrine did not produce emotional states, and it was not necessary for emotional expression. Epinephrine served the muscles, not the brain.

Although Cannon's theory is still widely quoted, its authority has been eroded by the flow of new data. For example, the theory does not account for those numerous occasions in animals and man when the visceral excitement of emotion is not accompanied by physical struggle or flight. Furthermore, Cannon believed that the metabolic effects of epinephrine served the "laboring muscles." It is now clear, however, that the metabolic responses to epinephrine are a mobilization of free fatty acids and glucose, and an inhibition of insulin secretion. This metabolic pattern results when epinephrine is infused (Porte *et al.*, 1966; Kris *et al.*, 1966) or when endogenous epinephrine is released during glucoprivation (Smith *et al.*, 1973), during defense reactions elicited by hypothalamic stimulation (Natelson *et al.*, 1973), or during the performance of a free-operant avoidance task (Mason *et al.*, 1968b). The metabolic pattern of a low concentration of insulin and a high concentration of fatty acids restricts glucose entry into skeletal muscle and tends to conserve glucose for the brain. Thus, recent evidence confirms the suggestion of Gaddum and Holzbauer (1957) that the primary purpose of epinephrine is to maintain the supply of sugar to the brain and not to the muscles. (See Natelson *et al.*, 1973, for further discussion.)

2. Epinephrine and Emotions

The possibility that epinephrine affects behavioral functions of the brain was not part of Cannon's theory, but this possibility has received considerable experimental attention. One recurrent hypothesis has been that the endogenous secretion of epinephrine produced emotional states. Despite what appeared to be the decisive results of Cannon *et al.* (1929) and of Sherrington (1900) which showed that removal of epinephrine by adrenalectomy plus bilateral sympathectomy (and vagotomy) did not abolish emotional expression in animals, the hypothesis has been repeatedly tested by administering epinephrine to human subjects and recording their symptoms and signs. Increasing technical sophistication and research design have merely confirmed the early report of Cantril and Hunt (1932) that the injection of epinephrine alone usually produced a state which did not mimic a real emotion ("cold") and which lacked constant affective correlates.

In 1962, Schachter and Singer (1962) provided an important perspective on the problem by demonstrating that when the social and cognitive aspects of the experimental conditions were appropriate, epinephrine intensified a variety of real emotional states. Thus emotions are specified by environmental cues and the experience of the organism. Epinephrine does not elicit any emotion, but epinephrine intensifies all emotions. This relationship of nonspecificity between emotions and epinephrine was also the relationship established by the work correlating epinephrine excretion and spontaneous or experimental emotional states (see Section II,A,2). The validity of this relationship is strengthened by finding it in two kinds of experimental results.

3. Epinephrine and Avoidance Behavior

A related, but more explicit, hypothesis for a behavioral function for epinephrine was put forward by Mowrer and Lamoreaux (1946) when they suggested that fear was an intervening variable in all conditioning experiments in which the UCS was noxious. Although they discussed fear as a hypothetical construct, they were optimistic that ". . . its reality and drive quality could almost certainly be independently confirmed." Mowrer and Lamoreaux suggested an experimental test for the embodiment of fear:

> Whether the paired presentation of a CS and a noxious UCS automatically results in the development of an avoidant CR, without the concomitant occurrence of fear, could be interestingly tested in animals which have been sympathectomized. Here one would have living

> organisms in which the central nervous system (including the so-called associative centers) and the afferent and efferent pathways are entirely intact but in which *the auxiliary autonomic mechanism which mediates the second drive of fear* had been eliminated. Here the opportunity for purely "associative learning" as traditionally conceived (and also "cognitive reorganization") would presumably be unimpaired; but our prediction is that actual avoidance conditioning would be strikingly depressed, if not altogether absent. (Italics are mine.)

Wynne and Solomon (1955) took up the experimental challenge by blocking the function of the peripheral sympathetic nervous system and adrenal medulla in dogs with surgical or pharmacological treatments and then training such dogs to avoid an intense, subtetanizing shock in a two-way shuttlebox situation. All seven sympathectomized dogs achieved the criterion of 10 avoidance responses in 10 trials, but four dogs showed abnormal acquisition and extinction, and one dog showed abnormal extinction. Two dogs, however, had normal acquisition and extinction. Treated dogs had decreased signs of emotional upset to electric shock and relatively little stereotyping of responses during extinction (Table III). Two dogs had peripheral sympathetic blockade *after* they acquired the avoidance response; their extinction behavior was normal.

Subsequent work analyzed the effects of increased or decreased epinephrine on fear, and on conditioned behaviors which are presumed to involve fear (conditioned emotional response, passive and active avoidance, Table III). Using a variety of measures and conditions, most investigators have reported that epinephrine increased fear or lowered the aversive threshold (Singer, 1963; Kamano, 1968; Leventhal and Killackey, 1968; Paré, 1969). Stewart and Brookshire (1968) failed to observe an increased suppression ratio during CER after epinephrine. Paré and Cullen (1971) observed slow acquisition of CER (with food) in demedullated rats, but Leshner *et al.* (1971) did not affect CER (with water) by demedullation.

The effects of epinephrine on active avoidance are much less consistent. Acquisition has been prolonged by epinephrine (Sines, 1959), by depletion of epinephrine with reserpine (Sines, 1959), and by removal of epinephrine by adrenal demedullation (Levine and Soliday, 1962). Conner and Levine (1969) restored normal acquisition in demedullated rats by injecting small doses of epinephrine. Acquisition has been enhanced by epinephrine in intact rats (Latané and Schachter, 1962), but Stewart and Brookshire (1967) failed to replicate this result. In a series of negative experiments, Moyer and Bunnell showed no effect of epinephrine, adrenalectomy, or adrenal demedullation (Moyer, 1958; Moyer and Bunnell, 1958, 1959) (Table III).

Moyer (1958) also reported that adrenalectomy did not alter performance; epinephrine did not affect (Stewart and Brookshire, 1968) or decreased performance (Kosman and Gerard, 1955). This deterioration of performance was probably due to toxic effects of epinephrine (Kosman and Gerard, 1955). Finally, neither epinephrine (Leshner and Stewart, 1966) nor adrenalectomy (Moyer, 1958) altered the rate of extinction of active avoidance.

Although the positive results noted above deserve our closest attention, the numerous negative reports suggest that the appropriate conditions are not easily arranged. The inconsistency of the results may derive not only from technical details but also from the mistaken hypothesis that epinephrine is the *dominant* mechanism underlying the acquired fear drive in active avoidance. This hypothesis is a constant theme in the papers cited, but if epinephrine, as we have seen, *increases the intensity* of emotional mechanisms, then we need an experimental strategy based on the parametric relationships of epinephrine to the biological mechanisms of active avoidance behavior.

Conner and Levine (1969) have suggested that the parametric relationship between epinephrine and active avoidance is an inverted U-shaped curve. They quote the following support for this suggestion: (*1*) removal of epinephrine (demedullation) slows acquisition (Conner and Levine, 1969); (*2*) small doses of epinephrine increase the rate of acquisition of demedullated rats (Conner and Levine, 1969) and of intact rats (Latané and Schachter, 1962); and (*3*) large doses decrease performance (Kosman and Gerard, 1955).

A corollary of this hypothesis has been tested in humans by Frankenhaeuser and Jarpe (1963). They infused epinephrine (.05, .10, .15 or .20 μg/kg per minute) into five subjects and recorded changes of blood pressure, heart rate, subjective reactions, recent memory for nonsense syllables, and performance of a timed mathematical task. The magnitude of the responses tended to be related to the dose of epinephrine, but the correlation of doses of epinephrine with the magnitude and duration of the responses varied greatly. Cardiovascular responses showed large changes (systolic blood pressure +27.5%, diastolic blood pressure—20.8% and heart rate +18.1%) which were maintained throughout the infusion. Magnitude estimates of subjective reactions increased 38.8%, but these large changes occurred primarily at the beginning of the infusion and were *not* sustained. Performance of the mathematical task improved slightly (+7.8%) and showed very little increase with doses above .10 μg/kg per minute. Retrieval of nonsense syllables immediately or 20 minutes later was not affected by any dose of epinephrine. These results are consistent with the hypothesis that epinephrine can alter be-

TABLE III

Behavioral Effects of Epinephrine

Investigator	Treatment	Test situation	Results
Wynne and Solomon (1955)	Surgical or pharmacological blockade of peripheral sympathetic system.	Acquisition and extinction of active avoidance.	Slower acquisition, more rapid extinction.
Kosman and Gerard (1955)	Epinephrine (6.0 mg/kg).	Performance of active avoidance.	Decreased performance, probably toxic effect.
Moyer and Bunnell (1958)	Epinephrine (.3, .6, or .9 mg/kg).	Acquisition of active avoidance.	No effect.
Moyer (1958)	Adrenalectomy.	Acquisition and extinction of escape.	No effect on acquisition, extinction, or latencies of escape responding.
Sines (1959)	Epinephrine (.2 or .4 mg/kg) or reserpine (.08 mg/kg).	Acquisition of active avoidance.	Both treatments slowed acquisition.
Moyer and Bunnell (1959)	Adrenal demedullation.	Acquisition of active avoidance.	No effect.
Sharpless (1961)	Epinephrine.	Negative reinforcement in T maze.	No effect.
Levine and Soliday (1962)	Adrenal demedullation.	Acquisition of active avoidance.	Poor acquisition (slower rate and lower asymptote).
Latané and Schachter (1962)	Epinephrine (.125 mg, .25 mg, or .50 mg/kg).	Acquisition of active avoidance.	Low dose (.125 mg/kg) improved acquisition (faster rate and higher asymptote).
Singer (1963)	Epinephrine (.05 mg or .10 mg/kg).	UCR to light, bell, and buzzer. UCR to test box alone.	Increased responsiveness to light, bell, and buzzer, but no effect on responsiveness to test box alone.

Leshner and Stewart (1966)	Epinephrine (.1 mg, 1.0 mg, or 3.0 mg/kg).	Extinction of active avoidance.	No effect.
Stewart and Brookshire (1967)	Epinephrine.	Acquisition of active avoidance.	No effect (failure to replicate Latané and Schachter).
Kamano (1968)	Epinephrine (.1 mg/kg).	Safe and fear compartment where received 20 shocks 3 weeks before.	Treated rats spent less time in fear compartment.
Stewart and Brookshire (1968)	Epinephrine (.1–7.0 mg/kg).	CER and performance of active avoidance.	No effect.
Leventhal and Killackey (1968)	Epinephrine (.08 mg/kg).	Light and buzzer.	Increased fear.
Paré (1969)	Adrenal demedullation or epinephrine (1.0 or 2.0 mg/kg).	Titration or Tilt cage estimate of aversive threshold.	No effect in demedullated rats; epinephrine (1.0 mg/kg) may lower aversive threshold.
Conner and Levine (1969)	Adrenal demedullation.	Acquisition of active avoidance.	Slower acquisition; normal acquisition was restored by epinephrine.
Paré and Cullen (1971)	Epinephrine (.05 mg); adrenal demedullation ± dibenzyline (.5 mg).	Titration estimate of aversive threshold, CER.	Epinephrine lowered threshold; demedullation ± dibenzyline raised threshold and slowed acquisition of CER.
Leshner et al. (1971)	Adrenal demedullation.	CER.	No effect.

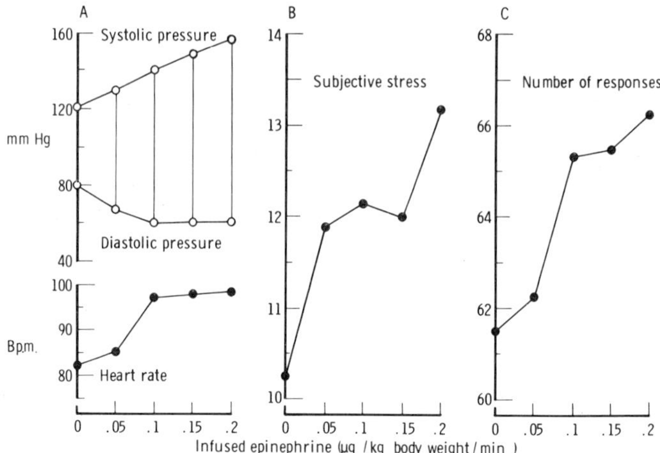

FIG. 13. Cardiovascular changes (panel A), subjective reactions (panel B), and performance of a timed mathematical task (panel C) of five subjects infused with four different doses of epinephrine. Mean values are plotted. Systolic blood pressure changes directly with dose of epinephrine, but none of the other responses do. Note that the displays of subjective stress and number of responses have exaggerated the very small changes of these parameters (redrawn from Frankenhaeuser, 1971).

havioral performance in a dose-related fashion, but they are not strong evidence. (Presumably, the range of doses tested here are on the ascending arm of the hypothesized inverted U-shaped curve.) I wish to emphasize the small mean change in performance in these experiments and the fact that individual data did not show orderly quantitative relationships between changes or response patterns of physiological, psychological, or performance variables.

4. Summary

Cannon's physiological work on emergency functions of the organism attracted attention to the role of epinephrine in emotions. Cannon and his students believed that during emotions, epinephrine mediated many emergency functions including the enhancement of skeletal muscular contraction and the mobilization of glucose to satisfy the increased metabolic requirements of the "laboring muscles." New data have demonstrated, however, that the emotional hyperglycemia elicited by epinephrine serves the brain, not the muscles.

New data have also demonstrated that epinephrine has important behavioral functions. Epinephrine intensifies emotions, but it does not elicit emotions. Emotions appear to be elicited and specified by environmental cues and the experience of the organism.

Since epinephrine intensifies emotional excitement, its role as a mechanism in emotional behavior has been extensively investigated. When epinephrine is removed by surgical or pharmacological techniques, acquisition of a variety of avoidance tasks is usually slower than normal. Epinephrine does not seem to affect performance or extinction except when large doses produce toxic symptoms. From the available data, Conner and Levine (1969) suggested that the shape of the parametric relationship between epinephrine and avoidance behavior was an inverted U-shaped curve. This hypothesis is consistent with some of the data, but it has not been tested with the quantitative rigor it requires.

B. ADRENAL GLUCOCORTICOIDS

1. Biological Significance of Corticoid Responses

The biological significance of the corticoid response to social and psychological stimuli which do not produce tissue damage has been debated. The prevailing view has been that these corticoid responses to potential conflict are vestiges of corticoid responses that served real conflict. Such an explanation can be traced through Cannon to Darwin. Modern proponents of this explanation often forget how much evidence Darwin assembled before asserting that a phenomenon was vestigal. Barcroft (1934) opposed this kind of explanation with characteristic eloquence:

> Accidents happen in nature as elsewhere, but having regard to the above and other considerations, I range myself on the side of those who regard a phenomenon as more likely to have a significance than not. Those who think with me must shoulder the burden of discovering what the significance may be, but on our opponents rests the much heavier burden of proving the phenomenon to be an accident, if indeed it be such.

If the increase of ACTH or corticoids observed during social or psychological threat improved neural function to facilitate behavioral adaptation, the search for biological significance could end. Liddell *et al.* (1935) made the seminal observation that adrenocortical extracts reduced the signs of experimental neurosis in sheep. Like so much of the good work on the biology of emotions done in the 1930's, these important results were not followed up.

Then in 1953 Mirsky and his colleagues reported that monkeys treated with ACTH showed much higher lever pressing behavior in a conflict situation with food reward (Mirsky *et al.*, 1953). Treatment with ACTH also increased the rate of extinction of free-operant avoidance behavior. This result during extinction is different from results with rats (see below); it has not yet been replicated.

2. ACTH, Corticoids, and Active Avoidance

In 1955, Applezweig and Baudry were stimulated by Mowrer's hypothesis of avoidance conditioning (see Section IV,A,3) to study the effect of hypophysectomy on the acquisition of two-way active avoidance (Applezweig and Baudry, 1955). The results were impressive: six of seven hypophysectomized rats failed to reach criterion. When four hypophysectomized rats were injected with ACTH, two rats reached normal criterion. The authors concluded that hypophysectomy interfered with, but did not abolish, the acquisition of active avoidance behavior. Of the many hormonal deficits produced by hypophysectomy, Applezweig and Baudry suggested that ACTH was particularly important. It was not clear in these experiments whether ACTH improved acquisition directly or whether the ACTH effect was due to the stimulation of adrenal steroids.

DeWied (1964) tested the suggested importance of ACTH in a careful study of acquisition of active avoidance by adenohypophysectomized rats. He confirmed that adenohypophysectomized rats had marked impairment of acquisition, although 6 of 21 adenohypophysectomized rats achieved criterion. Treatment with a long-acting ACTH preparation improved the rate of conditioning. But DeWied noted that the adenohypophysectomized rats were debilitated, and that they escaped a noxious stimulus in a runway more slowly than normal, indicating that the motor and sensory capacities of these rats were seriously impaired. Furthermore, improvement of avoidance responding was produced not only by ACTH, but also by a combination of cortisone, testosterone, and thyroxine. Thus, DeWied argued that the deficiency in learning capacity of adenohypophysectomized rats did not seem to depend on the absence of ACTH alone, but on the general debilitation resulting from the hormonal deficiencies produced by adenohypophysectomy.

DeWied reinvestigated the problem by treating hypophysectomized rats with synthetic fragments of ACTH devoid of metabolic or adrenocortical activity. Such fragments increased the rate of avoidance acquisition of hypophysectomized rats (DeWied, 1969). The smallest effective fragment was the heptapeptide comprising amino acids 4–10 of ACTH (Fig. 14). These results were strong evidence that the interference with avoidance learning observed in the hypophysectomized rat was not

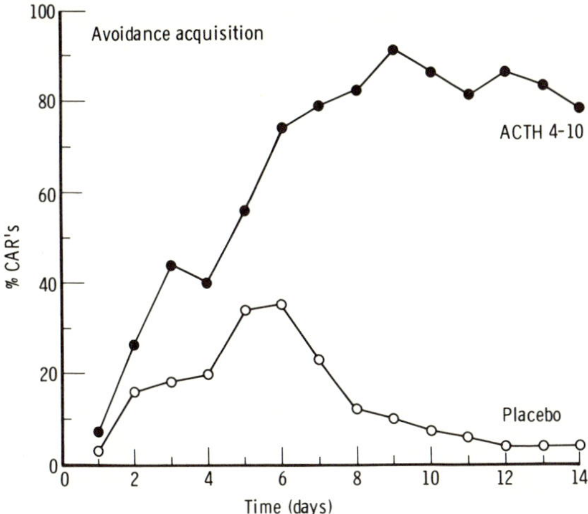

Fig. 14. Marked improvement of active avoidance by male hypophysectomized rats injected with a heptapeptide fragment of ACTH which had no adrenocortical stimulation activity. The lower curve traces the performance of male hypophysectomized rats treated with placebo injections (redrawn from DeWied, 1969).

caused by debilitation alone. Moreover, the behavioral action of ACTH was an extraadrenal effect which required only a small portion of the parent molecule. The possibility that the pituitary is a source of peptides distinct from ACTH or other known hormones and which enhance avoidance learning has been pursued with some success by DeWied *et al.* (1970). Simultaneous with DeWied's report, Bohus and Endroczi (1965) showed that ACTH increased active avoidance responses and decreased intertrial responses when administered on the second day of acquisition. This effect of ACTH was also extraadrenal because it occurred in adrenalectomized rats.

Beatty *et al.* (1970) showed that either adrenalectomy which produced high endogenous ACTH or the injection of large doses of ACTH improved the avoidance learning of rats trained with high intensity of shock (1.5 mA), but not those trained with low intensity (0.5 mA). These effects on avoidance were not due to changes in the reactivity to light (conditioned stimulus, CS) or to changes in spontaneous activity prior to training. The authors then performed the counterexperiment of suppressing endogenous ACTH by injecting large doses of the synthetic glucocorticoid dexamethasone. Despite low levels of circulating ACTH, dexamethasone-treated rats showed *normal* acquisition of avoidance. This result clearly demonstrated that the extraadrenal behavioral effect of endogenous ACTH in avoidance learning was neither necessary nor sufficient for normal acquisition. This conclusion is reinforced by the report of normal acquisition of active avoidance by hypophysectomized or adrenalectomized rats under certain conditions (Weiss *et al.*, 1970).

The review of these results emphasizes that poor acquisition is a necessary condition for the demonstration of an extraadrenal effect of ACTH on acquisition. ACTH treatment acts to normalize defective avoidance learning in hypophysectomized rats (DeWied, 1969) and in rats tested with high intensity shock (Beatty *et al.*, 1970), but ACTH does not improve normal avoidance learning (Murphy and Miller, 1955; Miller and Ogawa, 1962; Moyer, 1966).

The possibility that the interference with avoidance learning observed 1–4 hours after fear conditioning (Kamin effect) was related to decreased ACTH was suggested by the observation that the curves correlating plasma corticosterone or number of avoidance responses with intersession interval were U-shaped, with their nadirs at 1–4 hours after fear conditioning (Brush and Levine, 1966). When ACTH was injected at the time of the nadir, both the plasma corticosterone and number of avoidance responses increased (Levine and Brush, 1967). It was interesting that no behavioral effect was observed after ACTH injections at later times when avoidance responding was normal. Injections of hydrocortisone, but not corticosterone, also improved avoidance responding at the 1-hour intersession interval. These promising results have not been confirmed. Kasper-Pandi *et al.* (1970) failed to improve active avoidance at 1 or 4 hours with injections of dexamethasone. Furthermore, they found high corticosterone values (and assumed high circulating ACTH) in their control series of rats at the times (1 and 4 hours) of inferior performance. Suboski *et al.* (1970) reported that adrenalectomized rats (with high ACTH) displayed this incubation phenomenon 4 hours after initial training on CER, passive, or active (two-way) avoidance. Finally, manipulations of the pituitary-adrenal system by adrenalectomy, by dexamethasone administration, or a combination of these treatments failed to significantly change the poor active avoidance responding at 1 hour after original training (Barrett *et al.*, 1971). With this flurry of negative results, the hypothesis that low pituitary-adrenocortical secretion is causally related to the train-retest avoidance function does not seem worth pursuing.

3. ACTH, Corticoids, and Passive Avoidance

Koranyi *et al.* (1967) demonstrated an effect of ACTH on passive avoidance. When hypoactive mice received ACTH prior to being shocked in a passive avoidance test, the mice showed much greater suppression of the approach response than control mice. These data supported the idea that ACTH affected the acquisition of passive avoidance.

In a "step-out" passive avoidance test, Weiss *et al.* (1970) observed that hypophysectomized rats (low ACTH and low corticosterone) came out more readily and defecated less than normals or adrenalectomized rats (Table IV). Adrenalectomized rats (high ACTH, no corticosterone) came out slowest and defecated the most. When the shock compartment was disguised, both adrenalectomized and hypophysectomized rats entered readily, but the latency to enter differed. Hypophysectomized rats had significantly shorter latencies than normal, but adrenalectomized rats had abnormally long latencies. There was no difference in activity between the operated and normal rats. The authors interpreted these results as evidence that high ACTH (adrenalectomized rats) facilitated arousal or emotionality by an extraadrenal mechanism which potentiated fear responding. The effect was best seen when there were few experimental cues to elicit fear (disguised shock chamber). Because the hormonal states were maintained through the acquisition and extinction

TABLE IV

MEASURES OF THE BEHAVIOR OF NORMAL, HYPOPHYSECTOMIZED (HYPOX) AND ADRENALECTOMIZED (ADX) RATS IN A "STEP OUT" PASSIVE AVOIDANCE TEST[a]

		Fear tests			Environmental stimuli changed
Group	Before shock	1	2	3	
		Number rats entering shock compartment			
Hypox	20	11[a,d]	16[d]	12	20
Normal	20	4	13	12	19
Adx	20	5	9	11	14
		Median latency to enter shock compartment, seconds			
Hypox	7.3	263.2	176.5	161.7	16.1[c,e]
Normal	6.6	300.0	248.6	233.0	47.8
Adx	6.5	300.0	300.0	276.0	144.9[b]
		Mean number boluses defecated			
Hypox	.3	1.5[e]	2.2[d]	1.7	.3
Normal	.3	2.8	2.4	2.5	.5
Adx	.5	5.2[a]	4.4	2.8	1.2

[a] Adrenalectomized rats came out slowest and defecated the most. Superscripts denote statistical difference from normal rats ([a] = $p < 0.05$, [b] = $p < 0.01$, [c] = $p < 0.001$) and from adrenalectomized rats ([d] = $p < 0.05$ and [e] = $p < 0.001$) (data from Weiss *et al.*, 1970).

phases of the experiment, the results do not distinguish an effect on acquisition from an effect on extinction.

The results of Guth *et al.* (1971), however, provided elegant evidence for an effect of ACTH on acquisition of passive avoidance. They demonstrated that a single injection of ACTH 10 minutes before a punishment trial significantly strengthened the passive avoidance response acquired on that trial.

Thus, in contrast to active avoidance where ACTH improves defective acquisition, but does not change normal acquisition, ACTH potentiates the normal acquisition of passive avoidance. There is strong evidence that this effect of ACTH on acquisition of active or passive avoidance behavior is extraadrenal and is not due to changes in the behavioral responsiveness of rats to electric shock. Paré (1969) found that adrenalectomized rats were normally responsive to electric shock judged by a titration technique or by spatial preference. The shock threshold of adrenalectomized rats for flinching was observed to be slightly higher than hypophysectomized rats, and hypophysectomized rats had normal (Gibbs *et al.*, 1973) or slightly lower thresholds than normal (Gispen *et al.*, 1970). The decapeptide, ACTH 1-10, had no effect (Gispen *et al.*, 1970).

4. ACTH, Corticoids, and Extinction

In 1955, Murphy and Miller (1955) did an important experiment. They demonstrated that injections of ACTH prolonged extinction of active avoidance. Miller and Ogawa (1962) replicated this result in adrenalectomized rats. This indicated that the effect of ACTH on extinction was extraadrenal.

Levine and Jones (1965) produced a significant suppression of lever pressing for water after exposure to two single shock sessions by injecting ACTH each day prior, during, and after the shock sessions. If ACTH treatment was terminated after the second shock session, the suppression was not different than control rats. These data suggested that ACTH prolonged extinction of the suppression of lever pressing. Anderson *et al.* (1968) confirmed this effect of ACTH on extinction in hypophysectomized rats and reported that injections of hydrocortisone did not replicate it.

DeWied then demonstrated that extinction was prolonged by the high ACTH produced by adrenalectomy (DeWied, 1967). His investigation of the effect of corticosterone yielded a symmetrical behavioral result—corticosterone facilitated extinction. Corticosterone did not facilitate extinction by suppressing endogenous ACTH because corticosterone facilitated extinction of hypophysectomized rats (DeWied, 1967). These impressive results were quickly confirmed by Bohus *et al.* (1968) and by Bohus and Lissak (1968).

In a brilliant series of experiments, DeWied and his colleagues extended his initial observations in several ways. With the same synthetic fragments of ACTH which he had used in studying acquisition, DeWied found that the same heptapeptide (ACTH 4-10) prolonged extinction. The behavioral effect of the slightly larger peptide (ACTH 1-10) was shown to be independent of its thyroid-stimulating activity (DeWied and Pirie, 1968). Bohus and DeWied (1966) made the remarkable discovery that the heptapeptide ACTH (4-10) in which the amino acid phenylalanine in the seventh position is replaced by the D-isomer, had an opposite effect on extinction (Fig. 15). This D-isomer of ACTH 4-10 was even more powerful in hypophysectomized rats, so that its behavioral action was direct and not an antagonism of endogenous ACTH at receptor sites.

Van Wimersma Greidanus and DeWied established that the site of action of ACTH and corticosterone on extinction was central by demonstrating positive results after intracerebral implantation of ACTH or corticosterone (Van Wimersma Greidanus and DeWied, 1969, 1971). Corticosterone and dexamethasone were most effective in medial midline thalamic structures (particularly n. parafascicularis) and in the

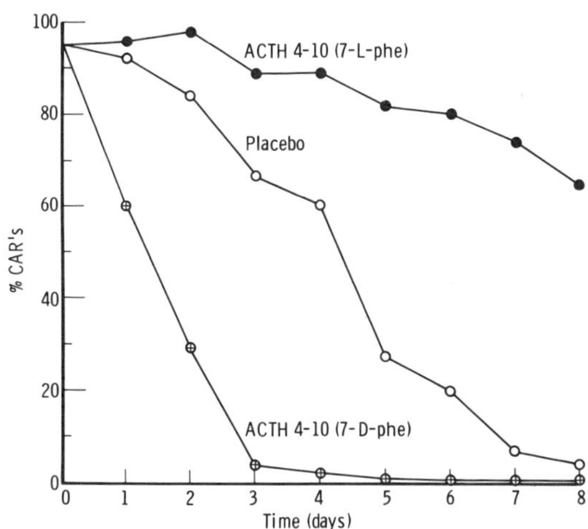

FIG. 15. The heptapeptide of ACTH (ACTH 4-10) which has the L-phenylalanine in position 7 prolonged extinction of avoidance. When D-phenylalanine was substituted into ACTH 4-10 at position 7, injection of the heptapeptide facilitated extinction. This is a remarkable demonstration of molecular specificity of behavioral effects (redrawn from DeWied, 1969).

lateral ventricle. ACTH (1-10) was effective in the same posterior thalamic region, in the region of the rostral mesencephalon and the caudal diencephalon, and also in the lateral ventricle. This work on extinction is the best experimental penetration into the daunting problem of the behavioral effects of ACTH and corticoids.

5. Summary

The biological significance of ACTH and corticoid secretion during social or psychological threat has been frequently considered vestigial— a failure of this neuroendocrine system to differentiate between threat and bodily injury. During the past decade, a number of investigators have entertained the possibility that these hormones have behavioral functions. The results are impressive. In active avoidance, ACTH improves defective acquisition but does not change normal acquisition. In passive avoidance, ACTH potentiates normal acquisition. In addition to these effects on acquisition, ACTH prolongs extinction. The corticoids do not have prominent effects in acquisition, but corticoids facilitate extinction. These behavioral effects of ACTH are not mediated by increased secretion of adrenal corticoids, and they are not due to changes in the behavioral responsiveness of rats to electric shock. At least in the case of extinction, the behavioral effects of ACTH or corticosterone can be obtained by treating the brain directly with small quantities of hormone. Most of the effective sites are in the diencephalon.

V. Formulation

A. Adrenal Catecholamines and Corticoids as Emotional Respondents

As emotional respondents, adrenal catecholamines and corticoids are reliable, nonspecific, and insensitive. They are reliable respondents because they always increase when there is a sufficiently large increase of emotional excitement. They are nonspecific respondents because they increase during a variety of emotional states. They are insensitive respondents because increases of catecholamines or corticoids do not sensitively reflect intensities of emotional excitement between threshold and maximal emotional stimulation. This insensitivity is the major limitation of catecholamines or corticoids as emotional respondents. Unfortunately, this insensitivity has not been widely recognized because urinary catecholamines or plasma or urinary corticoids have been frequently used to estimate the intensity of emotional excitement (stress) in the same individual at different times or in different individuals at the same time. Such research assumes that differences in catecholamines or corticoids sensitively reflect differences in emotional excitement, and we have seen that no currently available parameter of catecholamines or corticoids has such sensitivity.

Although currently available parameters of catecholamines or corticoids are not sensitive emotional respondents, it is possible that technical developments may improve their sensitivity. In the case of catecholamines, almost all of the respondent measurements have used urinary catecholamines. Since urinary catecholamine excretion is less than 6% of adrenal catecholamine secretion, a reliable technique for repetitive measurement of plasma epinephrine may permit a more accurate estimate of epinephrine secretion from the adrenal medulla and thus increase the respondent sensitivity of adrenal catecholamines.

In the case of corticoids, I do not think that methodological developments will increase their sensitivity as emotional respondents. The major reasons are (*1*) the range of corticoid response to ACTH is narrow (2- to 4-fold); (*2*) the response to ACTH is affected by the intensity of ACTH stimulation that has occurred in the preceding 6–8 hours; and (*3*) the response to ACTH is determined by the delivery of ACTH to the adrenal cortex which is dependent on the concentration of ACTH and adrenal blood flow. No one has attempted to control all of these factors during an investigation of emotions. Such an experiment will be very formidable.

In view of the problems with corticoids as respondents, the recent development of sensitive and reliable assays for ACTH is very welcome. These assays will permit the evaluation of ACTH as an emotional respondent. ACTH has several characteristics of a sensitive respondent: ACTH has a wide range of response (10- to 20-fold), a short half-life (less than 30 minutes), and is functionally close to the brain.

Even if measurements of plasma catecholamines and ACTH are used frequently as emotional respondents, a major problem remains. That problem is the relation between the activity of the neural systems controlling the rate of secretion of catecholamines or ACTH and the intensity of postulated central emotional states. We have reviewed the evidence that the adequate stimulus for both adrenal catecholamines and corticoids is not the intensity of the physical stimulus (electric shock, handling, gravitational stress, etc.), but the intensity of the *perceived stimulus*. There have been a variety of methods used to estimate intensity of the *perceived stimulus*. These include interviews, global clinical ratings, behavioral measurements, and scaling techniques. There has been very little attempt at cross-correlation of these techniques. There have been, however, frequent attempts to correlate such psychological estimates with urinary catecholamines or plasma or urinary corticoids. Because of the insensitivity of corticoids or catecholamines as emotional respondents, the meaning of these correlations is never clear. I believe one of the major obstacles to the study of emotions is the failure of investigators to develop, use, and validate an extensive battery of tests to scale the intensity of the *perceived stimulus*. Not only are such scaling techniques important in themselves, but they are essential for the determination of the sensitivity of any emotional respondent.

B. Adrenal Catecholamines, ACTH, and Corticoids as Mechanisms of Emotional Behavior

The role of epinephrine in emotions has been clarified. Epinephrine does not elicit specific emotions, but epinephrine intensifies the experience of a variety of emotions.

Since avoidance behavior builds on emotional excitement, a role for epinephrine in avoidance has been sought and found. Removal of epinephrine retards acquisition significantly, and replacement of epinephrine restores normal acquisition, at least under some conditions. Epinephrine has not been shown to have prominent effects on performance or extinction of avoidance.

The major discovery relating the pituitary adrenocortical system to behavior has been the dramatic effects of ACTH on active and passive avoidance. In active avoidance, ACTH improves defective acquisition but does not change normal acquisition. In passive avoidance, ACTH potentiates normal acquisition. But the most stunning effect has been the ability of ACTH to prolong extinction of avoidance, while corticoids facilitate extinction. All of these behavioral effects of ACTH are extra-adrenal, because they are produced by fractions of the molecule which have no stimulatory effect on the adrenal cortex. This finding has raised the possibility that there may be small peptides from the anterior pituitary gland with potent behavioral functions.

The effects of ACTH and corticosterone on extinction do not require systemic administration of the hormones. The effects can be obtained by hormonal treatment of small areas in the medial thalamus and posterior hypothalamus.

Important questions hover around the behavioral effects of catecholamines, ACTH, and corticoids. Are the endogenous concentrations of these hormones during acquisition or extinction of avoidance behavior adequate to produce these effects? What is the site(s) of action of epinephrine or ACTH, since neither of these hormones is known to penetrate the brain in significant amounts? If the classic action of hormones is to increase or decrease rates of intracellular reactions, what is the critical reaction(s) in which tissue(s) that results in such large behavioral effects? In their recent reviews, DeWied (1969) and Levine (1968) discuss numerous possible answers to these questions, but none of them persuade.

The startling results of the past decade, particularly the work concerned with ACTH, has proposed new behavioral functions for old hormones. To evaluate this proposal, we will have to be attentive to the quantitative aspects of the endogenous hormonal changes and the behavioral effects. But meticulous technique will only determine if the behavioral effects are physiological. To penetrate the problem, we require acts of the physiological imagination which bridge the chasm between the molecular and behavioral effects of these hormones.

Acknowledgments

I thank my colleagues W. T. Lhamon, P. R. McHugh, P. E. Stokes, J. Gibbs, and R. Young for criticizing an earlier version of the manuscript. Miss Lillian Wahrow, Medical Librarian for the Westchester Division of the New York Hospital, and the Brain Information Service of the University of California at Los Angeles provided bibliographic assistance. I am grateful to Mrs. Marion Jacobson and Mrs. Susan Sullivan for typing the manuscript. Preparation of this review and the experimental work from my laboratory which is referred to were supported by Public Health Service Grant NS 08042 and by Career Development Award 5 KO4 NS38601.

References

Ader, R., and Friedman, S. B. (1968). Plasma corticosterone response to environmental stimulation: Effects of duration of stimulation and the 24-hour adrenocortical rhythm. *Neuroendocrinology* 3, 378–386.

Ader, R., and Grota, L. J. (1969). Effects of early experience on adrenocortical reactivity. *Physiology & Behavior* 4, 303–305.

Ader, R., Friedman, S. B., and Grota, L. J. (1967). "Emotionality" and adrenal cortical function: effects of strain, test, and the 24-hour corticosterone rhythm. *Animal Behavior* 15, 37–44.

Anderson, D. C., Winn, W., and Taur, T. (1968). Adrenocorticotrophic hormone and acquisition of a passive avoidance response. *Journal of Comparative and Physiological Psychology* 66, 497–499.

Applezweig, M. H., and Baudry, F. D. (1955). The pituitary-adrenocortical system in avoidance learning. *Psychological Reports* 1, 417–420.

Ax, A. (1953). The physiological differentiation between fear and anger in humans. *Psychosomatic Medicine* 15, 433–442.

Axelrod, J. (1965). The metabolism, storage and release of catecholamines. *Recent Progress in Hormone Research* 21, 597–622.

Axelrod, J., Weil-Malherbe, H., and Tomchick, R. (1959). The physiological disposition of H³-epinephrine and its metabolite metanephrine. *Journal of Pharmacology and Experimental Therapeutics* **127**, 251–256.

Barcroft, J. (1934). "Features in the Architecture of Physiological Function," p. 357. Cambridge Univ. Press, London and New York.

Barrett, R. J., Leith, N. J., and Ray, O. S. (1971). The effects of pituitary-adrenal manipulations on time-dependent processes in avoidance learning. *Physiology & Behavior* **7**, 663–665.

Beatty, P. A., Beatty, W. W., Bowman, R. E., and Gilchrist, J. C. (1970). The effects of ACTH, adrenalectomy and dexamethasone on the acquisition of an avoidance response in rats. *Physiology & Behavior* **5**, 939–944.

Berson, S. A., and Yalow, R. S. (1968). Radioimmunoassay of ACTH in plasma. *Journal of Clinical Investigation* **47**, 2725–2751.

Bogdonoff, M. D., Estes, E. H., Harlan, W. R., Troit, D. L., and Kirshner, N. (1960). Metabolic and cardiovascular changes during a state of acute central nervous system arousal. *Journal of Clinical Endocrinology* **20**, 1333–1340.

Bohus, B., and DeWied, D. (1966). Inhibitory and facilitatory effect of two related peptides on extinction of avoidance behavior. *Science* **153**, 318–320.

Bohus, B., and Endroczi, E. (1965). The influence of pituitary-adrenocortical function on the avoiding conditioned reflex activity in rats. *Acta Physiologica* **26**, 183–189.

Bohus, B., and Lissak, K. (1968). Adrenocortical hormones and avoidance behavior of rats. *International Journal of Neuropharmacology* **7**, 301–306.

Bohus, B., Nyakas, C., and Endroczi, E. (1968). Effects of adrenocorticotropic hormone on avoidance behavior of intact and adrenalectomized rats. *International Journal of Neuropharmacology* **7**, 307–314.

Brady, J. V. (1964). Experimental studies of psychophysiological responses to stressful situations. *In* "Medical Aspects of Stress in the Military Climate," pp. 271–289. Walter Reed Army Inst. Res., Washington, D.C.

Bridges, P. K., and Jones, M. T. (1968). Relationship of personality and physique to plasma cortisol levels in response to anxiety. *Journal of Neurology, Neurosurgery and Psychiatry* **31**, 57–60.

Brush, F. R., and Levine, S. (1966). Adrenocortical activity and avoidance learning as a function of time after fear condi.ioning. *Physiology & Behavior* **1**, 309–311.

Cannon, W. B. (1915). "Bodily Changes in Pain, Hunger, Fear and Rage." Appleton, New York.

Cannon, W. B., Newton, H. F., Bright, E. M., Menkin, V., and Moore, R. M. (1929). Some aspects of the physiology of animals surviving complete exclusion of sympathetic nerve impulses. *American Journal of Physiology* **89**, 84–107.

Cantril, H., and Hunt, W. A. (1932). Emotional effects produced by the injection of adrenalin. *American Journal of Psychology* **44**, 300–307.

Conner, R. L., and Levine, S. (1969). The effects of adrenal hormones on the acquisition of signaled avoidance behavior. *Hormones and Behavior* **1**, 73–83.

Curtis, G. C., Cleghorn, R. A., and Sourkes, T. L. (1960). The relationship between affect and the excretion of adrenaline, noradrenaline and 17-hydroxycorticosteroids. *Journal of Psychosomatic Research* **4**, 176–184.

Dallman, M. F., and Yates, F. E. (1968). Anatomical and functional mapping of central neural input and feedback pathways of the adrenocortical system. *Memoirs of the Society for Endocrinology* **17**, 39–72.

DeWied, D. (1964). Influence of anterior pituitary on avoidance learning and escape behavior. *American Journal of Physiology* **207**, 255–259.

DeWied, D. (1967). Opposite effects of ACTH and glucocorticosteroids on extinction of conditioned avoidance behavior. *Proceedings of the International Congress on Hormonal Steroids, 2nd, Milan, 1966* pp. 945–951.

DeWied, D. (1969). Effects of peptide hormones on behavior. *In* "Frontiers in Neuroendocrinology, 1969" (L. Martini and W. F. Ganong, eds.), pp. 97–140. Oxford Univ. Press, London and New York.

DeWied, D., and Pirie, G. (1968). The inhibitory effect of ACTH 1-10 on extinction of a conditioned avoidance response: Its independence of thyroid function. *Physiology & Behavior* **3**, 355–358.

DeWied, D., Witter, A., and Laude, S. (1970). Anterior pituitary peptides and avoidance acquisition of hypophysectomized rats. *Progress in Brain Research* **32**, 213–220.

Douglas, W. W. (1968). Stimulus-secretion coupling: the concept and clues from chromaffin and other cells. *British Journal of Pharmacology* **34**, 451–474.

Elmadjian, F., Hope, J. M., and Lawson, B. A. (1957). Excretion of epinephrine and norepinephrine in various emotional states. *Journal of Clinical Endocrinology* **17**, 608–620.

Frankenhaeuser, M. (1971). Behavior and circulating catecholamines. *Brain Research* **31**, 241–262.

Frankenhaeuser, M., and Jarpe, G. (1963). Psychophysiological changes during infusions of adrenaline in various doses. *Psychopharmacologia* **4**, 424–432.

Frankenhaeuser, M., and Patkai, P. (1965). Interindividual differences in catecholamines excretion during stress. *Scandinavian Journal of Psychology* **6**, 117–123.

Frankenhaeuser, M., and Rissler, A. (1970). Effects of punishment on catecholamine release and efficiency of performance. *Psychopharmacologia* **17**, 378–390.

Frankenhaeuser, M., Sterky, K., and Jarpe, G. (1962). Psychophysiological relations in habituation to gravitational stress. *Perceptual and Motor Skills* **15**, 63–72.

Frankenhaeuser, M., Fröberg, J., and Mellis, I. (1965). Subjective and physiological reactions induced by electrical shocks of varying intensity. *Neuroendocrinology* **1**, 105–112.

Frankenhaeuser, M., Fröberg, J., Hagdahl, R., Rissler, A., Bjorkvall, C., and Wolff, B. (1967). Physiological, behavioral and subjective indices of habituation to psychological stress. *Physiology & Behavior* **2**, 229–237.

Frankenhaeuser, M., Mellis, I., Rissler, A., Bjorkvall, C., and Patkai, P. (1968). Catecholamine excretion as related to cognitive and emotional reaction patterns. *Psychosomatic Medicine* **30**, 109–120.

Friedman, S. B., and Ader, R. (1967). Adrenocortical response to novelty and noxious stimulation. *Neuroendocrinology* **2**, 209–212.

Friedman, S. B., Ader, R., Grota, L. J., and Larson, T. (1967). Plasma corticosterone response to parameters of electric shock stimulation in the rat. *Psychosomatic Medicine* **29**, 323–328.

Funkenstein, D. (1956). Nor-epinephrine-like and epinephrine-like substances in relation to human behavior. *Journal of Nervous and Mental Disease* **124**, 58–68.

Gaddum, J. H., and Holzbauer, M. (1957). Adrenaline and noradrenaline. *Vitamins and Hormones* 15, 151–203.

Gibbons, J. L., and McHugh, P. R. (1962). Plasma cortisol and depressive illness. *Journal of Psychiatric Research* 1, 162–171.

Gibbs, J., Sechzer, J. A., Smith, G. P., Conners, R., and Weiss, J. M. (1973). Behavioral responsiveness of adrenalectomized, hypophysectomized and intact rats to electric shock. *Journal of Comparative and Physiological Psychology* (in press).

Gispen, W. H., Van Wimersma Greidanus, T. J. B., and DeWied, D. (1970). Effects of hypophysectomy and ACTH 1-10 on responsiveness to electric shock in rats. *Physiology & Behavior* 5, 143–146.

Guth, S., Seward, J. P., and Levine, S. (1971). Differential manipulation of passive avoidance by exogenous ACTH. *Hormones and Behavior* 2, 127–138.

Hall, W. H., and Smith, G. P. (1969). Gastric secretory response to chronic hypothalamic stimulation in monkeys. *Gastroenterology* 57, 491–499.

Haltmeyer, G. C., Denenberg, V. H., and Zarrow, M. X. (1967). Modification of the plasma corticosterone response as a function of infantile stimulation and electric shock parameters. *Physiology & Behavior* 2, 61–63.

Hellman, L., Nakada, F., Curti, J., Weitzman, E. D., Kream, J., Roffwarg, H., Ellman, S., Fukushima, D., and Gallagher, T. F. (1970). Cortisol is secreted episodically by normal man. *Journal of Clinical Endocrinology* 30, 411–422.

Ingle, D. J., Higgins, G. M., and Kendall, E. C. (1938). Atrophy of the adrenal cortex in the rat produced by administration of large amounts of cortin. *Anatomical Record* 71, 363–372.

Johansson, G., Frankenhaeuser, M., and Lambert, W. (1969). Note on seasonal variations in catecholamine output. *Perceptual and Motor Skills* 28, 677–678.

Kamano, D. K. (1968). Enhancement of learned fear with epinephrine. *Psychonomic Science* 12, 331.

Kasper-Pandi, P., Hansing, R., and Usher, D. R. (1970). The effect of dexamethasone blockade of ACTH release on avoidance learning. *Physiology & Behavior* 5, 361–363.

Kendall, J. W. (1971). Feedback control of adrenocorticotropic hormone secretion. *In* "Frontiers in Neuroendocrinology, 1971" (W. F. Ganong and L. Martini, eds.), pp. 177–207. Oxford Univ. Press, London and New York.

Koranyi, L., Endroczi, E., Lissak, K., and Szepes, E. (1967). The effect of ACTH on behavioral processes motivated by fear in mice. *Physiology & Behavior* 2, 439–445.

Kosman, M. E., and Gerard, R. W. (1955). The effect of adrenaline on a conditioned avoidance response. *Journal of Comparative and Physiological Psychology* 48, 506–508.

Kris, A. O., Miller, R. E., Wherry, F. E., and Mason, J. W. (1966). Inhibition of insulin secretion by infused epinephrine in Rhesus monkeys. *Endocrinology* 78, 87–97.

Lashley, K. S. (1916). Reflex secretion of the human parotid gland. *Journal of Experimental Psychology* 1, 461–493.

Latané, B., and Schachter, S. (1962). Adrenalin and avoidance learning. *Journal of Comparative and Physiological Psychology* 55, 369–372.

Leshner, A. I., and Stewart, C. N. (1966). The effect of epinephrine on extinction of an avoidance response. *Psychonomic Science* 5, 89–90.

Leshner, A. I., Brookshire, K. H., and Stewart, C. N. (1971). The effects of adrenal demedullation on conditioned fear. *Hormones and Behavior* **2,** 43–48.

Leventhal, G. S., and Killackey, H. (1968). Adrenalin, stimulation and preference for familiar stimuli. *Journal of Comparative and Physiological Psychology* **65,** 152–155.

Levi, L. (1967). Sympatho-adrenomedullary responses to emotional stimuli: methodologic, physiologic and pathologic considerations. *In* "An Introduction to Clinical Neuroendocrinology" (E. Bajusz, ed.), pp. 78–105. Karger, Basel.

Levine, M. D., Gordon, T. P., Peterson, R. H., and Rose, R. M. (1970). Urinary 17-OHCS response of high- and low-aggressive rhesus monkeys to shock avoidance. *Physiology & Behavior* **5,** 919–924.

Levine, S. (1962). Plasma-free corticosteroid response to electric shock in rats stimulated in infancy. *Science* **135,** 795–796.

Levine, S. (1967). Maternal and environmental influences on the adrenocortical response to stress in weanling rats. *Science* **156,** 258–260.

Levine, S. (1968). Hormones and conditioning. *In* "Nebraska Symposium on Motivation" (W. J. Arnold, ed.), pp. 85–101. Univ. of Nebraska Press, Lincoln.

Levine, S., and Brush, F. R. (1967). Adrenocortical activity and avoidance learning as a function of time after avoidance training. *Physiology & Behavior* **2,** 385–388.

Levine, S., and Jones, L. E. (1965). Adrenocorticotropic hormone (ACTH) and passive avoidance learning. *Journal of Comparative and Physiological Psychology* **59,** 357–360.

Levine, S., and Soliday, S. (1962). An effect of adrenal demedullation on the acquisition of a conditioned avoidance response. *Journal of Comparative and Physiological Psychology* **55,** 214–216.

Liddell, H. S., Anderson, O. D., Kotyuka, E., and Hartman, F. A. (1935). The effect of extract of adrenal cortex on experimental neurosis in sheep. *Archives of Neurology and Psychiatry* **34,** 973–993.

Liddle, G. W. (1969). Physiological review of adrenocortical function. *In* "Hormonal Control Systems, Mathematical Biosciences Supplement 1" (E. B. Stear and A. H. Kadish, eds.), pp. 1–19. Amer. Elsevier, New York.

Liddle, G. W., Island, D., Rinfret, A. P., and Forsham, P. H. (1954). Factors enhancing the response of the human adrenal to corticotropin: Is there an adrenal growth factor? *Journal of Clinical Endocrinology and Metabolism* **14,** 839–858.

McCann, S. M., and Porter, J. C. (1969). Hypothalamic pituitary stimulating and inhibiting hormones. *Physiological Reviews* **49,** 240–284.

McHugh, P. R., and Smith, G. P. (1967). Negative feedback in adrenocortical response to limbic stimulation in *Macaca mulatta. American Journal of Physiology* **213,** 1445–1450.

McHugh, P. R., Black, W. C., and Mason, J. W. (1966). Some hormonal responses to electrical self-stimulation in the *Macaca mulatta. American Journal of Physiology* **210,** 109–113.

Malmejac, J. (1964). Activity of the adrenal medulla and its regulation. *Physiological Reviews* **44,** 186–218.

Mason, J. W. (1968a). A review of psychoendocrine research on the sympathetic-adrenal medullary system. *Psychosomatic Medicine* **30,** 631–653.

348   **Gerard P. Smith**

Mason, J. W. (1968b). A review of psychoendocrine research on the pituitary and adrenal cortical system. *Psychosomatic Medicine* **30**, 576–607.

Mason, J. W. (1971). A re-evaluation of the concept of "non-specificity" in stress theory. *Journal of Psychiatric Research* **8**, 323–333.

Mason, J. W., Brady, J. V., and Sidman, M. (1957). Plasma 17-hydroxycortico-steroid levels and conditioned behavior in the rhesus monkey. *Endocrinology* **60**, 741–752.

Mason, J. W., Mangan, G., Jr., Brady, J. V., Conrad, D., and Rioch, D. McK. (1961). Concurrent plasma epinephrine, norepinephrine and 17-hydroxy-corticosteroid levels during conditioned emotional disturbances in monkeys. *Psychosomatic Medicine* **23**, 344–353.

Mason, J. W., Brady, J. V., and Tolliver, G. A. (1968a). Plasma and urinary 17-hydroxycorticosteroid responses to 72-hr. avoidance sessions in the monkey. *Psychosomatic Medicine* **30**, 608–630.

Mason, J. W., Wherry, F. E., Brady, J. V., Beer, B., Pennington, L. L., and Goodman, A. C. (1968b). Plasma insulin response to 72-hr. avoidance sessions in the monkey. *Psychosomatic Medicine* **30**, 746–759.

Matsuyama, H., Ruhmann-Wennhold, A., Johnson, L. R., and Nelson, D. H. (1972). Disappearance rates of exogenous and endogenous ACTH from rat plasma measured by bioassay and radioimmunoassay. *Metabolism, Clinical and Experimental* **21**, 30–35.

Mendelson, J., Kubsansky, P., Leiderman, P. H., Wexler, D., DuToit, C., and Solmon, P. (1960). Catecholamine excretion and behavior during sensory deprivation. *Archives of General Psychiatry* **2**, 147–155.

Meyer, J. S., and Bowman, R. E. (1972). Rearing experiences, stress and adrenocorticosteroids in the rhesus monkey. *Physiology & Behavior* **8**, 339–343.

Miller, R. E., and Ogawa, N. (1962). The effect of adrenocorticotrophic hormone (ACTH) on avoidance conditioning in adrenalectomized rats. *Journal of Comparative and Physiological Psychology* **55**, 211–213.

Mirsky, A., Miller, R., and Stein, M. (1953). Relation of adrenocortical activity and adaptive behavior. *Psychosomatic Medicine* **15**, 574–588.

Motta, M., Fraschini, F., and Martini, L. (1969). "Short" feedback mechanisms in the control of anterior pituitary function. *In* "Frontiers in Neuroendo-crinology, 1969" (W. F. Ganong and L. Martini, eds.), pp. 211–253. Oxford Univ. Press, London and New York.

Mowrer, O. H., and Lamoreaux, R. R. (1946). Fear as an intervening variable in avoidance conditioning. *Journal of Comparative Psychology* **39**, 29–50.

Moyer, K. E. (1958). Effect of adrenalectomy on anxiety motivated behavior. *Journal of Genetic Psychology* **92**, 11–16.

Moyer, K. E. (1966). Effect of ACTH on open-field behavior, avoidance, startle and food and water consumption. *Journal of Genetic Psychology* **108**, 297–302.

Moyer, K. E., and Bunnell, B. N. (1958). Effect of injected adrenalin on an avoid-ance response in the rat. *Journal of Genetic Psychology* **92**, 247–251.

Moyer, K. E., and Bunnell, B. N. (1959). Effect of adrenal demedullation on an avoidance response in the rat. *Journal of Comparative and Physiological Psychology* **52**, 215–216.

Murphy, J. V., and Miller, R. E. (1955). The effect of adrenocorticotrophic hormone (ACTH) on avoidance conditioning in the rat. *Journal of Comparative and Physiological Psychology* **48**, 47–49.

Natelson, B. H., Smith, G. P., Stokes, P. E., and Root, A. W. (1973). Changes of plasma glucose and insulin during defense reactions in monkeys. *American Journal of Physiology* (in press).

Ney, R. L., Shimizu, N., Nicholson, W. E., Island, D. P., and Liddle, G. W. (1963). Correlation of plasma ACTH concentration with adrenocortical response in normal human subjects, surgical patients, and patients with Cushing's Disease. *Journal of Clinical Investigation* **42**, 1669–1677.

Nugent, C. A., Eik-Nes, K., Samuels, L. T., and Tyler, F. H. (1959). Changes in plasma levels of 17-hydroxycorticosteroids during the intravenous administration of adrenocorticotropin (ACTH). IV. Response to prolonged infusions of small amounts of ACTH. *Journal of Clinical Endocrinology and Metabolism* **19**, 334–343.

Paré, W. P. (1969). The effect of adrenalectomy, adrenal demedullation and adrenalin on the aversive threshold in the rat. *Annals of the New York Academy of Sciences* **159**, 869–879.

Paré, W. P., and Cullen, J. W. (1971). Adrenal influences on the aversive threshold and CER acquisition. *Hormones and Behavior* **2**, 139–147.

Patkai, P., and Frankenhaeuser, M. (1964). Constancy of urinary catecholamine excretion. *Perceptual and Motor Skills* **19**, 789–790.

Patkai, P., Frankenhaeuser, M., Rissler, A., and Bjorkvall, C. (1967). Catecholamine excretion, performance and subjective stress. *Scandinavian Journal of Psychology* **8**, 113–122.

Perkoff, G. T., Eik-Nes, K., Nugent, C. A., Fred, H. L., Nimer, R. A., Rush, L., Samuels, L. T., and Tyler, F. H. (1959). Studies of the diurnal variation of plasma 17-hydroxycorticosteroids in man. *Journal of Clinical Endocrinology and Metabolism* **19**, 432–443.

Persky, H., Hamburg, D. A., Basowitz, H., Grinker, R. R., Sabshire, M., Korchin, S. J., Herz, M., Board, F. A., and Heath, H. A. (1958). Relation of emotional responses and changes in plasma hydrocortisone level after stressful interview. *Archives of Neurology and Psychiatry* **79**, 434–447.

Poe, R. O., Rose, R. M., and Mason, J. W. (1970). Multiple determinants of 17-hydroxycorticosteroid excretion in recruits during basic training. *Psychosomatic Medicine* **32**, 369–378.

Porte, D., Jr., Graber, A., Kuzuya, T., and Williams, R. A. (1966). The effect of epinephrine on immunoreactive insulin levels in man. *Journal of Clinical Investigation* **45**, 228–236.

Porter, J. C., and Klaiber, M. S. (1965). Corticosterone secretion in rats as a function of ACTH input and adrenal blood flow. *American Journal of Physiology* **209**, 811–814.

Price, D. B., Thaler, M., and Mason, J. W. (1957). Preoperative emotional states and adrenal cortical activity. *Archives of Neurology and Psychiatry* **77**, 646–656.

Raisman, G., and Field, P. M. (1971). Anatomical considerations relevant to the interpretation of neuroendocrine experiments. *In* "Frontiers in Neuroendocrinology, 1971" (L. Martini and W. F. Ganong, eds.), pp. 3–44. Oxford Univ. Press, London and New York.

Rees, L. H., Cook, D. M., Kendall, J. W., Allen, C. F., Kramer, R. M., Ratcliffe,

J. G., and Knight, R. A. (1971). A radioimmunoassay for rat plasma ACTH. *Endocrinology* **89**, 254–261.

Rennick, B., and Yoss, N. (1962). Renal tubular excretion of dl-epinephrine-2-C^{14} in the chicken. *Journal of Pharmacology and Experimental Therapeutics* **138**, 347–350.

Rose, R. M., Mason, J. W., and Brady, J. V. (1969). Adrenal responses to maternal separation and chair adaptation in experimentally raised rhesus monkeys (*Macaca mulatta*). *Proceedings of the International Congress of Primatology, 2nd, Atlanta* **1**, 211–218.

Rushmer, R. F., Franklin, D. L., Van Citters, R. L., and Smith, O. A. (1961). Changes in peripheral blood flow distribution to healthy dogs. *Circulation Research* **9**, 675–687.

Sachar, E. J. (1967). Corticosteroids in depressive illness. *Archives of General Psychiatry* **17**, 554–567.

Sachar, E. J., Hellman, L., Fukushima, D. K., and Gallagher, T. F. (1970). Cortisol production in depressive illness. *Archives of General Psychiatry* **23**, 289–298.

Sassenrath, E. N., Hein, L. J., and Kaita, A. A. (1969). Social behavior and corticoid correlates in *Macaca mulatta*. *Proceedings of the International Congress of Primatology, 2nd, Atlanta* **1**, 219–231.

Sayers, G., Swallow, R. L., and Giordano, N. D. (1971). An improved technique for the preparation of isolated rat adrenal cells: A sensitive, accurate and specific method for the assay of ACTH. *Endocrinology* **88**, 1063–1068.

Schachter, S., and Singer J. E. (1962). Cognitive, social and physiological determinants of emotional state. *Psychological Review* **69**, 379–399.

Schumann, H. J., and Kroneberg, G., eds. (1970). "New Aspects of Storage and Release Mechanisms of Catecholamines." Springer-Verlag, Berlin and New York.

Sharpless, S. K. (1961). Effects of intravenous injections of epinephrine and norepinephrine in a choice situation. *Journal of Comparative and Physiological Psychology* **54**, 103–108.

Sherrington, C. S. (1900). Experiments on the value of vascular and visceral factors for the genesis of emotion. *Proceedings of the Royal Society of London* **66**, 390–403.

Silverman, A. J., Cohen, S. I., Shmavonian, B. M., and Kirshner, N. (1961). Catecholamines in psychophysiologic studies. *Recent Advances in Biological Psychiatry* **3**, 104–117.

Sines, J. O. (1959). Reserpine, adrenaline and avoidance learning in the rat. *Psychological Reports* **5**, 321–324.

Singer, J. E. (1963). Sympathetic activation, drugs, and fear. *Journal of Comparative and Physiological Psychology* **56**, 612–615.

Slusher, M. A. (1965). Influence of adrenal steroids on self-stimulation in rats. *Proceedings of the Society for Experimental Biology and Medicine* **120**, 617–620.

Smith, G. P., Gibbs, J., Strohmayer, A. J., Stokes, P. E., and Root, A. W. (1973). Effect of 2-deoxy-D-glucose on insulin response to glucose in intact and adrenalectomized monkeys. *Endocrinology* **92**, 750–754.

Smith, U., Smith, D. S., Winkler, H., and Ryan, J. W. (1973). Exocytosis in the adrenal medulla demonstrated by freeze-etching. *Science* **179**, 79–82.

Stewart, C. N., and Brookshire, K. H. (1967). Shuttle box avoidance learning and epinephrine. *Psychonomic Science* 9, 419–420.

Stewart, C. N., and Brookshire, K. H. (1968). Effect of epinephrine on acquisition of conditioned fear. *Physiology & Behavior* 3, 601–604.

Stokes, P. E. (1972). Studies on the control of adrenocortical function in depression. *In* "Recent Advances in the Psychobiology of the Depressive Illness" (T. A. Williams, M. M. Katz, and J. A. Shield, Jr., eds.), pp. 199–220. U.S. Gov. Printing Office, Washington, D. C.

Suboski, M. D., Marquis, H. A., Black, M., and Platenius, P. (1970). Adrenal and amygdala function in the incubation of aversively conditioned responses. *Physiology & Behavior* 5, 283–289.

Sydnor, K. L., and Sayers, G. (1954). Blood and pituitary ACTH in intact and adrenalectomized rats after stress. *Endocrinology* 55, 621–636.

Uretsky, E., Kling, A., and Orbach, J. (1966). Plasma 17-hydroxycorticosteroid levels following intra-cranial self-stimulation in rats. *Psychological Reports* 19, 891–901.

Urquhart, J. (1965). Adrenal blood flow and the adrenocortical response to corticotropin. *American Journal of Physiology* 209, 1162–1168.

Van Wimersma Greidanus, T. J. B., and DeWied, D. (1969). Effects of intracerebral implantation of corticosteroids on extinction of an avoidance response in rats. *Physiology & Behavior* 4, 365–370.

Van Wimersma Greidanus, T. J. B., and DeWied, D. (1971). Effects of systemic and intracerebral administration of two opposite acting ACTH-related peptides on extinction of conditioned avoidance behavior. *Neuroendocrinology* 7, 291–301.

Vendsalu, A. (1960). Studies on adrenaline and noradrenaline in human plasma. *Acta Physiologica Scandinavica, Supplementum* 173.

von Euler, U. S. (1964). Quantitation of stress by catecholamine analysis. *Clinical Pharmacology and Therapeutics* 5, 398–404.

von Euler, U. S., and Luft, R. (1951). Noradrenaline output in urine after infusion in man. *British Journal of Pharmacology* 6, 286–288.

von Euler, U. S., and Lundberg, U. (1954). Effect of flying on the epinephrine excretion in Air Force Personnel. *Journal of Applied Physiology* 6, 551–555.

von Euler, U. S., Luft, R., and Sundin, T. (1954). Excretion of urinary adrenaline in normals following intravenous infusion. *Acta Physiologica Scandinavica* 30, 249–257.

von Euler, U. S., Luft, R., and Sundin, T. (1955). The urinary excretion of noradrenalin and adrenalin in healthy subjects during recumbency and standing. *Acta Physiologica Scandinavica* 34, 169–174.

Weiss, J. M., McEwen, B. S., Silva, M. T., and Kalkut, M. (1970). Pituitary-adrenal alterations and fear responding. *American Journal of Physiology* 218, 864–868.

Wynne, L. C., and Solomon, R. L. (1955). Traumatic avoidance learning: Acquisition and extinction in dogs deprived of normal peripheral autonomic function. *Genetic Psychology Monographs* 52, 241–284.

Yates, F. E., Brennan, R. D., and Urquhart, J. (1969). Adrenal glucocorticoid control system. *Federation Proceedings, Federation of American Societies for Experimental Biology* 28, 71–83.

Author Index

Numbers in italics refer to the pages on which the complete references are listed.

A

Abraham, F. D., 12, 33, *75*

Adams, T., 156, 160, 162, 187, 188, 189, 198, *203*, 208

Adler, N. T., 270, 272, 279, 280, *291*, *292*, *297*

Ader, R., 316, 317, 318, 322, *343*, *345*

Ades, H. W., 89, *115*, *120*, *122*

Adey, W., 58, *66*

Affanni, J., 22, 26, *64*

Agranoff, B. W., 134, *153*

Ainsworth, A., 86, *117*

Aitkin, L. M., 14, 15, 47, 50, *73*, *75*

Albe-Fessard, D., 27, *73*

Alcaraz, M., 10, 11, 21, 25, *64*, *68*, *69*, 258, 261, 281, *292*

Allen, C. F., 307, *349*

Allman, J. M., 86, 89, 111, *115*

Altman, I. A., 8, 9, 10, 47, 48, 49, *64*

Anderson, C. H., 255, *292*

Anderson, D. C., 338, *343*

Anderson, F. D., 283, *292*

Anderson, K. V., 90, *115*

Anderson, O. D., 333, *347*

Anderson, W., 223, *251*

Angel, A., 226, *252*

Applezweig, M. H., 334, *343*

Aquino-Cias, J., 23, 25, 47, 48, 49, *67*

Arden, G. B., 24, 47, *64*

Arduini, A., 33, *64*

Armengol, V., 22, *72*

Artemiev, V. V., 6, *64*

Arthur, R. P., 190, *203*

Askew, H. R., 54, *64*

Auerbach, P. P., 133, 139, 140, 151, *152*

Avis, H. H., 126, 136, 139, *152*

Ax, A. F., 182, *203*, 311, *343*

Axelrod, J., 250, 254, *293*, 301, 302, *343*

B

Babineau, L.-M., 221, *247*

Bach-y-Rita, G., 9, 10, 44, *64*

Bagshaw, M. H., 78, 80, *115*, *121*

Bailey, P., 78, 79, 85, 88, *115*, *123*

Baker, H., 187, 188, *203*

Ball, J., 271, 272, 275, 279, 280, *292*

Balvin, R., 33, *73*, 259, *297*

Bamford, J. L., 182, *203*

Barbizet, J., 150, *152*

Barcroft, J., 333, *344*

Bard, P., 281, 288, *292*

Bare, J. K., 260, 261, *296*

Barfield, R., 270, 287, *292*, *297*

Barondes, S. H., 125, *152*

Barraclough, C., 258, *292*, *294*

Barrett, R. J., 336, *344*

Barry, J., 80, *121*

Basowitz, H., 324, *349*

Battersby, W. S., 80, *121*, *122*

Baudry, F. D., 334, *343*

Baust, W., 17, *64*

Beach, F. A., 253, 265, 276, 288, *292*, *295*

Beatty, P. A., 335, 336, *344*

Beaver, W., 165, *204*

Beer, B., 326, *348*

Begg, R. W., 239, 240, *247*

Bell, C., 55, 58, *64*

Bell, D., 272, *292*

Bell, F., 58, *66*

Bender, D. B., 80, 99, 100, 103, 108, 109, 110, 112, *115*, *116*, *118*, *122*

Bender, M. B., 80, *121*, *122*

Bennett, G. S., 134, *152*

Berlucchi, G., 17, *64*

Berlyne, D. E., 156, *203*

Bermant, G., 265, 270, *292*

Bernardis, L., 244, *247*

Bernstein, A. S., 4, *65*

Berry, C. M., 283, *292*

Berson, S. A., 304, 305, 307, 308, *344*

Bever, J., 198, *207*

Beyer, C., 258, 281, *292*, *293*

Bierman, H. R., 230, *247*

Bjorkvall, C., 314, 316, *345*, *349*

Subject Index

S

T

V

W